The Woman Reader

The Woman Reader

1837 – 1914

KATE FLINT

CLARENDON PRESS · OXFORD

Oxford University Press, Walton Street, Oxford OX2 6DP

Oxford New York Toronto
Delhi Bombay Calcutta Madras Karachi
Kuala Lumpur Singapore Hong Kong Tokyo
Nairobi Dar es Salaam Cape Town
Melbourne Auckland Madrid
and associated companies in
Berlin Ibadan

Oxford is a trade mark of Oxford University Press

Published in the United States
by Oxford University Press Inc., New York

First published 1993
Reprinted (with corrections) 1994

British Library Cataloguing in Publication Data

Data available

Library of Congress Cataloging in Publication Data

Flint, Kate.
The woman reader, 1837–1914/Kate Flint
Includes bibliographical references and index.
1. Women—Great Britain—Books and reading—History—19th century.
2. Women—Great Britain—Books and reading—History—20th century.
3. Women and literature—Great Britain. I. Title.
Z1039.W65F57 1993
028'.9082—dc20   93–18195
ISBN 0–19–811719–1

Printed in Great Britain
on acid-free paper by
Bookcraft Ltd.
Midsomer Norton, Bath

For Linda

Preface

This book had its origin in a particular act of reading. In 1981, I was invited to write an Introduction to Anthony Trollope's *Can You Forgive Her?* (1864–5) for the World's Classics. I pondered for some time on that title. Can *you* forgive *her*? That interrogative form involves the reader, and provokes a response. The pronoun with which the short query ends suggests, even before we open the novel, that we are to engage our moral judgement with the dubious behaviour, the peccadilloes of a specific, female individual. Assessment of her conduct is necessarily related to her gender. Moreover, the novel proves to be concerned, throughout, with the specific conditions governing a woman's life in the mid-nineteenth century. Very soon, I came to see that the gender not just of the title's 'her', but also of the 'you', might matter. To what degree, I asked myself, could one postulate a difference in response between a woman and a man reading this story at the time of its original publication?

The text of *Can You Forgive Her?* itself draws attention to the fact that women and men may read with different priorities. Although Trollope usually uses the male form—'The reader will be right in his surmise'—as a 'neutral' norm, there are occasions when he specifically addresses the 'delicate reader' or 'my male friend and reader'. In the first instance, I was led to what Trollope wrote elsewhere about gender and reading, particularly in his two lectures 'Higher Education' and 'On English Prose Fiction as a Rational Amusement'. In doing this, I quickly became aware that Trollope was but one of the very many commentators on the issue of women and reading in the nineteenth century: commentators who addressed themselves to questions of what women should read, and what they should be protected against reading; how they should read; where and when they should indulge in this occupation. Moreover, I found that the issue of reading was not just returned to repetitively by literary critics and the writers of advice texts, but was continually raised within fiction (the literary form which invariably gave rise to the most anxiety), and was frequently referred to by autobiographers. More intriguing yet was the number of times it was referred to by writers of medical and psychological texts, indicating that the preoccupation with a woman's mind and conduct was also intimately linked to presuppositions about the innate functioning of her body.

The more evidence of debates about reading which I amassed, the more instances which I gathered of individual reading practices, made me reformulate my initial questions. Asking 'how a woman might read' became increasingly problematical, indeed unanswerable, as I came to recognize the great heterogeneity among nineteenth- and early twentieth-century women readers. Although many commentators chose to believe or desire that women read in certain ways, documentary material tends to suggest that the practice of reading provided a site for discussion, even resistance, rather than giving grounds for assuming conformity. Instead of my initial formulations about the possible relations of women and texts, I came to be fascinated by *why* the polemic should prove so pervasive and long-lasting (for its roots lie way before the Victorian period). And so, rather than write what I had initially conceived of as a work of critical interpretation (and rather than write a materialist history of women and reading in the nineteenth century—something which remains to be done), I chose to examine the topos of the woman reader, and its functioning in cultural debate between the accession of Queen Victoria and the First World War.

Many people have helped, in a variety of ways, with the writing of this book. First, I would like to thank all those who have participated in discussions following papers which I have given on the Woman Reader, and who have helped me to clarify my ideas, in particular at the California Institute of Technology; the conference of the Collège des anglicistes Romands (Lausanne); the Istituto Universitario Orientale, Naples; Manchester, Middlesex, and Sheffield Polytechnics, and the Universities of Birmingham, Konstanz, Leeds, Princeton, Sacramento, Sheffield, Southampton, and York.

My students, undergraduate and graduate, have contributed significantly to the making of this book, both by their stimulating, searching, and imaginative conversation and questions and by supplying a range of references. I am especially grateful to Karen Avenoso, Laura Chrisman, Fiona Giles, Jennie Kassanoff, Margot McCarthy, Julie Peavyhouse, and Peter Stoneley. I owe a special debt of thanks to all the public librarians who took the trouble to reply to my queries, and to the staff of the Bodleian Library, the British Library, the London Library, and the Witt Library.

Among those friends and colleagues who have given indispensable advice, criticism, and encouragement, I wish to thank in particular Joe Bristow, Christopher Butler, Maria Teresa Chialant, Stephen Gill, Anne Hudson, Alastair and Florence Minnis, Frank Romany, Elaine Showalter, and John Sutherland. My parents, Joy and Ray Flint, have been wonderfully supportive and enthusiastic throughout. Gillian Beer's comments on the first draft were not just thoughtful and knowledgeable, but helped me greatly in preparing the final version. Linda Cookson has been an exacting reader, has posed some searching questions, and has warmly spurred on the project since its inception. I owe a great deal to John House, both for methodologically rigorous discussions concerning cultural history, and for his iconographic interest in women readers. Kim Scott Walwyn has been an ideal editor: sympathetic, rigorous, and unflaggingly encouraging. Finally, Nigel Smith's combination of enthusiasm and intellectual precision has been both inspirational and invaluable.

All errors, inconsistencies, and infelicities are, of course, my own.

K. F.

Contents

PART V.

List of Illustrations

Part I

1 *Introduction*

I begin with five images. What these images have in common is the depiction of women readers absorbed in texts, apparently oblivious to artist and observer. Immersed uncritically in the material which preoccupies them, they are made to manifest no self-awareness of their own status or activity as readers.

First, Edward Ward's *Girl Reclining on a Sofa* (1854) (Fig. 1): a small canvas, informal both in dimensions (210 x 240 mm. 8¼ x 9½ in.) and in subject, the girl's posture suggesting that she is reading for recreation, idly, passively, rather than engaging in any scheme of programmed self education. In contrast, the figure in Robert Martineau's *The Last Chapter* (1863) (Fig. 2) is far more alert, although still reading for escapist pleasure. She is unmistakably caught up in one of the fashionably controversial 'sensation novels'. As we watch her consuming the text avidly, by firelight, we conclude that the book has the power to keep her up and awake beyond the customary hour at which the house goes to bed. Her pose is testimony to the compulsive nature of these fictions: moreover, the lighting of the picture and the angle from which she is portrayed invest her with something of the melodramatic mystery and self-importance of the heroines about whom she reads.

Reading, in the case of these two women, is presented as an essentially private activity. Yet it had its social implications, as one finds in Thomas Brooks's *Tales of the Sea* (1867) (Fig. 3). Here mother and daughters are bonded not just by their vacationing but by the activity of reading aloud, sharing tastes, values, interests, narratives. The painter is privileging the sense of continuity between generations, something which Victorian commentators increasingly presented as being under assault. William Rothenstein's *The Browning Readers* (1900) (Fig. 4) again shows reading within the home. It dates from a time when there was a growing amount of debate concerning the difference between domestic and academic reading practices, and the responsible demeanour of these two girls suggests that they, at least, have not been so staled by study that they are unable to appreciate literature read in their own time. Nor are they fulfilling a contemporary stereotype by finding recreational solace in magazine stories, nor in the polemical 'New Woman' writing of the 1890s, but the poetry they read forms part of a comfortable environment in which the reproductions and ornaments testify to a belief in cultural durability. Finally, we see the consumption of print in the least private of environments, a public library. The title of Ralph Hedley's *Seeking Situations* (1904) (Fig. 5) indicates, on this occasion, a functional, rather than a leisure activity. It alludes tangentially to the polemic, recurrent from the mid-nineteenth century onwards, concerning the woman who was financially obliged to seek work, or who chose to do so. Additionally, the presence of women and men together evokes those discussions which accompanied the growth in public libraries, about whether women and men readers should share the same reading-spaces. Moreover, in this unequivocally mixed-sex reading-room, the fact that this young woman is separated only by a newspaper stand from a not unattractive, equally respectable young man—a step sideways would ensure that their eyes met—suggests a potential submerged narrative, especially since libraries were recognized trysting spots. Hedley's painting thus also serves to alert one to the proximity of textuality and sexuality in discourses of reading throughout the Victorian and early Edwardian period.

The image of the woman reader makes an apt starting-point for several reasons. First, its very presence in these and many other paintings points to the wide range of contexts in which 'the woman reader' was constructed as a discrete topic throughout the period. These included articles in newspapers and periodicals; medical and psychological texts; advice manuals for young girls, wives, servants, governesses; educational and religious works; autobiographies; letters; journals; fiction; and verse, as well as paintings, photographs, and graphic art. Second, the self-absorption of the readers depicted implies some of the reasons why the private activity of reading tended so persistently to come under scrutiny. It hints at the subject's vulnerability to textual influence, deaf and blind to all other stimuli in her immediate environment. It suggests the potential autonomy of her mind, mirrored in her self-sufficient postures. The very relaxation of outward social awareness which we observe in the first two of these pictures prompts the idea of another element: the eroticism of the female subject for the male spectator or commentator, provoking questions which indicate his own fascination with the woman's mental processes. What is she reading about? What are her fantasies? What relation might he hold to such a fantasy? Furthermore—and this tended to be the line publicly taken on the subject—what moral, sexual, religious, ideological dangers may lie in a woman's being absorbed by so preoccupying a pursuit?

The essence of this paternalistic surveillance is exemplified in an article of 1859 by the critic and moral crusader W. R. Greg, entitled 'False Morality of Lady Novelists'. He notes how:

novels constitute a principal part of the reading of women, who are always impressionable, in whom at all times the emotional element is more awake and more powerful than the critical, whose feelings are more easily aroused and whose estimates are more easily influenced than ours, while at the same time the correctness of their feelings and the justice of their estimates are matters of the most special and preëminent concern.[1]

---

[1] [W. R. Greg] 'False Morality of Lady Novelists', *National Review*, 8 (1859), 144.

1. Edward Ward, *Girl Reclining on a Sofa*, (1854)

2. Robert Martineau, *The Last Chapter*, (1863)

3. Thomas Brooks, *Tales of the Sea*, (1867)

4. William Rothenstein, *The Browning Readers*, (1900)

5. Ralph Hedley, *Seeking Situations*, (1904)

This keeps before us certain important points: the assertion that women's and men's responses to what they read were widely and popularly believed to differ from one another for reasons which went far beyond their various social experiences and expectations; the degree to which much of this debate concentrated on the consumption of fiction; and the fact that much, though certainly not all, discussion about women's reading was conservative in its gender politics. Whether conducted by men or by women, this discussion was very frequently used to uphold and reinforce dominant patriarchal structures. Those women who voiced their anxieties about how vulnerable girls could be to certain types of reading helped to circulate and make familiar these conservative attitudes and terminology. To do this gave them access to cultural capital, in Pierre Bourdieu's sense of the term: commenting on and censoring the behaviour of their own sex was one means by which they could readily wield authority in a society where direct access to public expression of opinion could be difficult for a woman.[2] At the same time, the form this advice-giving often took was to adopt the caring voice of the wise mother. This could be found reflected in book titles, such as Matilda Pullan's *Maternal Counsels to a Daughter* (1855). Moreover, the voicing of domestic expectations was not confined to the household. In the later part of the century, when publications dealing with girls' reading were frequently composed by people, such as Dorothea Beale and Lucy Soulsby, who were professionally involved with education, writers were still often at pains to stress the part which reading should play in relation to a young woman's presumed future role at home.

One aim of the present book is to offer suggestions as to why 'the woman reader' was an issue addressed with such frequency throughout the period. To be able to do this involves considering reading at all periods of a woman's life, whilst bearing in mind that childhood and adolescence were considered to be the times when the young mind was most susceptible and suggestible. It demands treating reading both as a leisure activity—an assertion and organization of private space—and as an essential component of more formal education, whether this education was home based or, increasingly, obtained at school. The study of literature, in particular, became an area for discussion as girls' education widened in availability and seriousness in the second half of the century. Should it be aimed at preparing a young woman for her future

[2] See Judith Newton, 'Making—and Remaking—History: Another Look at Patriarchy', *Tulsa Studies in Women's Literature*, 3 (1984), 125–42, for the argument that women as well as men have been extremely efficient at propagating their own versions of patriarchal and bourgeois ideology.For the notion of cultural capital, see Pierre Bourdieu, 'Cultural Reproduction and Social Reproduction', Richard Brown (ed.), *Knowledge, Education and Cultural Change: Papers in the Sociology of Education* (1973), 71–112. Bourdieu, however, restricts his understanding of cultural capital to the way in which access to high culture functions to maintain pre-existing social distinctions and hierarchies. Although this is how I, too, am employing the term in this instance, I believe that the notion of cultural capital may also function in a wider, enabling sense within feminist criticism. It can be used to show how women can have access to a system of shared and circulating ideas relating to the power to be found within coalition in a politics of resistance.

matrimonial role, by encouraging her sympathetic nature; at preparing her, even, as a future mother within the Empire by enhancing her conception of the English heritage to which she belonged? Or should such study be geared towards the increasing professionalism of attitude on which some public school headmistresses were placing a growing amount of emphasis? Innovation in women's education was accompanied by cautious rhetoric, which attempted to forestall contemporary fears about the different types of damaging effect created by different types of reading. Thus Emily Davies, writing of women's claim to university study, maintained that serious reading would neither corrupt nor de-sex: 'the fast women and the masculine women are not those who sit down to their books and devote themselves to an orderly course of study'.[3]

This work offers a dual, though continually intersecting focus. Attempts to legislate about reading and its effects can be seen on the one hand as a means of gaining control over subjectivity, and, on the other, as a means of obtaining access to different types of knowledge, and through this, to different social expectations and standards. Thus, recognizing the potency of 'the woman reader' as a subject within cultural discussion is not a self-sufficient end. It illuminates important networks of ideas about the presumed interrelations of mind, body, and culture. It shows how notions about reading fed off attempts to define women's mental capacities and tendencies through their physical attributes, and, in turn, appeared to contribute to the validation of these very definitions. Furthermore, it demonstrates contradictions and paradoxes which inhered within nineteenth-century notions of gender. From one point of view, reading was a form of consumption associated with the possession of leisure time, and thus contributed to the ideology, if not always the practices, which supported the ideal of the middle-class home. Yet it could also be regarded as dangerously useless, a thief of time which might be spent on housewifely duties. Although a means of extending one's knowledge and experience beyond the bounds of one's personal lot—hence, perhaps, becoming a fitter marital companion in the process—reading was often, none the less, unavoidably associated with woman's 'inappropriate' educational ambition. 'Book-love' itself, according to the language of a contributor to *Fraser's Magazine*, 1847, on the one hand possessed feminine attributes, yet was nevertheless not the 'natural' preserve of women:

Book-love is a home-feeling—a sweet bond of family union—and a never-failing source of domestic enjoyment. It sheds a charm on the quiet fireside, unlocks the hidden sympathies of human hearts, beguiles the weary hours of sickness or solitude, and unites kindred spirits in a sweet companionship of sentiment and idea. It sheds a gentle and humanising influence over its votaries, and woos even sorrow itself into a temporary forgetfulness.

[3] Emily Davies, 'The Influence of University Degrees on the education of women', *Victoria Magazine* (1863), repr. ead., *Thoughts on Some Questions Relating to Women, 1860–1908* (Cambridge, 1910), 59.

Book-love is the good angel that keeps watch by the poor man's hearth, and hallows it; saving him from the temptations that lurk beyond its charmed circle; giving him new thoughts and noble aspirations, and lifting him, as it were, from the mere mechanical drudgery of his every-day occupation. The wife blesses it, as she sits smiling and sewing, alternately listening to her husband's voice, or hushing the child upon her knee. She blesses it for keeping him near her, and making him cheerful, and manly, and kindhearted,—albeit understanding little of what he reads, and reverencing it for that reason all the more in him.[4]

In 'The Ideological Work of Gender', which forms the introductory chapter to *Uneven Developments* (1989), Mary Poovey reminds one that, contrary to the belief of many Victorians, 'the representation of biological sexuality, the definition of sexual difference, and the social organisation of sexual relations are social, not natural, phenomena'. She chooses to discuss in her study certain representative topics which feature gender as a crucial factor, such as the 1857 Matrimonial Causes Act, the position of the governess (especially in relation to *Jane Eyre*), and Florence Nightingale. For her, these provide 'sites at which struggles for authority occurred, as well as the locus of assumptions used to underwrite the very authority that authorized these struggles'.[5] The issue of reading, as the example just cited illustrates, is another such site, and Poovey's attempt to use the potential of her chosen topics to expose the artificiality of the binary logic which underpinned the Victorian symbolic economy, to expose the limits of ideological certainty, and to challenge '*the* opposition upon which all other oppositions claimed to be based—the opposition between men and women',[6] is particularly relevant, in both methodology and practice, to the theme of this book.

In Part II, I shall be concerned primarily to reconstruct the contexts of the Victorian and Edwardian debate. To do this will not only show the contradictions it encompassed, but will indicate the ceaseless passage between, on the one hand, preoccupations based on woman's interlocking physiological and psychological constitution, and on the other, preoccupations based on social factors. Early in the period, the co-presence of these two angles is neatly encapsulated in a review article of 1842:

The great bulk of novel readers are females; and to them such impressions (as are conveyed through fiction) are peculiarly mischievous: for, first, they are naturally more sensitive, more impressable, than the other sex; and secondly, their engagements are of a less engrossing character—they have more time as well as more inclination to indulge in reveries of fiction.[7]

---

[4] [R. A. Willmott] 'Book-Love', *Frasers Magazine*, 36 (1847), 199.

[5] Mary Poovey, *Uneven Developments: The Ideological Work of Gender in Mid-Victorian England* (Chicago, 1988), 2.

[6] Ibid. 12.

[7] 'Moral and Political Tendency of the Modern Novels', *Church of England Quarterly Review*, 11 (1842), 287–8.

The range of authoritative voices cited in this book passes from medical and psychological theorists to writers of advice manuals, reviewers and periodical journalists, and educationists. Yet none of the advice or educational texts, nor the books and magazines they discussed, nor the opinions which constituted their currency, circulated in a commercial vacuum. The awareness of Victorians and Edwardians of that discrete category, 'the woman reader', and the hypotheses about her special characteristics, as well as her presumed needs and interests, affected the composition, distribution, and marketing of literature. The category was continually drawn upon by reviewers, who could use the figure of 'the woman reader', or 'the young person' (by implication almost invariably female), as a touchstone against which to place fiction with undesirably explicit sexual content, or as a marker to suggest a work's sentimentality and presumed appeal. Sexual division in reading expectations is most apparent in relation to romantic fiction, in both novel and novelette form; certain types of religious fiction, verse, and devotional prose; and works which deal explicitly with the position of woman within society. Such works range from *Jane Eyre* to the so-called 'New Woman' fiction of the 1890s; from a volume like Mrs Newton Crosland's *Lives of Memorable Women* to the polemical publications of the suffrage movement. This is not to say that men never read these types of writing. What it indicates, however, as we shall see, is that such books were not only frequently directed outwards towards notional women readers, but were received, classified, and interpreted by both publishers and critics within a context of what women should and should not be reading, and what they expected from their books. Gaye Tuchman develops this point in *Edging Women Out* (1989), quoting, for example, Geraldine Jewsbury, in her role as publisher's reader in the 1860s, reinforcing the belief that women preferred light stuff.[8] This prescriptive attitude had further ramifications. The restrictive influence of the circulating libraries, for example, with their avowed intent to provide reading material suitable only for the entire family circle, has already been well documented.[9] The debate about access to appropriate reading material extended to the literature surrounding the growth of the public libraries movement, and to discussions about the provision of books in working girls' clubs and recreational evening homes, as well as to where books were, and should be, located within the middle-class home. Especially (but by no means exclusively) after the passing of the 1870 Education Act, the reading of the working classes came under close scrutiny. Here, notably, boys' as well as girls' reading materials and habits were at issue. Class difference, as well as difference of gender, provided the distance which allowed comment, prescription, and the manipulation of stereotypes concerning reading to play a part in broader social debates. But in every class, as separate studies have already indicated, children's literature, books aimed specifically at girls and young

[8] Gaye Tuchman, *Edging Women Out: Victorian Novelists, Publishers, and Social Change* (1989), 83.
[9] See esp. Guinevere Griest, *Mudie's Circulating Library and the Victorian Novel* (1970).

women, and women's magazines had their contents determined to a significant extent by assumptions about gender difference and role expectations, present and future. Judith Rowbotham's *Good Girls Make Good Wives* (1989) has examined extensively the content of didactic fiction for girls, showing how the nature of the stereotype changed throughout the Victorian period, as educational and employment opportunities for girls improved, how girls' stories increasingly contained impressions of a variety of contemporary issues and movements, and, significantly, how the range of social spheres and situations which was found in such fiction enabled girls to internalize the crucial nature of their role.[10]

A clear question follows from the presentation of this material: what difference did—or does—the hypothesis of a woman reader (whether constructed according to the prevalent norms of the time, or according to internal textual evidence) make to one's understanding of the ways in which certain texts may have been read at the time of their first publication? To pose this question, however, is to assume, erroneously, that theory necessarily reflected practice. In fact, evidence of actual reading activity calls many of the theoretical assumptions presented in Part II into question. In the last section of this part, it is in fact demonstrated that towards the end of the nineteenth century, as reading became an area increasingly scrutinized by sociological methods, a range of articles with titles like 'Do Our Girls Take an Interest in Literature?' and 'The Reading of the Modern Girl' attempted to classify changing tastes not just through impressionistic observation based upon popular stereotypes, but through elementary statistical inquiry, analysing evidence gathered through questionnaires. In Part III, a variety of accounts of reading are offered, providing evidence of the wide-ranging practices of particular girls and women throughout the period; their opportunities for obtaining books and the differing degrees of supervision exercised over their consumption of print. The conspicuous variety to be found in these autobiographical testimonies emphasizes, unsurprisingly, the dichotomy in many cases between theory and practice, ideal and actual, although the belief in the affective power of print is constant. Additionally, and importantly, these accounts indicate how the activity of reading was often the vehicle through which an individual's sense of identity was achieved or confirmed. This frequently involved the assertion of practices or preferences which opposed that which was conventionally expected of the young woman within the family circle. At the same time, to recount these moments of rebellion which took place through reading is, none the less, to reinscribe the original violation, celebrating

[10] Judith Rowbotham, *Good Girls Make Good Wives: Guidance for Girls in Victorian Fiction* (Oxford, 1989). See also Gillian Avery, *Childhood's Pattern: A Study of the Heroes and Heroines of Children's Fiction, 1770–1950* (1975); J. S. Bratton, *The Impact of Victorian Children's Fiction* (1975); Mary Cadogan and Patricia Craig, *You're a Brick, Angela! The Girls' Story 1839–1985* (1986); Kimberley Reynolds, *Girls Only? Gender and Popular Children's Fiction in Britain, 1880–1910* (Hemel Hempstead, 1990).

the author's capacity to overthrow received notions of femininity and encouraging the continuing need for transgression.[11] Moreover, these steps towards awareness and achievement of individuated subjecthood provide detailed evidence of how such individuation inevitably and necessarily takes place within slowly changing social and ideological structures including, but stretching beyond, the family. It is with this incessant mediation between the individual and the social in mind that I examine more closely the reading beliefs and practices of the Suffragettes, who whilst publicly acknowledging themselves as women-identified readers in a way ostensibly disruptive to dominant patriarchal lines of thought, yet, none the less, failed to challenge some of patriarchy's central values as expressed in literature.

Much of the evidence concerning individual readers comes from those who are self-evidently reflective about their own actual practices. They incorporate their personal histories of reading into autobiographical material in ways which may be rhetorically important to their construction of an autobiographical self, rather than possessing value as quasi-objective accounts of reading practice. This, therefore, perhaps calls into question their claim to typicality. But there remains the evidence of the primary reading matter itself. Throughout the whole period, two types of fiction were notable for causing concern: the 'sensation novels' of the 1860s, with their foregrounding of adultery, bigamy, disguise, and crime, and the so-called 'New Woman' fiction of the 1890s, debunking romantic expectations, and emphasizing, among other things, prevalent double standards in respect to sexual behaviour and 'purity'. Whilst much differentiates these two widely consumed fictional forms, they nevertheless share a tendency to acknowledge, even flatter, the literary and social alertness of their readers. Like much Victorian fiction, they incorporate metatextual references, which are employed sometimes for ostentatiously didactic purposes, and sometimes serve the ends of mimetic realism. But both sensation and 'New Woman' fiction mock within themselves the belief that women read uncritically, unthoughtfully: the very characteristics which their authors were accused of engendering. They challenge, head on, the assumption that a woman will automatically identify with the central female character in the novel she is reading. They refute the idea that a woman reader is mentally passive and accepting of what she consumes, and emphasize her capacity to act as a rational, rather than as an emotional, being. This is not to say that they do not rely, to some extent, on encouraging a sympathetic, identificatory response on the part of their consumers, but they stimulate, simultaneously, their readers' capacity for self-awareness and social analysis and judgement.

[11] I am here drawing on some of the ideas concerning the representation of unorthodox lives in women's autobiography proposed by Nancy K. Miller, 'Writing Fictions: Women's Autobiography in France', *Subject to Change: Reading Feminist Writing* (New York, 1988), 52.

Whilst the greater part of *The Woman Reader* will address itself to Victorian and Edwardian contexts, the debate about what women should, and should not read, and how they read, was not a new one, nor has it disappeared. I begin the next chapter, therefore, with an outline of the debates over women's reading practices which the Victorians inherited: and follow this with a consideration of some more recent approaches. 'Woman as reader' is a fashionable topic in feminist criticism, but I contend that with a few notable exceptions, most of the current debate has either focused on the practice of women reading today, or has looked at the construction of the woman reader primarily as a textual phenomenon divorced from a fuller socio-historical context. Both approaches have had the effect of de-historicizing the concepts of 'woman' and of 'reading' alike.

2   Theory and Women's Reading

We get no good
By being ungenerous, even to a book,
And calculating profits—so much help
By so much reading. It is rather when
We gloriously forget ourselves, and plunge
Soul-forward, headlong, into a book's profound,
Impassioned for its beauty and salt of truth—
'Tis then we get the right good from a book.

Elizabeth Barrett Browning, *Aurora Leigh*
(1857), i, 702–9

Suppose the informed reader of a work of literature is a woman. Might not this make a difference . . . to 'the reader's experience'?

Jonathan Culler, *On Deconstruction* (1982), 43

Early in his career, Dante Gabriel Rossetti produced two paintings in which women and books figure prominently together. In the first of these, *The Girlhood of Mary Virgin* (1848–9) (Fig. 6), the young Mary sits with her mother, Saint Anne. Under a two-handled vase containing her personal emblem, a white lily, stands a pile of thick volumes: not the named works of individual authors, but emblems of the virtues which she embodies. Each tome is bound in the colour traditionally associated with its quality: gold for Charity; blue for Faith; grey for Prudence; green for Hope; white for Temperance; and red for Fortitude. The picture depicts the Virgin being instructed by her mother in the womanly art of embroidery, but the presence of the books does not indicate the learning which she will pursue in the future, but symbolizes the codification of the knowledge which she has locked up inside herself. To quote one of the sonnets which Rossetti appended to the catalogue of the 1849 Free Exhibition, where the painting was first shown, and which also appears on the frame:

The books (whose head
Is golden charity, as Paul hath said)
Those virtues are wherein the soul is rich.[1]

But the reading material of *Paolo and Francesca da Rimini* (1855) (Fig. 7) is turned to no such divine purpose. The two lovers illustrate Dante's lines, inscribed, on the lower member of the frame, in Cary's translation:

[1] Quoted by Virginia Surtees, *The Paintings and Drawings of Dante Gabriel Rossetti (1828–1882): A Catalogue Raisonée*, 2 vols. (Oxford, 1971), ii. 10. For the symbolic tradition of Mary being compared to a closed book, see Anna Jameson, *Legends of the Madonna* (1852), pp. xlviii–xlix.

> One day,
> For our delight we read of Lancelot,
> How him love thrall'd. Alone we were, and no
> Suspicion near us. Oft-times by that reading
> Our eyes were drawn together, and the hue
> Fled from our alter'd cheek. But at one point
> Alone we fell. When of that smile we read,
> The wished smile so rapturously kiss'd
> By one so deep in love, then he, who ne'er
> From me shall separate, at once my lips
> All trembling kiss'd.[2]

Inflamed by the text, the reading is abandoned in favour of mutually impassioned embraces. These are far more fervent than those depicted in a slightly earlier painting of the same couple by William Dyce, where Francesca, her hand still resting demurely on the book's pages, adopts an attitude of passive submission rather than wholehearted rapture (Fig. 8).[3] In Rossetti's water-colour, the all-encompassing sexual swoon renders the lovers apparently oblivious to the little flickering, decorative flames of the circle of the lustful which Dante and Virgil observe with sorrowful fascination as they look towards the right-hand panel. Ruskin, who offered the water-colour to his protégée Ellen Heaton, expressed some doubt concerning the boldness of the scene: 'Prudish people might perhaps think it not quite a young lady's drawing. I don't know. All the figures are draped—but I don't quite know how people would feel about the *subject* . . . '.[4]

Rossetti's two paintings embody two major possibilities for the cultural representation of women and reading during the period. Either the woman is improved and educated through access to approved knowledge, which builds on the innately valuable characteristics which she was presumed to retain within her own body; or reading of the forbidden leads to her downfall. Moreover, their compositions suggest differing forms of reading. Looking at the first of the pictures, the spectator is placed at a distance, both by the formality of the scene, and by the demands of interpreting the iconographic significance of the lily and the rose, the lamp, the dove, the palm frond and the branch of thorns, the carefully tended vine, and the colours of High Church ecclesiastical vestments.

[2] *The Vision; or Hell, Purgatory, and Paradise, of Dante Alighieri* trans. Revd. Henry Francis Cary (new ed., 1850), 28–9. Cary's translation, which first appeared in 1814, remained the standard English version of Dante for most of the nineteenth century. The text continues: 'The books and writer both | Were love's purveyors. In its leaves that day | We read no more.' The choice of subject-matter may also have been influenced by Leigh Hunt's 'The Story of Rimini' (1816).

[3] Similarly, in Alexander Munro's marble sculpture of 1852, Francesca remains demure, with downcast eyes, in contrast to Paolo's decidedly fervent advances. See Benedict Read and Joanna Barnes (eds.), *Pre-Raphaelite Sculpture: Nature and Imagination in British Sculpture 1848–1914* (1991), 111–12.

[4] John Ruskin to Ellen Heaton, Heaton collection, quoted by Surtees, *Paintings and Drawings of Dante Gabriel Rossetti*, ii. 37.

6. Dante Gabriel Rossetti, *The Girlhood of Mary Virgin*, (1848–9)

7. Dante Gabriel Rossetti, *Paolo and Francesca da Rimini*, (1855)

8. William Dyce, *Francesca da Rimini*, (1837)

She or he has to be both alert and knowledgeable: ideal characteristics in a reader. *Paolo and Francesca*, on the other hand, invites one to read a narrative in which the focus is on human self-absorption to the exclusion of even the most immediate features of the environment. But we are invited to enjoy the aesthetics of the depiction without—even if one is instantly familiar with Dante—entering into conscious moral judgement. In other words, the spectator is positioned in a relation to Paolo and Franscesca analogous to that which they themselves experienced towards Lancelot and Guinevere. This position encourages sympathy and emotional identification, rather than critical detachment.

There was nothing new for the Victorians in proclaiming woman's affectability, nor in recommending that she should be protected from reading certain texts, as she should be encouraged to read others. These recommendations were based on paradoxical grounds. First, the argument ran, certain texts might corrupt her innocent mind, hence diminishing her value as a woman. Second, it was often put forward that she, as woman, was peculiarly susceptible to emotionally provocative material. This paradox serves above all to heighten the importance that woman's reading has held, historically, as a site on which one may see a variety of cultural and sexual anxieties displayed.

The latter half of the sixteenth century seems to have been, as Caroline Lucas has lucidly argued, the first time in English literary history that women were recognized as constituting a specific secular readership.[5] Following the publication of William Painter's *Palace of Pleasure* (1566), the growing number of romances, focusing on love and courtship rather than on chivalric adventure as their predecessors had done, were usually directed, sometimes specifically dedicated, to women. Warnings about the pernicious effects of romance reading had already been uttered, notably by Juan Luis Vives: 'a woman should beware of all these books, like as of serpents or snakes'.[6] They might, such imagery suggests, allow evil to enter the woman insidiously whilst her mind is off guard. Vives marvelled 'that wise fathers will suffer their daughters, or husbands their wives, or that the manners and customs of people will dissemble

---

[5] For a full discussion of this phenomenon, and of the relationship between Elizabethan romance and current theories about women and romance reading, see Caroline Lucas, *Writing for Women: The Example of Woman as Reader in Elizabethan Romance* (Milton Keynes and Bristol, Pa., 1989). Renaissance books which seem to have been intended specifically for women have been identified by Suzanne Hull, *Chaste, Silent and Obedient: English Books for Women, 1475–1640* (San Marino, Calif., 1982). Hull also suggests some reasons why the women's readership should have increased so suddenly at this time: the growth of a middle class, bringing with it increased leisure opportunities; increased educational opportunities; the rise of professional writers dependent on book purchasers as well as patrons; and the need of booksellers for new markets. See also Ruth Kelso, *The Doctrine for the Lady of the Renaissance* (Urbana, Ill., 1956; 1978).

[6] Juan Luis Vives, *The Instruction of a Christian Woman*, trans. Richard Hyrde (c.1540); ed. Foster Watson, *Vives and the Renascence Education of Women* (1912), 61. For a discussion of Vives's work, see Valerie Wayne, 'Some Sad Sentence: Vives' *Instruction of a Christian Woman*', in Margaret Hannay (ed.), *Silent but for the Word: Tudor Women as Patrons, Translators, and Writers of Religious Works* (Ohio, 1985), 15–29.

and overlook, that women shall use to read wantonness',[7] and he consolidated his emphasis that men possess the authority which enables them to determine what women should or should not read, by claiming that since women have only a small amount of learning, they should not trust their own judgement as to what it is proper and 'wholesome' for them to read, but should defer to men's superior knowledge and wisdom.

Vives, coming to England in 1523 as a member of Katherine of Aragon's court, was primarily concerned with the education of princesses and aristocratic young ladies. Later Renaissance advice about women and reading was largely written with a growing middle-class audience in mind, but the emphasis was essentially the same. It was clearly stated that women should not choose their own reading material; and that it should be chosen for them with care. Thus Thomas Salter, in *A Mirrhor mete for all Mothers, Matrones, and Maidens* (1579), wishes that girls be forbidden from reading 'lascivious Songes, filthie Ballades, and undecent books'—indeed, he condemns fathers who give their daughters this type of material—and that rather 'our wise Matrone, shall reade or cause her Maidens to reade, the examples and lives of godly and vertuous Ladies'.[8] He claims that: 'you shall never repeate the vertuous lives of any such Ladies as, *Claudia, Portia, Lucretia* and such like were, but you shall kindle a desire in them to treade their steppes, and become in tyme like unto them.'[9] The patterns of reasoning which lay behind Renaissance prescriptive remarks concerning woman's reading were remarkably close, in outline, to ones which were repeated during the next three centuries, linking together preoccupations with bodily and mental fitness. Whilst too great an acquaintance with light reading might lead her sexually astray, either in imagination or reality, it would also distract her from developing intellectually and spiritually. Edward Hake makes this point in *A Touchestone for this time present* (1574): 'Eyther shee is altogither kept from exercises of good learning, and knowledge of good letters, or else she is so nouseled in amorous bookes, vaine stories and fonde trifeling fancies, that shee smelleth of naughtinesse even all hir lyfe after.'[10] Yet the parental responsibility and practical education recommended by Salter and Hake in relation to the young woman are not to be understood as a means towards encouraging her own independent growth into self-knowledge, confidence, and articulacy.[11]

[7] *Vives and the Renascence Education of Women*, 58.

[8] Thomas Salter, *A Mirrhor mete for all Mothers, Matrones, and Maidens, intituled the Mirrhor of Modestie* (1579), sig. C iii; sig. Bii^v.

[9] Ibid. sig. Bii_j.

[10] Edward Hake, *A Touchestone for this time present . . . Whereunto is annexed a perfect rule to be observed of all Parents and Scholemaisters, in the trayning up of their Schollers and Children in learning* (1574), sig. C^4.

[11] See Joan Kelly-Gadol, 'Did Women have a Renaissance?', in R. Bridenthal and C. Koonz (eds.), *Becoming Visible: Women in European History* (Boston, 1977), 137–64, for critiques of the assumption that the general growth of humanist learning in the Renaissance period led to greater intellectual independence for women. For a general discussion of advice to women in this period, see Ann Rosalind Jones, 'Nets and Bridles: Early Modern Conduct Books and Sixteenth-Century Women's Lyrics', in Nancy Armstrong and Leonard Tennenhouse (ed.), *The Ideology of Conduct: Essays on Literature and the History of Sexuality* (1987), 39–72.

Like the utilitarian characteristics praised by Guazzo in 'Domestic Conversation', the third book of his *Civil Conversation*, or like the obedient, subordinate, but useful wife commended in William Gouge's frequently reprinted collection of sermons, *Of Domesticall Duties* (1622; 1627; 1634), the tastes and attitudes stimulated by a girl's reading were, right through the seventeenth century, habitually ideally seen as preparation for her role within marriage. Romances, on the other hand, could instil false expectations, 'insinuate themselves into their unwary readers', even 'instruct in the necessary Artifices of deluding Parents and Friends, and put her ruine perfectly in her own power'.[12] Nor did escapist reading provide the sole cause for anxiety. Particularly in the mid-decades of the century, the relationship between gender and the authority of interpretation was highlighted through the debates concerning women preachers and prophets.[13]

Notwithstanding these and other references, it is difficult to reconstruct a coherent body of theory concerning women and reading before the eighteenth century, or even to observe the persistent recurrence of stereotypes. It is still harder to collect accounts by women of their reading experiences, except in the case of those who possessed and left records of their exceptional degree of learning. Women's libraries were catalogued relatively seldom in comparison with men's. Although, of course, many women would have had access to the collections of their fathers or husbands, it is, again, difficult to state with any certitude the extent to which they made use of family libraries. However, the volume of commentary on women's reading increased dramatically during the eighteenth century and the early years of the nineteenth. It can be found within general studies of literature, especially those examining the rapid growth of novel production; within the growing number of advice manuals aimed specifically at young girls and their mothers, and within fiction itself.[14] As in the earlier period, the anxieties expressed fall into easily identifiable categories. In particular, one encounters the familiar fear that young women will be corrupted by what they read, and, becoming preoccupied with the importance of romance, will seek perpetually for excitement; and the criticism that reading fiction, especially when carried to excess, wastes time which may more valuably be employed elsewhere. In the later years of the eighteenth century a new apprehension appears: that reading may teach politically seditious attitudes, especially, but not exclusively, challenging the role of the family and the position of woman in relation to authority. Mrs Mowbray, for example, in the conservative novelist Amelia Opie's *Adeline Mowbray* (1804), reads Locke's *The*

---

[12] [R. Allestree] *The Ladies Calling. In two parts* (Oxford, 1673), ii. 9, 10.

[13] See Elaine Hobby, *Virtue of Necessity: English Women's Writing 1649–88* (1988), 26–53; Nigel Smith, *Perfection Proclaimed: Language and Literature in English Radical Religion, 1640–1660* (Oxford, 1989), 45–53; Keith Thomas, 'Women and the Civil War Sects', *Past and Present*, 13 (1958), 42–62.

[14] See Theodor Wolpers (ed.), *Gelebte Literatur in der Literatur: Studien zu Erscheinungsformen und Geschichte eines literarischen Motivs*, Abhandlungen der Akademie der Wissenschaft in Göttingen, Philologisch-Historische Klasse, Folge 3, Nr.152 (Göttingen, 1986).

Conduct of the Understanding as a child and then oversteps her filial place by recommending it to her parents as a text which will teach them how to 'think'. Her daughter, Adeline, finds that the reading to which she has been introduced by her mother encourages her to believe that marriage is something consecrated merely by mutual 'honour', without the need for civil ceremony. Inevitably, this leads to disaster.

In the final pages of her *Vindication of the Rights of Women*, Mary Wollstonecraft criticizes sentimental fiction for encouraging 'a romantic twist of the mind', a false view of human nature, and for teaching women to articulate 'the language of passion in affected tones', placing more reliance on their sensations than on their reason. The best way to correct a fondness for novels, she believes, 'is to ridicule them'.[15] This, of course, had already been done during the eighteenth century, and an examination of this ridicule is as revelatory of the growing variety of stereotypes, anxieties, and prescriptions concerning women and reading as is the range of more conspicuously serious material which is to be found in the rapidly growing advice literature and periodical reviews of the time.[16] Taken together, all these genres demonstrate the mid-eighteenth-century consolidation of the grounds on which Victorian attitudes to women's reading were to be based.

Charlotte Lennox anticipated Wollstonecraft's request for ridicule in *The Female Quixote* (1752), satirizing the influence of the heroic romance tradition, and concluding with the moralizing dialogue of the doctor on the dreadful effects such reading may have: 'The immediate tendency of these books . . . is to give new fire to the passions of revenge and love: two passions which, even without such powerful auxiliaries, it is one of the severest labours of reason and piety to suppress.'[17] The theme of the mental stultification and blunted judgement which is induced by reading fiction was a recurrent one in the second half of the century. It was not necessarily central to a narrative, but used as a pointer to the interpretation of character. In Eliza Hamilton's *Letters of a Hindoo Rajah* (1796), for example, we find not only the deplorable example of the niece of the Dewan who had become addicted to novels, which 'by giving constant fuel to the vivid flame of youthful imagination, created such an

---

[15] Mary Wollstonecraft, *Vindication of the Rights of Women* (1792; repr. Harmondsworth, 1975), 305–9.

[16] For full discussions on attitudes to reading, esp. women and reading, in the eighteenth century, see Peter de Bolla, *The Discourse of the Sublime: History, Aesthetics and the Subject* (Oxford, 1989), ch. 10; W. F. Gallaway, Jr., 'The Conservative Attitude Toward Fiction, 1770–1830', *PMLA* 55 (1940), 1041–59; Winfield H. Rogers, 'The Reaction against Melodramatic Sentimentalism in the English Novel, 1796–1830', *PMLA* 49 (1934), 98–122; Kathryn Shevelow, *Women and Print Culture: The Construction of Femininity in the Early Periodical* (1989); John Tinnon Taylor, *Early Opposition to the English Novel: The Popular Reaction from 1760 to 1830* (New York, 1943); Ioan Williams (ed.), *Novel and Romance 1700–1800: A Documentary Record* (1970). Eighteenth-century advice literature, and its relation to the education of girls, is discussed by Mitzi Myers, ' "A Taste for Truth and Reading": Early Advice to Mothers on Books for Girls', *Children's Literature Association Quarterly*, 12 (1987), 118–24.

[17] Charlotte Lennox, *The Female Quixote* (1752; repr. Pandora: Mothers of the Novel, 1986), 420.

insatiable craving for novelty, as rendered every other sort of reading, tasteless and insipid', but the fate of another susceptible novel-reader, Julia, who:

has, it seems, suffered much from the unexpected metamorphosis of a charming swain; who, soon after he had introduced himself to her acquaintance, as a hero of exalted sentiment and tender sensibility, was unfortunately recognized by certain sagacious men, from a place called Bow-street, to be one of the tribe of Swindlers . . . [18]

A specific target is offered, famously, when the Radcliffean Gothic is mocked in *Northanger Abbey* and Henry Tilney, as part of his debunking, shows up to Catherine 'the liberty which her imagination had dared to take'.[19] If Austen is double-edged in her mockery here (for Catherine has plenty of justification for being apprehensive of her actual, rather than her imaginary, situation, given the undramatic but humanly damaging bigotry and selfishness that it contains), she returns with another twist in *Sanditon*. Here, she shows that it would be misguided to presume that only women might be affected adversely by what they read. The fanciful plot of seduction which Sir Edward develops, Austen indicates, was partly attributable to particular aspects of his indolent lifestyle:

The truth was that Sir Edw: whom circumstances had confined very much to one spot had read more sentimental Novels than agreed with him. His fancy had been early caught by all the impassioned, & most exceptionable parts of Richardsons; & such Authors as have since appeared to tread in Richardson's steps, so far as Man's determined pursuit of Woman in defiance of every opposition of feeling & convenience is concerned, had since occupied the greater part of his literary hours, & formed his Character.[20]

The trope of satirizing human (and usually women's) gullibility when it comes to confusing the fictional world with the real is, of course, dependent for its didacticism on a further fiction: that the worlds which Arabella, Catherine, and others inhabit are, in their turn, 'real'. They are presented by the novel with a serious aim in view, such as warning the heroine/reader of the folly of eloping, or of not distinguishing carefully enough between love and passion.

But if these women novelists are anxious about the naïve vulnerability of their readers, different sorts of worries are voiced by their male counterparts: worries which seem to be stimulated by the growing number of women readers, and, especially, by the phenomenon of the growth of the circulating library.[21] It is in

[18] Eliza Hamilton, *Translation of the Letters of a Hindoo Rajah*, 2 vols. (1796), ii. 38, 337.
[19] Jane Austen, *Northanger Abbey* (1818); repr. *The Works of Jane Austen*, ed. R. W. Chapman, vol. V., (1969), 199.
[20] Ead., *Sanditon* (written 1817); *Works*, vi. (1972), 404.
[21] Paul Kaufman, in *Libraries and their Users* (1969), draws on archival material to prove that in Bath, at least, in the latter half of the eighteenth century, over 70% of subscribers were men, concluding that 'the imposition of the burden of responsibility upon women is an irresponsible and essentially arrogant male slander' (p. 225). He also explodes the general assumption that the stock of the average library was predominantly fiction. On the other hand, he does not explore the probability that many women readers would have borrowed on a subscription taken out in their husband's or father's name.

relation to this 'ever-green tree of diabolical knowledge' that another recurrent vein of satire develops, reliant on the fear, as Sheridan's Sir Anthony Absolute goes on, 'that they who are so fond of handling the leaves, will long for the fruit at last.'[22] Great play is made on titles and their associations, both of actual works and of invented texts. Lucy, in *The Rivals*, is unable to obtain *The Reward of Constancy*, *The Fatal Connection*, *The Mistakes of the Heart*, *The Delicate Distress* or *The Memoirs of Lady Woodford* for her mistress: the last of these titles reminding one that it was not just the novels stocked by circulating libraries which gave rise to anxiety, but the volumes which dealt with contemporary scandals or *causes célèbres* or which contained the supposed biographies of actresses or prostitutes. The Reverend Horace Homespun, one of the letter-writers in Courtney Melmoth's *The Pupil of Pleasure* (1777), similarly rails against the fact that the bookseller-cum-haberdasher at the fashionable resort of Buxton 'has nothing in his shop but the trash that circulates at a watering place amongst the women', and lightly hints at the links between reading and behaviour: a gaggle of ladies entered the shop:

in great anxiety to find THESE MISTAKES OF THE HEART had been carried off last season, by a person who took the road to GRETNA GREEN—the Scotch marrying village—with her footman, in her way to London; though some (said the haberdasher archly) may think *that* was going a round-about way too.[23]

In these male-derived caricatures, there is blatant class anxiety about the cultural levity of these social parvenues. Though derogatory, it is not, perhaps, as constricting in its implications as contemporary attacks on 'blue-stockings',[24] for the suggestion is not that women should not read, but rather that they should read something less frivolous. Such reading as they might be permitted to undertake, however, should not hamper their social usefulness, but should, whilst endeavouring 'to call forth the reasoning powers of girls into action' enrich 'the mind with useful and interesting knowledge suitable to their sex', to quote Thomas Gisborne.[25] Then, the very titles of the books in these satiric pieces suggest that a 'natural' affinity between women and the sentimental is being taken for granted. This criticism was shared by more overtly serious writers, women as well as men. Clara Reeve, for example, in the preface to *The School for Widows* (1791) writes of the 'rage for SENTIMENT' which had prevailed recently, and had 'given rise to a great number of whining, maudlin stories, full of false sentiment and false delicacy, calculated to excite a kind of morbid sensibility, which is to faint under evry ideal distress, and every fantastical trial'. Readers consume such fiction 'disarmed of that strength and for-titude'—traditional characteristics of the chivalric romance *hero*—which should

---

[22] Richard Brinsley Sheridan, *The Rivals* (1775), ed. Richard Little Purdy (Oxford, 1935), I. ii. 17.

[23] Courtney Melmoth, *The Pupil of Pleasure* (1777), 30.

[24] For 'bluestockings', see Sylvie Harstack Myers, *The Bluestocking Circle: Women, Friendship, and the Life of the Mind in Eighteenth-Century England* (Oxford, 1990).

[25] Thomas Gisborne, *An Enquiry into the Duties of the Female Sex* (1797), 58.

be used to encounter and vanquish difficulties. At worst, it breeds the reaction exemplified by the 'poor lady, whose sensibility was excited by the broken leg of an unfortunate wheelbarrow!'[26] Wollstonecraft, too, presents, by 1792, women's responses to such fiction, or to its language, as not only undesirably anti-rationalist, but as liable to render them weak or confirm them in a subordinate position. She wishes, she states in her introduction to the *Vindication*, 'to persuade women to endeavour to acquire strength, both of mind and body, and to convince them that the soft phrases, susceptibility of heart, delicacy of sentiment, and refinement of taste, are almost synonymous with epithets of weakness'.[27] By the last chapter, it is clear where she locates at least one source of women's familiarity with such powerless language when she writes of 'the women who are amused by the reveries of the stupid novelists, who, knowing little of human nature, work up stale tales, and describe meretricious scenes, all retained in a sentimental jargon, which equally tend to corrupt the taste, and draw the heart aside from its daily duties'.[28] For Wollstonecraft, it was a political imperative to fight assumptions, whether satirically expressed or otherwise, about the way women's 'natural' delicacy and sensitivity renders them vulnerable to the appeal of fiction. This imperative throws into strong relief the very relationship between the natural and the cultural which was to be central to the entire issue of women's writing and reading for the next century.

The debate about women as readers in the latter half of the eighteenth century overlapped with a broader discussion concerning the status of the novel and its possible effects. The Reverend Vicesimus Knox, in his essay, 'On Novel Reading', presumed, as many since him have done, that the young reader will 'identify' with the experiences and feelings of a story's central character, even if the novel is, like one of Samuel Richardson's, written with an ultimately didactic end: 'It is to be feared, the moral view is rarely regarded by youthful and inexperienced readers, who naturally pay the chief attention to the lively descriptions of love, and its effects; and who, while they read, eagerly wish to be actors in the scenes which they admire.'[29] Sentimental fictions, once again, are likely to inflame undesirable activity, since they 'tend to give the mind a degree of weakness, which renders it unable to resist the slightest impulse of libidinal passion'. Although an implied reference to femininity may be detected through the associations surrounding a word like 'weakness', there is no clear evidence that Knox has either sex specifically in mind. The equal vulnerability, in theory, of men and women in relation to what they read is made explicit in the conversation which takes place on Evening XII in Clara Reeve's *The Progress of*

[26]   Clara Reeve, *The School for Widows*, 3 vols. (1791), i, pp. [v]–vii.
[27]   Wollstonecraft, *Vindication*, 81–2.
[28]   Ibid. 306.
[29]   Vicesimus Knox, 'On Novel Reading', *Essays Moral and Literary*, 3 vols. (Basle and Strasburg, 1800), i. 101–2.

Romance (1785) between Hortensus, Sophronia, and Euphrasia. Hortensus talks of the 'evils' of novel reading: 'The seeds of vice and folly are sown in the heart,—the passions are awakened,—false expectations are raised.—A young woman is taught to expect adventures and intrigues,—she expects to be addressed in the style of these books, with the language of flattery and adulation.'[30] Euphrasia comes back at these and other complaints, asking 'is all this severity in behalf of our sex or your own?':

HORT. Of both.—Yet yours are most concerned in my remonstrance for they read more of these books than ours, and consequently are most hurt by them.

EUPH. It seems to me that you are unreasonably severe upon these books, which you suppose to be appropriate to our sex, (which however is not the case):—not considering how many books of worse tendency, are put into the hands of the youth of your own, without scruple.

HORT. Indeed!—how will you bring proofs of that assertion?

EUPH. I will not go far for them. I will fetch them from the School books, that generally make part of the education of young men—They are taught the History—the Mythology—the morals—of the great Ancients, whom you and all learned men revere.

She continues by telling how Lucretius teaches the false notion that the indulgence of passions and appetites is the truest wisdom; that Juvenal and Persius 'describe such scenes, as I may venture to affirm that Romance and Novel-writers of any credit would blush at: and *Virgil*—the modest and delicate *Virgil*, informs them of many things, they had better be ignorant of.' Hortensus is gratifyingly overwhelmed by the cogency of this argument:

I am astonished—admonished—and convinced!—I cannot deny the truth of what you have advanced, I confess that a reformation is indeed wanting in the mode of Education of the youth of our sex.

SOPHRONIA. Of both sexes you may say.—We will not condemn yours and justify our own.

The conclusion, as voiced by Euphrasia and echoed by Reeve in her conclusion to the whole work, is that it is essential for parents and guardians to pay attention to the formation of good taste in reading, teaching children, from their infancy, 'to despise paltry books of every kind'.[31]

Yet despite the attempt made in Evening XII at levelling the terms of anxiety concerning reading, it is ultimately suggested by Reeve, like so many of her contemporaries, that it is the female who is most at risk. *The Progress of Romance* concludes with a list of recommended 'Books for Young Ladies', ranging from

[30] Clara Reeve, *The Progress of Romance*, 2 vols. (1785), ii. 78.
[31] Ibid. 80–3.

Dr Percival's *A Father's Instructions* through the *Spectator* and the *Rambler* and Richardson to Moore's *Fables for the Female Sex* and *Mrs Talbot's Meditations for every Day in the Week*. Moreover, the connection between women, reading, and moral responsibility is underlined still further by the concluding remarks in which Reeve tells us that 'It is certainly the duty of every Mother, to consider seriously, the consequences of suffering children to read all the books that fall in their way indiscriminately.'[32] The role of the mother, which was to become such a prominent theme in the Victorian period, was emphasized by others, too, in both published and private contexts. Mary Hays, for example, writing to a woman friend in 1793, advised her not to be too alarmed at her daughter's predilection for novels and romances. More, Hays thinks, would be lost by forbidding these than by taking the opportunity to discuss the books with her, since this would damage the daughter's confidence without correcting her taste. Rather like Wollstonecraft maintaining in the *Vindication* that, on balance, any reading is better than no reading, Hays claims that 'The love of the marvellous, or of extraordinary and unexpected coincidences, is natural to young minds, that have any degree of energy and fancy.' To avoid risking the loss of these characteristics, a mother should read with her daughters, should converse with them about the merits of various authors, and should 'accustom them to critical and literary discussions'. Eventually, they, like their mothers, should disapprove of anything that has 'an improper and immoral tendency'.[33]

Notably, the protests of Wollstonecraft, Reeve, and others about women being 'naturally' more susceptible to being manipulated by their reading matter are couched in the abstract, if politically loaded language of eighteenth-century debate. They are largely arguing within assumed categories which can be proved or disproved by appeals to observable social behaviour. Yet during the 1830s and 1840s, whilst the relation between a woman's reading and her social behaviour was still of central interest, attention shifted towards those biological characteristics of woman which make her different from a man. She was considered less able, for example, to withstand the rigours of a demanding educational programme, due to the assumption that she had energies which needed conserving for her crucial task as mother.[34] As we shall see, physiological, rather than social factors were increasingly under scrutiny. Maternity was no longer regarded, in relation to women's reading, simply as a function which ensured close social guiding of one's offspring. Rather, its

---

[32] Clara Reeve, *The Progress of Romance*, 101.

[33] Mary Hays, *Letters and Essays, Moral and Miscellaneous* (1793), quoted Williams, *Novel and Romance*, 383.

[34] For the argument that the apparent authority offered by Victorian science and 'arguments from nature' served to disengage the feminism of the time (with the exceptions of Harriet Taylor and John Stuart Mill) from its Enlightenment philosophical roots, as exemplified by Wollstonecraft's non-fictional prose, see Flavia Alaya, 'Victorian Science and the "Genius" of Woman', *Journal of the History of Ideas*, 38 (1977), 261–80. Persuasive though Alaya's argument is, she underplays the emphasis laid by a range of Victorian women writers on the importance of women being rational, rather than exclusively emotional, beings.

'natural' concomitant, the ability to venture with sympathetic identification into the lives of others, guaranteed that women's susceptibility to identificatory modes of reading was perceived to be related to the inescapable facts about the way in which her biological make-up influenced the operations of her mind.

In recent years, woman as reader has again become a prominent topic in literary criticism. Some of this discussion has reappropriated familiar preoccupations, albeit from a feminist angle. Thus romantic fiction has once again come under scrutiny for encouraging the myth that falling in love is the supreme adventure, with marriage the end of the story, and for making women regard themselves as dependent on men, and on male values, for their sense of their own value and the terms in which they express it.[35] Such condemnations of the genre tend to view the production of romance fiction in terms of conspiracy theory: a means, to quote Helen Taylor, 'of keeping women quiet, complaisant, heterosexual and home-and-family oriented'.[36] Deriving, largely, from the early years of the current wave of the women's movement, these studies were not able to take on board either the increasing sexual explicitness of some titles within the genre, nor of a more interesting phenomenon: the growth of the blockbuster featuring women who are materially and emotionally successful and strong in their careers as well as in their personal lives.[37] Nor did they fully consider the role played by women in producing such fictions, nor, except for some passing acknowledgement that romances sometimes supply an imaginative need, did the early critics dwell on the consideration that reading romances might have a positive function in women's lives which makes them more than a substitute for librium.

More recently, though, the romance form has had its defenders.[38] Starting, once again, from the premiss that a woman will most probably identify with the interests of her sex as depicted within writing, they have interrogated the implications of entering the realm of fantasy through such reading matter. Rather than accept that the reader is trapped into the belief that a successful relationship with a man should be rated above all other forms of self-validation and fulfilment, Janice Radway and others have argued that entering the

[35] For particularly energetic critiques, see Germaine Greer, *The Female Eunuch* (1970; repr. 1971), 198–218; Shulamith Firestone, *The Dialectic of Sex* (1970), 139.

[36] Helen Taylor, 'Romantic Readers', in Helen Carr (ed.), *From My Guy to Sci-Fi: Genre and Women's Writing in the Postmodern World* (1989), 60. Taylor's article provides an excellent summary of debates about women readers and romance fiction in the 1980s.

[37] For discussions of these new developments in the genre, see Carol Thurston, *The Romance Revolution: Erotic Novels for Women and the Quest for a New Sexual Identity* (Urbana, Ill., and Chicago, 1987).

[38] See e.g. Janet Batsleer, 'Pulp in the Pink', *Spare Rib*, 109 (1981) 52–5; Jan Cohn, *Romance and the Erotics of Property: Mass-Market Fiction for Women* (Durham, NC, 1985); Valerie Hey, 'The Necessity of Romance', *Women's Studies Occasional Papers*, 3 (1983); Tania Modleski, *Loving with a Vengeance* (1982); and, to my mind, the most lucid, stimulating, and sophisticated study yet to appear, Janice Radway, *Reading the Romance: Women, Patriarchy, and Popular Literature* (Chapel Hill, NC, 1984).

romance actually allows the woman to feel, imaginatively, at the powerful centre of her own life. She occupies the place of a woman in relation to whom men, for once, allow and accept that the private, emotional, caring sphere is more important than an external world of publicly acknowledged success. Such theories, indeed, can plausibly be applied retrospectively to most nineteenth-century romantic plots.

The most evident limitation of these theories, however, is that they restrict themselves to the thought of reading as a form of escapism:[39] escape into imagined lives more active and interesting than the reader's own, and into fictional spaces where 'feminine' values are granted more weight than is often the case in 'real' life. Alternatively, as we shall see, in the nineteenth century, escape might be into a world which would free the woman reader from the immediate and particular pressure to live up to such values. The prevalence of romance in the contemporary novel, and the limitations of the home life of the middle-class girl which made fiction eminently suitable as a vehicle for escape were, of course, painfully obvious to some nineteenth-century readers. Florence Nightingale asked, in *Cassandra*:

What are novels? What is the secret of the charm of every romance that ever was written? The first thing in a good novel is to place the persons together in circumstances which naturally call forth the high feelings and thoughts of the character, which afford food for sympathy between them on these points—romantic events they are called. The second is that the heroine has *generally* no family. These two things constitute the main charm of reading novels.[40]

Yet, in this unpublished protest against the lot of many home-based women forced to lead a sedentary life of crushing boredom, she wrote of their lives in a simile which consolidates the impression that the mind-numbing effects of fiction were seen as offering a means of escape: 'They are exhausted, like those who live on opium or on novels, all their lives—exhausted with feelings which lead to no action.'[41]

But the issue of women's reading goes far beyond their consumption of fiction. One of the earliest examples of research into nineteenth-century women readers, Amy Cruse's wide-ranging but infuriatingly unreferenced *The Victorians and their Books* (1935) demonstrates, through the weight of detail that it offers, that women not only read material which it would be hard to subsume under the category of escapism, but read in a way which was often critically and intellectually alert to the issues raised within texts: issues of religious debate and controversy over evolution; of sexuality and education. Two subsequent pioneering studies of reading trends are, however, virtually silent on the topic of

[39] Although Radway, at least, acknowledges the appeal, and the empowering quality, of the historical, geographical, and working-environmental knowledge which is conveyed by these novels.

[40] Florence Nightingale, *Cassandra* (1852, rev. 1859); repr. in Ray Strachey, *The Cause* (1928), 397.

[41] Ibid. 407.

women as readers: Richard Altick's *The English Common Reader* (1957) and Louis James's tellingly titled *Fiction for the Working Man* (1963) do, none the less, provide invaluable information concerning the spread of literacy and the rapidly increasing availability of printed material among the skilled working classes and lower middle classes. And James, to be sure, has a chapter on 'The Paradox of the Domestic Story', showing the conventions on which the domestic genre depends, and indicating that, after the decline of the Gothic, it became the dominant form of popular fiction: 'a logical form of fiction for a "democratic" age. Its stories tell of people one can recognize. The reader can feel at home with it, place him (or more usually her) self in the picture. At the same time the realism is illusory. The situations are romanticized, the people less complicated, the horizon always, finally, bright.'[42] But he does not pause to consider that the demands of female and male readers might be different; that they might hold different responses to the situations and values depicted. Not until Sally Mitchell's work on a recurrent theme in popular fiction—and, indeed, in middle-class fiction—*The Fallen Angel: Chastity, Class and Women's Reading 1835–1880* (1981) is the issue of a woman's perspective in relation to James's prime concern, the periodical fiction of the period, treated fully.

This silence concerning woman as reader is found not only in historical work on readership, but, as is now notorious, reverberates through almost all the reader-response criticism of the 1960s and 70s, together with a uniform absence of references to differences created by class and race.[43] Norman Holland goes so far as to suggest that gender difference in reading applies only to popular writing, to 'the magazines of romance for women or adventure for men', tracing what he terms the 'deep' appeal of serious literature primarily to 'the fantasies of the developmental phases prior to latency, before fantasies and reading choice become markedly different for boys and girls'.[44] The best readers, like the best texts, this implies, are without gender: a suppression of difference which, as countless feminist critics have pointed out in relation to issues of literary value within and outside the curriculum, only serves to sustain, unchallenged, a status quo of dominant interests and biases.

[42] Louis James, *Fiction for the Working Man 1830–50: A Study of the Literature Produced for the Working Classes in Early Victorian Urban England* (1963; repr. Harmondsworth, 1974), 134. James does, however, consider aspects of working-class women's reading in 'The trouble with Betsy: Periodicals and the Common Reader in Mid-Nineteenth-Century England', in Joanne Shattock and Michael Wolff (eds.), *The Victorian Periodical Press: Samplings and Soundings* (Leicester, 1982), 349–66.

[43] See the cogent critique offered by Patrocinio P. Schweickart, 'Reading Ourselves: Toward a Feminist Theory of Reading', in Elizabeth A. Flynn and Patrocinio P. Schweickart (eds.), *Gender and Reading: Essays on Readers, Texts, and Contexts* (Baltimore, Md., and London, 1986), 31–62. As well as a variety of stimulating, relevant essays, this volume contains a valuable annotated bibliography on works published concerning the relationship between gender and reading up to 1983.

[44] Norman Holland, *The Dynamics of Literary Response* (New York, 1968), 51. For a critique of Holland which draws attention to his treatment of gender difference in reading, see Judith Kegan Gardiner, 'On Female Identity and Writing by Women', *Critical Inquiry*, 8 (1981), 347–61.

Michael Riffaterre, Wolfgang Iser, and Hans Robert Jauss, among others, have of course maintained that the text is the dominant force in creating the expectations and responses of a reader. The last two, at least, indicate in their writings that these expectations are going to be differently encoded according to the period at which text was written, and according to the audience originally envisaged for it and its particular 'horizon of expectations', to use Jauss's phrase.[45] But gender—whether of writer or reader—is, like the individual psychology of any reader, apparently assumed to be of little importance. Necessary revisionism is provided by Sally Mitchell, again, and by Elaine Showalter. Mitchell addressed the question of middle-class reading in an important article of 1977, 'Sentiment and Suffering: Women's Recreational Reading in the 1860s'. In this, she makes various convincing claims for the emotional part played by reading in women's lives. Above all, she argues, it offered them 'vicarious participation, emotional expression, and the feeling of community that arises from a recognition of shared dreams'.[46] She substantiates this point in *The Fallen Angel* with reference to a slightly different, less ubiquitously middle-class readership, when she maintains that 'literally millions of people were provided with emotional experiences that they held in common because they read the same fiction'. This must have been especially important to the wives of skilled working men: relatively house-bound, but not freed from their chores by hordes of servants, nor of a class which had habitual recourse to the gin-shop like the 'non respectable poor'.[47]

Further useful pointers to a study of the woman reader are offered by Elaine Showalter in *A Literature of their Own* (also published in 1977). Some of her hypotheses concerning the choices made by women novel writers during the Victorian and Edwardian periods may be extended to indicate the preferences of their readership. Showalter suggests, for example, that whilst they had little difficulty imagining heroines who were extensions of themselves, they had genuine problems in figuring suitable men to be companions for them: hence the proliferation of blinded, wounded, lame, sick, even temporarily transvestite men who are produced as possible mates: 'Men, these novels are saying, must learn how it feels to be helpless and forced unwillingly into dependency. Only then can they understand that women need love but hate to be weak. If he is to be redeemed and to rediscover his humanity, the "woman's man" must find out how it feels to be a woman.'[48] Like Mitchell, Showalter is interested in why the sensation fiction of the 1860s should have had such an appeal for the woman

---

[45] Hans Robert Jauss, 'Literary History as a Challenge to Literary Theory', *New Literary History*, 2 (1970), 14.

[46] Sally Mitchell, 'Sentiment and Suffering: Women's Recreational Reading in the 1860s', *Victorian Studies*, 21 (1977), 45.

[47] Ead., *The Fallen Angel: Chastity, Class and Women's Reading 1835–1880* (Bowling Green, Ohio, 1981).

[48] Elaine Showalter, *A Literature of their Own: British Women Novelists from Brontë to Lessing* (Princeton, NJ, 1977; repr. 1978), 152.

reader. She hypothesizes that the domestic crime and violence which the novels depicted, albeit in an exaggerated fashion, expressed a wide range of suppressed female emotions, the authors skilfully articulating 'the fantasies of their readers, fantasies that they themselves fervently shared'. At the same time, the writers, according to her, were subverting many of the premises of the traditional 'feminine' novel, substituting one set of fulfilled desires for an earlier, more conservative formulation.[49]

What, it is useful to ask at this point, might the imaginative fulfilment of desires through reading entail? Many nineteenth-century commentators, and the vast majority of novelists—including, up to a point, the sensation novelists—assumed that women wished for romantic fulfilment above all. This was a socially based assumption pre-dating, and doubtless feeding into, Freud's observation in 'The Relation of the Poet to Day-Dreaming' (1907) that male fantasies concentrate on dreams of ambition, female fantasies on erotic themes, figuring themselves as objects of desire.[50] In *Becoming a Heroine* (1982), Rachel Brownstein, fascinated by her own fascination with novels both as an adolescent and in later life, uses Freud, too, in developing the idea that admiration of the heroine of a romantic novel—'beautiful, wise, beloved, and lucky—is love for an idealized image of oneself'.[51] She quotes Freud's description of the feminine form of erotic life:

Women, especially if they grow up with good looks, develop a certain self-contentment which compensates them for the social restrictions that are imposed upon them in their choice of object. Strictly speaking, it is only themselves that such women love with an intensity comparable to that of the man's love for them. Nor does their need lie in the direction of loving, but of being loved; and the man who fulfils this condition is the one who finds favour with them.[52]

Accepting Freud's viewpoint, however, as Brownstein (just like many earlier readers) seems happy to do, means abandoning oneself as reader, and as woman, to a state of passive receptivity.

Yet, as Nancy Miller has asked, albeit again with writers rather than readers in mind: since Freud allows a small space in male egocentric fantasy for erotic wishes, may not egocentric, ambitious desires exist within woman's fantasy? She finds evidence for such desires not in specific forms of social achievement recorded in realist fiction, but in the way in which a female character manages to negotiate a plot with a self-exalting dignity, proving to be better than her victimizers. Such triumphant negotiation would be sustained by a reading of Mary Braddon's *Aurora Floyd*, for example, although the deaths of the heroines

[49] Ibid. 159.
[50] Sigmund Freud: 'The Relation of the Poet to Day-Dreaming', *Pelican Freud Library*, 14, 131–41.
[51] Rachel M. Brownstein, *Becoming a Heroine* (1982; repr. Harmondsworth, 1984), p. xiv.
[52] Freud, 'On Narcissism: An Introduction' (1914), *Pelican Freud Library*, 11, 82.

in certain other sensation novels (*Lady Audley's Secret*, or *East Lynne*, to take the two most obvious examples) would have to be explained away in the same manner that Miller deals with *The Mill on the Floss*: as necessary given the social context of reading and representation. In the fictional economy which Miller encourages her own readers to recognize, she maintains that:

egoistic desires would assert themselves paratactically alongside erotic ones. The repressed content, I think, would be, not erotic impulses, but an impulse to power: a fantasy of power that would revise the social grammar in which women are never defined as subjects; a fantasy of power that disdains a sexual exchange in which women can participate only as objects of circulation.[53]

Miller's comments are important to my later argument. However, there is little sign that she, or Mitchell, or Showalter conceive of their implied nineteenth-century readers as being consciously aware of what was happening to them as they read. In fact, they, like almost every commentator on nineteenth-century women's fiction, tacitly accept that readers identify almost automatically with the most attractive—if not the most conventional—central woman character available.[54] In assuming the ease with which identification takes place when reading, they are, of course, replicating a crucial nineteenth-century social and educational assumption. That identification was believed to happen when one read, and that it was thought that reading could powerfully instil and confirm desirable moral and social qualities, is exemplified particularly clearly in the numbers of brief biographical compilations produced during the period, and in the language of their prefaces and introductions. John Maw Darton's 1880 edition (18th, expanded) of *Famous Girls, who have become Illustrious Women*, a counterpart to *Brave Boys who have become Illustrious Men of our time* (1880), for example, ranges from Margaret Roper, 'The Loved Daughter of Sir Thomas More' and Fanny Burney, through Madame de Staël and Harriet Martineau, to Jenny Lind, the Princess of Wales, and Angela Burdett Coutts. Darton claims, in his editor's note, that his aim was 'to stimulate the minds of the daughters of England to courses of action as noble and intellectual as those which have made famous the heroines of my volume'.[55] Despite his predilection for the well-connected at birth, Darton does go to lengths to point out that 'wealth has its duties no less than its opportunities',[56] although little comfort could be drawn by some readers from the comment that 'It is not very wonderful, but certainly true, that all great men and women have had, with few exceptions, good, if not

---

[53] Nancy K. Miller, 'Emphasis Added: Plots and Plausibilities in Women's Fiction', *Subject to Change: Reading Feminist Writing* (New York, 1988), 35.

[54] For a consideration of the implications of the concept of identification as a mechanism of character formation, see W. W. Meissner, 'Notes on Identification. III. The Concept of Identification', *Psychoanalytic Quarterly*, 41 (1972), 224–60.

[55] Editor's note, J. M. Darton, *Famous Girls Who Have Become Illustrious Women of Our Time: Forming Models for Imitation by the Young Women of England* (1880).

[56] Ibid. 286.

distinguished, parents',[57] unless they were to derive from this a lesson as to the importance of their own future familial duties. However, throughout the volume the stress lies on the importance of taking individual, decisive action in whatever sphere lies before one. Such a point is reinforced in the numerous role-modelling articles offered in the *Girl's Own Paper*, featuring heroines as diverse as Florence Nightingale and Grace Darling on the one hand, and Renaissance women scholars in Bologna on the other.[58]

By and large, a much more passive model is proposed for identificatory imitation in Catherine Mary MacSorley's *A Few Good Women, and What They Teach Us* (1886). She takes a smaller number of examples through which to celebrate particular characteristics: the scientist Mary Somerville, to illustrate 'perseverance'; Agnes Jones, pioneer of nursing among the poor, to demonstrate 'thoroughness'; the Princesse de Lamballe, superintendent of the Queen's household at the time of the French Revolution (loyalty); the Marchioness de la Rochejaquelin, whose Christian patience enabled her to bear life in the Vendée during the Revolution (endurance); the Royalists Lady Russell (unselfishness) and the Countess of Derby (courage); St Monica (patience), and Hilda of Whitby (helpfulness). The introductory chapter emphasizes that Christ's life is the most significant and worthy example possible and that the qualities of courage, loyalty and endurance, in the abstract, are of course as applicable to men as they are to women. Yet MacSorley emphasizes that these particular examples, full of instances of women's trials and sorrows, offer specific instances of the brave self-sacrifice which is likely to be demanded of women in less sensational contexts:

you each of you know what kind of woman God meant you to *be*—what the very fact of your Christianity calls you to be; not a weak, selfish woman, living a colourless life, but strong, loving, helpful, unselfish; working for others, raising them, cheering them, making the world better and happier for your presence in it.

Will you not try to be such a woman as this?[59]

Similarly, the writer of *Girls and their Ways* (1881), in advocating the reading of Female Biography, reminds us that 'we cannot accomplish the great deeds, cannot make the signal discoveries of which we read; but we can emulate the patience, the tenacity, the resolution, the energy which led to such results'.[60] The headmistress Frances Buss underlined the particular importance to women of copying abstract virtues, claiming in one of her weekly addresses to the girls at the North London Collegiate School that:

One hears and reads of heroic women; every woman and girl is heroic who strictly does her daily duty lovingly, tenderly, cheerfully. There can be no greater mistake than to

---

[57] Ibid. 144.
[58] See e.g. Sylvia Thorne, 'Female Heroism', *Girl's Own Paper*, 1 (1880), 4–45; 'The Learned Ladies of Bologna', ibid. 147–9.
[59] Catherine Mary MacSorley, *A Few Good Women, and what they teach us. A Book for Girls* (1886), p. xvi.
[60] 'One Who Knows Them', *Girls and Their Ways* (1881), 189.

suppose that to be heroic we must go outside the bounds of our little circle; one's family duties are often enough to prove our energy, our fitness, our tenacity of purpose.[61]

Different yet again is Marie Trevelyan's *Brave Little Women*, a fictionalized set of tales founded on fact, each presenting a dramatic episode: a girl who rides for help when a beggar woman, let into the house on a stormy night, turns out to be a burglar—and, indeed, a man—in disguise; a strong swimmer who manages to rescue two children and their mother in a Hungarian flood; a Dakota girl and her brother who divert a prairie fire from engulfing the house in which their sick mother lies; a girl who saves the Royal Mail from being robbed by highwaymen. Trevelyan's preface explicitly informs us that many deeds of heroism by girls take place, but go unrecognized. Hers is an exercise in retrieval as well as didacticism:

courage and self-sacrifice are more likely to be fostered in the characters of girls by means of stories from real life, in which heroism plays a prominent part, than by sentimental fiction relating to commonplace events. Boys are stimulated in their efforts by records of thrilling adventures, and it would be satisfactory if similar circumstances awakened the latent heroism of our own little women.[62]

As we will see in Part II, the woman reader was expected, according to the terms of the contemporary psychological and physiological tenets which stressed her innate capacity for sympathy, to find it far easier than a man would do to identify with characters and incidents from her reading material. As is apparent from the examples of didactic biographies quoted above, this assumption could readily be deployed to underpin certain desired social beliefs, notably the development and consolidation of a bourgeois society structured around patriarchal ideologies, with women playing a crucial supportive, complementary role in the maintenance of such structures. But at the same time, of course, women, as both writers and readers, were far from innocent of the existence and functioning of these structures.

To introduce this range of popular educational biographical material does not just serve as an angle from which to examine the question of identificatory practices. It also reinforces the impression of the restricted nature of earlier studies of nineteenth- and early twentieth-century women readers. For it is very evident that, despite the anxieties generated by the practice of novel-reading, women read, and were encouraged to read, much more widely besides. A

[61] Grace Toplis (ed.), *Leaves from the Note-Books of Frances M. Buss, being Selections from her weekly addresses to the Girls of the North London Collegiate School* (1896), 9.

[62] Marie Trevelyan, *Brave Little Women: Tales of the Heroism of Girls. Founded on Fact* (1888), Preface. The examples cited here are representative, and far from exhaustive. For a further sample of the many works presenting positive images of women, see Jabez Burns, *The Mothers of the Wise and Good* (1846); Ellen Clayton, *Women of the Reformation* (1861); *English Female Artists* (1876); *Female Warriors* (1879); Henry Ewart, *True and Noble Women* (1888); Julia Kavanagh, *Women of Christianity exemplary for acts of piety and charity* (1852), and Louisa Menzies, *Lives of the Greek heroines* (1880).

significant task of this study, therefore, will be to examine the role and impact of this broader reading, and, in particular, to investigate the function both of the knowledge, and of the methods of expressing thought and understanding, which were thereby gained.

As will become clear, I am here interpreting knowledge not in the sense of the accumulated facts which might be amassed through, say, the thorough learning of those dissociated snippets of information to be found in the despairing refuge of the under-prepared governess and schoolmistress, *Mangnall's Questions*; the type of education insisted upon by Aurora Leigh's aunt:

> I learnt the royal genealogies
> Of Oviedo, the internal laws
> Of the Burmese empire,—by how many feet
> Mount Chimborazo outsoars Teneriffe.
> What navigable river joins itself
> To Lara, and what census of the year five
> Was taken at Klagenfurt,—because she liked
> A general insight into useful facts.[63]

Rather, I am employing the concept in the sense used by H. T. Buckle in 1858, when he stated that 'our knowledge is composed not of facts, but of the relations which facts and ideas bear to themselves and to each other'.[64] In more contemporary terms, I am falling in line with Foucault's view that forms of knowledge (*savoir*, in this context, rather than *connaissance*) are not characterized by positivities, whether these be a priori conditions or forms of rationality, but rather that knowledge should be regarded as consisting of a combination of factors, a group of elements 'formed in a regular manner by a discursive practice'. One must consider not just the object or objects with which this discursive practice treats, but 'the types of enunciation that it uses, the concepts that it manipulates, and the strategies that it employs'. Knowledge, for Foucault, is, moreover, 'defined by the possibilities of use and appropriation offered by discourse . . . there is no knowledge without a particular discursive practice; and any discursive practice may be defined by the knowledge that it forms'.[65] What constitutes knowledge, or what is considered legitimate knowledge, or useful knowledge, at any specific historic moment is, of course, going to be determined in part by who has the authority both to make such distinctions, and to have them accepted. But at the same time, this does not prevent the challenging of such authority through the assumption and manœuvring of knowledge in various ways, as with the development of the

---

[63] Elizabeth Barrett Browning, *Aurora Leigh*, i. 407–14.

[64] Henry Thomas Buckle, 'The Influence of Women on the Progress of Knowledge', *Fraser's Magazine for Town and Country*, 57 (1858), 397.

[65] Michel Foucault, *The Archaeology of Knowledge* (*L'Archéologie du savoir* (1969)), trans. A. M. Sheridan Smith (1972), 182–3.

politically articulate women's movement in the nineteenth century, and with the changes which took place within women's writing for women. On the one hand, women can be seen entering into traditionally masculine structures of knowledge, most particularly within education and the sciences: not just learning men's factual knowledge, but, more particularly, taking on board their understanding of the structuring of authority and power. On the other, they are to be observed constructing and maintaining alternative discursive systems which emphasize their comprehension of social practice: in the fiction of Olive Schreiner or Sarah Grand, say; in the dramatic monologues of Augusta Webster; or in magazines like the *Woman's Signal* or *Shafts*. Sometimes these systems operated according to the dominant definitions of what should constitute women's roles, but with increasing frequency, they functioned as a powerful, and shared critique on these definitions.

A central point in the argument of this book is to stress the importance of knowledge, and of awareness of the possession and employment of knowledge, to Victorian and Edwardian women's reading practices. Gaining knowledge, however, as should be clear from the terms I outline above, is not exactly a question of donning men's clothing, using their linguistic systems, putting on men's knowledge with their power. For in addition to the definitions proferred above, knowledge, for Foucault, and for the purposes of my argument, 'is also the space in which a subject may take up a position and speak of the objects with which he deals in his discourse.'[66] By 'subject' Foucault does not, of course, intend one to understand an identifiable individual, but rather 'a position that may be filled in certain conditions by various individuals'.[67] Foucault deliberately underplays, even discounts, the role played by subjectivity in perception: far more than I intend to do in the coming chapters. But what his words here implicitly invite one to consider is the space, or rather the spaces, which may be occupied by the reading, as well as by the writing subject. These spaces may to some degree be products of the texts themselves, constructing the responses of the ideal reader. Simultaneously, readers may bring their own assumptions to them. The same texts, in other words, may elicit complicity or resistance; the same reading subject, for that matter, cannot be relied upon to be a stable identity, responding in a predetermined way to each text that she encounters.

Using Foucault's work helps one to identify further limitations to the investigation which has so far been carried out in relation to women readers of the period. By stressing the way in which fiction, in particular, dramatized unvoiceable desires, Showalter and Mitchell have not made the naïve assumption that their readers are fully integrated subjects: they are alert to the constant interplay of ideology and unconscious in the reading process. However, they do not fully consider the part which reading may play in the

---

[66] Michel Foucault, *The Archaeology of Knowledge* 182.
[67] Ibid. 115.

continuing formation of the subject. The assumption that it *could* play a crucial part was central to the vast majority of nineteenth- and early twentieth-century commentators. The assumption that it had in fact done so, and could continue to do so, was expressed by many of the subjects themselves.[68]

Recent feminist theories about the development of the subject have tended to emphasize the difference between male and female subject formation. There has been, they argue, a tendency when describing the formation of men to stress the importance of individuation, following the model outlined and consolidated by Freud; whilst, in our culture, the woman has tended to develop her sense of subjecthood through a pattern which includes identification and bonding as well as differentiation. Nancy Chodorow's remarks have been particularly influential here, notably her belief that girls tend to keep a primary attachment to their mothers even as they pass into the Oedipal phase:

Mothers tend to experience their daughters as more like, and continuous with, themselves. Correspondingly, girls tend to remain part of the dyadic primary mother-child relationship itself. This means that a girl continues to experience herself as involved in issues of merging and separation, and in an attachment characterized by primary identification and the fusion of identification and object choice.[69]

The role played by the family structures of Western society is emphasized in the theories developed by Chodorow, and by Carol Gilligan,[70] giving their work the social and historic specificity necessary to remove the authors from accusations of essentialism, and ensuring that they operate very interestingly when tested against nineteenth-century reading theories. For throughout that century, it was commonly believed that women exercised a stronger role than anyone else when it came to establishing future reading habits: 'On them, as mothers and sisters, rests a great responsibility, for, as is well known, they are childhood's first teachers. In these days it is as important to teach our children what to read, as how to read, and thus it is imperative that a mother should read, so that she might direct her family in their choice of books.'[71] As Part III demonstrates,

---

[68] I am, of course, aware that in writing of the 'self' or of 'subjecthood' I am entering a minefield. I want, therefore, to make it clear that I am not proposing that the 'self' is to be understood as some unified, integral concept. A subject possesses both conscious and unconscious; and the 'self' is frequently divided, uncertain, and changes over time. Broadly speaking, however, it may be defined as the place from which any given individual perceives and speaks or writes, and against which it defines anything that it conceives of as 'other'. For further discussion of this topic, see esp. Paul Smith, *Discerning the Subject* (Minneapolis, 1988). In the context of this book, it is perhaps particularly useful to cite Elizabeth A. Flynn, 'Gender and Reading', *College English*, 45 (1983), 236: 'reading involves a confrontation between self and "other", the text, and the nature of that confrontation depends upon the background of the reader as well as upon the text'. 'Subjectivity and Feminism', ch. 2 of Rita Felski, *Beyond Feminist Aesthetics* (1989), 51–85, also provides a useful set of formulations in relation to women's writing.

[69] Nancy Chodorow, *The Reproduction of Mothering: Psychoanalysis and the Sociology of Gender* (Berkeley, Calif., 1978), 166.

[70] Carol Gilligan, *In a Different Voice: Psychological Theory and Women's Development* (Cambridge, Mass., 1982).

[71] 'Female Influence on Reading', *Library Journal*, 3 (1878), 380–1.

fathers as well as mothers played an important role in developing girls' reading practices, and reading could be a means by which distance from, as well as closeness to, the mother might be established. But whatever the reality, Victorian and Edwardian commentators repeatedly drew a connection between maternal nurturing responsibilties and the daughter's ingestion of print. This assumption has been consolidated by some twentieth-century psychoanalysts. James Strachey developed Freud's statement that books and paper are female symbols[72] into a claim (admittedly constructed with a male model of psycho-sexual development in mind) that reading has the unconscious significance of taking knowledge from the mother's body.[73] Melanie Klein adds to this 'that it is essential for a favourable development of the desire for knowledge that the mother's body should be felt to be well and unharmed'.[74]

But as I shall go on to argue, one need not just see the formation of the female subject through bonding and self-identification with others as taking place in relation to her biological mother. Reading, whether in the company of one's biological mother or not, is a means (as we have already seen Mitchell suggest) of becoming part of a broader community. Such a community may stretch far beyond the reader's immediate social world to incorporate other readers whom she may never meet in person, but with whom she shares horizons of expectations which have to a significant extent been built up through their common reading material.

Or rather, the woman reader becomes part not just of one single community of readers, but has the choice of many. For it would be most misleading, as I have been arguing, to take 'the woman reader' as if this term presupposed a fixed set of responses. It is because each woman reader is constituted by a complicated set of material, ideological, and psychoanalytic forces that recent text-based definitions and discussions of women readers—by, say, Jonathan Culler, or Paul Smith, or Mary Jacobus[75]—tend to fall down. The view that it may be possible to 'learn to read as a woman' (as women have for academic generations had to learn to read as men) provides one with terms which allow one to articulate that extension of textual and personal understanding which it is possible to achieve through consciously taking up a reading position differing from that which one has socially and institutionally been trained to adopt. However, it still allows no space for the difference between the fifteen-year-old or the grandmother, the woman on a Yorkshire farm or the society hostess. As

---

[72] Freud, *Papers on Psycho-Analysis* (2nd edn., 1918), 676.

[73] See James Strachey, 'Some Unconscious Factors in Reading', *International Journal of Psychoanalysis*, 11 (1930), 322–31.

[74] Melanie Klein, 'A Contribution to the Theory of Intellectual Inhibition' (1931) in *Love, Guilt and Reparation and Other Works 1921–1945* (1975; repr. 1988), 241.

[75] Jonathan Culler, 'Reading as a Woman', *On Deconstruction: Theory and Criticism after Structuralism* (1982); Paul Smith, 'Men in Feminism: Men and Feminist Theory', in id. and Alice Jardine (eds.), *Men in Feminism* (1987), 33–46 (and, indeed, many of the other pieces in this volume); Mary Jacobus, *Reading Woman* (1986). Robyn R. Warhol's interesting discussion in *Gendered Interventions. Narrative Discourse in the Victorian Novel* (New Brunswick and London, 1989) came to my attention too late for me to engage with it during the writing of this book.

the rest of this book will show, Victorian and Edwardian woman readers formed a variety of reading communities according to class, and to religious and political allegiances, including allegiances to the growing women's movement itself. Such different groupings were recognized, and commercially catered for. Even within them, one should note, however, there was a prevalent, though not ubiquitous assumption that the woman reader was invariably heterosexual, and that romance, marriage, and maternity were not just motivating factors in her life, but could be relied upon to provide captivating features of a fictional plot, or ready emotional catalysts within poetry. What forms of identification were available, I shall be asking, for those women who overtly or unconsciously resisted such social models?

The study of reading, in this as in any period, involves examining a fulcrum: the meeting-place of discourses of subjectivity and socialization. Of pressing concern to those who wished to understand how the individual mind might work, and how it might develop, reading was simultaneously perceived as a prime tool in socialization; in moulding a conformist, or for that matter a questioning, member of society. It is therefore centrally bound in with questions of authority: authority which manifests itself in a capacity for judgement and opinion based on self-knowledge (so far as this may be possible, both in psychological terms and within the social framework of language); and authority to speak, to write, to define, to manage, and to change not just the institutions of literature, but those of society itself.

Part II

3   Victorian and Edwardian Reading

The issue of reading and its effects did not concern women alone. It centred around the widely held belief in the affective powers of what was read. On the one hand, the beneficial potential of reading was celebrated: 'a good book is "the precious life-blood of a master-spirit," and possesses a wonderful potency of encouragement and inspiration.'[1] On the other, it was feared that 'desultory reading is very mischievous, by turning the memory into a common sewer for rubbish of all sorts to float through, and by relaxing the power of attention'.[2] In general, it was believed that reading had more effect on an individual's private and moral life than on his or her public concerns: discussion about it tended to belong, in other words, to the domestic sphere. 'The songs of a nation, to quote once more the poor old truism, affect men's manners more than their laws', wrote Leslie Stephen in 1875, expressing his view that culture is producer, as well as product, of society: 'The poems which they learn by heart, the novels with which they amuse their leisure, the pictures which hang upon their dwelling-rooms, affect their whole theory of life and conduct, or they do nothing.'[3] By the mid-century, certain reviewers and essayists were speculating about the general dangers specifically attendant on the rapid proliferation of print. In 1879, Ellen Higginson reminded her schoolgirl readers of the books around them in school, at home, in libraries, in shop-windows, on stalls in the streets, on railway stations, in public conveyances of all kinds, as a prelude to telling them that 'most good things have some dangers belonging to them, and this blessing of cheap literature has many dangers'.[4] The availability of reading material might be a sign of social progress: none the less, girls must take the utmost care in exercising a privilege of choice which would have been undreamed of by their grandmothers Excessive indiscriminate reading was condemned as morally debilitating. 'Doubleday', for example, questioned in 1859 'whether the craving for books may not be a disease, and whether we may not live too little in ourselves, and too much in others', censuring those who read a book merely because it is fashionable.[5] This factor was also remarked on by Francis Palgrave, writing four months later. He claimed that people, unless motivated otherwise by profession or scientific inquiry, 'go to books for

---

[1] W. H. Davenport Adams, *Woman's Work and Worth* (1880), 140.

[2] Archdeacon Hare, *Guesses at Truth* (1827), quoted by S.G.G., 'The Best Hundred Books', *Leisure Hour*, 35 (1886), 268.

[3] [Leslie Stephen] 'Art and Morality', *Cornhill Magazine*, 32 (1875), 92.

[4] Mrs Alfred [Ellen] Higginson, *The English School-girl: her position and duties. A Series of Lessons from a Teacher to her Class* (2nd edn., 1879), 67–8.

[5] 'Doubleday' [Alfred Ainger] 'Books and Their Uses', *Macmillan's Magazine*, 1 (1859), 110.

something almost similar to what they find in social conversation. Reading tends to become only another kind of gossip'. Condemnatory vocabulary here links lightweight reading with 'feminine' modes of passing the time in trivial, unenduring ways. Repetitive reading of 'the best books', is Palgrave's advice to someone who wishes to study, enjoy, and judge fairly what they read. This advice was given not only to men, but explicitly directed towards 'a woman who wishes to claim her natural mental rights and position'.[6]

But what, indeed, might one consider to be 'the best books'? Above all, could works of fiction safely be included among them? For what Henry James called, in 'The Art of Fiction', the 'old superstition about fiction being "wicked"' was not entirely dispelled, even by the time James's essay was published in 1884. Based in part, as he points out, on the 'old evangelical hostility to the novel', such antagonism rested in the first instance on a belief on the importance of conveying literal fact. A novel which did not explicitly 'renounce the pretension of attempting really to represent life', pointing out in apologetically jocular fashion that it was only make-believe, 'only a joke', laid itself open to condemnation from religious quarters, and even from utilitarians.[7] Although perhaps James was somewhat overstating his case in this respect, some of his complaints were perfectly valid ones, such as the impossibility (which Hardy, George Moore, and others were to echo) of writing honestly about sexual relations. So, too, was the stress he placed on the uncertain social and critical status of fiction.

Yet by the mid-nineteenth century, the popularity, the prevalence of fiction had become widely remarked upon. 'The present age is the age of novels', asserted Percy Greg, reviewing Trollope in 1858;[8] 'We have become a novel-reading people', maintained Trollope himself. 'Novels are in the hands of us all; from the Prime Minister down to the last-appointed scullery-maid'.[9] 'The Victorian has been peculiarly the age of the triumph of fiction', claimed Edmund Gosse in his provocatively entitled piece 'The Tyranny of the Novel' (1892).[10] If Leslie Stephen, in Ruskinian manner, could assert in general terms

[6] F. T. Palgrave, 'On Readers in 1760 and 1860', *Macmillan's Magazine*, 1, (1860), 488–9.

[7] For an excellent discussion of Henry James's awareness of such antagonism to the novel, and of his identification of the novel with history as a way of claiming the ability of fiction to represent life truly, and of justifying a serious attitude towards it, see Roslyn Jolly, '*History and Fiction: Modes of Narrative in the Works of Henry James*' (D.Phil. thesis, Univ. of Oxford, 1990). Jeremy Bentham's utilitarian objections to fiction are presented by C. K. Ogden, *Bentham's Theory of Fictions* (1932). The most sustained discussion of the changing status of fiction in the mid-Victorian period is that offered by Richard Stang, *The Theory of the Novel in England 1850–1870* (1959). Richard Altick points out in *The English Common Reader: A Social History of the Mass Reading Public 1800–1900* (Chicago, 1957) that, even when novels started to be met with a more consistently tolerant reception by the middle classes, anxiety continued to be expressed about working-class reading: such protectionism, as we shall see, extended towards women readers as well (pp. 64, 76).

[8] [Percy Greg] 'Mr Trollope's Novels', *National Review*, 7 (1858), 416.

[9] Anthony Trollope, 'On English Prose Fiction as a Rational Amusement' (1870), *Four Lectures*, ed. Morris L. Parrish (1938), 108.

[10] Edmund Gosse, 'The Tyranny of the Novel', *National Review*, 19 (1892), 164.

the influence of culture on a nation's morals, so fiction was specifically accredited with influencing both ideas, and people's access to knowledge: moreover, of doing so in a way that had become almost imperceptible. Baldwin, a character in Vernon Lee's 'A Dialogue on Novels' (1885) articulates this assumption:

I believe that were the majority of us, educated and sensitive men and women, able to analyze what we consider our almost inborn, nay, automatic, views of life, character, and feeling; that could we scientifically assign its origin to each and trace its modifications; I believe that, were this possible, we should find that a good third of what we take to be instinctive knowledge, or knowledge vaguely acquired from personal experience, is really obtained from the novels which we or our friends have read.[11]

A key issue here is the question of knowledge. If fiction appeared to have a manifestly utilitarian end, offering the reader empirical information about historical events or geographical settings, then its defence was not hard, even if the exploration voyaged no further than London's East End. Nor was it hard to justify reading it even if the useful knowledge it imparts was more nebulous, inviting one to examine the complexities of social existence and the moral attitudes and actions most conducive to successful and honourable survival within it—'the extension of man's sympathies beyond the bounds of our personal lot', to quote George Eliot; providing 'the humanizing education found in fictitious narrative', as Thomas Hardy put it.[12] Yet it was seldom easy to find defenders of the type of narrative considered most liable to corrupt: 'penny fiction', particularly that aimed at working-class young men (especially after the 1870 Education Act had been passed), which, with its unqualified celebration of violence, was frequently held to be one of the factors inciting both urban and domestic crime.[13] But much fiction published with a specifically female readership in mind (and, as we saw in the Introduction, there was a popular perception that women, particularly young women, formed the most likely readership for novels) fell into neither category. Although concern about the effects of novels on women was constantly expressed, it is not easy to locate a critical vocabulary for it which does not assume a distanced, patronizing air of disdain for the texts themselves.

The main exception to this generalization lies in the fact that the importance of escapism as motivating a reader was increasingly remarked upon. Reading fiction, wrote Edward Dowden in 1865, may be justified since it cultivates the sympathetic faculties, but its primary function is 'to amuse us, to give us agreeable relaxation', particularly when the reader has returned from a hard day

[11] Vernon Lee [Violet Paget] 'A Dialogue on Novels', *Contemporary Review*, 48 (1885), 390.
[12] [George Eliot] 'The Natural History of German Life', *Westminster Review* NS 10 (1856), 54; Thomas Hardy, 'The Profitable Reading of Fiction', *Forum*, 5 (1888), 66.
[13] See e.g. Hugh Chisholm, 'How to Counteract the "Penny Dreadful"', *Fortnightly Review*, NS 58 (1895), 771; [Francis Hitchman] 'Penny Fiction', *Quarterly Review*, 171 (1890), 170; A[lexander] Strahan, 'Bad Literature for the Young', *Contemporary Review*, 26 (1875), 985–6.

at work.[14] When the *Saturday Review* praised George Meredith's *The Egoist* (1879), it was on the grounds that its very difficulty contradicted the customary assumption that novel-reading is an unintellectual purging of the passions, usually in the context of 'armchairs, pipes, and slippers'.[15] These two examples focus, clearly enough, on the role fiction could play for the hard-pressed man. But other commentators offer hypotheses about the appeal of novels which allow a space for the woman reader (although rarely acknowledging that she, too, might be increasingly likely to go out to work). Herbert Maxwell, in 'The Craving for Fiction' (1893), claimed that:

the truth about the popularity of novels is that most people, being discontented with their environment, find relief in contemplating an ideal society where tedium is unknown and disappointment is generally circumvented . . . Has a woman been denied the gift of beauty? she is free to identify herself for the time with the fortunes of Di Vernon or Tess of the D'Urbevilles.[16]

A writer in the *Spectator* the following year remarked on the numbers of men and women who use fiction as 'mental sedatives', which steady their nerves not through inducing total inaction, but which keep their thinking mechanisms just, but only just, ticking over.[17] Blatantly escapist reading continued, however, to come under frequent attack, especially from religiously motivated sources. Thus a writer in the journal of the Mothers' Union in 1893 noted that:

The practice of self-indulgence by young women was rather aptly illustrated at the Conference of Schoolmistresses the other day at Southsea, where a speaker described a young woman's idea of a comfortable Saturday morning by saying 'she liked to be in bed with a shilling shocker and a shilling's worth of sweeties.' This is the sort of reckless waste of hard-earned money which can best be arrested by the suggestion in early life of something better worth doing.[18]

The quotations in the first paragraph of this chapter typify the common equation made between bodily and mental health; the censorious words of the last commentator fall equally on the ingestion of story and sugar. Many Victorians wrote of reading as an activity as natural, as essential, as eating, supplying the food of the mind. For this, they frequently and predictably drew on Bacon as their authority: 'Some *Bookes* are to be Tasted, Others to be Swallowed, and Some Few to be Chewed and Digested.'[19] Characterized as a physical appetite, reading became a form of ingestion to be carefully controlled, in order to avoid temporary indigestion or more long-term damage to the system. When Ruskin claimed (in 1876) in *Fors Clavigera* that 'Gluttonous

[14] 'Decem' [Edward Dowden] 'Fiction and its Uses', *Fraser's Magazine*, 72 (1865), 747.
[15] *Saturday Review*, 48 (1879), 607–8.
[16] Herbert Maxwell, 'The Craving for Fiction', *Nineteenth Century*, 33 (1893), 1057.
[17] 'Novels as Sedatives', *Spectator*, 73 (28 July 1894), 108.
[18] Hon. Mrs Joyce, 'Need of a Mothers' Union in all Classes', *Mothers in Council*, 3 (1893), 113.
[19] Francis Bacon, 'Of Studies', *The Essayes or Counsels, Civill and Morall*, ed. Michael Kiernan (Oxford, 1985), 153.

reading is a worse vice than gluttonous eating', he was drawing on familiar terminology.[20] Matilda Pullan, for example, had written in *Maternal Counsels to a Daughter* (1855) that the appetite for fiction, 'like that of a child for cakes, must be restrained within due bounds, or it will be injurious. No pastry will ever be a proper substitute for a solid joint.'[21] A writer in *All the Year Round* in 1863 described how the 'hungering after' sensation in fiction and drama was erroneously spoken of as 'a new and unhealthy greed—a diseased craving, an unwholesome fancy', whereas in reality (for he looks back to Gothic fiction and drama in the very early nineteenth century) there is little of novelty in 'this taste for fiery sauces, and strongly-seasoned meats and drinks'.[22] Writing to Mary Smith, schoolmistress and poet, in 1865, Jane Welsh Carlyle indicates that the gastronomy of reading had found its way into private discourse, claiming that: 'the appetite for magazine *Tales* and three-volume novels is getting to be a positive lupus—? something! I forget the full medical name of that disease which makes the victim gobble up, with unslaked voracity, pounds on pounds of raw beef and tallow candles! or anything else that comes readiest.'[23] In order to emphasize the social importance of reading aloud within the home, Charlotte Mason, in 1886, suggested that to keep an entertaining volume all to oneself was 'an act of selfish greediness on a par with secretly indulged gluttony': 'to read "The Newcomes" to yourself is like sitting down to a solitary feast of strawberries and cream; every page has that in it which demands to be shared'.[24] Towards the end of the century, J. E. C. Welldon, in claiming that 'it is more important to read wisely than to read widely', maintained that 'intellectual health, like physical, depends not upon the amount of food consumed, but upon the digestion',[25] whilst J. J. Wright, in a pamphlet advocating the joining of the National Home Reading Union, maintained that 'we live in an age of dyspepsia', and that one should no more try to read everything than attempt to swallow every dish at a banquet.[26] Such advice had, naturally, plenty of physiological support from medical authorities, regularly reminding one that 'it is not from what we *eat*, but from what we *digest*, that beneficial results are desirable'.[27] Lady Laura Ridding, opening a debate on 'What Should Women Read?' in the *Woman at Home* made the metaphor of consumption the structuring pivot of her article. Anxious to put readers off

[20] John Ruskin, *Fors Clavigera*, 6. Letter 61 (Jan. 1876), *The Works of John Ruskin*, ed. E. T. Cook and Alexander Wedderburn, xxviii. 501.
[21] Matilda Pullan, *Maternal Counsels to Daughters* (1855), 51–2.
[22] 'Not a New "Sensation"', *All the Year Round*, 9 (1863), 517.
[23] Jane Welsh Carlyle to Mary Smith, 10 Apr. 1865, in Mary Smith, *The Autobiography of Mary Smith Schoolmistress and Non-conformist* (1892), 315.
[24] Charlotte M. Mason, *Home Education* (1886), 232–3.
[25] J. E. C. Welldon, 'The Art of Reading Books', *National Review* 23 (1894), 217. See also Captain Dawson, *Give Attention to Reading: A Talk on the Reading of Books* (1892), 17 for the advice not to gobble one's reading any more than one would gobble one's food.
[26] J. J. Wright, *So Many Books! So Little Time! What to Do?* (Birmingham, 1892), 8.
[27] Alfred Beaumont Maddock, *Practical Observations on Mental and Nervous Disorders* (1854), 121.

'morbid, pessimistic, coarse, flippant, irreverent . . . bigoted controversial books'—the fiction of the 'New Woman', indeed—she wrote that minds should be fed:

a wholesome variety of food—well cooked, well digested, nourishing . . . The strawberry ices of literature glow on every railway bookstall in the shape of the lighter magazines, the society and comic papers, fashion journals, sensational stories. These are harmless occasional reading, but a mind glutted with them needs medicine as much as a greedy child after a surfeit of sugar-plums.[28]

Lucy Soulsby, in *Stray Thoughts on Reading*, advised in much the same tone that 'Poetry should not form the staple of our reading, any more than sugar-plums of our food'.[29] Such metaphors continued into the twentieth century. In 1908 Dorothy Owen addressed a question to those whom she feared might greet her pious book of advice, *Letters to School-girls*, with a 'contemptuous sneer':

If your ordinary, every-day meals consisted of nothing but sweets and delicacies, with no plain or solid food, is your body likely to be in the strong, healthy state it was meant to be? You naturally answer, 'No.' Well, then, I put it to you—Is your *mind* likely to be in a strong, healthy condition if you persist in feeding it on nothing but delicacies?[30]

The next chapter addresses in more detail the medical assumptions which support this ready popularisation of the idea that medical and physical processes are intimately, indeed inseparably, connected.

[28]   Lady Laura Ridding, 'What Should Women Read?', *Woman at Home*, 37 (1896), 29.
[29]   Lucy Soulsby, *Stray Thoughts on Reading* (1895), 75.
[30]   Dorothy Owen, *Letters to School-girls* (1908), 12.

4 Medical, Physiological and Psychoanalytic Theory

Throughout the period, theories about how women's modes of reading differed from those of men, and why they should be affected so strongly by what they read, were inseparably linked to those developments in physiology and psychology which found, demonstrated, and utilized evidence for the intimate interrelations of mind and body. These hypotheses about the assumed connections between psychology and physiology passed readily from specialist scientific research into more widely circulating discourse. This process was aided by the publication of many of the medical findings not in specialist journals, but in magazines with a far broader readership, particularly the *Westminster Review* and the *Fortnightly Review*. No body was perceived as being more vulnerable to impure mental foods as that of the young woman.

Women's experience of their bodies in social relations is inevitably different from that of men, and women's bodies unarguably are distinct from men's in terms of their separate reproductive systems. More controversially, however, biological difference was asserted to lie behind unalterable gender differences in the physical constitution of the brain, and hence in its operation. And, as has been well documented by socio-medical historians of the nineteenth century, the fact of differing reproductive systems was widely believed to determine specific, innate mental characteristics.[1] Moreover, for the duration of the nineteenth century, most medical and psychological commentators were unable to distinguish between the workings of the brain and the mind. Robert M. Young, in *Mind, Brain and Adaptation in the Nineteenth Century*, has indicated the long-lasting influence of Franz Joseph Gall's *Sur les fonctions de cerveau* (6

[1] See, in particular, Paul Atkinson, 'Fitness, Feminism and Schooling' in Sara Delamont and Lorna Duffin (eds.), *The Nineteenth Century Woman: Her Cultural and Physical World* (1978), 92–133; Flavia Alaya, 'Victorian Science and the "Genius" of Woman', *Journal of the History of Ideas*, 34 (1977), 261–80; Joan Burstyn, 'Education and Sex: The Medical Case Against Higher Education for Women in England, 1870–1900', *Proceedings of the American Philosophical Society*, 117 (1973), 79–89; Lorna Duffin, 'Prisoners of Progress: Women and Evolution', in Sara Delamont and Lorna Duffin (eds.), *The Nineteenth Century Woman: Her Cultural and Physical World* (1978), 57–91; Carol Dyhouse, *Girls Growing up in Late Victorian and Edwardian England* (1981), esp. ch. 4 (115–38); Brian Harrison, 'Women's Health and the Women's Movement in Britain: 1840–1940', in Charles Webster (ed.), *Biology, Medicine and Society 1840–1940* (Cambridge, 1981), 15–71; Ludmilla Jordanova, 'Natural Facts: A Historical Perspective on Science and Sexuality', in Carol MacCormack and Marilyn Strathern (eds.), *Nature, Culture, and Gender* (Cambridge, 1980), 42–69; Thomas Laqueur, *Making Sex: Body and Gender from the Greeks to Freud* (Cambridge, Mass., and London, 1990), esp. chs. 5 and 6, (149–243); Ornella Moscucci, *The Science of Woman: Gynaecology and Gender in England, 1800–1929* (Cambridge, 1990).

vols; 1822–5) on European physiology and psychology. Gall argued in this that 'the brain is the organ of the mind' and that both the brain's structure and functions could adequately, and concomitantly, be analysed by observation.[2] On such an assumption rested the debate about the correlations between brain size, weight, body size, and capacity for intelligence which were consolidated during the second half of the century, and which were preoccupied with, and came to have serious implications for, the growth of women's educational opportunities.[3] Gall, however, whilst authoritative about *what* consist the functions of the brain, had little to say about *how* the brain functioned. This area of investigation was developed in Britain, in particular, by Alexander Bain, one of the first in this country to apply to psychology the results of physiological investigations. His books *The Senses and the Intellect* (1855) and *The Emotions and the Will* (1859) constituted the standard British texts on these subjects for nearly half a century, as well as putting forward his strong belief in the laws of association. With the near-universal acceptance of the inescapable relation of brain and body, it is unsurprising that focusing on the physiological difference between women and men formed the basis for a number of apparently authoritative theories concerning women and reading.

Evidence for the prevalence of assumptions about woman's greater sensitivity and sensibility, and the biological grounds on which such assumptions could be based, can be found across a range of texts in the early Victorian period, both those which laid claim to medical status in their own right, and those which seem to have been intended for a non-specialist readership. Alexander Walker, in *Woman Physiologically Considered* (1840) is illustrative of these early hypotheses. He argued that the organs through which we receive our sensory perceptions are larger in the woman than in the man, basing this assumption on the belief that such organs are contained in the frontal part of the brain. Since the measurements he recorded showed that women habitually had larger foreheads than men, there must consequently be less room in them for the reasoning faculties, situated further back in the skull. The results, he wrote, of this anatomical difference are that 'the *sensibility* of woman is excessive; she is strongly affected by many sensations, which in men are so feeble as scarcely to attract attention'; that 'the IMAGINATION, a peculiarly and strongly marked function in woman, is highly susceptible of excitement, and yields easily to every excess'; that woman, 'by the intensity, rapidity and variety of her sensations . . .

---

[2] Robert M. Young, *Mind, Brain and Adaptation in the Nineteenth Century: Cerebral Localization and its Biological Context from Gall to Ferrier* (Oxford, 1970), 9–53.

[3] The standard nineteenth-century source concerning the relationship of the brain's size and weight to intelligence was Henry Charlton Bastian, *The Brain as Organ of Mind* (1880), esp. ch. 18; and further concerning the brain as organ of the mind, George Trumbull Ladd, *Elements of Physiological Psychology* (1887), pt. ii, ch. 1. See also David Ferrier, *Functions of the Brain* (2nd edn., 1886); Michael Foster, *A Text-Book of Physiology* (2nd edn., 1878), iii, p. ii; G. H. Lewes, *The Physiology of Common Life*, 2 vols. (1859; 1860); id., *Problems of Life and Mind*, ser. 1, 2 vols. (1873); ser. 2 (1877); ser. 3, 2 vols. (1879); Henry Maudsley, *The Physiology and Pathology of the Mind* (1867).

is of course incapable of thought separated from all external things, of *trains of connected ideas*, and of *connected modes of reasoning*.[4]

The terms of the discussion about women's mental operations were not just concerned with whether or not brain size or shape was a determinant in establishing intelligence, but involved consideration of the differing ways in which the brain was believed to receive its stimuli. G. H. Lewes, in 1865, wrote of how in certain 'feminine natures' there is an unusual development of the direct connection between brain and heart. He himself was unusual, incidentally, in voicing this hypothesis that gender is effectively established through a categorization of mental and physical manifestations, rather than being a biological given. A sensation of any kind—such as that produced by reading an exciting novel, for example—would invariably transmit its agitating influence to the heart, and in the 'feminine nature' this would the more readily be passed along the pneumo-gastric nerves, those filaments which connect heart with spinal cord and hence with brain. Thus it could be argued that anyone of a 'feminine nature' (most probably, though not exclusively, also biologically female) would by her very physiology be especially liable to the perturbing effects of literature calculated to shock and surprise.[5] Whilst Lewes makes no reference to the works of Braddon, Broughton, or Wood, it is worth noting that the formulation of his theory coincides with the extensive debate about the effects of reading the sensation novel. As will be seen in Chapter 10, the craze for this fiction was considered a suitable topic for discussion in medical journals. Thus the *Medical Critic and Psychological Journal* in 1863 considered the possible reasons lying behind its obsessive consumption, and the terms employed indicate how readily current populist social theories fed into professional discourses. The author located the reasons for this mania as lying on the one hand within a wider 'morbid craving for excitement' which was liable to be found among 'the idle members of prosperous communities', and which was deliberately fed by those out to make profits from various forms of publishing; and on the other reports, with no apparent irony, the suggestion that the fashion for the crinoline might have helped to determine the fact that in the present generation this craving for excitement was particularly to be found in their interest in sexual immorality. The crinoline, the writer argues, is a fashion destructive of modesty, since it necessitates the habitual display of women's legs, whether they are walking up or down hills, climbing into a railway carriage, or getting over a stile. Trained to this display from their infancy, the result in the rising generation of young women and girls 'is the utter destruction of that modesty which is one of the strongest outposts of virtue'.[6]

The hypotheses concerning the functioning of a woman's response mechanism worked in two ways. First, one was asked to consider the effect that

---

[4] Alexander Walker, *Woman Physiologically Considered as to Mind, Morals, Matrimonial Slavery, Infidelity and Divorce* (1840), 12, 28, 36.

[5] Editor [G. H. Lewes] 'The Heart and the Brain', *Fortnightly Review*, 1 (1865), 66–74.

[6] 'Sensation Novels', *Medical Critic and Psychological Journal* 3 (1863), 513–19.

women's reproductive organs, and the characteristics which accompany them, may have on the mind; and second, to consider the effect which may be created by stimuli, such as reading, on the reproductive organs, and on the particular organization of the nervous system in women. Joan Burstyn has argued that medical discussion about the effects of the reproductive system on women's intellectual capacity became far more gynaecologically specific during the 1870s than had previously been the case. Those who were opposed to the changes taking place in women's education decided that they stood a stronger chance of defeating them if they discussed medical details more openly. It was far from irrelevant, of course, that medicine was itself the first occupation to be assailed by women in their attempts to enter the professions, and specialists in gynaecology and obstetrics were the first to feel threatened by women doctors. Henry Maudsley, in his controversial, influential *Fortnightly Review* essay of 1874, 'Sex in Mind and in Education', wrote again about the relation of the brain to other organs of the body. Although elsewhere Maudsley did not underestimate the importance of environmental influence, this is an article which refutes the ideas put forward by, for example, Lydia Becker, who, in a paper read before the British Association for the Advancement of Science in 1868, maintained that 'the attribute of sex did not extend to mind; that there was no distinction between the intellects of men and women corresponding to and dependent on the special organisation of their bodies', and that any such distinction which was evident at the present time could be attributable to environmental and educational factors.[7] However, Maudsley claimed that the brain was in the closest physiological sympathy with the body's vital parts, having 'special correspondence with them by internuncial nerve-fibres; so that its functions habitually feel and declare the influence of the different organs. There is an intimate consensus of functions.' Alteration, or disorder, in one part of the body will automatically lead to alteration within the mind. The most striking instance of this is given, he claimed, 'by the influence of the reproductive organs upon the mind; a complete mental revolution being made when they come into activity'.[8]

Although Maudsley was advancing this as a proof that women and men should have different types of education, which in each case should aim at the 'drawing out of the internal qualities of the individual into their highest perfection', these ideas can be seen to have their place, also, in the construction of an implicit theory of reading. If woman's 'natural', biological function is presumed to be that of childbearing and rearing, of the inculcation of moral

---

[7] 'Miss Becker's Paper read before the British Association for the Advancement of Science: The Equality of Women', *Englishwoman's Review*, 9 (1868), 51. See also 'Miss Becker on the Mental Characteristics of the Sexes', *Lancet*, 2 (1868), 320–1.

[8] Henry Maudsley, 'Sex in Mind and in Education', *Fortnightly Review*, NS 15 (1874), 469–71. Burstyn, 'Education and Sex', 81, indicates the dependence of Maudsley's theories on those of the American Edward H. Clarke, thus indicating that the English debate shared much in common with contemporary discussion on the other side of the Atlantic.

beliefs along with physical nurturing, with the ensuing presumption that she is thus especially constructed by nature so as to have a close, intuitive relationship with her offspring, then such instincts as sympathetic imagination, and a ready capacity to identify with the experience of others, are unalterable facts about her mental operations, and hence, by extension, about her processes of reading.

Maudsley's article has frequently been cited, by Burstyn and others, as a crucial contribution to the rapidly growing debate concerning women's education: an authoritative voice which had to be assimilated or countered by other commentators. What was in fact new, and important, about the discussion generated during the 1870s was the degree to which it spread from specialist texts to a range of publications with the potential to reach a wider readership.[9] For Maudsley, as we will see, was building on medical commonplaces which had become established during earlier decades. Thomas Laycock, in *A Treatise on the Nervous Diseases of Women* (1840) emphasized the importance which the reproductive organs had come to assume in the assessment of the anatomy and functions of the brain and nerves over the previous thirty years, stating categorically that now, 'by universal consent the nervous system of the human female is allowed to be sooner affected by all stimuli, whether corporeal or mental, than that of the male.'[10] And in 1847, J. G. Millingen wrote that: 'Woman, with her exalted spiritualism, is more forcibly under the control of matter; her sensations are more vivid and acute, her sympathies more irresistible. She is less under the influence of the brain than the uterine system, the plexi of abdominal nerves, and irritation of the spinal cord.' This combination of factors, he believes, means that she is inescapably predisposed to hysteria from the time that she reaches puberty, and particularly liable to look for her emotional satisfaction either in love or, later, in religion.[11] Such comments as these, partly based on long-standing medical tradition, were on occasion supported by empirical evidence such as that supposedly taken from observing the effects of reading.

Among the stimuli it was considered advisable for the young woman to avoid, novels figure consistently. We see this theory advanced, for example, by E. J. Tilt, in *On the Preservation of the Health of Women at the Critical Periods of Life* (1851). Proposing the theory that the highest life forms are those which take the longest to develop, Tilt argues that achieving 'the full perfection of womanhood' must therefore be dependent on retarding '*as much as possible the*

[9] This tendency did not, itself, pass without comment and anxiety. Herbert Cowell, for example, complained in *Blackwood's*, in a review of Maudsley's piece, E. Garrett Anderson's reply, and Edward H. Clarke's *Sex in Education* (Boston, 1875) that 'Considerations of delicacy and decency are usually held to impose some reserve both upon editors and authors, and it is not in the interest of English literature and the English public that any violations of them should pass unnoticed and unchallenged'. 'Sex in Mind and Education: A Commentary', *Blackwood's Edinburgh Magazine*, 115 (1874), 737.

[10] Thomas Laycock, *A Treatise on the Nervous Diseases of Women* (1840), 76.

[11] J. G. Millingen, *Mind and Matter, illustrated by Considerations on Hereditary Insanity and the Influence of Temperament in the Development of the Passions* (1847), 157.

appearance of first menstruation'. Since Tilt regarded mental and physical disturbance as interdependent, this could best be achieved through a combination of 'rational food, rational hours of rest and of rising, and rational exercise at judicious times . . . the absence of sofas to lounge on—the absence of novels fraught with harrowing interest'.[12] Similar advice could still be found in popular manuals into the Edwardian period. The 1910 edition of George Black's *The Young Wife's Advice Book*, for example, claimed that: 'a lazy, listless life; undue mental excitement, either caused by the reading of sensational novels, by conversation or the like; late hours, irregular habits of sleep, highly seasoned articles of diet, and stimulants, have all a tendency to accelerate the occurrence of menstruation in the girl.'[13]

E. J. Tilt also advised against too many balls, concerts, theatres, and opera, before returning to fiction as a possible cause of that mid-century focus of fascination for specialists in women's medicine, hysteria:

> Novels and romances, speaking generally, should be spurned, as capable of calling forth emotions of the same morbid description which, when habitually indulged in, exert a disastrous influence on the nervous system, sufficient to explain that frequency of hysteria and nervous diseases which we find among the highest classes.[14]

Reading features in writings on hysteria both as a contributory cause of insanity, and as an activity to be monitored closely in the hysteric herself. That reading should regularly appear as a topic within the literature of hysteria is significant. It demonstrates the intensity with which some specialists believed the affective qualities of print could operate. Additionally, it is a manifestation of their general reluctance to examine some of the social and personal factors which underlay the withdrawal from socially 'acceptable' forms of behaviour, and which permitted the designation of the hysteric. Reading's provision of an outlet for frustration and boredom, a channel for forms of individualism, may be understood retrospectively as a symptom of the malaise behind types of hysteria, rather than as causative in its own right. But the concern shown by the specialists provides one strand of contributory evidence for the degree of anxiety exhibited by some mid-nineteenth-century parents and educationists about the tendency of young women to adopt compulsive reading habits. Moreover, it shows how uncertain the line between 'hysteric' and 'normal' behaviour could be.

Once hysteria had been diagnosed, according to Robert Carter, a mid-century authority on the condition, reading 'will only be found advantageous under peculiar circumstances. Silent reading encourages reverie; and reading

---

[12] E. J. Tilt, *On the Preservation of Health of Women at the Critical Periods of Life* (1851), 31.

[13] George Black, *The Young Wife's Advice Book* (1st pub. 1880; issued as an 'entirely new edition' 1910), 5.

[14] Tilt, *Preservation of Health*, 40. For an account of medical attitudes towards hysteria in the Victorian period, see Elaine Showalter, *The Female Malady: Women, Madness and English Culture, 1830–1980* (1985).

aloud, unless it be particularly well done, is a nuisance to everybody within hearing, while the matter read is at least as likely to be injurious as beneficial.' He recommends that moderate reading should not be interfered with, but 'excessive reading' should be carefully watched, suitable authors and books suggested, and the reader frequently examined to ensure that she is reading in a 'satisfactory' way. He goes on to suggest that if enquiries about the patient's reading fail to satisfy, then whoever has care of the hysteric should attempt to divert the attention. 'This may be done by obtaining a book upon some practical subject; such, for instance, as bee keeping . . . '.[15] Precisely what Carter may understand by 'satisfactory' is clarified later in the book, when he writes at length about reading in a section entitled 'Regulation of the Studies and Accomplishments', something which he sees as necessary to the healthy mind. Although he writes in general terms, one may take his comments in this section as particularly relevant to women since the greatest emphasis of his study falls upon them. Reading should cultivate interpretation and be used to train the memory. It should teach method in comprehension, for the reader should never skim the difficult parts of texts and trust to the future to provide understanding. He cautions against those works, such as biographies and travel books, which aim to combine instruction with amusement, since frequently all that is retained consists of anecdotal material rather than valuable moral reflection. Nor does he see any merit in accumulating a superficial selection of facts. More damaging yet is fiction, and he makes clear his objections to this:

It will be difficult to find a better illustration of complete automatic attention than is constantly furnished by a child with a novel; and this attention, interfering, as it does, with a volitional fixing of the thoughts, is not at all to be desired. The strong emotions too, which, in a susceptible mind, may be called forth by fiction, and, especially, by accounts of situations to which the events of daily life afford no parallel, are often hurtful; and good novels may serve only to excite a craving, which, with an immature judgment, bad ones will be sufficient to satisfy.[16]

What is significant about this is not the ideas in themselves, which are commonplace enough, but their location within a medical manual dealing with the condition of the hysteric. They serve to link what we might regard as the escapism offered by fiction, the release of desires which its consumption may afford, the access which it gives to experiences and situations lying outside the immediate circumstances of its reader, with the hypothesis advanced by Elaine Showalter among others, that nineteenth-century hysteria itself may be regarded as 'a mode of protest'—however ineffectual—'for women deprived of other social or intellectual outlets or expressive opinions'.[17] The degree to which this hypothesis was not taken on board by many major physicians is made manifest by the fact that 'demanding' reading was one of the crucial things to be

[15] Robert Brudenell Carter, *On the Pathology and Treatment of Hysteria* (1853), 135–6.
[16] A. B. Carter, *Diseases of the Nervous System* (1855), 429.
[17] Showalter, *The Female Malady*, 147.

banned for those 'hysteric', nervous, or depressed patients prescribed the notorious rest 'cure'. Winnie Seerbohm, who left Newnham College, Cambridge in November 1885 after only one term's study, suffered from what seems retrospectively to have been nervous asthma combined with a pathological inability to swallow. Instead of there being an investigation into any possible psychological causes for this, she was ordered total rest: she was allowed only to read *Punch* and the *Illustrated London News*, she told a college friend in a letter. Whilst she wished to be read Ruskin's *Stones of Venice* aloud, her sisters desisted after a couple of chapters, thinking that it was too heavy for the invalid. She never recovered.[18] However, views on this matter were, slowly, to change. By 1912, Sir Thomas Clouston was recommending 'suitable literature, as well as suitable company' as a major means of curing 'hereditary brain-weakness, moral or physical', drawing for support on the theories of G. Stanley Hall and the German physiologist Paul Flechsig.[19]

In making this recommendation, Clouston seems to be acknowledging that reading, like people, can extend one's horizons, take one away from preoccupation with oneself. In doing this, he was countering the Victorian tendency which presumed that few, if any, women were capable of practising such detachment. For the capacity for intuitive response on a woman's part was considered 'natural', backed up by biological facts, and reinforced by Darwin's statement in *The Descent of Man* (1871) that 'it is generally admitted that with women the powers of intuition, of rapid perception . . . are more strongly marked than in man'.[20] As we have seen, the majority of the medical theorists cited so far in this chapter assume explanations for woman's susceptibility which are closely linked to her reproductive functions, and hence with her capacity for motherhood. They thus connected very readily with more widely held social expectations, especially those concerning the nature of the nurturing process. In 1845, for example, Sarah Stickney Ellis emphasized the especial fitness of women for reading aloud, since 'the female perceptions' are 'more quick, and the female character altogether more easy of adaptation, more sympathizing, and therefore more capable of identifying itself with the thoughts and feelings of others'.[21] Elizabeth Strutt, in *The Feminine Soul: Its Nature and Attributes* (1857), a Christian work designed to make women aware of the importance of recognizing, and hence gaining control over, their own feelings, described how 'woman is invariably influenced by her affections, rather than by her understanding; and accordingly as these affections are well or ill directed, she finds her own happiness or misery'.[22] She goes on to record that 'the

[18] Victoria Glendinning (ed.), *A Suppressed Cry: Life and Death of a Quaker Daughter* (1969), 89, 101.
[19] Sir Thomas Clouston, *Morals and Brain* (1912), 28–9.
[20] Charles Darwin, *The Descent of Man, and selection in relation to Sex*, 2 vols. (1871), ii, 326.
[21] Mrs. Ellis (ed.), *The Young Ladies' Reader* (1845), 4.
[22] Elizabeth Strutt, *The Feminine Soul: Its Nature and Attributes, with Thoughts Upon Marriage, and Friendly Hints Upon Feminine Duties* (1857), 20.

peculiarly feminine fact of seeing into character, and divining what is passing in other minds, has frequently been the saving of a family'.[23] Henry Thomas Buckle, lecturing to the Royal Society in 1858, argued that woman had a special 'genius' for deductive and intuitive modes of thought: it was because of this that she has a special role to play in ensuring the progress of knowledge, since the emotion, imagination, quickness of perception, and insight into character which she can provide will join with men's more inductive capacities. However, he is not postulating some androgynous type, but an acknowledgment for woman's central role in an evolutionary process, for true genius will develop when 'unconsciously, and from a very early period, there is established an intimate and endearing connection between the deductive mind of the mother and the inductive mind of the son'.[24] Not quite sharing the same terms as Buckle, but coming to highly similar conclusions, William Roscoe, writing in the *National Review* the following year, commented on the power of woman's intuitive, rather than deductive faculties; on her capacity to see significance in detail which escapes men; and on the phenomenon of 'the more instinctive nature of the woman finding its life among personal relations . . . her gracious prerogative and happiest attribute—the power to live in others'.[25] A decade later, Anne Mozley claimed in *Blackwood's* that 'the ideal woman does not reason; her processes of thought are intuitive so far that she can give no account how she arrives at them', whilst 'clever women'—not, it would seem, a category to be aimed at—'throw intuition over and aim at logic', not accepting 'a limited province as especially her own'.[26] It was woman's 'imagination, memory, and quickness of perception' as distinct from 'power of sustained thought, judgement, and creativeness', to quote the *Lancet*'s classification of male/female attributes in 1868, which could be assumed to make the consumption of such genres as fiction and poetry so appealing to her in the first place.[27] Yet such innate faculties could simultaneously be perceived as rendering women particularly vulnerable. Annie Swan, writing in the 1890s, claimed that to pander too much to woman's 'imaginative and emotional side is to create the morbid'.[28]

Clouston was not, however, the first to oppose the enduring equation between intuition and womanhood. Dr Elizabeth Blackwell wrote in *Counsel to Parents on the Moral Education of their Children in Relation to Sex* (2nd edn, 1879) that whilst the instinctive life of the body necessarily exists, and therefore constantly strives to make itself felt, it is none the less important to cultivate in all children, female as well as male, the growth of Reason as a controlling force. She believed in the dominance of the mind over the senses and muscles, rather

[23] Ibid. 43–4.
[24] Buckle, 'The Influence of Women', 399, 405.
[25] [William Caldwell Roscoe] 'Woman', *National Review*, 7 (1858), 342.
[26] [Anne Mozley] 'Clever Women', *Blackwood's Magazine*, 104 (1868), 411–12.
[27] 'Miss Becker', *Lancet*, 321.
[28] Annie Swan, 'What Should Women Read?', *Woman at Home*, 37 (1896), 31.

than vice versa, and quotes a large section from Carpenter's *Physiology* in support of the power of the Will to 'exercise a determining power, keeping in check every automatic impulse, and repressing the promptings of emotional excitement'.[29] Above all, since the faculty of sex 'comes into perfection when the mind is in full activity, and when all the senses are in their freshest youthful vigour', and since its operation affects not just the well-being of the individual but social life as a whole, it is important that the will must control this function more than any other.[30] The development of this faculty is dependent on securing healthy, strengthening influences during youth, whilst 'the permanent and incalculable injury which is done to the young mind by vicious reading, is proved by all that we now know about the structure and methods of growth of the human mind'. This knowledge leads, she argued, to the belief that: 'the moral sense itself, may be affected by the constant exercise of the brain in one direction or another, so that the individual standard of what is right or what is wrong, will be quite charged, according to whether low or high ideas have been constantly recorded in the retentive substance of the brain.'[31] Blackwell does, however, get into something of a tangle when indicating with more precision what may be learnt directly from literature. She points out on the one hand that Balzac, 'a modern writer of unsurpassed genius', attributed his own powers to the fact that he led a remarkably chaste life, while remarking on the other that his 'writings are injurious because they are such wonderfully vivid representations of horrible social disease'.[32] But her main point is clear: that women, and men, can learn to have control over their responses, which are not to be seen in the light of involuntary, physiologically determined acts.

Nor was Blackwell the only woman to attack the line of argument articulated by Maudsley. Notably, Elizabeth Garrett Anderson, in her reply published in the *Fortnightly* later the same year, claimed that study was extremely unlikely to weaken a woman's health at any period of her life. Equally notably, however, she is far from defending indiscriminate reading: indeed, her argument underscores yet further the belief in fiction's undesirable capacity for over-stimulation. Rather, Anderson saw formal education as undeniably healthier than the alternative effects of leisure activities, which contribute towards:

a life directly calculated to over-stimulate the emotional and sexual instincts, and to weaken the guiding and controlling forces which these instincts so imperatively need. The stimulus found in novel-reading, in the theatre and ball-room, the excitement which attends a premature entry into society, the competition of vanity and frivolity, these involve far more real dangers to the health of young women than the competition

---

[29] William Carpenter, *Principles of Human Physiology* (1842), quoted by Dr Elizabeth Blackwell, *Counsel to Parents on the Moral Education of their Children in Relation to Sex* (2nd edn. , 1879), 16. Blackwell, an American, trained at Geneva College in New York, and was permitted to register in England since she had practised medicine prior to the qualifying date of 1 Oct. 1858.
[30] Blackwell, *Counsel to Parents*, 18–19.
[31] Ibid. 91.   [32] Ibid. 74.

for knowledge, or for scientific or literary honours, ever has done, or is ever likely to do.[33]

Lack of study, as she sees it, is likely to lead to boredom and ennui, and thus to the probability of making a hasty and foolish marriage: something which itself carries physiological risks. The connection between novel-reading and physical lassitude, incidentally, filtered down to the level of popular medicine. An 1892 advertisement for Caffyn's Liquor Carnis, Malto-Carnis, and allied Products of Raw Beef Juice claimed that these would cure 'bloodlessness in girls' who 'pore for hours over novels and sickly sentimental stories, becoming weaker and weaker, until at last their friends take notice of their condition, and the tedious work of repair has to be commenced', with healthy substances being substituted for the ingestion of unsuitable print.[34]

Some later nineteenth-century psychologists were to express a growing insistence on the separation of the psychical and the physical. Thus James Sully stated firmly in the opening pages of *The Human Mind* (1892) that 'psychical processes cannot be included in and studied as part of the functional activities of the bodily organism'. Neither this work, nor his *Outlines of Psychology* (1884) which it largely superseded, nor *Studies of Childhood* (revised edn. 1903) devote themselves in any degree to differentiation between the sexes. When Sully remarks in passing on 'the peculiar strength of feeling which binds together the mother and her offspring', he attributes it not to innate qualities but to habitual proximity and sustained physical contact, both inside and outside the womb.[35] But despite the airing of these views, they had but limited immediate currency and influence, for the major exponents of girls' education continued to rely on theorists whose view of women's intertwined psychology and physiology best served their social beliefs. Thomas Smith Clouston, for example, delivering two lectures entitled *Female Education from a Medical Point of View* at the Philosophical Institution in Edinburgh in 1882, continued to promote the argument (familiar from Maudsley, and before him to be found in Spencer and in Edward H. Clarke) that any individual has only a certain fixed amount of energy at their disposal, and that it is dangerous to make demands upon this resource which will deplete the stock available for the full 'ripening' of the woman's body, culminating in her childbearing.[36] He was more specific than Maudsley, however, about the mental, as well as physical changes which take place during a girl's adolescence. Whereas bread and butter and sweets used to satisfy her, now she craves stronger and more stimulating foods, and, as ever

[33] E. Garrett Anderson, 'Sex in Education: A Reply', *Fortnightly Review*, NS 15 (1874), 590.

[34] Advertisement in *Our Mothers and Daughters*, 1 (1892), p. vii.

[35] James Sully, *The Human Mind: A Text-book of Psychology*, 2 vols. (1892), ii. 118.

[36] Herbert Spencer e.g. claimed in *Education: Intellectual, Moral and Physical* (1861) that 'Nature is a strict accountant; and if you demand of her in one direction more than she is prepared to lay out, she balances her account by making a deduction elsewhere' (p. 179). Such theories upheld the danger posed to a woman's fertility by excessive study during—even before—puberty; recommended rest at the time of menstruation; and provided medical arguments to support cases for separate examinations for women and men.

when gastronomic issues are mentioned, the analogy between physical and mental desires, the 'direct action and interaction between body and mind', is present. Thus 'Literature and poetry begin to be understood in a vague way, and the latter often becomes a passion.'[37] In 1899, Lucy Soulsby, despite her considerable experience in girls' secondary education, could generalize easily that 'It is true that the human interests of life are the only satisfying ones to a woman, whose emotions are probably a more vital part of her than her reasoning faculties.'[38]

By the 1890s, circumstantial evidence was increasingly threatening these particular medical and physiological arguments. Sufficient women had proceeded to higher education and subsequently successfully produced children to begin to refute alarms about educational pressure placing an unacceptable strain on a woman's fertility. Moreover, as more women entered the labour market, and overtly or implicitly allied themselves with working-class wage-earning women, who had never formed part of the discussion about the desirability of energy conservation, so such a discussion could come to look increasingly irrelevant in relation to the medical and psychological well-being and development of the individual.[39] But among social and educational conservatives, emphasis shifted from concern for the individual, or the immediate family circle, to the condition of the species; or, as Herbert Spencer put it in *The Principles of Ethics* (1892), 'the ultimate truth that the interests of the race must predominate over the interests of the individual'.[40] Hence, a range of authorities attempted to convince women that the most important contribution which they could make to social progress was through their role as mothers: the movement towards women's emancipation came under fire as running contrary to the future good of the race. Eugenicist ideas influenced educational policy, providing justification for domestic science and home economics constituting a notable part of a girl's curriculum. Moreover, as we shall see in Chapters 6 and 7, such assumptions fed readily into commentary on girls' and women's reading, which was perceived as helping to form not just a morally and socially desirable individual, but a worthy representative of a race.[41]

---

[37] T. S. Clouston, *Female Education from a Medical Point of View* (Edinburgh, 1882), 14–15. Clouston was not himself averse to making literature a mainstay of his argument, however. Countering the argument in favour of higher education for women that 'it makes them fitter companions for highly-educated men', he engages in a highly selective reading of a variety of literary examples, from Shakespeare's heroines to Gwendolen Harleth and Romola, in an attempt to prove that the most desirable women—in every sense of the word—are not necessarily the most highly educated. Ibid., 20–5.

[38] Lucy H. M. Soulsby, *Happiness* (1890), 14.

[39] See Burstyn, 'Education and Sex', 89.

[40] Herbert Spencer, *The Principles of Ethics*, 2 vols. (1892–3), i. 554.

[41] For detailed discussion of ideas relating to women and eugenics in the later nineteenth century, see Lorna Duffin, 'Prisoners of Progress: Women and Evolution', in Delamont and Duffin, *Nineteenth Century Woman*, to which my brief account is considerably indebted; Carol Dyhouse, *Girls Growing up*, ch. 5, 'Feminist Perspectives and Responses', 139–75; and Anna Davin, 'Imperialism and Motherhood', *History Workshop Journal*, 5 (1978), 9–65.

In the later decades of the nineteenth century, particularly after the publication of Patrick Geddes and J. Arthur Thomson's *The Evolution of Sex* (1889), evolutionary science offered a substantial confirmation to those psychological and educational theories which stressed the importance of social progress. Social conformity, and the ensuing improvement of the race, was foregrounded at the expense of individual growth. In its turn, this meant a deepening of the connection between women and altruistic and sacrificial virtues.[42] 'Females,' claimed Geddes and Thomson, 'especially as mothers, have indubitably a larger and more habitual share of the altruistic emotions.' The woman:

has what may be called the greater integrating intelligence; the man, introducing new variations [due to his 'greater cerebral variability';] is stronger in differentiation. The feminine passivity is expressed in greater patience, more open-mindedness, greater appreciation of subtle details and consequently what we call more rapid intuition. The masculine activity lends a greater power of maximum effort, of scientific insight, or cerebral experiment with impressions, and is associated with an unobservant or impatient disregard of minute details, but with a stronger grasp of generalities. Man thinks more, women [*sic*] feels more. He discovers more, but remembers less; she is more receptive, and less forgetful.[43]

Havelock Ellis, in *Man and Woman* (1894), whilst highly dismissive of the brain-weight debate which had been for some years a recurrent feature of educational discussions, and determined to show woman's difference *from* man, rather than her inferiority or superiority in relation to him, devotes a chapter to woman's 'affectibility'.[44] 'Women', he wrote, 'respond to stimuli, psychic or physical, more readily than men.' Convinced that an emotion is not a purely mental phenomenon, that it cannot exist until an impression has passed into the body and become mixed with a convulsion of blood and muscle and heart and other organs, and looking to recent authorities, such as chapters 23–5 of William James's *The Principles of Psychology* to support him, Ellis puts forward several physiological factors for assuming woman's greater affectibility. He maintains it is due to the fact that her circulatory system, her viscera and glands are differently composed; her vaso-motor system is more readily stimulated; and that her possession of a smaller average proportion of red blood corpuscles in relation to men allows the more rapid circulation of stimuli throughout the body.[45] He seeks proof for the greater excitability of women's hearts in the fact that there is a distinctly greater increase in the number of pulsations on awaking

[42] For discussion of the intersection of evolutionary science and theories of gender, see Alaya, 'Victorian Science and the "Genius" of Woman'.

[43] Patrick Geddes and J. Arthur Thomson, *The Evolution of Sex* (1889), 271.

[44] For Havelock Ellis's contribution to the gender debate, see Alaya, 'Victorian Science and the "Genius" of Woman', 272–6, and more generally, Phyllis Grosskurth, *Havelock Ellis: A Biography* (New York, 1980).

[45] Havelock Ellis, *Man and Woman: A Study of Human Secondary Sexual Characteristics* (1894), 298–304.

from sleep in women; for the more spontaneous, more excitable nature of woman's vaso-motor system in the fact that blushing is far more frequent in her than in a man. He suggests that training, and greater attention to the physical culture of women, may diminish these forms of affectibility to some extent, but nothing will alter her tendency to anaemia, nor, above all, her monthly periods, which give her a broader basis for the play of emotion than is the case with men. The suggestibility of women, to some extent organically based, influences, according to Ellis, some of her habits of thought. He asserts that she more frequently accepts statements and opinions than does a man. She is a readier observer of detailed social phenomena: this leads her to be 'organically fitted' as a writer, and, one might adduce, consumer of fiction.[46] Her physiology even determines her tastes in philosophical reading:

Ladies' philosophers, according to the experience of a well-known West End bookseller, are Schopenhauer, Plato, Marcus Aurelius, Epictetus, and Renan. That is to say, that women are attracted to the most concrete of all abstract thinkers, to the most poetic, to the most intimately personal, above all to the most religious, for every one of these thinkers was saturated through and through with religious emotion.[47]

Cautiously, and somewhat inconsistently, however, Ellis adds that it is impossible to tell what part social and educational differences may play in determining such differences in tastes between women and men.

A debate on women's education in the *Englishwoman* in 1896 conveniently encapsulated the different arguments current at the end of the century which controlled the predominating presuppositions about how women read. This debate was launched by Sir James Crichton Browne, expressing his concern for the stress produced on schoolgirls by study and academic pressure. He supported his claim that housewifery should be included in the curriculum, preparing woman for her future role as wife and mother, by drawing attention to the way the flow of blood within the brain predisposes her towards loving, altruistic tendencies: whilst men's vascular supply flushes with blood the regions concerned with 'involition, cognitions, and ideo-motor processes', those governing the 'sensory functions' are most generously served in women.[48] However, Crichton Browne was challenged in the next number by Maud

[46] Havelock Ellis, *Man and Woman: A Study of Human Secondary Sexual Characteristics* 324. The idea that women were innately more disposed to pay attention to close detail than were men was a commonly voiced assumption throughout the Victorian period. See e.g. M. A. Stodart, *Female Writers: Thoughts on their Proper Sphere, and on their Powers of Usefulness* (1842) where, in addition to writing of woman's closeness of sympathy, of her facility in associating ideas, and on the want of much separation between her moral and mental faculties, she comments, rather less than flatteringly, on her 'closeness of observation and the power of entering into minute details. The sphere is confined, and the view is microscopic' (p. 21). Later (p. 131), she claims that it is precisely this combination of factors which gives women writers, 'for some species of novels, peculiar advantages'.

[47] Stodart, *Female Writers*, 189–90. Ellis is citing *Westminster Gazette* (13 May 1893): neither Ellis nor the *Westminster Gazette*'s correspondent pauses to consider what a woman's response to Schopenhauer's notorious misogyny might be.

[48] Sir James Crichton Browne, 'Should Women Be Educated?', *Englishwoman*, 2 (1896), 456.

Venables Vernon, who cited Emmanuel Bonavia and H.C. Bastian to show that different ideas about brain functions were to be found in respectable scientific circles, indicating that such references were readily accessible in Ellis Ethelmer's *Woman Free* (1893), a long poem heavily annotated with a compilation of pro-feminist extracts.[49] Moreover, she asks the reader to consider that many of the differences between men and women which have hitherto been taken as 'natural' are in fact the result of generations having accepted, unquestioningly, the socially inherited occupation of motherhood, 'no matter what a woman's tastes and inclinations may be'.[50] Finally H. S. Drayton, whilst conceding that medical examinations of the brain revealed no real differences between those of men and of women 'by which any distinction of functional capacity can be discovered', none the less, and confusingly, sustains the belief that the parts of the brain which govern 'the affectional sentiments and moral emotions', rather than the intellect, are greater in the woman. He ends on a plea that this 'superior endowment of the psychic emotions and . . . gentle instincts . . . tenderness, kindness, reverence, affection, devotion, self-sacrifices, the qualities recognised in true womanhood' should not be taken at a lesser evaluation than intellectual capacities.[51]

In the developing field of experimental psychology, the earliest experiment which actually directs itself to establishing a difference between women and men as readers would seem to be that which George Romanes conducted in the latter half of the 1880s. Romanes presented the same paragraph in turn to a group of well-educated individuals of both sexes, ten seconds being allowed for twenty lines. When the reading time was up, the paragraph was removed, and each reader was immediately asked to write down what she or he remembered of it. Nine times out of ten, not only did the women read more quickly—up to four times as quickly, indeed—but they were better at recollecting the content. However, Romanes expressly consoles his male readers by adding 'that rapidity of perception as thus tested is no evidence of what may be termed the deeper qualities of mind—some of my slowest readers being highly distinguished men'.[52] Romanes notably paid almost no attention to factors of social conditioning. Nor did he approach his researches with an open mind: since on average a woman's brain weighs 5 oz. (140 g) less than a man's, he claimed that 'we should be prepared to expect a marked inferiority of intellectual power in

---

[49] The identity of Ethelmer has been the subject of debate: it has been argued (by Sheila Jeffrys, *The Spinster and her Enemies: Feminism and Sexuality 1880–1930* (1985), 29) that this was the pseudonym of the feminist Elizabeth Wolstenholme Elmy, and with more plausibility, Sylvia Pankhurst (*The Suffragette Movement* (1931; repr. 1977), 31) attributed it to Elmer's husband, Ben Elmy. Possibly, suggests Lucy Bland, it was a joint work (Lucy Bland, 'The Married Woman, the "New Woman" and the Feminist: Sexual Politics of the 1890s', in Jane Rendall (ed.), *Equal or Different: Women's Politics 1800–1914* (1987), 154.

[50] Maud Venables Vernon, 'How Should Women be Educated?', *Englishwoman*, 3 (1896), 179–80.

[51] H. S. Drayton, 'Is the Brain of Woman Inferior?', *Englishwoman*, 3 (1896), 463–5.

[52] George J. Romanes, 'Mental Differences between Men and Women', *Nineteenth Century*, 21 (1887), 655–6.

the former'. Additionally, he started from a position where he accepted the views of Crichton Browne: that the cortex of the female brain is shallower than that of the male; that the general physique of woman is less robust than that of a man and therefore 'less able to sustain the fatigue of serious or prolonged brain action'; that woman's 'inferiority' particularly expresses itself in a comparative absence of originality; that 'there is a greater power of amassing knowledge on the part of the male'; and that when it comes to issues of judgement, women are more apt than men to make a superficial assessment of circumstances. None the less, in women the 'sense-organs' are more evolved, and hence women's perception tends to be more rapid.[53] His experiments were specifically designed to measure speed in perception, and tended to confirm Crichton Browne's last point. Romanes' findings are used to support the assertions he goes on to make: that in women, the emotions are almost always less under the control of the will than in the man; that there is in the feminine, 'as compared with the masculine mind, a greater desire for emotional excitement of all kinds',[54] and that women, through their maternal instincts, are more prone to displays of affection and sympathy than are men, but that such attributes do not fit them for intellectual pursuits.[55]

The degree to which reading, among other activities, may function as a substitute for woman's 'natural' outlets for emotion was taken up by the American psychologist G. Stanley Hall, who exercised a considerable influence on educational policy in both the United States and England in the early years of the twentieth century.[56] Many of his assumptions are familiar, such as his insistence that the characteristic differences of women from men in every organ and tissue designate the female's primary importance in continuing the race; and his attribution of intuition, feeling, and greater intensity of emotions to women. More novel, in terms of its relevance to the reading process, are his postulations about the nature of woman to desire what she does not possess, to have the capacity of living almost permanently 'in what is really a suppressed semi-erotic state', and of needing, and seeking, absorbing occupations.[57]

[53] George J. Romanes, 'Mental Differences between Men and Women', 657.

[54] Ibid.

[55] Romanes was relatively unusual in stressing the different results obtained by each sex within reading experiments, since on neither side of the Atlantic did sexual difference tend to figure in the work of theorists of perception. E. B. Huey's *The Psychology and Pedagogy of Reading* (Boston, 1908), for example, treats his subject, even implicitly, as though there is no need to make any distinction between girls and boys. Romanes' theories seem to have had little bearing on the development of his own daughter, Ethel, who was extremely well read as a schoolgirl, absorbing her father's evolutionary and historical arguments, and reducing Winifred Peck to tears, when they were both pupils at Wycombe Abbey, by telling her that her whole family was descended not just from apes but from jellyfish, and that the date 4004 BC as the date of creation was an invention of James I's reign. Winifred Peck, *A Little Learning or A Victorian Childhood* (1952), 132.

[56] For the importance of G. Stanley Hall to the theories of the nature of female adolescence and its educational consequences, see Carol Dyhouse, *Girls Growing up*, 121–31. See also Dorothy Ross, *G. Stanley Hall, The Psychologist as Prophet* (Chicago, 1972).

[57] Hall, *Adolescence*, 572, 578.

Notoriously, Hall suggests that women remain all their lives in a kind of natural adolescence, but some of the characteristics which he attributes to this state are particularly relevant to the habit of reading, especially what he terms the 'convertibility of the emotions', and the capacity for sympathy and appreciation.[58] However, these tendencies only seem unequivocally praiseworthy if they are directed towards marriage and maternity, for, in focusing on the 'disappointed woman', Hall writes of how she attempts to assert her own individuality, transmuting a desire for love into a desire for knowledge. Independence, seen as synonymous with competition with men, becomes a substitute for the 'legitimate expression' of her feelings in childbirth as she turns, instead, 'successively to art, science, literature, and reforms'.[59]

The growth of woman's educational opportunities, and the simultaneous broadening of discussions on the one hand about the varied positions she might play within society, and on the other about her capacity for sustained intellectual work and analysis are themes which feature prominently in the chapters to come. The expansion of women's opportunities took place, however, right until the First World War, against an undercurrent of conservative disapproval and anxiety from many medical authorities. These continued to assert their belief in the importance of woman's role, above all, as mother. This emphasis on presumed maternal functions is the one, ultimately, which has the most bearing on the question of women and reading.

The issue of identification with fictional characters is one which has already been raised and to which we shall return, but it is useful to introduce into this context Janice Radway's theories concerning the reading of romantic fiction. As we have seen, the identificatory process was, for many of the authorities cited in this chapter, presented as a 'natural' attribute of woman, related to the 'intimate and special sympathies which a mother has with her child'.[60] But Radway postulates that reading the romance, putting oneself vicariously into a passive relationship with a caring, nurturant, powerful male in fact encourages an abandonment of any such sense of duty: the heroine/reader:

is required to do nothing more than *exist* as the center of this paragon's attention. Romantic escape is, therefore, a temporary but literal denial of the demands women recognize as an integral part of their roles as nurturing wives and mothers. It is also a figurative journey to a utopian state of total receptiveness where the reader, as a result of her relationship with the heroine, feels herself the *object* of someone else's attention and solicitude.[61]

If one accepts this plausible hypothesis, it becomes possible to see how, for many Victorian commentators, reading the right type of material involved and

[58] Ibid. 64.
[59] Ibid. 629.
[60] Maudsley, 'Sex in Mind and in Education', 472.
[61] Radway, *Reading the Romance*, 97.

encouraged the use of certain desirable 'natural' faculties. But at the same time the misuse of women's intrinsic attributes for sympathetic identification did not just carry with it the possibility that she might morally be led astray, but constituted in itself a transgression of the proper function of her innate characteristics. The aim of training women for their 'proper function' in a wider social sense lay behind, as we shall see in the next section, the way in which reading was presented in the many books and articles of advice aimed at the young woman reader.

5 Advice Manuals, Informative Works, and Instructional Articles

The status and function of the advice manual changed only slowly during the nineteenth century. In its manifestations early in the period covered by this book, such as Elizabeth Sandford, *Woman and Her Social and Domestic Character* (1831) and *Female Improvement* (1836), Anna Jameson, *Characteristics of Women* (1832), Sarah Lewis, *Woman's Mission* (1839), and C. M. Sedgwick, *Means and Ends or Self-Training* (1840), it may be seen as contributing to the establishment of 'the cult of domesticity'.[1] Aimed largely at middle-class girls in their mid- to late teens, these books formed a genre written for women, and largely by women, thus ensuring the commercial circulation and dissemination of various types of domestic advice and information. Some of this, relating to routine household matters and questions of health, amplified or substituted for knowledge habitually supplied to daughters by their mothers (or, in the case of publications aimed at servants, which increased in number during the century, by older housekeepers, even employers). Much of the conversational, occasionally sententious, guiding prose worked towards establishing the centrality of motherhood itself, the home and family, to a woman's life. At once caring and authoritative, these texts implicitly claimed for themselves something of the ideological role of the mother which was constructed within their own covers, bonding the reader, at least in theory, into a framework of categorical self-definition: learning, and playing out, the part of the receptive yet obedient daughter, and thus ensuring the transmission of values and practices from one generation to the next. Such a function was made explicit in certain mid-century titles, such as Matilda Pullan's *Maternal Counsels to a Daughter* (1855), and Mary Bayly's *An Old Mother's Letter to Young Women* (1885). It is embedded, implicitly, in other advice texts. In Mary Stodart's *Principles of Education* (1844), for example, the final chapter, on 'Maternal Influence', emphasizes the importance of a mother being able to take an overview of all aspects of her daughter's education. The book itself has just provided a model of the different

---

[1] For further discussion about the status and function of advice manuals, see Mary Poovey, *The Proper Lady and the Woman Writer: Ideology as Style in the Works of Mary Wollstonecraft, Mary Shelley, and Jane Austen* (Chicago, 1984), 3–47; Nancy Armstrong and Leonard Tennenhouse (eds.), *The Ideology of Conduct: Essays on Literature and the History of Sexuality* (1987), esp. Armstrong and Tennenhouse, 'The Literature of Conduct, the Conduct of Literature, and the Politics of Desire: An Introduction', 1–24; and Armstrong, *Desire and Domestic Fiction: A Political History of the Novel* (New York and Oxford, 1987), esp. ch. 2, 'The Rise of the Domestic Woman', 59–95, and the first section of ch. 3, 'The Rise of the Novel', 96–108.

categories of advice which she should be considering, offering an authority on which the mother can safely base her own practice.

Although the stress on religious motivation, on doing one's duty by God, becomes markedly less prominent throughout the period (at least in those texts aimed at the middle-classes) the overall tenor remains the same: that girls are, in learning how to care for and present themselves, how to assist in the home, and how most profitably to occupy their leisure hours, in some way fitting themselves to be, eventually, good wives and mothers. The continual assumption is that theirs is an individual character to be brought out and developed, but that this individualized subjecthood is only acceptable when constructed within certain carefully defined paradigms. Despite the importance given to the cultivation and maintenance of female friendships, and the implicit sense that these books of advice offer a range of shared information with the capacity to bind its readers together, the dominant order which is served is, inevitably, the patriarchal order of the Victorian and Edwardian bourgeois economy, co-joined, in the later decades of the century, to the demands of nation and empire. This role was acknowledged within the years covered by this book, when Elizabeth Robins looked back in 1908 to the 'wide popularity' enjoyed by some of these works of guidance, which 'had their share in maintaining, if not increasing, the conditions we are face to face with to-day'. She singled out for particular condemnation the manuals of Sarah Stickney Ellis's, such as *The Women of England* (1838), *The Daughters of England* (1842), *The Mothers of England* (1843), and *The Wives of England* (1843). Robins deplored Ellis's advice to bring 'every rebellious thought to subservience', to be impartially polite to all and willing to bend to circumstance, to revere the angelic power and sublimity to be found in 'the truly good man', and, most debasing of all, to demand pity and compassion from an unfaithful husband rather than challenging his actions.[2]

The specific contexts in which advice was given changed, however, alongside developments in educational opportunity, and the growing acknowledgement of the possibility of the middle-class girl going out to work, not only for reasons of economic necessity, but, on occasion, out of choice. These factors were major contributors to the marked increase in expressions of anxiety about a growing gap between mothers and daughters as the nineteenth century drew to a close: anxiety which will be examined more closely in the next chapter. Moreover, there was considerable discussion about the demands being made on girls by organized education, which was leaving them less time than before for serious leisure pursuits, including reading, and this discussion was supplemented by a series of complaints against rather loosely defined 'tendencies of the age, outside forces, beating like waves against the door of every happy home in

[2] Elizabeth Robins, 'The Suffrage Camp Revisited', *Way Stations* (1913), 52–9. This paper was originally given as a lecture in the Portman Rooms in March 1908.

England'.[3] Despite the alleged 'revolt of the daughters' however, to use Mrs Crackanthorpe's phrase,[4] the genre of the advice manual itself showed no sign of decline: it was, after all, probably not the revolting daughters themselves who were the prime purchasers of these texts as gift books and prizes. This fact in itself should, of course, make one wary about assuming that girls or women necessarily followed the advice laid down in the pages of these books and articles in exemplary fashion. It is worth noting the findings of Carl Degler, who, whilst analysing the evidence of a survey concerning women's sexuality in late nineteenth- and early twentieth-century America, learnt that a considerable proportion of the women interviewed seemed to have read similar prescriptive texts, but that this reading had had an insignificant effect on their attitudes towards sex.[5] But I am not making the claim, in this chapter, that the advice texts cited reflect actual reading habits. My concern, throughout, is with the rhetoric of reading practices, and the degree to which it is possible to build up a picture of widespread assumptions about what, when, and how a woman should read.

Recreational Reading

Throughout the period, novels were at the centre of discussions concerning women and reading: 'the medium through which moral poison is frequently administered', complained the *Saturday Review* in 1867 about this genre with the capacity to blunt a 'woman's sense of the broad demarcation between right and wrong'.[6] Whilst acknowledging the long-standing reservations about novel-reading in general, we must consider why, in particular, this genre was regarded as being so dangerous to women. W. R. Greg's article, 'False Morality of Lady Novelists', quoted in the introduction, emphasized women's impressionability, and the ready capacity of women's feelings and emotions to respond to external influences. Claiming that 'it is not easy to over-estimate the importance of novels',[7] he went on to give various reasons why one should take the genre so seriously. First, novels are primarily read by those who are wealthy enough to enjoy leisure time. By extension, they are thus especially likely to influence those who, in their turn, have the most influence within the country, either at first hand, if men, or through their husbands. Second, since they are invariably read in leisure time, when the brain is comparatively passive, the critical faculties are asleep, so that material is ingested without being judged or sifted.

    [3] Lucy H. M. Soulsby, *Home Rule, or Daughters of To-day* (Oxford, 1894), 6–7.
    [4] B. A. Crackanthorpe, 'The Revolt of the Daughters', *Nineteenth Century*, 35 (1894), 23–31.
    [5] Carl Degler, 'What Ought To Be and What Was: Women's Sexuality in the Nineteenth Century', *American Historical Review*, 79 (1974), 1478.
    [6] 'Novel-Reading', *Saturday Review* (16 Feb. 1867), 196.
    [7] [W. R. Greg] 'False Morality of Lady Novelists', *National Review*, 8 (1859), 144.

Third, novels form, in Greg's view, an unfortunately large part of the habitual reading of the young, at a time when the memory is fresh, when what he calls the 'moral standard' is largely fluctuating and unformed, and experience has not yet been great enough to afford 'a criterion whereby to separate the true from the false in the delineations of life'.[8]

Greg was unusual in the concern which he expressed about the far-reaching social and political effects of novel-reading. Generally, the emphasis fell on the damage the practice would have on the developing individual, and considered her reading patterns and expectations in relation to her immediate social environment. The perennial expectation, throughout the period, was, as we noted in the last chapter, that women read uncritically, readily identifying with the central characters in their fictions. Tellingly, novel-reading was warned against because of its capacity to raise false expectations, and engender dissatisfaction with one's present mode of life. Ruskin's words in the popular *Sesame and Lilies* (1865) proved useful ones for subsequent commentators to draw upon. 'The best romance', Ruskin wrote, 'becomes dangerous, if, by its excitement, it renders the ordinary course of life uninteresting, and increases the morbid thirst for useless acquaintance with scenes in which we shall never be called upon to act.'[9] Ruskin reminds his readers that a girl's intellect ripens faster than that of a boy, and that she should be led, earlier than her male counterpart, into 'deep and serious subjects'; 'her range of literature should be . . . calculated to add the qualities of patience and seriousness to her natural poignancy of thought and quickness of wit', all working together to prepare her for her function as moral guardian of the hearth and home. The social prescriptiveness is underscored by the fact that he implicitly sets himself up to protect women against the potential invasion of the sanctity of their own bodies by unsuitable reading matter, for his language is heavily charged with resonances of male sexuality as he describes how a girl must be shielded from the textual pressures on her. One must be sure that 'her books are not heaped up in her lap as they fall out of the package of the circulating library, wet with the last and lightest spray of the fountain of folly'.[10]

Advice manual writers continually stressed the vulnerability of the young, unprepared, inexperienced girl, who early learnt from novels, it was thought, that she must 'fall' in love. Hence, in her own life, she would quickly become apt to magnify any slight attentions paid to her, mistaking flutterings of vanity in her own breast for emotions of real love. As W. H. Davenport Adams put it: 'This fictitious sentiment she nourishes by novel-reading, idleness and indulgence in day-dreaming.'[11] Romantic fiction remained suspect throughout

---

[8] [W. R. Greg] 'False Morality of Lady Novelists', 145.

[9] John Ruskin, *Sesame and Lilies* (1865), *The Works of John Ruskin*, ed. E. T. Cook and Alexander Wedderburn, 39 vols. (1903–12), xviii. 129.

[10] *Works*, xviii. 129.

[11] W. H. Davenport Adams, *Woman's Work and Worth* (1880), 97.

the period. George Bainton, in *The Wife as Lover and Friend* (1895) complained that such novels are damaging since they portray difficulties as ending at the marriage altar, ignoring all reference to the subsequent effort which a marriage necessarily involves: ' "They married, and were happy ever afterwards," is a loving tradition, which, though devoutly to be wished, will yet, in too many instances, if dragged into the revealing sunshine of prosaic, every-day life, show how unsubstantial is its origin, and how unreliable its philosophy.'[12] But the damage which novels were suspected of inducing went further than the generating of foolish romantic expectations, or worse, than the assimilation of material which might devalue a girl's marketable values as a bride, causing 'her simplicity and innocence, which should be her chief charm, [to be] lost for ever'.[13] Generally consumed in passivity, as Greg acknowledged, fiction was accused of encouraging lethargy, narcolepsy, and at worst of creating drug-like habits of dependence. Thus Annie Swan, herself a prolific romantic novelist, claimed that too much novel-reading turned a 'recreation' into a 'dissipation', and what followed was 'the loss of that discriminating power which is the prized possession of the cultured reader who is able to exercise the right amount of self-control'.[14]

Yet, controversial though the practice could be, it would be wrong to assume that novel-reading was habitually regarded with suspicion. First, many maintained that it was better to establish a reading habit of any kind than none at all. Phyllis Browne warns that to stop a girl reading story-books is all too frequently a means to 'destroy the love for reading that the story books were helping to form'. She tells a cautionary tale to prove her point of the mother who proudly proclaimed that if ever she saw her daughters with a book in their hands, she set them instantly to needlework. 'You might have trained them to be domesticated,' comments Browne, 'but you had no business to forbid them to read. It is your fault that your daughter, though married to an intelligent, thoughtful young fellow, is gradually losing all influence over her husband, and is nothing of a companion to him.'[15] Whereas the taste for story-books will pass away, the taste for reading, she confidently maintains, will not. In the meantime, she recommends stories in which the moral is suggested rather than direct, in which the heroine is not improbably virtuous, and which are cheerful, rather than sad, sadness being an area of the emotions best dealt with at first hand: 'We want feeling to be called forth only by real suffering, to pass as a matter of course into action, and to dictate helpful conduct.'[16] John Robertson's advice of 1904 was in a similar vein. 'To mothers in particular I would say, do not fret if your daughter in her spare hours shows a passion for novels. If you can only

[12] George Bainton, *The Wife as Lover and Friend* (1895), 22.
[13] Dorothy Owen, *Letters to School-girls* (1908), 53.
[14] Annie Swan, 'What Should Women Read?' *Woman at Home*, 37 (1896), 31.
[15] Phyllis Browne, *What Girls Can Do* (1880), 102–3.
[16] Ibid. 106.

lead her taste upwards on that path—and the best plan is always to travel that way yourself—she will grow wiser and better, not more flighty and indolent.'[17]

For since it was believed that reading could influence for the bad it must also, if of the right kind, be presumed to influence for the good. We saw earlier how this assumption was put forward in one of its most blatantly didactic forms, the biography: it was further supported by a variety of commentators on fiction and drama. Trollope, for example, believing in the morally educative power of fiction, advised his female listeners in a lecture of 1868 that if they: 'will take some little trouble in the choice of your novels, the lessons which you will find taught in them are good lessons. Honour and honesty, modesty and self-denial, are as strongly insisted on in our English novels as they are in our English sermons.'[18] Davenport Adams prefaced his highly popular *Woman's Work and Worth*, designed, he maintained, as 'an aid to Self-Culture', with the claim that he has selected, throughout, 'those types which best deserve admiration and imitation':[19]

The fancy of many a youth has been worthily kindled by contemplation of the heroic as presented in poem and romance; and there is no reason, we repeat, why our girls, our maidens, should not profit by a similar inspiration. There is much virtue in a good poem or a good novel. Why should not a girl strive to model herself by the fine patterns set before her? All depends upon the choice of model.[20]

Davenport Adams is not short of possible examples, taken from a range of genres. In Shakespeare, there are Juliet, Cordelia, Rosalind; Miranda, with her 'virgin openness of heart', or 'the lofty maidenhood of Isabella'.[21] Similarly, Elizabeth Wordsworth, Principal of the Oxford college, Lady Margaret Hall, advocated that a 'well-educated girl ought to be, at twelve or fifteen years old, in love with Miranda, Cordelia, Desdemona, Portia, and Perdita, with Nausicaa and Andromache, and many another heroine. She ought to catch some of their beautiful feeling, their dignity.'[22] Moving from drama to poetry, Herbert's *Parentalia* provide for Adams a catalogue of the virtues one might hope to find in the perfect mother (it appears not to matter to him that the poems are in Latin). More up to date, he offers Tennyson's Dora, and, unsurprisingly, the heroine of what he terms 'Mr Coventry Patmore's fine panegyric of the domestic affections, that beautiful poem of "The Angel in the House"'. Among novelists, he acknowledges that heroines cannot always be accepted as

[17] John M. Robertson, *What to Read: Suggestions for the Better Utilisation of Public Libraries* (1904), 9.

[18] Anthony Trollope, 'The Higher Education of Women' (1868), repr. in *Four Lectures*, ed. Morris L. Parrish (1938), 85.

[19] Davenport Adams, *Woman's Work and Worth*, p. xvii.

[20] Ibid. 142. Selected parts of Davenport Adams's work, presenting specific examples, were issued as a separate volume, *Exemplary Women: A Record of Feminine Virtues and Achievements* (1882), published in John Hogg's 'The Secret of Success' series.

[21] Ibid. 123.

[22] E. Wordsworth, *First Principles in Women's Education* (Oxford, 1894), 9.

embodying the ideas of 'perfect maidenhood', since their actions and character must be adapted to the exigencies of the plot. However, he recommends Mary Barton and Molly Gibson, among Elizabeth Gaskell's creations, for their 'constant pursuit of a higher and nobler life', their 'strenuous endeavour to fulfil the law of duty';[23] he praises the purity and almost saintly resignation of Amyas Leigh's mother in Kingsley's *Westward Ho!* and the piety, dutifulness, grace, and cultivation of Lady Armine in Disraeli's *Henrietta Temple*, and warns his readers against emulating 'the loud-speaking, fast-going, essentially vulgar heroines of the sensational school'.[24]

However, rather than acquiescing in the theory that a reader will habitually and uncritically identify herself with the central character in a work, Adams offers a more active mode of reading. He suggests that she should continually be matching herself up against protagonists, asking herself if she has the heroism of Charlotte Brontë's Shirley, or the 'glowing piety' of Dinah, in *Adam Bede*, or the 'amiability' of Evelina.[25] Moreover, Davenport Adams suggests that the readiness of women to identify themselves with the central characters in the texts they read is, in fact, a consequence of what he terms their 'defective mental training', since the imagination and passions have, according to him, been developed at the expense of judgement. 'We have allowed our girls to read poetry and fiction, and subjected them to the sensuous influences of art, while taking no pains to cultivate the reasoning faculties or the practical intellect';[26] and he goes on to recommend—using Maria Grey and Emily Shirreff's *Thoughts on Self-Culture* (1850) as a model—a methodically organized, industrious course of study, with 'understanding' as the eventual aim of all reading. That self-cultivation can lead to great things, Adams is in no doubt. He provides a lengthy study of the impressive contribution which women have made to English literature, singling out, above all, the novels of George Eliot: 'to all time they will remain an eloquent vindication and irresistible support of the intellectual claims of woman'.[27] Nor does his support for women's intellectual efforts confine them to the home: chapter 7 of his book, 'The Higher Education of Woman', warmly supports the availability of university and college courses.

Whilst the greatest amount of anxiety about the effects of novel-reading centred on the young woman, reading the romance was not her prerogative alone. 'It is beyond question', noted Annie Swan, 'that a love-story has yet the power to charm even sober men and women of middle age, for whom the romance is mistakenly supposed to be over.'[28] Yet whilst current research has addressed the role which such reading plays in the adult woman's life, it remained largely undiscussed during the period covered by this study. Swan,

---

[23] Davenport Adams, *Woman's Work and Worth*, 135.   [24] Ibid. 136.
[25] Ibid. 136.   [26] Ibid. 159.   [27] Ibid. 196.
[28] Swan, *Courtship and Marriage and the Gentle Art of Home-Making* (1893), 9.

however, gives a hint of fiction's potential advantages to more mature women. Writing of 'The Ideal Wife', she praises the value of unselfishness, and the frequent necessity for woman to blend her individuality with that of another person. But a woman should not lose sight of her individuality, even whilst she takes care not to usurp her husband as head of the house. She certainly should avoid succumbing to 'the sickly thrall of sentimentality'—Swan specifically cites Thackeray's Amelia as a heroine with whom nobody would, in the 1890s, have sympathy—but rather should be more 'robust', 'sound of body and sound of mind'.

Despite this concentration on fiction, poetry also received its share of attention, albeit in less contentious fashion. The commonly-held implicit distinction between the two genres was brought to the fore in *Thoughts on Self-Culture*. In this work, Grey and Shirreff place much emphasis on the importance of developing that susceptible faculty, the imagination. This should not be allowed, like an unweeded garden, to 'run riot', but rather should be cultivated by 'careful training, and the supply of worthy objects to excite it'.[29] Prime among these objects was poetry, which they believed contained enough manifestations of strong emotion for a reader to be able to associate herself readily with its contents. Yet poetry, in its tendency for idealization, avoided the pitfall engendered by fiction: the tendency for a reader to take a novel's events and presentation of material circumstances as manifestations of fact and probability which act as standards against which to measure one's own life. Rather, poetry leads one, valuably, away from the actual. The distinction which they make is fundamentally a Cartesian one, in which poetry is equated with a conceptual level of apprehension, fiction with a lesser form of perception which is irrevocably linked to the body:

In a poem, the wildest language of passion, though it may appeal to the feelings, is generally called forth in circumstances remote from the experience of the reader; but in works which profess to paint real life, a regard to probability is so necessary, that there is nothing to prevent the young reader placing herself in the position of any favorite personage, and should she feel or fancy any resemblance in her own mind and circumstances to those portrayed, she is easily led to expect a similar course of events to draw forth the virtues or the talents, or to give scope to the feelings of which she is conscious. . . . The grand conceptions of the poet are true in ideal beauty; the novelist's pictures of real life are false, because necessarily covered with an unreal gloss. The object of the poet and artist is to embody their own lofty view of the truly beautiful; that of the novelist to present us with an imitation of what we see around us, and therefore to mingle with the beautiful all that generally detracts from it in real life, even shrinking from portraying such excellence as we actually *have* known and loved, lest it should

[29] Maria Grey and Emily Shirreff, *Thoughts on Self-Culture Addressed to Women*, 2 vols. (1850), ii. 218. For Grey and Shirreff, and the role which they played in the development of educational opportunities for women in England, see Edward W. Ellsworth, *Liberators of the Female Mind: The Shirreff Sisters, Educational Reform, and the Women's Movement* (1979).

appear to border on romance. The one sublimes the soul by lifting it above the present to the contemplation of eternal beauty; the other increases the interest of the actual and the present already too engrossing, enamouring us of the chain which binds the soul to earth. . . . The poet, in short, elevates the thoughts, while the novelist excites the feelings, and this one difference sufficiently expresses how admirable is the one and how pernicious the other kind of reading for women.[30]

For Mrs Ellis too, poetry was particularly suited for women precisely because it is removed from the 'realities of material and animal existence'. The poetry to be found in the written word, she maintained, is analogous to the expansiveness which lies dormant within the passive exterior of the woman:

whose world of interest is as wide as the realm of humanity, boundless as the ocean of life, and enduring as eternity! For woman, who, in her inexhaustible sympathies can only live in the existence of another, and whose very smiles and tears are not exclusively her own—for woman to cast away the love of poetry, is to pervert from their natural course the sweetest and loveliest tendencies of a truly feminine mind, to destroy the brightest charm which can adorn her intellectual character, to blight the fairest rose in her wreath of youthful beauty.[31]

Matilda Pullan, in *Maternal Counsels to a Daughter* (1855), recommended that poetry be learnt by heart, both as a means of training the memory and in order to store up a source of pleasure: 'Poetry, indeed, can be learnt in odd minutes,—from an open book while working, or whilst brushing the hair at night, or at many other periods that are too often wasted.'[32] She, too, advises against attempting anything off-puttingly difficult, confessing that she suspects she is not the only person who read *Paradise Lost* '*as a duty*'.[33] Dorothy Owen, maintaining that as a schoolgirl she hated 'the very thought of reading poetry', claimed that this is still—in 1908—the case with many girls. She believes this is because they have started with something too difficult, like a Shakespeare play, or one of Scott's poems, and advises instead Macaulay's 'Lays of Ancient Rome' for young girls, along with Longfellow (especially 'Evangeline' and 'The Courtship of Miles Standish') and Adelaide Procter's work.[34] Lucy Soulsby recognized that one might well progress from 'simple' poetry like that of Mrs Hemans and Longfellow to writing, such as that of Browning, which encourages the pleasure of 'hard thought'. But she cautions against dismissing Tennyson, Herbert, or Vaughan as 'too intelligible', since their achievement is in large part due to their apparent simplicity, which conceals intensity and complexity.[35]

---

[30] Grey and Shirreff, *Thoughts on Self-Culture*, ii. 224–6.
[31] Mrs Ellis, *The Daughters of England* (1845), 161–2.
[32] M. Pullan, *Maternal Counsels*, 45.
[33] Ibid. 55.
[34] Owen, *Letters to School-girls*, 58.
[35] Soulsby, *Stray Thoughts on Reading* (1895), 83–4.

Reading as Social Education

For many commentators, the most important text was, of course, the Bible: 'certainly no day should be allowed to pass by any young girl, without her having made some addition to her Biblical knowledge'.[36] This recommendation was also made by C. M. Sedgwick, although she warned against reading the Bible 'as a mere habit, from an impression that you perform a religious act, if you read a certain portion of the holy book'.[37] The positive aspects of providing religious education ranked far higher in many lists of priorities than issuing warnings against reading fiction or poetry—although writers were swift to supply these when appropriate. The lessons offered, particularly in the New Testament, set down the moral foundation by which all other forms of reading might be judged or interrogated. And, when it came to considering other theological writing, the Bible, as Mary Ann Stodart put it, ' "the whole Bible, and nothing but the Bible," may be set forth as the motto upon our banner—the simple rule, the perfect standard in what we designate religious education'.[38] She recommends it not just for the broad 'treasure-house of wisdom' which it offers, but because of the examples it gives of 'the true place of the female sex . . . the holy women of Scripture, domestic women', and, through the teaching of St Paul, of the especial duties of women.[39]

That girls were, especially in the first half of the period, expected to read the Bible, and to do so carefully and thoughtfully, comes as no surprise. But warnings proliferated against uncritical acceptance of no matter what form of Christian writing. Sedgwick, again, for example, advised that one should not believe that one is automatically performing a religious act if one is simply choosing a religious text to read for such an activity is merely conformity to the letter, and 'the letter killeth'.[40] And, despite the numerous tracts and pieces of sentimental religious fiction which circulated, she warned against too much reading of such literature. Why read that which may be polluted, she inquires, when one may have access to the clear, unmuddied stream of the Scriptures? Sedgwick lacks, however, the intonation of panic with which Stodart, in *Every Day Duties*, deters her reader from 'religious novels, that froth and scum upon which thousands of professed Christians feed, or rather starve their minds'.[41]

[36] Pullan, *Maternal Counsels*, 47.

[37] C. M. Sedgwick, *Means and Ends; or, Self-Training* (1839), 236, Sedgwick's work, explicitly aimed at girls between ten and sixteen, was originally produced for the American market, but was brought out in an English edition with an additional preface. Compared with English works, this and other advice texts by Sedgwick, such as *Morals or Manners; or, Hints for Our Young People* (1846) make great play of stressing the democracy of opportunity to be found in America, claiming that the New is not as the Old world, where a person's life course may be determined by being born with a pewter, rather than a silver spoon in their mouth.

[38] Mary Ann Stodart, *Principles of Education Practically Considered; with an especial reference to the Present State of Female Education in England* (1844), 29.

[39] Ead., *Every Day Duties: in letters to a young lady* (1840), 3, 17.

[40] Sedgwick, *Means and Ends*, 236–7.

[41] Stodart, *Every Day Duties*, 123.

In asking their female readership to pay careful attention to the Bible, these commentators were encouraging them to think about the connections between their reading material and how they approached their lives. The argument that consuming literature functioned as a substitute for social education was advanced in relation to many other types of texts. It was particularly useful to those who looked for plausible grounds on which to defend fiction. Reading Trollope, maintained the *Saturday Review* in 1867, 'is only to most girls "coming out" a season or two earlier than they would have done, and "coming out" under the auspices of a careful drawing-room chaperon, who will not introduce them to more objectional characters than he thinks unavoidable.'[42] At this level, reading is seen as operating in a socially mimetic way, introducing the girl vicariously to situations which she might well come across in her own life, or which she would do well to avoid; or, for that matter, ensuring that she experiences imaginatively what it would be like to move in certain circles which lie outside the range of her probable circumstances. Thus rules of etiquette and good behaviour, and above all, the capacity to make moral judgements, may be inculcated, if only by reiteration. This factor necessarily involves the reader projecting herself into friendships and family relationships which may well grant emotional satisfactions, as well as social experiences, unavailable to her in her daily life. The issue of social propriety is played upon further by the injunction to look on books themselves as possible friends, and on occasion to regard their authors as people to whom proper behaviour must be shown. There are frequent references to books as 'people', as 'companions', as 'intimate friends', as safeguards against loneliness, as 'a solace . . . in times of sorrow and trouble'. 'Books are like people', claimed Matilda Pullan. 'Some should be minutely studied; some may be just glanced through; but every one should leave a certain definite impression on the mind.'[43] The rhetorical manipulation of books as people allows for advice to be given in a way which plays on received upper-class social codes, reinforcing them through the initial assumption that they are as authoritative a set of guidelines when applied as metaphors as in real life. This further leads the middle-class reader into imaginary situations where these guidelines can be seen to be tested and applied, and invites her to participate in the social rules of a strictly demarcated ritual from which she would probably have been excluded in actual terms, at least until the very end of the nineteenth century.[44]

In this way, gaining knowledge about, for example, what it would be appropriate to read, and the methods to be adopted when reading, could be

---

[42] 'Novel-reading', *Saturday Review*, 23 (1867), 196.

[43] Pullan, *Maternal Counsels*, 47.

[44] For the way in which etiquette may be understood as a set of strictly structured access rituals to 'good' society, acting as a safeguard for that society at a time of rapid social change and increased geographical mobility, and ensuring its continuity through familial connections rather than through wealth, see Leonore Davidoff, *The Best Circles: Society Etiquette and the Season* (1973).

written about in the terms of the correct etiquette governing social introductions. Cowper's lines:

> Too careless often as our years proceed,
> What friends we sort with, or what books we read[45]

provided a suitable aphorism to this end. 'It is said that a man or woman may be known by the company he or she keeps; a truer index to character is the books they read', confidently asserted Davenport Adams.[46] Dorothy Owen, after announcing that 'Books . . . are like people', with the capacity to exert an enormous influence on one's outlook on life, claimed that she made a point, even as an adult, 'of never reading any book unless I know something of the author, or have had it recommended to me by someone whose judgement I trust; and I think every girl would do well to do the same'.[47] Amy Barnard, in advising girls to pay attention when they read, reminds one that if Macaulay or Emerson or Shakespeare were here in person we would not give divided attention to what they said: hence if one does not concentrate single-mindedly on what one reads, 'rudeness is done to the author'.[48] The *Girl's Own Paper* informed its audience that reading 'good books':

raises the tone of the mind and purifies the morals in much the same way as the frequenting of good society. . . . A girl becomes a reflection of the graces of her favourite authors, and though she may have no wealthy or aristocratic friends, if she moves at home in the society of Shakespeare and Milton she can never be commonplace, and will always make herself respected.

The article goes on to suggest, moreover, that one should judge one's potential husband, and estimate the success of future home life, by his attitude to books: 'never marry a husband who has not a collection of books of more general interest than his cash-book and ledger. The reading young man makes a stay-at-home fireside-loving husband. Like to like.'[49] Moreover, in the second of his articles, Mason reminds the reader that others will judge her own tastes and character by the books which she possesses: one's little library:

should be such that a stranger coming in and looking at it might say with confidence either, 'There are many points of contact between that girl's mind and mine;' or, 'I am sure that girl and I will never get on, for she cares for nothing that I like and likes nothing I am keen upon'.[50]

When we come to consider sensation fiction in Chapter 10, we shall see the anxiety expressed by some reviewers that the appeal of this fiction transgressed

[45] William Cowper, 'Tirocinium: or, a review of schools' (1784), ll. 113–14.
[46] Adams, *Woman's Work and Worth*, 140–1.
[47] Owen, *Letters to School-girls*, 52–4.
[48] Amy B. Barnard, *The Girl's Encyclopaedia* (1909), 80.
[49] James Mason, 'How to Form a Small Library', *Girl's Own Paper*, 2 (1881), 7.
[50] 'How to Form a Small Library—II', ibid. 123.

clearly demarcated class lines. This concern for the maintenace of social hierarchies can also be located in advice manuals. Phyllis Browne, for example, claims:

I was very much grieved the other day in going into a large circulating library, where a number of young ladies were choosing books to read, to find that not one of them asked for anything but the most miserable trash, with no thought of anything better. When their wants were satisfied, the girls compared notes rather loudly of the books they had read, and it was pitiable to find their taste lay exclusively in the direction of literature unreal, unhealthy, sensational and false. I hoped these girls were not types of their class. Good books were there, but they never thought of opening them any more than if they had been written in a foreign tongue. As Mr. Ruskin said, it seemed as though they preferred to gossip with housemaids when they might have discoursed with the wise and good.[51]

Choice of Books

How should one choose one's books—fiction or otherwise—wisely? Throughout the period, it was widely assumed that a girl's mother was the best person to give advice: 'In the choice of books to be read for the instruction or amusement of her daughters, a mother should always be consulted', wrote Sarah Stickney Ellis in *The Mothers of England*, continuing, 'A novel read in secret is a dangerous thing; but there are many works of taste and fancy, which, when accompanied by the remarks of a feeling and judicious mother, may be rendered improving to the mind, and beneficial to the character altogether.'[52] Ellis's supervisory standards seem to have been strict ones. She warns in *The Young Ladies' Reader* (1845) that:

It is scarcely possible to imagine a prudent and judicious mother allowing the unrestrained and private reading of Shakespeare amongst her children; but if herself a good reader, thoroughly imbibed with a sense of the beautiful and the pure, it *is* possible to imagine her reading passages from Shakespeare to her family in such a manner, as to improve the taste of those around her, and to raise their estimate of what is great and good.[53]

'Nothing should induce a daughter to read such as are not sanctioned by her mother', wrote Pullan.[54] Reading—and this takes us back to Wollstonecraft and Hays—could actively be invoked as a means of consolidating a potentially

---

[51] Browne, *What Girls Can Do*, 253. The allusion is to Ruskin's rhetorical questioning: 'Do you know, if you read this, that you cannot read that—that what you lose to-day you cannot gain to-morrow? Will you go and gossip with your housemaid, or your stable-boy, when you may talk with queens and kings?' *Sesame and Lilies, Works*, xviii., 62.

[52] Mrs Ellis, *The Mothers of England: Their Influence & Responsibility* (1843), 338–9.

[53] Ead. (ed.), *The Young Ladies' Reader* (1845), 289–90.

[54] Pullan, *Maternal Counsels*, 52.

fragmenting bond between mother and daughter. Crackanthorpe, writing of the difficulties she alleged mothers were having in the 1890s with their grown-up daughters demanding freedom, suggests that this sense of division could be averted if mothers made friends of their daughters in childhood. She quotes approvingly a woman at a recent gathering who 'assured the company that half an hour's daily reading with her daughter had placed her in safety out of the reach of the flowing tide'.[55] Such a viewpoint necessarily elevated maternity to the level of unerring correctness. Whilst thus reinforcing the Victorian bourgeois ideal of mother as wise guide and protector, it shows little logical consideration of the simultaneously advanced propositions of the power of texts to influence or corrupt, for no claim is made that the fact of mothering undoes all past bad effects of that mother's own reading. Some commentators, none the less, stress the need for mothers to carry on learning themselves about the importance, the sacredness, even, of their own duty. Thus John Angell Jones, in *Female Piety* (1852), not only recommended the Bible to all women as the chief guide to female excellence, but advises the mother in particular to supply her deficiencies through reading Mrs Ellis, Mrs Sandford, *Woman's Mission*, Eugene Monod, and the *British Mother's Magazine*.[56] None the less, it was also suggested that mothers would be ill-advised to be too overtly managerial, needing to practise as much tact in determining their daughters' reading as in organizing other areas of their lives. For their task was not to induce dependency, but ultimate self-sufficiency and sound judgement. According to Charlotte Mason, author of a number of educational texts which dealt with school as well as with home education, if the mother is too ready to settle the employments and amusements of everyone about her, then 'the girl's only chance of getting a few minutes at her own disposal is to dawdle; and this leads to small deceptions, furtive readings of story-books, any of the subterfuges of the weak in dealing with the strong'.[57] By the same token, by the time a daughter reaches young womanhood, she should be allowed, according to Mason, to choose her own reading, albeit having been made fully conscious of the risks lying in wait for her mental and physical health: 'the girl who sits for hours poring over a novel to the damage of her eyes, her brain, and her general nervous system, is guilty of a lesser fault of the nature of suicide.'[58]

[55] B. A. Crackanthorpe, 'The Revolt of the Daughters (No. I): A Last Word on "The Revolt"', *Nineteenth Century*, 35 (1894), 427. Other contributors to the debate disagreed, however. M. E. Haweis, whilst admitting her own ideas in the matter of literature are relatively old-fashioned—'I object to both "Dodo" and "Barbara"'—replies to Crackanthorpe that however much the mother might have been a 'friend' to her daughter, encouraged her talents, taken her out, dressed her well, 'deprecated, but not fiercely prohibited, the unwholesome book, the music-hall and the songs that sail near the wind', the daughter will still devise complaints: 'most girls of a certain age seem to like a grievance' ('No. II: Mothers and Daughters', 430).

[56] John Angell James, *Female Piety: or the Young Woman's Friend and Guide through Life to Immortality* (1852), 285.

[57] Charlotte M. Mason, *Home Education: A Course of Lectures to Ladies* (1886), 255.

[58] Ibid. 258.

The role of fathers in selecting and interpreting a girl's reading is seldom addressed in all this advice, although, as the autobiographical material in Part III shows, the paternal influence frequently seems to have been as influential as the maternal in literary matters. The purchase of books as presents is, however, written about. The gesture is perceived as an important one, a potential means of communication: 'A well selected book, given by some near one, may prove a turning point in life. It may say to them what we cannot say, may advise where we cannot, and the voice will be as our own.'[59]

A number of the advice texts provided lists of their own of suggested reading material. Two of the most detailed of these can be found in Lucy Soulsby's *Stray Thoughts on Reading* (1897) and in chapter 7 of *Girls and their Ways*, 'The Girl's Library—What to Read': titles which, we are told, 'fairly represent such a course of English literature as may be accessible to most English maidens'.[60] The author of *Girls and their Ways* offers a daunting compilation under the heads of English Poetry (from *Piers the Plowman* to 'The Angel in the House'), Fiction, History, Biography, Travel and Discovery, English Theology, Miscellaneous Reading (ranging through Foxe's *Book of Martyrs*, 'notwithstanding its occasional blots of coarseness and credulity'[61], the *Compleat Angler*, Bunyan, Landor, Emerson, Ruskin, and Leslie Stephen), and Scientific Reading. This last category included Mary Somerville's *Physical Geography*, Herbert Spencer's *Education: Intellectual, Moral, and Physical*, John Tyndall's *Glaciers of the Alps*, and Charles Darwin's *On the Origin of Species*. Women, the writer says, are often censured for their irregular and uncertain processes of thought, for their supposed incapacities in following up a definite line of reasoning, and for their habits of drawing unfounded inferences and making deductions from assumptions which have not been proved; scientific reading may prevent them from falling into such errors.[62] For this author, the girl's mind is itself a blank page which may be inscribed: it does not start off with any innate tendencies to one direction or another.

Certain of the recommendations come with brief comments. Thus we learn of Longfellow's 'purity of tone' and that 'Tennyson is another poet whose poems may be put before "virginibus puerisque"'; 'that there is not one of Scott's long series of fictions which may not be put into the hands of a young girl'; that Bulwer Lytton's later fiction may be recommended, but of his earlier novels, 'their sentiment is false; their views of life are unsound; and their style is meretricious and affected'; that Margaret Oliphant's novels 'may safely be recommended . . . though in some of them one could desiderate a more hopeful

---

[59] W. L., 'Some Hints on Giving Presents', *Girl's Own Paper*, 4 (1883), 591.

[60] 'One Who Knows Them', *Girls and their Ways* (1881), 161. Soulsby and 'One Who Knows Them' were far from being unique in providing detailed lists. See also e.g. the two articles by James Mason in the *Girl's Own Paper*, 2 (1881), 7–8 and 122–3 on 'How To Form a Small Library'; J. P. Mears, 'How To Improve One's Education.-II', ibid. 794–6.

[61] 'One Who Knows Them', *Girls and their Ways*, 202.

[62] Ibid. 207.

tone, and a firmer expression of belief'. The writer also notes, when speaking of the younger reader, that 'Even what are called Boys' Stories, when good, will help to strengthen her moral nature, and counteract the effeminate and enervating tendency of a great part of female education.'[63] Certain comments seem designed with dangerous certitude to send an inquisitive reader to books which the author of this work clearly designates as unsuitable ('I cannot recommend "Pamela" because of its false morality; and the story of "Clarissa Harlowe" is unfortunate in itself, and not worked out with sufficient delicacy or reticence'; 'Not one of Smollett's works can I indicate as wholesome reading for young folk. Indeed, to every refined mind their coarseness must be objectionable').[64] These remarks, when coupled with the overall tone of the whole book, suggest that in fact the intended audience may more probably be parents than the young girl herself.

Soulsby, in her turn, offers a list of books which, she claims, her reader could easily work through during her first five years after leaving school, with the result that 'you would be intellectually in a far better position for facing the world, at twenty-two or twenty-three, than most girls of that age'.[65] She, incidentally, is well aware that she is taking on the role of proxy mother in giving advice, writing that very probably many of her readers have at home someone who is just as capable as she is of giving them a good, if not better, selection of titles. But none the less, she observes, perhaps in a rhetorical manœuvre to gain the confidential ear of her reader, 'girls sometimes go abroad for confession and direction, when their own mother is fully qualified to meet all their requirements'.[66] And thus prepared, she goes on to tell them what perhaps their own mother will not: that their future life will inevitably have dull, even depressive stretches in it; that if they marry their husband will be no fairy prince, and will be out all day, and that they will miss the company of their sisters and girl-friends. A thorough, steady course of reading will prevent them from an apparent ready means of escape which in fact only serves to trap them in a further predictable circle of boredom, the rehashed plot of yet another novel from the circulating library: 'Dante's sinners, who ran their ceaseless round over burning sand, had hardly a worse lot than one who by mental self-indulgence has doomed herself to incapacity for reading anything but a ceaseless round of novels, whose plots she knows beforehand, from long and dreary experience.'[67] The stock of learning she lists for her readers' self-improvement ranges through history—including Froissart, Voltaire, Carlyle, Clarendon, and much Mrs Oliphant; travels—from Marco Polo to Arthur Young, Sir Richard Burton to Pierre Loti, Darwin and Hakluyt; biography; and essays (Marcus Aurelius, Bacon, de Quincey, Ruskin, and Emerson, among

[63] 'One Who Knows Them', *Girls and their Ways*, 166–7.
[64] Ibid. 170.
[65] Soulsby, *Stray Thoughts on Reading*, 3.
[66] Ibid. 3.
[67] Ibid. 16.

others). Whole chapters are devoted to novels, poetry, and 'Sunday reading'. By no means does she discount reading fiction for escapist reasons, but she suggests that we must resolve 'to sandwich our books', reading one 'good' book for each work of sensation fiction. She does not disapprove of such novels for moralistic reasons, but rather because they stunt the imagination by leaving it little room for play. By preference, she would have the reader extend her imaginative scope through vicarious travel, via Cooper's *The Last of the Mohicans* or Gogol's *Dead Souls*. Writing in 1897, she is particularly interesting for the survey she offers of fashions in young women's reading during the previous half-century. *The Heir of Redclyffe* was the popular choice of the 1850s; Helen Mathers' *Comin' Thro' the Rye* of the 1860s, of which she remarks, turning the tables on the usual route for the transmission of influence, that it 'is rendered quite harmless, and even instructive, if it be read aloud to an unsympathetic elder'.[68] *Middlemarch* was the book for the early seventies; *John Inglesant* for the following decade. Whilst she does not directly address the phenomenon of New Women fiction, she does remark that it is strange that readers who forty years ago would know only such heroines as Ethel May and Ethel Newcome should now be familiar with the likes of Trilby and Dodo, and notes 'the turbid seas of Passion (with a particularly large P) which meet us in every novel', coupled with Psychology, Pain, and Protoplasm.[69] She recommends *Sir Charles Grandison* and Ann Radcliffe's fictions as forms of historical escapism, and because such works have certain advantages not to be found within the modern novel. They do not tamper with one's faith, having nothing to offer in exchange (an attack is made on *Robert Elsmere*, without naming Mrs Humphry Ward's novel). The idea that one is only fit to cope with such works as Ward's own after submitting oneself to a fairly strict course of training in religious reading is amplified by the stress which she places in her chapter on Sunday reading on women's need for knowledgeable theology, as opposed to emotionalism. Additionally, she speaks out with feeling against a familiar nineteenth-century bugbear, the French novel: 'I wish you would read *no* French novels without a warrant from some old-fashioned person',[70] since these, even when not outwardly disgusting, have a tendency towards 'moral vulgarity' which tends to numb one's own powers of moral discrimination:

Every doubtful book that you read kills a certain amount of the virtue of purity, which might have come out of you, and might have helped some one in their battle against evil, of which you may be unconscious. By every such book you deliberately put a veil between your soul and the Beatific Vision. You cannot be as much shocked at the end of a book which offends your taste, or your sense of right and wrong, as you were at the beginning: such indulgence must blunt our feelings.[71]

---

[68] Ibid. 31.   [69] Ibid. 38.
[70] Ibid. 51.   [71] Ibid. 53–4.

Soulsby supplies a long list of suitable novels 'it becomes a young woman to know', ranging from Susan Ferrier and Maria Edgeworth, through Thackeray, Dickens (*Martin Chuzzlewit, Bleak House,* and *Our Mutual Friend*), and George Eliot (*Scenes of Clerical Life, Romola,* and *Silas Marner*) to Trollope, Sarah Fraser-Tytler, and Mrs Oliphant.

Such lists of recommended reading material could in their own right become sites for debate about the educational presuppositions lying behind them. Many of the lists were, indeed, outrageously over-idealistic. Thus Salmon wrote scathingly of the list given in *Girls and their Ways*, consisting of over fifty poets, nearly seventy histories, ninety biographies, twenty-five works of travel, and so on, pondering over the omission of the Bible and Shakespeare, and suggesting that such a surfeit of prescription would lead to the dangerous practice of skimming.[72] The *Academy* was equally disparaging both about the content of the course of reading offered by Miss Lumby in Dorothea Beale's *Work and Play in Girls' Schools*—surely a girl would prefer Tennyson's 'The Grandmother' and 'Dora' and 'The May Queen' to the tale of bigamy, 'Enoch Arden'; and Stevenson's *Travels with a Donkey* to Milton's *Areopagitica* and Burke's speeches—and about the nine or ten pages of dated historical fiction which Miss Beale herself cites as an advisable compliment to history lessons.[73]

All the modes of advice so far drawn on in this chapter emphasize the vulnerability of the young woman, and her potential to be influenced, for good or disaster, by what she read. The maternal claims, whether made implicitly or directly, by the writers of advice manuals reinforced the sense that some gently protective form of advice was thought desirable. But a further, though far less common line of approach was to assert the girl's 'natural' purity, claiming that some innate sense of propriety—or maybe simply effective education in the home and schoolroom—will teach her what to avoid. Immorality is thus invested in writer, rather than reader, at least when pre-contemporary writing is concerned. Thus, in her contribution to 'What Should Women Read?', Mrs Lang claimed that girls under twenty-one could safely be turned into any old-fashioned library:

Rare, very rare, will be the girls who would care to open 'Humphrey Clinker,' or give a second glance to Beaumont and Fletcher, still less Wycherly or Congreve. 'Pamela' they would find a bore (the unconscious humour of the performance only occurs to the maturer mind), Boccaccio would weary them. But 'Dr Faustus,' and 'Hero and Leander,' and perhaps even 'The Broken Heart,' would draw them with their magic, as surely as would the Utopia or even the Arcadia. Any coarseness they would pass by as if it were written in a foreign language—for it is not one girl in a million who is of the traditional temperament that will give itself the trouble to learn Greek in order to read the notes in Gibbon.[74]

[72] Edward G. Salmon, 'What Girls Read', *Nineteenth Century*, 20 (1886), 525.
[73] 'Little Maids at School', *Academy*, 54 (1898), 189.
[74] Mrs Lang, 'What Should Women Read?', *Woman At Home*, 37 (1896), 30.

Far better that she reads Elizabethan drama, or Horace Walpole's letters, than 'about the vulgar and missish young ladies who people modern fiction'. Annie Swan, the editor of the magazine, confirms this point in the next piece in the debate, returning to the familiar theme that a wise mother will keep much of modern fiction out of her young daughter's hands, 'else she will have her standing handicapped on the very threshold of her life'.[75] But the idea that girls had an innate (or inculcated) purity which, if called upon, would act as a means of censorship was commonly found alongside warnings about what would happen if one did not cease reading unsuitable material. Soulsby writes that 'If we get up from a novel, dissatisfied with that state of life to which we have been called, and inclined to pity ourselves, then we may be sure that such a novel is our poison, and should be laid aside.'[76] Marianne Farningham advocated self-censorship as a means of arbitrating between the many 'absolutely bad and degrading' books available. Her advice—'If you come to a passage which you could not read aloud to your father or brothers without a blush, lay down the book, it is not fit for you'[77]—was typical. The involuntary blush was invoked by Barnard, too—'Do *not* read what you would blush to say aloud.'[78] None the less, it is worth noting that blushing itself came to be recognized as a socialized response, rather than as a manifestation of an innate capacity for shame. As Darwin acknowledged, blushing: 'depends in all cases on the same principle; this principle being a sensitive regard for the opinion, more particularly for the depreciation of others, primarily in relation to our personal appearance, especially of our faces; and secondarily, through the force of association and habit, in relation to the opinion of others on our conduct.'[79]

The proliferation of advice directed towards protecting girls from unsuitable books was tempered, however, by the caution which was also expressed about the effects of too heavy a hand in prohibiting and censoring reading. Emily Shirreff shared the view that most young girl readers would probably pass over, unheeding, many passages which would offend an older reader. Far more damaging, since it excites undesirable curiosity, is to shroud particular books or passages in mystery:

If certain books are prohibited,—perhaps justly,—or the young reader inconveniently asks for an explanation of expressions she has met with, the tone adopted often conveys the idea of an undue degree of importance attached to the subject, which in some minds may rouse curiosity; while a simple and frank answer might have prevented any willing recurrence to the subject. Explanations cannot, of course, always be given, but it is easy to answer in a manner that satisfies the questioner and does not violate truth; as, for instance, to say in a simple tone and manner, that such or such expressions are coarse words, now utterly banished from decent society and from good writing, used in less

---

[75] Swan, 'What Should Women Read?', 31.
[76] Soulsby, *Stray Thoughts on Reading*, 49.
[77] Marianne Farningham, *Girlhood* (1869), 46.
[78] Barnard, *The Girl's Encyclopaedia*, 80.
[79] Charles Darwin, *The Expression of the Emotions in Man and Animals* (1872), 337.

refined periods, or as describing a ruder state of society, or alluding to vices which, fortunately, women in the educated classes do not come in contact with, &c. Answers of this kind leave the mind untainted by any needless acquaintance with impropriety, and in the very great majority of girls educated with refined and delicate habits, will create a disagreeable association with the subject matter which will prevent any recurrence to it.[80]

As we shall see, Shirreff's apprehension that to forbid a book was to encourage a girl to read it was borne out by a number of autobiographers. There is little evidence, however, that the adoption of her advice to provide rational models of explanation was effective in stopping girls from closely scanning the Bible or *Adam Bede* to see what details they could glean.

Methods of Reading

It was not just the identity of what was read which concerned commentators. It was also considered essential to practise the right *methods* in reading. 'You should no more begin to read a book without some definite object, than you would enter upon a road without knowing to what point you wished to be conducted', warned C. M. Sedgwick, obviously not encouraging her American girl readers to share in the pioneering spirit of their male counterparts.[81] These methods foster the development of several primary perspectives: the deepening of contemplation, the broadening of knowledge, and the growth of sympathy. To use the terms adopted by Louise Rosenblatt, 'aesthetic' reading—that which involves experiencing a text fully, imaginatively living through its events as they are encountered—is eschewed in favour of 'efferent' reading, which involves taking something away from the reading, making use of it.[82] However, thought, or the inculcation of the belief that one had the capacity to identify and express one's *individual* ideas, reached through one's own inward processes, usually was seen as more important than the mere acquisition of knowledge. 'Girls read too much and think too little' was a common complaint. Indiscriminate consumption was believed to weaken the mind and turn the necessity for print into a drug-like craving. Rather than abandon self to the seduction of the printed word, the example of the slow-reading Harriet Martineau was invoked as someone who perhaps takes an hour to read a page, but 'what she reads she makes her own'.[83] 'Read to think', exhorted Marianne Farningham, and Amy Barnard claimed that: 'A book fails in its purpose if it does not rouse thought; even the youngest girl reader must have some opinion

[80] Emily Shirreff, *Intellectual Education and its Influence on the Character and Happiness of Women* (1858), 316–17.
[81] Sedgwick, *Means and Ends*, 244.
[82] Louise Rosenblatt, *The Reader, the Text, the Poem: The Transactional Theory of the Literary Work* (Carbondale, Ill., 1978), 22–47.
[83] F. W. Robertson, quoted by S.G.G., 'The Best Hundred Books', *Leisure Hour*, 1 (1886), 268.

of the book she has just finished reading. Let her write down that opinion, honestly, giving her reasons for it.'[84] Practical knowledge as well as growth in self-definition may well ensue. Studying 'the style of the best authors' is a means of improving one's own essay style—providing that also makes use of one's own individuality.[85] When it came to absorbing knowledge, an article in the first volume of the *Girl's Own Paper* in 1880, for example, advises that even the reading of fiction can be far more than a pleasant way of passing a leisure hour. If one is reading a historical novel, or a novel dealing with a foreign country, one should verify and amplify all the details given; one should note down all unfamiliar quotations, and hunt their sources, check unusual words, and above all analyse the text, considering the author's intentions, style, degree of probability in characterization, and achievement. Looking at a work in this way, the reader should gain 'some faint notion of the difficulties of authorship, and, better still, imbibe a lesson in humility'.[86] These recommendations function, of course, in contradictory ways. They justify novel-reading as a serious activity, yet betray anxiety over its power of social mimesis. They exploit the factual element in fiction, turning its consumption into an educational opportunity, yet warn the reader against dangerously confusing fiction with mimetic representation through making her alert to the artificial structuring of the text.

The author of *Girls and their Ways* draws attention to the importance of developing a girl's sympathy. Drawing on Arthur Helps, with his belief that the greatest merit of fiction is that 'it creates and nourishes sympathy',[87] she or he claims that this is a faculty which is particularly needed in the present times, full 'of narrowness and hardness, of hasty and arbitrary judgment, of violent and indiscriminate censure'. Despite the reservations expressed about indiscriminate novel-reading, and despite the clear advice that it should be regarded as an amusement, and not allowed to interfere with more serious studies, 'It is because the higher Fiction cherishes and enforces Sympathy that I plead for it as an agency in the moral and intellectual culture of our Girls.'[88] As we shall see

[84] Barnard, *The Girl's Encyclopaedia*, 79.

[85] 'C.P.', 'How To Write an Essay', *Girl's Own Paper*, 1 (1880), 174. A further article in this series gave detailed advice on 'How to Read the Bible', ibid. 483.

[86] 'A.M.', 'How to Read a Story to Advantage', ibid. 615. The attitude towards fiction taken by the *Girl's Own Paper* was initially highly contradictory. Despite such articles as the one quoted here, and despite its habitual incorporation of stories into each month's number, 'Advice to Correspondents' notes that 'we cannot recommend novel-reading at any time as a profitable thing'. Ibid. 591. By 6 Aug. 1881, 'Advice to Correspondents' reassured readers that 'if we considered it wrong for young girls to read fictitious stories, we should not supply them in THE GIRL'S OWN PAPER' (2 (1881), 720), although a fortnight later a young wife was warned to put aside all amusing books for six months (with the exception of the *Girl's Own Paper*) and devote herself to practising and learning household duties. 'At the end of six months a habit of industry will have been formed, and you might indulge in an hour's reading daily with advantage'. Ibid. 751.

[87] [Sir Arthur Helps] *Friends in Council: A Series of Readings and Discourse Thereon*, 2 vols. (1847), 90.

[88] 'One Who Knows Them', *Girls and their Ways*, 170.

in the next chapter, this attitude was one which informed the growing emphasis placed on the teaching of English literature in girls' schools.

The emphasis on the importance of right methods in reading, and their desirable effects (rather than primarily commentating on the importance of content) emerged in other forms. The prevalent advice, as we have already seen, was that the ingestion of sentiments and expectations through the medium of fiction should be heavily monitored, whether this discipline was imposed from within or without. The recommendation to self-discipline given in 'A Chat with Girls who have Just Left School' in the *Girl's Own Paper* (1883), was typical in its dual emphasis. Having emphasized that habitual reading of sensation novels is 'barely one degree removed from the bathos of entire idleness', sowing 'a variety of poisonous mental weeds', the writer recommends: '1st . . . you will never touch a novel before luncheon, and second that you will only read such as your mother, or motherly elder sister, approves and permits! These two rules . . . will prove invaluable—the one by setting a limit to quantity, the other to quality, of the mental poison imbibed.[89] Nor, incidentally, was it advisable to read *during* lunch, or any other meal. This was not just a question of politeness, but, as Amy Barnard put it, one should abstain from studying following eating heavily, for 'while the body is busy digesting, the brain must rest from deep thought. For the same reason, it is unwise for a girl to read any book, even a novel, at meal-time.'[90]

The lure of fiction itself could be turned to positive advantage if recognized as a temptation to be shunned, or temporarily withstood. Marianne Farningham's *Girlhood* (1869) was one of the most widely circulating of all advice manuals. It was specifically advertised as suitable for Sunday School prizes, and in 1907 Farningham claimed proudly of the way it was passed from generation to generation like family lore: when it first came out, 'Mothers and fathers bought it for their girls, many of whom have now become mothers themselves, and are still buying it for their daughters.'[91] She did not advise against novels, although she recommended that a course of 'more solid reading' be followed simultaneously, and also cautioned against the practice of reading for the plot only, and skipping the serious parts. But Farningham explicitly acknowledged the fact that books have the capacity to:

be so bewitching that everything else is neglected for them. There have been such things as periodicals, or small volumes, stowed away in the pocket, to be snatched out and devoured every minute there was a chance, while the untouched task and neglected duty arose condemningly before the eyes, and almost hid the page . . . Even though the plot were intricate, and the descriptions marvellous; and the love-making delicious beyond expression, they could scarcely make up for an ill-cooked dinner or a displeased mother.

[89] ' "If I Were You!" A Chat with Girls who have Just Left School', *Girl's Own Paper*, 4 (1883), 471.
[90] Barnard, *The Girl's Encyclopaedia*, 24.
[91] Farningham, *A Working Woman's Life: An Autobiography* (1907), 114. A new and revised edition of *Girlhood* came out in 1895.

Farningham suggests that this power be exploited: 'The girl who can see her favourite magazine arrive with the tale "To be continued", which has kept her in a small fever of excitement for several months, and who can resolutely lay it aside till work is finished and recreation may begin, has some honour in her; and is capable of exercising that very valuable quality—self-control.'[92] She advises that a certain portion of each day be set aside for reading, and that one postpone the pleasure until the legitimate time arises. This will bring 'positive strength and stability' to the character, whilst, additionally, reading is much more likely to be effective if carried out in a regular, systematic way. Elizabeth Wordsworth also used the practice of the difficult art of self-denial in relation to reading as a touchstone of female worthiness: the important thing being to realize how trifling is print when compared with human priorities:

You are sitting, let us suppose, by a sleeping invalid, the third volume of your novel with its thrilling *dénouement* is on the mantel-piece just out of your reach. Your boots creak, or your dress rustles, you dare not stir; there you have to sit, perhaps in growing dusk, and you dare not light a candle. These are the kind of little self-denials that really touch us.[93]

Mary Bell, in *A Book of Counsels for Girls* (1888), when recommending practices of self-denial in general, suggests 'if you are very fond of story-books, why not give up fiction during Lent?'[94]

The advice that 'it is not *what* we read, but *how* we read, that makes us learned, or leaves us ignorant', as Pullan put it,[95] applied, of course, to nonfictional as well as fictional texts. Here, too, advice proliferated. Young women were exhorted to keep a written record of their reading, with résumées of its contents; to note discrepancies between different authors, and to ascertain how far these arise from the characters of the authors themselves. They were advised to underline or to mark in the margin important passages, or—towards the end of the period—practise their shorthand by taking notes. Historical questions should be studied from more than one point of view.[96] Browne recommends reading slowly, noting one's opinions immediately one has concluded a book, and then to estimate one's intellectual development by

[92] Ead., *Girlhood*, 44–5.

[93] E. Wordsworth, *First Principles in Women's Education* (Oxford, 1894), 11–12.

[94] Mary Bell, *A Book of Counsels for Girls* (1888), 9.

[95] Pullan, *Maternal Counsels*, 51. Pullan echoed, and was echoed by, many other commentators e.g. Sedgwick: 'Next to "what to read," comes the great question, "how to read;" and I am not sure the last is not the weightier of the two', *Means and Ends*, 242; and '*How* to read is, for society, more important than *what* we read', *The Habits of Good Society: A Handbook of Etiquette for Ladies and Gentlemen* (new edn., 1890), 65–6.

[96] Pullan, *Maternal Counsels*, 49–50 gives a specific instance of this: 'our Protestant histories of England speak strongly of the cruelties exercised by Queen Mary on her reformed subjects, but they totally overlook the equal atrocities perpetrated by her sister Elizabeth, on the Roman Catholics.' Yet if one reads two histories written from opposing perspectives: 'we find out how little real religion had to do with the crimes for which it was made a cloak, and we arrive at such a knowledge of the truth as may not only teach us the history of past ages, but furnish us with a hint for our future guidance in many a difficulty.'

reading it again some six or eight months later, and comparing one's later with one's earlier notes.[97] Amy Barnard, in *The Girl's Encyclopaedia*, placed particular emphasis on developing the memory, something which, she believed, depended on acknowledging the vividness and clarity of the initial impression, on being able to associate it with some other fact, and on repetition.[98] Readers were instructed to use a dictionary: 'If a word that we do not understand is used by an author or speaker, we should at once search for it in the dictionary and make it our own. One advantage of culture is the enlarged vocabulary it gives us, thus enabling us to express and to comprehend shades of meaning that would otherwise be altogether beyond us.'[99] They should keep an atlas and dictionary by them, note down additions to their knowledge, and keep a list of books to be read, compiled from reviews in current literature, the National Home Reading Union's lists, and so on. If it is not immediately convenient to search for the information, an entry should be made in a small memorandum-book, and the subject enquired about before interest has had time to die away.[100] The very act of reading could be turned into an opportunity to develop other capacities, particularly the memory, the habit of summarizing arguments, and the tracing of patterns of reasoning. Pullan considers the genre of letter-writing, claiming that reading published correspondence can offer hints for one's own models. She particularly recommends Cowper's letters, and adds that 'as specimens of taste and wit, Lady Mary Wortley Montagu's are unrivalled; but in her brilliancy she sometimes forgets her womanhood'.[101] Fictional and non-fictional reading could usefully be dovetailed: Amy Barnard recommends reading historical novels alongside a historical period which is being studied, referring one to J. Nield's *A Guide to the Best Historical Novels and Tales* (1902) for information.[102]

Readers were frequently advised to copy into a commonplace book passages of memorable sentiment or description, 'passages which appeal to us because of their striking beauty, wise thought, scientific laws'.[103] For Shirreff, the keeping of a commonplace book trained the memory, through encouraging one to organize important points and passages from one's reading. She recommends that one page of the book be reserved for actual notes, whether quotations, references to passages, or summaries of arguments or facts, whilst the page opposite should be used for one's original remarks, such as the difficulties one may have in accepting the views that are advanced.[104] An article in the *Girl's Own Paper* gave detailed advice about how to keep a commonplace book in order to preserve things which one wishes to remember: a half-way house between one's journal and an academic notebook. Instructions are given for

---

[97] Browne, *What Girls Can Do*, 111.
[99] Browne, *What Girls Can Do*, 111.
[101] Pullan, *Maternal Counsels*, 58.
[103] Ibid. 81.

[98] Barnard, *The Girl's Encyclopaedia*, 70.
[100] Ibid. 112.
[102] Barnard, *The Girl's Encyclopaedia*, 85.
[104] Shirreff, *Intellectual Education*, 287.

entering quotations and references neatly, indexed first by initial letter of the key topic, then by the first vowel in this word. One is advised to practise cross-referencing, invited to consider collecting references that bear a particular relationship to one's own occupations and interests, and counselled to turn its pages frequently: 'By such means as this, girls, we become more useful members of society, and enjoy what is best worth enjoying—a vigorous, intellectual life.'[105] An alternative scheme is proposed by Lydia Child in *The Girl's Own Book* which, her rather circumlocutory prose suggests, was initially a formulation of her own mother's:

an original suggestion of one to whom we owe the foundation of all our knowledge, as well as our life. Write daily (if it may be) an English noun, attach to it its synonyms, its meaning, and the corresponding French, Italian, or German word. Then give quotations from the several authors who have used it, in one, or in all three languages, as you have means and ability.[106]

Lucy Soulsby proposed that instead of putting together a commonplace book of poetry—the most usual form of compilation—one could make one 'of sound maxims of practical philosophy? The thought of them may come to your aid at many a pinch when animal spirits will fail you, and when higher motives . . . refuse to be evoked at will.' She recommends an eclectic set of sources: the ever-popular Epictetus and Marcus Aurelius, plus Gratian, l'Abbé Roux, The Book of Ecclesiasticus, Trench's book on Proverbs, Sir Henry Taylor's *Notes on Life,* and Charles Buxton's *Notes of Thought.* 'Those of a philosophical turn may read Kant and Hegel, but all would find life easier for the mild metaphysics and shrewd worldly wisdom of *Friends in Council*.'[107] Soulsby also produced a notebook, ready for filling in, entitled *Record of a Year's Reading*, in which girls were invited to complete three categories: (1) 'Good Intentions: or Books Specially Recommended' (divided into Sunday books, sensible books, stories), (2) 'List of Books Read' (divided into Title of Book, Author, Reason, Remarks), and (3) a 'Monthly Classification', replicating the Sunday, sensible books, stories categories.[108]

Justification for Reading

The crucial question remains: *why* were women advised to read in this way? Whilst the dread of 'uselessness' hangs over much of the advice, the question itself was seldom directly addressed, except in generalized moral terms. Even 'the most trivial' book ought, according to Pullan, 'to teach us some lesson of

---

[105] James Mason, 'How to Keep a Commonplace Book', *Girl's Own Paper*, 3 (1882), 602.
[106] Lydia Child, *The Girl's Own Book* (1869), 375.
[107] Soulsby, *Happiness* (1899), 26–7.
[108] Ead., *Record of a Year's Reading*, (1903), unpaged.

morals or manners; to confirm or alter some opinion'. Sometimes, as she
suggested, the mere gathering of information and opinions could bring its own,
rather nebulous, rewards, since the very discipline involved strengthens
character.[109] Such a point was also made by Soulsby, who encourages even the
reluctant reader. For her, to read half an hour steadily each day for a year will
promote self-denial and discipline, and will 'strengthen your moral fibre in a
way no manual drudgery could have done'.[110] To some extent, the indications
of the future use to which reading may be put will remain vague because the
young woman's future is equally indeterminate. Browne, whilst acknowledging
that if a girl needs to work for her living, 'it would be necessary for her to give
special attention to the particular study that would help her calling', continues,
far more generally, to imply that it will be far more likely that her reader will
'not know what position she will fill in the future, but be it what it may, she can
best prepare herself for it by trying to cultivate every faculty she possesses'.[111]
None the less, orderly methods are bound to stand her in good stead. The
young woman's mind, she maintains, will become like an infinite number of tidy
pigeon-holes, each containing a neatly labelled, correctly recorded fact. Such a
mental filing system might do little for one's speculative capacities; yet, Browne
maintains, it will prevent one 'from speaking and writing at random'.[112] Other
writers make it explicitly clear that reading may be turned to social advantage.
The Girl's Encyclopaedia, asking 'What can a girl talk about?', strongly condemns
chit-chat about dress or neighbours, 'which easily degenerates into foolishness
and narrows her mental horizon'. Rather, she should find topics for discussion
in magazine articles, newspapers, biographies, books of travel and politics, and
the girl is advised to sharpen up her powers of defence, reason, and self-
assurance when launching and sustaining these subjects by gaining experience
talking in such terms to her father and brothers.[113] An acquaintance 'with the
best current literature is necessary to modern society', claimed *The Habits of
Good Society: A Handbook of Etiquette for Ladies and Gentlemen* in 1890:

and it is not sufficient to have read a book without being able to pass judgement on it.
Conversation on literature is impossible, when your respondent can only say, 'Yes, I like
the book, but I really don't know why.' Or what can we do with the young lady whose
literary stock is as limited as that of the daughter of a late eminent member of
Parliament, whom a friend of mine had once tried to take down to dinner?

He had tried her on music and painting in vain. She had no taste for either. Society
was as barren a theme, for papa did not approve of any but dinner parties.

'Then I suppose you read a great deal?' asked my friend.

'Oh, yes! we read.'

'Light literature?'

---

[109] Pullan, *Maternal Counsels*, 48, 52.
[110] Soulsby, *Suggestions on Reading*, 13.
[111] Browne, *What Girls Can Do*, 109, 110.
[112] Ibid. 112.
[113] Barnard, *The Girl's Encyclopaedia*, 107.

'Oh, yes! light literature.'
'Novels, for instance?'
'Oh, yes! novels.'
'Do you like Dickens?'
'We don't read Dickens.'
'Oh! I see you are of Thackeray's party.'
'We never read Thackeray.'
'Then you are romantic, and devoted to Bulwer Lytton?'
'Never,' replied the young lady, rather shocked.
'Then which *is* your favourite novelist?'
'James,' she replied triumphantly.
'Ah!' said my friend, reviving a little, 'James is exciting.'
'Oh, yes! we like his books so much! Papa reads them aloud to us, but then he misses out all the exciting parts.'
After that my friend found his knife and fork better company than his neighbour.[114]

The author of this text goes on to say that, none the less, the young lady should avoid too displeasingly self-righteous a display of learning, and she is recommended to cultivate, instead, 'an artless gaeity, tempered by refinement'.[115] Edward John Hardy, in *The Five Talents of Woman* (1895) commended the initiative of some young ladies in Chicago, who had set up a newspaper-reading circle, in order to make themselves better aware of current events. Once again, however, he envisaged a clearly defined social end for the knowledge thus acquired: a woman equipped with a variety of topics of conversation 'would be more companionable to her partners of the other sex at the dinner-table and in the ball-room, who are often driven to their wits' end for something to say other than mere trivialities about the weather or the last new novel or play'.[116] In the same way, learning furthers a woman's community of tastes with her husband, and prepares her 'for forming the tastes and minds of her children, thus improving the stock of national talents'.[117] But he warns against being too learned. Disposition and character are more important than acquired culture, a point which he enforced through organic imagery which places womanhood in a pre-lapsarian state of continual spring and summer:

Health is the soil, intelligence the branches, and disposition the leaves, buds, and blossoms—the robe of living beauty, fragrance, and sweetness with which a young woman is to clothe her life. Without heart-culture the finest mental culture is like a tress with nothing but cold, leafless limbs.[118]

It is often made extremely clear that the function of this gained cultural capital is for it to be fed back into the domestic economy. Ruskin's comment,

---

[114] *The Habits of Good Society*, 65–66. The James in question is undoubtedly G. P. R. James, author of historical novels such as *Richelieu* (1829) and *Philip Augustus* (1831).
[115] *The Habits of Good Society*, 270.
[116] [Edward John Hardy] *The Five Talents of Woman* (5th edn., 1895), 239.
[117] Ibid. 268.
[118] Ibid. 269.

that 'A woman, in any rank of life, ought to know whatever her husband is likely to know, but to know it in a different way', was drawn on by a number of writers,[119] and this belief endured the century. Lydia Child, in *The Girl's Own Book* (1869), claimed that 'it is most desirable in the present day, that they should possess such an amount of literary and scientific knowledge as may fit them for appreciating the pursuits, and sharing the interests of their brothers, fathers, or (hereafter) their husbands'.[120] Judicious reading would enable woman, as Dorothea Beale put it, 'to enter into the subjects of study and thought which occupy the minds of their fathers, husbands, sons'.[121] Similarly, E. B. Kirk, including a section on reading in the conclusion of what is basically a sex-education book, *A Talk With Girls About Themselves* (1905), links one of the main anxieties of his time concerning girls' reading, the habit of skimming magazine articles, to apprehension that such a practice builds up insufficient resources against her future: 'A girl who wastes her thought power in this idle, careless way, will have but an empty mind to give to her children, and will also make a very poor companion for her husband.'[122] George Bainton described how culture and home-making were not mutually exclusive, and that a woman might simultaneously develop the 'range and vigour of her mind', and gain possession of material which will enable her to serve 'in the highest ways her husband, children, and friends'. By perseverance and methodical effort, a wife ought to be able to set aside an hour or so each day for reading, music, and general intellectual improvement: her reading, he expected, would be in the subjects 'in which her husband is most interested'. Nor is this desideratum limited to the middle-class woman:

Even in the cottage of the poor, the hard-working wife, struggling with poverty, plotting and planning to make two ends meet upon the scantiest income, has yet maintained her place at her husband's side by keeping abreast with him in the study of the Bible, Foxe's 'Book of Martyrs,' Bunyan's 'Pilgrim's Progress,' 'The Illustrated History of England,' and whatever other literature came their way.[123]

After marriage, it would seem, a woman is being tacitly encouraged to seek self-recognition in relation not just to the general structures of patriarchal discourse, but to their individual representative within her life. She is also encouraged to think, even as a young woman, about her future role, as a 'future teacher of the beautiful and useful', as the editor of *The Young Lady's Book* (1876) put it, to the children she may herself bear.[124]

[119] Ruskin, *Sesame and Lilies, Works*, xviii. 128.
[120] Lydia Maria Child, *The Girl's Own Book* (1869), 507.
[121] Dorothea Beale, introd. to Beale, Soulsby, and Jane Frances Dove, *Work and Play in Girls' Schools* (1898), 5.
[122] E. B. Kirk, *A Talk With Girls About Themselves* (1905), 61.
[123] George Bainton, *The Wife as Lover and Friend* (1895), 99, 106.
[124] Mrs Henry Mackarness (ed.), *The Young Lady's Book: A Manual of Amusements, Exercise, Studies, and Pursuits* (1876), 41.

But not all portrayals of the future are so socially optimistic. Lucy Soulsby regarded the development of good reading habits as a form of insurance against boredom in the leisure time that one inevitably will have in life. She advises, in a tone which seems to assume that the reader shares, or may be invited to assume, her relatively worldly knowledge, forward planning against the time when girls 'will sadly detect a novel's plot in its first chapter, and when even a young man's conversation will seem to them to have its limitations!'[125] Elsewhere, she suggested that reading may be another form of preparation. She recommended that one make a system of rules (no novels in the morning; reading something sensible every day) and stick to it: 'I say to you, read doggedly; the snare of a free life is desultory reading. Make any plan of stiff reading you like, and stick to it for one year, writing out notes of what you read, and you will be fitter for real work if it comes, as come it will.' Explicitly, she is preparing for unmarried, as well as married later life. At the same time, a girl's books, and self-disciplined plan, should not obtrude, but should remain 'a secret hair shirt, and not a red flag flaunted in your family's face'. She is advised to seem at leisure, willing to socialize, within the home, whilst retaining 'an inner life of thought and work'.[126] Hardy, too, sees reading as a form of preparation for the future, for 'the days which may come—days of pain, illness, or enforced seclusion because of weakness and advancing years . . . Determine that you will be bright and pleasant, even when the beauty of youth is gone', quoting Swift on Stella:

> Such is the fate of female race,
> With no endowments but a face
> Before the thirtieth year of life,
> A maid forlorn, or hated wife

in support of his point.[127] He advises consistent reading, however little may be possible at a time—'Ten minutes each day, five or six solid books a year'—and thinking about what one has read when one is at work.[128]

As one might anticipate, few commentators stress the importance which reading can play in shaping a writer's future career, although, as we shall see in Part III, plenty of writers were themselves willing to acknowledge their debt to early acquaintance with books. Perhaps a surprising exception to this, given her habitual emphasis on the importance of cultivating domestic virtues, is Mary Ann Stodart. In *Female Writers* (1842), she singles out the present time as a 'writing age' in which 'women have caught the mania, a disease which is most easily caught'. She recommends that, since the malady is unlikely to be cured, it is important not to start to write—at least not for publication—until one has learnt to read to advantage. The book interleaves a reasonably comprehensive history of women writers from Sappho to de Staël with comments on the moral

---

[125] Soulsby, *Happiness* (1899), 28–29.
[126] Ead., *A Home Art, or Mothers and Daughters* (Oxford, 1890), 9, 11.
[127] Hardy, *The Five Talents of Woman*, 260–1.
[128] Ibid. 263.

and religious dangers which Stodart sees as besetting the woman writer's path. It contains, indeed, an impressive range of models who have lived up to her standards of scholarly steadiness, principled searches after truth, and a love of beauty. Since a woman's talents should be employed as effectively as possible, she recommends studying Latin for style and logic, in order to counteract women's tendency to reason badly. However, she would not restrict the study of classical literature to potential authors, for she, like others, writes emphatically of the void which many women feel in their lives. One needs:

something to put to flight that ugly little sprite, Ennui, with her attendant train of what used to be yclept vapours and spleen, but which are now known and stigmatized under the general designation of nervousness. Want of employment is the source of much that is evil in women; of much that is prejudicial to health. Real study, continued employment, is often found one of the best medicines for many who account themselves invalids; and if it be a cure for physical, it is also one of the best antidotes against moral evils.[129]

Yet by the end of the period, and following the widespread recognition of the power of reading to provide necessary relaxation and escape, an entirely different image of its domestic function could be promoted. Maud Churton Braby, in *Modern Marriage and How to Bear It* (1909), whilst very much supporting the institution of marriage, thinks it a good idea for the husband to go out to his club once or twice a week, for 'on these occasions the wife can have a picnic dinner—always a joy to a woman—with a book propped up before her, can let herself go and let her cook go out'.[130]

The linking of reading and domesticity raises, incidentally, the frequently remarked on advantages of reading aloud within the home. This practice would necessarily check the dangerous delights of *solitary* reading; was believed to aid family unity, and—as many autobiographies testified was indeed the case—served to introduce children to valued works of literature. It promoted domestic harmony, as imaged in the frontispiece to the family reader, *Evenings at Home: A Variety of Miscellaneous Pieces for the Instruction and Amusement of Young Persons* (1838), compiled by Dr Aikin and Mrs Barbauld. (Fig. 9) A similar scene was envisaged by Sarah Stickney Ellis in *The Mothers of England* (1843) when she commented that it was not possible: 'to imagine a scene of much greater enjoyment, than is presented by a thoroughly united and intelligent family, the female members of which are busily at work, while a father or brother reads aloud to them some interesting book approved by the mother, and delighted in by her daughters.[131] Reading aloud could function, moreover, as a means of enhancing a woman's natural or trained assets, and of consolidating domestic virtues. Thus in *The Young Ladies' Reader* (1845), Mrs

---

[129] Mary Ann Stodart, *Female Writers* (1842), 6, 61.
[130] Maud Churton Braby, *Modern Marriage and How to Bear It* (1909), 220.
[131] Mrs Ellis, *The Mothers of England* (1843).

9. Frontispiece to Aikin and Barbauld, *Evenings at Home: A Variety of Miscellaneous Pieces for the Instruction and Amusement of Young Persons*, (1838)

Ellis claimed that the practice provided a means of imparting interest and ideas to the home, 'and of investing with the charm of perpetual freshness the conversation of the family circle, the intercourse of friendship, and the communion of "mutual minds" '.[132] If well done, it 'tends to promote family union and concord', being a safe rallying point around which various tempers, feelings, and constitutions can group. Especially, it is important to women, she maintains, since the mind is so little employed in so many of a woman's daily occupations that she has plenty of time for idle and unprofitable thoughts whilst physically engaged on mundane tasks. Reading aloud is therefore a means of engaging with her family, and perhaps of imparting valuable moral education to her children, whilst activating her own mind. It is a far more valuable activity, for her, than escaping into 'the solitary and indiscriminate devouring of novels', which 'beguile the restless craving of a diseased imagination'. Private reading, Ellis makes clear, is ultimately a self-centred activity: one of the great values of reading aloud is that it leads to the 'entire forgetfulness of self'. In other words, one's own desires cannot be focused on: if one enters, as she suggests one does, into the life and feelings of another—when, say, reading aloud biography, or Mrs Jameson on Shakespeare's heroines—one is, in her eyes, not primarily consolidating one's own sense of identity, but establishing shared and acknowledged values with the group of people to which one is closest.[133] The idea that reading aloud was one means through which woman employed her presumed capacity for influence lasted throughout the century, despite an increasing number of lamentations that the practice was becoming less and less common. 'A musical voice', the readers of the *Girl's Own Paper* were told in 1881, before being given detailed instructions as to how to deliver and emphasize their chosen recitation pieces, 'can carry its persuasive eloquence to the heart'.[134]

Reading within the Home

The question of the provision of books and reading material within the home raises a number of issues, which include, but go far beyond, the identity of the books themselves. If reading is seen as a means of claiming personal space for oneself, this needs to be considered in terms of its connections with real locations, as well as with the metaphoric spaces of the mind. To designate certain areas specifically for reading, or to prohibit or advise against the presence of books in others, can be interpreted as attempts, deliberate or otherwise, to prescribe or limit the terms in which access to personal space was granted within the physical and ideological structures of Victorian homes.

[132] Ead. (ed.), *The Young Ladies' Reader* (1845), 1.
[133] Ibid. 9, 13, 15, 77–8.
[134] Revd Canon Fleming, 'How to Recite a Poem', *Girl's Own Paper*, 2 (1881), 307.

The most clearly contested areas were the library—in those houses large enough to have one—and the bedroom. Robert Kerr, in *The Gentleman's House; or How to Plan English Residences, from the Parsonage to the Palace* (3rd edn., 1871), reminds one that, of course, the library is not the only location in the house where books may be found; conversely, the way in which he writes of the room emphasizes its role as social space as well as for book storage:

It is primarily a sort of morning-room for gentlemen rather than anything else. Their correspondence is done here, their reading, and, in some measure, their lounging;—and the Billiard-room, for instance, is not unfrequently attached to it. At the same time the ladies are not exactly excluded[135]

—although Kerr's grudging vocabulary suggests that they are not exactly welcome, either. Moreover, when he describes how, 'for a man of learning', one must either constitute the library itself as a study, or add one, with a secluded position, no door of intercommunication with any other room '(except possibly the Gentleman's-room)', so that it becomes 'now essentially a private retreat', the assumption that serious reading customarily takes place within male-designated spaces is consolidated.[136] However, Jane Panton, in *A Gentlewoman's Home* (1896) is adamant that the library should not remain sacred to 'the master of the house'. The more public duties and offices, indeed, which are subsumed under that title, such as interviewing tenants or business men, she recommends be delegated to a separate 'business room'. Moreover, since the library is also a room in which the father will lecture his offspring, she suggests a certain 'prettiness' in the décor, both on the grounds that 'then his womenfolk would feel they had a right to be with him', and that the surroundings would diminish his masculine sternness. Perhaps it is on these grounds, too, that she feels it correct to have novels in the library. Additionally, she advises one never to put an embargo on any of the contents of the library so far as younger members of the family are concerned, reiterating the viewpoint which had so incensed Hardy, and others, that 'if a book is not fit for the children it isn't fit for us'. Thus she would include *Tess of the d'Urbervilles*, but keep out E. W. Benson's *Dodo* and Sarah Grand's *The Heavenly Twins*.[137]

Sharing a room is no substitute, however, for a room of one's own: a requirement which became increasingly accepted as desirable, if at all possible, as the century progressed (Fig. 10). An article in the *Young Woman* in 1892 makes this point firmly:

One of my strongest convictions is that every grown-up girl should have a little place in her father's house that is altogether her own. Let it be only a glorified attic, let it be only

[135] Robert Kerr, *The Gentleman's House; or How to Plan English Residences, from the Parsonage to the Palace* (3rd edn., rev., 1871), 116.

[136] Ibid. 118.

[137] J. E. Panton, *A Gentlewoman's Home: The Whole Art of Building, Furnishing, and Beautifying the Home* (1896), 220–4.

10. Alice Squire, *Young Girl Reading in an Attic Bedroom*, (1861)

11. Augustus Leopold Egg, *The Travelling Companions*, (1862)

a bedroom,—but let it be exclusively hers where she can retire when so disposed, where extracts from favourite authors can be copied, where letters can be written, or anything that requires special attention can be read, or where an hour's quiet can be attained if the occasional need, which now and then besets every thinking human being, is felt for a brief spell of solitude.[138]

Panton uses the guise of her advice on housebuilding and furnishing to convey her opinions about the role of governesses, emphasizing the difficulty of keeping spaces and the lives of those who occupy them separate. Great care should be taken that the governess receives the daily and weekly papers (such as the *Graphic*, *Punch*, and the *Illustrated London News*), because Panton believes in the importance of her keeping up to date with current affairs. Moreover, one should remember 'that the governess is a real live woman, not a dry collection of propriety and facts', so one should be sympathetic to her need, at times, to read novels, to rest during the day, or to go to bed later in summer than winter. Her worth may, however, be judged by the novels she reads. Test her before employing her:

She should have read Dickens and Thackeray, Walter Scott and Jane Austen, and be able to stand a good examination on them; she should like to read poetry, she should not understand what 'decadent' and *fin-de-siècle* mean: the implication being that if such information is not imported into one area of the house, its contamination cannot spread.[139]

Moving away from the home, incidentally, reading could also have its uses as a means of establishing personal space. Anne Bowman, in *The Common Things of Every-Day Life* (1857) recommends books as bodyguards when travelling. One should be cautious about entering into conversation with strange fellow-travellers: 'Civilities should be politely acknowledged; but, as a general rule, a book is the safest resource for "an unprotected female".'[140] In relation to travelling, Bowman warns that it is not a good thing to try and look at the countryside through which the train is passing whilst it is in motion, otherwise 'the eyes and head usually become confused'.[141] Reading is recommended as the most rational mode of employing the time, a piece of advice which, if reflecting common opinion, perhaps goes some way towards explaining the indifference to the scenery of the Riviera exhibited by Augustus Egg's *Travelling Companions* (1862) (Fig. 11). Yet primarily, the painting is a satiric commentary both on the unadventurous propriety of the young English girl abroad, and on the capacity of fictional artifice to absorb a reader's attention to the exclusion of the attractions of the real world. It finds its prose counterpart in one of Ruskin's letters in *Fors Clavigera*, when he writes angrily against two American girls

[138] 'What shall we read?', *Young Woman*, 1 (1892), 26.
[139] Panton, *A Gentlewoman's Home*, 321–2.
[140] Anne Bowman, *The Common Things of Every-Day Life: A Home Book of Wisdom for Mothers and Daughters* (1857), 163.
[141] Ibid. 162.

whom he met on a train from Venice to Verona. Their behaviour was symptomatic, for him, of the disastrous way in which his contemporaries ignored their environment:

They pulled down the blinds the moment they entered the carriage, and then sprawled, and writhed, and tossed among the cushions of it . . . they had French novels, lemons, and lumps of sugar to beguile their state with; the novels hanging together by the ends of string that had once stitched them, or adhering at the corners in densely bruised dog's ears, out of which the girls, wetting their fingers, occasionally extracted a gluey leaf.

Yet outside could be seen 'blue against the southern sky, the hills of Petrarch's home. Exquisite midsummer sunshine, with low rays, glanced through the vine-leaves; all the Alps were clear, from the Lake of Garda to Cadore, and to farthest Tyrol.'[142]

Reading Clubs and Circles

In *What Girls Can Do*, Phyllis Browne strongly advised the girl who had left school not to plan a course of solitary study, retreating to her room to pursue it. Such a path would lead to her becoming 'either a bookworm or conceited. She would do far more if she studied with some one.'[143] Moreover, company is a great strengthener of self-will, especially if the improvement of one's mind leads to no particularly tangible immediate goal.[144] Browne tells of some young women acquaintances of hers who formed themselves into a Society for Mutual Culture, meeting weekly to read and discuss a paper or papers on previously agreed topics. According to her description, this was a good way of disseminating information, although the prior socialization of the girls involved restricted the range of possible educational benefits, as, without passing judgement, she points out:

When first this society was established, the rule was laid down that the members were to criticise one another's performances, and so endeavour to arrive at a just estimate of the value of their work. This part of the plan did not answer. It might have been successful with boys, for they enjoy speaking their minds and rubbing the gilt off a friend's gingerbread, but the girls were too polite for this. They were afraid of wounding the feelings of the members, and so contented themselves with general applause. After a time it was found that criticism had degenerated into compliments all round, and was therefore discontinued.[145]

Browne's anecdote reminds us that not all the impetus for a woman to organize her reading was self-sustained. Not only did the existence of a formal pattern

---

[142] John Ruskin, Letter 20 (Aug. 1872), *Fors Clavigera, Works* xxvii. 346.
[143] Browne, *What Girls Can Do*, 107.
[144] Ibid. 109.   [145] Ibid. 108.

and programme of reading help her to apportion and direct her time, the very presence of an organization to which she could belong might have its uses. As Emily Davies put it in 1878, Reading Societies, and Essay Societies, and Societies for the encouragement of Home Study, could be resorted to not only as a defence against woman's 'own idleness and desultoriness', but also as something of 'an outward and visible sign', 'something which can be held up to relations and friends as a plea for the concession of a little slice of quiet time'. Davies's tone is a mixture of sympathy and condescension: sympathy at the limitations which drive women to such measures, coupled with a sadness at the limitations of their educational vision, as she notes hearing of one Reading Society which 'compels its members under penalties to read for a certain time every day'.[146] Penalties—a penny per day for those who omit to read, unless suffering from illness or a severe and incapacitating headache—are, indeed, mentioned by the popular novelist Edna Lyall, describing a private reading society with which she was personally familiar. She provides the additional information that four weeks' annual holiday may be taken from the society's strictures; that members should read for half an hour a day, in sessions at least as long as ten minutes at a time; that fiction and newspapers are excluded from this, and that poetry must not be read for more than six weeks in the year. Writing in *Our Mothers and Daughters*, a magazine with a practical emphasis, and a conservative, Christian, temperance slant, addressing itself specifically to 'the Busy and Tired', she emphasized the importance of this reading time for those, particularly mothers and grown-up daughters, who were in danger of exhausting themselves with domestic duties.[147]

There also existed a variety of types of specific reading groups and circles where views could actively be compared. The furthest reaching, and probably the best organized of all the self-help reading schemes was undoubtedly that run by the National Home Reading Union, which specifically intended to act as a continuation of the guidance given through formal education. It was thus particularly suitable for, and followed by, young women of the middle classes who had ended their formal education, but were neither obliged to seek employment, nor had yet got married: a condition leading frequently, commentators maintained, to depression, 'deteriorating amusement, trivial letter writing, and random reading'.[148] The idea that intellectual capacity degenerated if the brain were not used gained firm scientific support towards the end of the Victorian period.[149] But members of the NHRU were not

[146] Emily Davies, 'Home and the Higher Education' (lecture delivered 1878), *Thoughts on Some Questions Relating to Women, 1860–1908* (Cambridge, 1910), 154.

[147] Edna Lyall, 'A Quiet Half-Hour', *Our Mothers and Daughters*, 1 (1892), 45–6.

[148] Mondy, *Reading as a Means of Education*, 7.

[149] See E. M. Bonavia, 'Women's Frontal Lobes', *Provincial Medical Journal*, 11 (1892), 358–62, where not only does he reiterate Darwin's important lesson that there is no such thing as fixed, unalterable tissue or organism, but cites—with a certain irony—Sir James Crichton Browne's experiment which proved that the brain of a wild duck was larger and more developed than that of a domestic duck.

confined to this sector. Its secretary, Miss Mondy, suggested that they be sought from Juvenile Clubs and Guilds, Sunday Schools, Girls' Friendly Societies, and Associations for Befriending Young Servants: indicative of a strong base among the working classes. Thomas Greenwood, in his seminal *Public Libraries* (4th edn., 1894) records how branches were frequently attached to these institutions. None the less, its membership was not vast. C. S. Bremner, whilst speaking very highly of the Union in *Education of Girls and Women* (1897) regretted that membership was not greater than 8,000. She also noted that 'Culture, not class, is the standard of the Union', and that its members ranged from those who had only attended elementary schools, and whose reading needed direction, to university graduates.[150]

Mondy envisaged giving half an hour a day at home to systematic reading, with 'the formation of will and character' (rather than the acquisition of knowledge) the desired result. She also gives clear recommendations for the conduct of meetings, which she believed would have a social as well as an educational function. The NHRU disseminated its programme by means of a journal, and on the first evening of each term, a lecture presenting a general outline of the term's reading, perhaps accompanied by a magic lantern show, should be given. Each subsequent meeting, she advises, should open with singing, followed by a discussion of that week's reading, with members quizzed as to whether they gained any new ideas from what they read; if anything had surprised them, and what passages they had liked best and why. 'Draw attention to descriptions of natural scenery, to choice language, word pictures, to heroic action, to the finer touches of character, and, above all, to the poetry of every-day life.' Answers to questions set in the Journal should, if possible, be written up at home.[151] As so frequently was the case in the latter decades of the nineteenth century, however, this personal character-building was placed within a wider eugenicist horizon. The corrective to 'desultory reading' offered by the NHRU would, it was envisaged, prevent the formation of 'a race of flabby-souled men and women'.[152] Mondy is specific about the ultimate end of the reading, offering temporary enlightenment only to close in the social parameters again:

Through and by reading our girls should learn to steer safely between the praises rendered to women by poets, artists and sages on the one hand, and the repression, injustice, slavery and contempt of the world on the other. They should learn to distinguish between the true and the false, between selfish expediency and noble honour, and while weighing these in the balance, should acquire a just estimate of the many eulogies and criticisms to which we women are subject—a self-respect, and a calm determination to be free to realise their lives as God meant them to be. The most

---

[150] Bremner, *The Education of Girls and Women*, 109.
[151] Mondy, *Reading as a Means of Education*, 28.
[152] David Balsillie, *The National Home Reading Union* (Edinburgh, 1889), 10.

difficult and noble of all life's responsibilities is theirs—motherhood, and only freed souls can be faithful in the fullest sense to such a high duty.[153]

Reading aloud might form part of the activities on other occasions. At Dorcas meetings, it was a common accompaniment to the sewing: the *Girl's Own Paper* indicated that the reading of 'a lighter kind of literature, or poetry' at these events might in fact be undertaken by a father or brother.[154] Advice was not just given about attending reading meetings, but about organizing the opportunities for those less socially and educationally favoured than oneself to gain access to print. Frequently, such provision was linked to parish work. Charlotte M. Yonge, in *What Books to Lend and What to Give* (1887), writes of the need to provide reading material within rural communities. Her sense of what it is apposite to provide is strongly reflective of her clearly-defined assumptions about gender-roles. Thus 'men . . . must have manly books. Real solid literature alone will arrest their attention', such as travel, biography, and 'classical' fiction. Their wives, 'in these days of education', 'generally love fiction':

They do not want to be improved, but they like to lose their cares for a little while in some tale that excites either tears or laughter. It is all very well to say that they ought to have no time for reading. An industrious thrifty woman has little or none, but the cottager's wife who does as little needlework, washing, or tidying as possible, has a good many hours to spend in gossip or in reading. She may get cheap sensational novels, and the effects on a weak and narrow mind are often very serious. The only thing to be done is to take care that she has access to a full supply of what can do her no harm, and may by reiteration do her good.[155]

She is well aware that we should not be quick to condemn 'frivolous tastes', since reading is, for working women, often a necessary relaxation. However, books which foster enthusiasm for courage and truth, 'and show religion as the only true spring of life', are the ones with which a village library should be stocked. Yonge suggests a number of titles—including a large number of her own—which indicate her alertness to the kind of situation with which women are most likely going to identify (Maggie Symington, *Through Trial to Triumph*: 'the troubles of a wife who cannot understand her husband'); ones which are likely to prove popular, and harmless, despite their imperfections (Annette Lyster, *My Lonely Lassie*: 'the governess is a very pretty character. We could dispense with her becoming a marchioness in her own right, but no doubt it renders her the greater favourite'); and ones which offer a countering effect to other tendencies (F. Stockton, *Rudder Grange*: 'this most quaint and diverting American story is, among its other perfections, a good protest against romance derived from penny dreadfuls').[156]

[153] Mondy, *Reading as a Means of Education*, 17.
[154] J. P. Mears, 'How to Improve One's Education', *Girl's Own Paper*, 2 (1881), 638.
[155] Charlotte M. Yonge, *What Books to Lend and What to Give* (1887), 7–8.
[156] Ibid. 71–4.

Whilst Yonge's work seems primarily directed at those with responsibilities in a rural area, Lady John Manners's articles about making reading and recreation rooms easily available, which first appeared in the *Queen*, were separately reprinted, and make suggestions for reading provisions for the urban working classes. She notes the opposition with which she met in allowing women as well as men into the reading-rooms which she helped establish, but this does not seem to have diminished her enthusiasm for advising the facilitating of reading possibilities wherever practicable. She suggests supplying books in ladies' waiting-rooms at stations, which might also be used by the young women who serve in the railway refreshment bars, and she recommends that reading-rooms, whether set up under the auspices of the Girls' Friendly Society, Parochial Missions, or other organizations, are as comfortably furnished and welcoming as possible. They should provide an invaluable environment to those who live in lodgings. She advises that heads of families subscribe to circulating libraries for their servants. In organized reading-rooms, she proposes that 'a matronly kindly woman of the lower middle classes' be put in charge, 'because she understands what is needed by working people', although she recommends that a man be within call, 'as sometimes the spirits of the hobbledehoys become rather uproarious'.[157] When it comes to the choice of books, her emphasis falls partly on fiction, and partly on practical works, especially those 'intended for women who wished to be really help-mates to their husbands or their families'. The eclectic list she provides seems to presume a wide variety of reading needs and abilities:

I name a few: Mrs Valentine's 'Domestic Economy;' 'Enquire Within upon Everything;' Miss Nightingale's 'Notes on Nursing;' Miss Octavia Hill's 'Homes of the London Poor;' Lady Hope's 'Our Coffee-Room;' Miss Weston's 'Our Blue-Jackets;' 'The Early Choice,' a book for daughters; 'Friendly Words for Our Girls' by Lady Baker; 'Thoughts for Young Women in Business,' by Mrs W. H. Wigley. I must strongly recommend this most useful little book to the attention of shop-assistants; it is published by Nisbet. 'Letters to Young Women in Mills and Factories,' Parker, published by Messrs Hatchards, contain advice applicable to all young women; so do 'Letters to Young Women,' by J. M. Carr. 'Common-Sense for Housemaids,' by Jane Tytler, is a really diverting and practical book (mistresses and maids ought to read it). 'An Old Mother's Letter to Young Women,' by Mrs Bayly, is valuable, and so is her 'Letter on Temperance Work,' addressed to our serving friends. 'Lectures on Health,' by Caroline Hallett, may be bought for a shilling, and will save the purchaser many pounds, if understood. The Girls' Friendly Society papers should be placed in the room; Warne's 'Cookery Book for the Million' contains two hundred useful recipes, and its cost is twopence; 'Cookery Recipes for the Million,' published by the Ladies' Sanitary Society, are very good. The 'Life of Princess Alice,' if it comes into a cheap edition, would be most suitable; for it would show many busy, harassed women that their Queen's

---

[157] Lady John Manners, *Some of the advantages of easily accessible reading and recreation rooms and free libraries with remarks on starting and maintaining them, and suggestions for the Selection of Books* (1885), 77. See also her *Encouraging Experiences of Reading and Recreation Rooms* (1886).

daughter worked for her children, nursed them devotedly, and found time to care for the sick and needy, while managing her household and cultivating her mind.[158]

The accounts given by other women in their autobiographies are on occasion employed to give an idea of some of the practical implications of setting up such ventures. Marianne Farningham, in the late 1880s, established evening meetings, and a library, for working girls in Nottingham, these readers coming mostly from the shoe factories. She tells how indebted they were to Mr Clarke, editor of *The Christian World*, who gave them, among other books, all those by Emma Jane Warboise, and who inserted an appeal in his paper on Farningham's behalf, to which publishers, particularly Hodder and Stoughton, were quick to respond. Farningham—again, possibly, with didactic intent as well as self-justification of her enterprise—chose to present the attenders as keen and pious: 'Many had pocket editions of the Gospel of St. John—"little John's" they called them—with which they began, continued, and ended their days of work.'[159] Ellice Hopkins, also writing about Nottingham, described the operation of the 'Girls' Movement' there, with educated girls coming forward to help the poor ones. She claimed that Recreative Evening Homes were an alternative to pubs, and described how the girls were fond of being read to, 'listening quietly to a pathetic or comic story, either in prose or poetry. The "library night" is always well attended; the girls take home the books not only for themselves to read, but to lend to fathers and brothers.'[160] M. C. Mondy expressed, none the less, some disquiet about why Sunday School readers enjoyed certain texts: 'they always wanted those on naughty children, and practised the naughty tricks suggested by the reading, on parents, teachers, and companions'. To counteract this, Mondy read the same books 'and gave the early part of the afternoon to talking over what they had read, the point being to draw their attention to some things they had overlooked, for example:—the consequences of mistaken pleasure'. Better books for the Sunday School—which meant more instructional ones of a practical nature—improved matters, and this writer's faith in the power and specific role of literature is demonstrated by the claim that 'Two girls of the class became thoughtful readers, and were better mothers in consequence', whilst of the two who left early, 'One became a hopeless drunkard, the other, something worse. Yet, had they been longer in the class, they would have been saved.'[161] Incidentally, Mondy did not just consider that it was the content of reading which had the power to impart lessons. Having started a reading circle, she noted that employers were willing to let lads read at work, when opportunities occurred, and allowed them to leave work early for circle meetings; girls, on the other hand, still had all the 'drudgery and responsibility' of home duties:

[158] Ead., *Advantages of Easily Accessible Reading and Recreation Rooms*, 24–5.
[159] Farningham, *A Working Woman's Life*, 127.
[160] Ellice Hopkins, *Girls' Clubs and Recreative Evening Homes* (1887), 33.
[161] Mondy, *Reading as a Means of Education*, 5.

and the lads of the circle also felt that something was not right when they realised that the girls—simply because they were girls—could not receive the full benefits of the circle; and it was pleasing to see the look of regret that passed over their countenances. Is not this an example of the indirect moral and social training which may be imparted through reading circles?[162]

Elsewhere within the parish, reading aloud was a familiar activity at mothers' meetings, and both Yonge and Lady Manners offer advice in this area. Yonge writes compassionately of the need of 'weary, hardworked women' for some 'wholesome amusement'. Whilst, she warns, they are suspicious, if not resentful, of tales with an overtly didactic intent, they 'like nothing better' than stories which feature the joys or sorrows of an infant, 'and there is no better mode of conveying indirect lessons'. These stories need not necessarily be aimed at an audience of adult women in the first place. Thus, for example, a work entitled *My Little Patient* is 'Full of pathos, which touches mothers more than it does children'; Laura Lane's *Harry's Discipline* is summarized: 'A good-natured careless young railway porter neglects his mother till she is almost starved. The lesson is chiefly meant for the sons, but it deeply affects the mothers, and is a warning to them not to spoil their boys.'[163] She notes, however, the difficulty in presenting any continuous course of reading material, since women rarely attend regularly. Advising on the organization of mothers' meetings in the *Girl's Own Paper*, Alice King tailored the recommended programme to the idea that women were unlikely to attend as a matter of routine from week to week, suggesting that they always begin with a prayer and Bible-reading, and that the subsequent reading continue for about two hours—the most the mothers can and should afford to spend away from home—'with sunny little intervals of chat and laughter . . . We think that, in general, story books, with good religious teaching in them, suit best'.[164]

Advice for Working-class Girls

The bulk of texts discussed in this chapter were, broadly speaking, aimed at a middle-class readership. However, particularly following the 1870 Education Act, the reading of the working-class girl and woman was, as we have seen in the preceding section, also a matter for comment and advice. Whilst the remarks of Yonge, Manners, and others were designed for the middle-, even upper-class woman reader, the subjects of their philanthropic intentions were also addressed in their own right. Much of this advice was religious in nature

---

[162] Mondy, *Reading as a Means of Education*, 9.

[163] Yonge, *What Books to Lend*, 77–9.

[164] Alice King, 'About Mothers' Meetings', *Girl's Own Paper*, 3 (1881), 85. The particular structure of mothers's meetings stimulated the publication of texts aimed explicitly at them, such as Florence Wilford, *Short Stories for Mothers' Meetings* (1883) and Mrs G. E. Morton and A. Hankey, *Addresses and Stories for Mothers' Meetings* (1883).

and origin. Moreover, the content and tone of works aimed at working-class girls were greatly influenced by the increased activity of Social Purity movements, fuelled, in their turn, by eugenicist anxiety. Edward Bristow has pointed to the large number of anti-sexual lectures, tracts, books, lantern-shows, and films appearing between 1880 and the inter-war period. Although much of this publicity was aimed at boys and young men, these years saw such phenomena as the Snowdrop Bands, originating in Sheffield but spreading throughout the North, composed of young women pledged to 'discourage all wrong conversation, light and immodest conduct and the reading of foolish and bad books'.[165]

The long-established Society for Promoting Christian Knowledge was, in 1871, quick to seize the opportunity for exploiting the growth in literacy. This is illustrated when the writer of *A Mistress' Counsel; or A Few Words to Servants*—a small book entirely aimed at women—turns to the subject of reading. Doubtless, she says, a girl who 'has passed the highest standard required by Government . . . considers herself to be rather highly educated', but education is not much good, she continues, if it has not taught one what to read and what to avoid. She claims that nowadays 'in all ranks of life young women and girls are too careless as to what they read', and recollects that in her youth if a newspaper or book unsuitable for women came into the house, it was put out of the way. However, the contents of these were unlikely to be as pernicious as the material which is customarily offered to servants. Injudiciously casting aspersions on her audience's intelligence, she writes of the sensational, addictive appeal of some publications which are brought to the back doors of gentlemen's houses. Some of these are full of impurity, others of silly sensational stories, which unsettle the weak minds of those who read them:

It is delightful to a kitchen-maid to be told of a rich gentleman who once fell in love with and married a kitchen-maid. Of course it sets her wondering why the same thing should not happen to herself, and immediately her work becomes hateful to her. Why should she not ride in a carriage and wear silk dresses? These publications generally come out in numbers, and the last page invariably leaves off at some thrilling point of the story. Thus these lying tales rest on the mind, and, at last, this kind of reading becomes to the young people who indulge in it exactly what brandy and gin are to the drunkard. They crave for it, and will have it: they no longer crave for good, wholesome reading any more than he does for good, wholesome food.[166]

The effects of reading of 'wickedness' in books are incalculable, and the writer presents them in awesomely melodramatic terms: 'none of us know how it may burn the soul as with a red hot iron, and how the effect of it may never be fully known until we stand at the judgement seat.'[167] It is notable that the anxiety

---

[165] *Prevention* (1911), quoted by Edward J. Bristow, *Vice and Vigilance: Purity Movements in Britain since 1700* (1977), 131.

[166] *A Mistress' Counsel; or A Few Words to Servants* (1871), 49–50.

[167] Ibid. 52.

which underlies this terrifying scenario is not so much centred, from the writer's point of view, on sexual corruption (although the subject-matter of her hypothetical story shows this is clearly present) but on the threat which reading improbable fiction poses to the class structure. When she speaks of how reading about one crime in the newspaper may lead to the committal of further crimes, again she is as much concerned with society as with the individual soul.

There is no need to read 'trash', as the author of this advice text puts it, when so many good books, including story-books, are published: she suggests seeking direction from the local clergyman, and finding out whether there is a parish lending library which contains suitable volumes. Books *may* be provided in the house for servants, but otherwise should never be taken without leave. It is a dishonest treatment of property to read books lying about on a drawing-room table—'they are not intended for your use'—and she tells cautionary tales centring around a missing volume of a novel being found in a greasy kitchen drawer, and another being taken up to a servant's bedroom to be read in secret. Whereas the Bible is the best of all possible reading, she does not advocate it exclusively. However, she indicates how to tell what else is suitable, what not: 'There are some books you would hide instantly if anyone you respected were to look over your shoulder. Depend upon it, these are the books you should ever put from you. Avoid them as you would avoid deadly poison.'[168] Using the same metaphor of corruption, Mrs Bayly, in her pamphlet *An Old Mother's Letter to Young Women* (1884) beseeches her readers, whom she specifies are most likely to be domestic servants or shop assistants: 'to avoid, as you would poison, all books, papers, and pictures, which can raise the thought of impurity in the mind. We know the real struggle of your lives will not be so much for bread and butter, for "places," or to get money in the savings bank; it will be to resist the tempter and keep yourselves pure.'[169] More directly, Mary Bell, in a general section on resisting temptation, offers a firm guideline: 'If a book, or paper, has put bad thoughts into your head—don't touch it again.'[170]

The Bible figures prominently in other advice manuals for servants. It is central to *The Young Servant's Own Book, intended as A Present for Girls on First Going Into Service* (1883), a pamphlet which bore the injunction on the title-page: 'Please to read this little book, then put it in your box, and take it out once a year to read over again.' The young servant was advised to look—in what little time she would have available for this—'in such books as are improving and useful'. The Bible is 'the best book': she should study chiefly in the New Testament, since the Old Testament contained some practices formerly allowable, but forbidden to Christians. She should always read the Bible in a serious frame of mind, with heart uplifted in prayer. The Countess of Aberdeen also counselled careful daily Bible reading, encouraging her readers to draw on

168 *A Mistress' Counsel; or A Few Words to Servants* (1871).
169 Mrs Bayly, *An Old Mother's Letter to Young Women* (1884), 16.
170 Mary Bell, *The Lowly Life: A Simple Book for Girl-Workers* (1892), 24.

biblical promises of help when tempted to say an angry word or complete their work carelessly, and to take all commands as given to themselves personally.[171] The author of *The Young Servant's Own Book*, like the SPCK writer, and using the same vocabulary of bodily contamination, warns against the 'very foolish books' which may be found in some families, as well as condemning the 'foolish ballads' which may be brought to the back door. A fail-safe guide is offered to judging the books which the girl might encounter: 'Should you at any time meet with a book in which the Bible, or our blessed Saviour, are spoken of with irreverence, in a way to make people laugh, you may be sure that is a bad book; avoid it as you would a cup of poison; such books are poison to the mind.'[172] Ella Welby, writing in 1895 for members of the Girls' Friendly Society,[173] asked them if they laughed when bad words were spoken, laughed at coarse jokes, if they read 'bad books? or accounts of bad things in the papers?' An affirmative answer to any of these was a prompt to kneel before God and ask him to wash one's soul.[174] Furthermore, she attempts to appeal to some of her readers' literary assumptions by posing the question: 'What do we understand by a favourite book?' Is it one with a brilliant, beautiful binding, to be taken out and aesthetically admired, or one with a 'well-worn though tenderly handled cover', a 'friend to whom we turn for counsel, for sympathy, or for pleasant converse, just as we do to a human friend?' She acknowledges a common current desire to 'improve ourselves, as we call it', and notes the part reading books can play in this, even if patience and instruction are needed to overcome some of their difficulties. The assembled 'correct' responses to this gentle catechism about reading attitudes unsurprisingly led to the point when the ideal book for the addressee of Soulsby's advice is revealed to be the Bible.[175]

But not all the advice offered was explicitly religious in its basis. E. A. Walker, in *Friendly Hints to Our Girls* (1889), acknowledges that many of her addressees enjoy reading, but accuses them of consuming solely 'sugar plums', paying attention only to the stories in such magazines as *Friendly Leaves*, *Home Visitor*, or *Our Own Gazette*, and ignoring the remainder of the text. Such a habit will breed compulsive, sensation-seeking reading habits, and it would be far better, she advises, to peruse the whole of each magazine, and also to try and find some real biographies and travel books to read, which, unlike stories, 'may be of use to you, instead of turning your head to nonsense, and making you discontented with your position'.[176] The same writer, in *Womanhood; or*

---

[171] The Countess of Aberdeen, *Mistresses and Maid-Servants: suggestions towards the Increased Pleasure and Permanence of their Domestic Relations* (Aberdeen and London, 1884), 13–14.

[172] *The Young Servant's Own Book, intended as A Present for Girls on First Going Into Service* (1883), 5.

[173] For the Girls' Friendly Society, see Brian Harrison, 'For Church, Queen and Family: The Girls' Friendly Society, 1875–1920', *Past and Present*, 61 (1973), 107–38; M. Heath-Stubbs, *Friendship's Highway, Being The History of the Girls' Friendly Society 1874–1920* (1926).

[174] [Ella Welby] *Every Day: Thoughts on the G.F.S. Rules of Life* (1895), 2.

[175] Ibid. 35–8

[176] E.A.W. [E. A. Walker] *Friendly Hints to Our Girls* (1889), 12–13.

Thoughts for Young Women (1891) urges her readers to spend half an hour a day in thoughtful reading, continuing the beginnings which they had made at Parish and Board Schools. She condemns 'tales full of unnatural scenes, murders and suicides', since 'such novels are like brandy-drinking; they make the mind feverish and exhaust its powers'. Instead, she recommends obtaining books from the depots of the National Society, the Society for Promoting Christian Knowledge, or the Tract Society. She specifically mentions, among other texts, Mrs Markham's *History of England*, the *Short Biographies* produced by the Religious Tract Society, Wood's works on Natural History, and a book called the *Thousand and One Gems of Poetry*. Rather, however, than implying that such works will lead girls to become resigned and content with their position, she exhorts her readers to adopt a forward-looking individualism: 'These are days of intellectual culture! Do not be left behind in the race!'[177]

Advice was not just on offer to servants themselves, but to those who employed them. In some houses, it was evidently the practice to provide books for the servants. Mrs Eliot James, in *Our Servants: Their Duties to Us and Ours to Them* (1882) incorporated the recognition of this practice with an acknowledge-ment of the importance of leisure space, advising her readers to see that their servants 'are supplied with pleasant, sensible literature . . . for their evening's reading, a comfortable place in which to sit when their work for the day is over, and liberty every now and again to see their friends openly.' Whereas, she claimed, few servants were unable to read and write, she indicates that a good housewife will spare her personal time to offer appropriate instruction. Moreover, although the idea of reading aloud to servants may seem old-fashioned, she suggests that 'with a little self-denial on the mistresses part', the afternoons when servants are employed in household mending might be 'made to pass quickly and pleasantly' by her reading aloud to them. Incidentally, she advises against servants reading instruction manuals, believing that practical knowledge is taught by experience alone, and such books are likely to promote 'a lingering sort of consciousness that *all* in the reader's own house is not quite as it should be'.[178]

It would be improbable to think that many nineteenth-century readers actually set about following the instructions preferred in these manuals in any systematic way. But their impact may be thought of as several-fold. The reiteration of the views about a woman's proper role, and the way in which reading helps form her social function and attitudes must have served as a confirmation and consolidation of the dominant ideology of the period. A resisting reader might have asked herself why such repetition and codification was necessary, and what anxieties it masked. But to assume that the function of such manuals was entirely pernicious would be mistaken. They can be seen as

---

[177] Id., *Womanhood; or Thoughts for Young Women* (1891), 32–4.
[178] Mrs Eliot James, *Our Servants: Their Duties to Us and Ours to Them* (1882), 30, 34.

potentially enabling fictions in their own right, alluring for the sense of achievement which they hold out to the reader. This is the type of attraction which Kenneth Burke recognized, writing of a descendant of the genre, the Dale Carnegie type of manual aimed at struggling white-collar workers in post-Second World War America:

The reading of the book on the attaining of success is in itself the symbolic attaining of that success. It is while they read that these readers are 'succeeding.' . . . The lure of the book resides in the fact that the reader, while reading it, is then living in the aura of success. What he wants is easy success; and he gets it in symbolic form by the mere reading itself. To attempt applying such stuff in real life would be very difficult, full of many disillusioning difficulties.[179]

It would also, of course, entail an impossible eradication of differences between readers.

[179] Kenneth Burke, 'Literature as Equipment for Living', in *The Philosophy of Literary Form* (Berkeley, Calif., 1973), 299.

6   Reading at School

The growth of women's education during the nineteenth century has been well chronicled.[1] The claim that change at the level of secondary and tertiary study for girls and women was the most marked of all the developments which took place in nineteenth-century education was justifiably advanced in the Preface to one of the earliest of these accounts, Christina Bremner's *Education of Girls and Women in Great Britain* (1897).[2] But it is not the place, in this chapter, to rehearse again the expanding educational possibilities for women, but to show how the issue of reading, and, in particular, the special aptitudes and skills associated with the reading of literature, supplied an arena in which current sociological and medical debates could be seen as having a practical application.

Reading, inevitably, was a central topic when discussing education, whether the education in question took place in the home schoolroom, a private girls' school, or according to state provision. Debates focused on what knowledge it would or would not be useful for a girl to possess; on how literature should best be studied; and on the relation—indeed the division—within a curriculum between formal and leisure reading. The practice of reading played a part in the disputations concerning the relations between study and health. As we saw earlier, the opinions of medical specialists intersected with widely-held views about the social role of women, which in turn fed into the educational theories and practices which characterized some dominant aspects of the debate surrounding the growth of women's education.

Despite the development of educational opportunities, the idea that marriage and maternity would be the most important elements in a girl's future remained the underlying assumption informing most sectors of secondary education until the First World War. Charles Eyre Pascoe, in his highly informative *Schools for Girls and Colleges for Women* (1879), which strongly advocated the development of serious academic teaching for the daughters of the middle classes, saw this as ultimately enhancing the woman's place at her husband's side, so that 'she may add to his happiness by her ability to appreciate and share his highest intellectual pursuits, and lessen his cares by her power to aid in the education of

---

[1] See e.g. Gillian Avery, *The Best Type of Girl: A History of Girls' Independent Schools* (1991); Carol Dyhouse, *Girls Growing up in Late Victorian and Edwardian England* (1981), 40–78; Sheila Fletcher, *Feminists and Bureaucrats: A Study in the Development of Girls' Education in the Nineteenth Century* (Cambridge, 1980); Josephine Kamm, *Hope Deferred: Girls' Education in English History* (1965); Barry Turner, *Equality for Some: The Story of Girls' Education* (1974); Martha Vicinus, *Independent Women: Work and Community for Single Women* (1985), 121–210.

[2] Preface by Miss E. P. Hughes to C. S. Bremner, *Education of Girls and Women in Great Britain* (1897), p. vi.

his children'.[3] This view paralleled the common assumption, met with in the previous section, that the knowledge and potential conversational material which might be acquired through reading would serve to make a woman a fitter, more companionable wife and mother. Even by 1907, Sara Burstall, Headmistress of Manchester High School for Girls and historian of girls' education, whilst acknowledging that many girls would have to work for money (either before marriage, or because they would never marry, or because they would not wish to waste their premarital days in vacuous anticipation) nevertheless confidently maintained that: 'We see clearly now that the normal work of a woman is to be the maker of a home, to be a wife, and above all a mother. Does a liberal education fit her for this? The answer is surely yes, if it makes her a better woman, abler and stronger in body, in intellect, and character.'[4] Similarly, Dorothea Beale believed in the importance of training girls so that they would be able to supply 'healthy intellectual companionship' in marriage.[5] The study of literature in particular could be recommended, since, to quote the *School Board Chronicle*, it need not necessarily be laid aside after marriage, because it is the form of study 'which is linked the closest with daily duties, sympathies, and pleasures', and renders the reader 'not only a delightful companion but a delightful member of society'.[6]

Most of the material I shall here be discussing deals with the reading of the middle- and upper-class girl, since it was on her that the focus of the debate invariably fell. But practice in working-class schools bore out, even more forcibly, the existence of these prevalent assumptions. Anna Davin has shown in effective detail how the reading textbooks in board schools, which on the whole served the poorer end of the working class, were habitually didactic in the way in which the extracts, stories, and poems which they contained imparted homely moral 'truths'. More than this, she demonstrates, they were rigorously gendered in their assumptions: 'their tendency, both through the behaviour they advocated—unselfishness, compassion, devotion to housewifely industry and family duty—and through the situations which they presented as natural to women, was to direct girls towards an exclusively domestic role, even at the expense of school.'[7] Moreover, girls were less likely to spend time on reading than were boys, devoting instead many hours to the manual skill of sewing, important for the girl going into service. School log books show that the

[3] Charles Eyre Pascoe, *Schools for Girls and Colleges for Women: A Handbook of Female Education chiefly designed for the use of persons of the upper middle classes* (1879), 83.

[4] Sara A. Burstall, *English High Schools for Girls* (1907), 13.

[5] Dorothea Beale, Lucy H. M. Soulsby, and Jane Frances Dove, *Work and Play in Girls' Schools* (1898), 5.

[6] *School Board Chronicle*, reproduced in *Victoria Magazine*, 19 (1872), 437.

[7] Anna Davin, ' "Mind that you do as you are told": Reading Books for Board School Girls, 1870–1902', *Feminist Review*, 3 (1979), 89–98. For examples of representative Board School readers, see Phebe Lancaster, *National Thrift Reader* (1880); Henry Major, *Little Mothers* (1893); Margaret Sandford, *The Girls' Reading Book* (1876).

demands of housework and sibling care made girls' attendance at school more irregular than that of their brothers.[8]

But it would be misguided to believe, even when a girl's future role as wife and mother was considered in relation to her educational experience, that she was only being prepared for a life cocooned within the family. In the case of board schools, the texts often involved an inculcation of hierarchized class stability through emphasizing the importance of knowing one's place and doing one's duty. Among the middle and upper classes, many women heads of public schools considered themselves, unlike private schoolmistresses, professional people in their own right. Not only did they place a certain amount of emphasis on the academic achievements of their pupils, but they saw themselves as training and preparing their girls for public life—not necessarily in the sense of teachers or members of a school-board or the medical profession, but as women who had a sense of responsibility not just to family but to the wider community.[9] Beale herself acknowledged that individual and social development should go hand in hand, proclaiming that the dual aim of education was 'the perfection of the individual and the good of the community'.[10]

Without a sense of purpose which stretched outside the family circle, education too frequently prepared a girl for nothing other than the 'elegant leisure' or 'the state of wholesome rust', as Emily Davies described the enforced under-activity which led to indolent habits, and to the vapid emptiness of society talk. Parents were accused of setting too much store by the acquisition of materially quantifiable 'accomplishments', and not appreciating 'that an inquiring spirit, a love of reading, and an increasing interest in high and worthy subjects are of infinitely greater importance'[11] for what they bring to the individual in her own right, rather than as a social commodity. As early as 1864, Davies was arguing that one can judge the standards of education in women's schools by looking at the finished product, and material which formed women's habitual reading was one of her yardsticks:

Of literature, women of the middle class know next to nothing. I am not speaking of religious literature, which is extensively read by some women and to which they owe much. I speak of general literature, and of ordinary women, whose reading is for the most part confined to novels, and of novels not the best. The catalogue of a book seller's circulating library, in which second-rate fiction largely preponderates, is a fair criterion

[8] See June Purvis, 'The Experience of Schooling for Working-class Boys and Girls in Nineteenth-Century England', in Ivor F. Goodson and Stephen J. Ball (eds.), *Defining the Curriculum: Histories and Ethnographies* (1984), 107; and Purvis, 'The Double Burden of Class and Gender in the Schooling of Working-class Girls in Nineteenth-Century England, 1800–1870', in L. Barton and S. Walker (eds.), *Schools, Teachers and Teaching* (Lewes, 1981), 97–116.

[9] See Joyce S. Pedersen, 'Schoolmistresses and Headmistresses: Élites and Education in Nineteenth-Century England', *Journal of British Studies*, 15 (1975), 135–62.

[10] Beale *et al.*, *Work and Play in Girls' Schools*, 2.

[11] J. G. Fitch, 'The Education of Women', *Victoria Magazine*, 2 (1864), 437.

of the range and the taste of middle class lady readers. Newspapers are scarcely supposed to be read by women at all. When the *Times* is offered to a lady, the sheet containing the advertisements, and the Births, Deaths, and Marriages, is considerately selected.[12]

Similar statements were expressed by Davies when she gave evidence to the Schools' Inquiry of 1867–8. She declared that schoolmistresses of her acquaintance claimed that the ignorance of girls who came to them from home, or from the average run of schools serving the middle classes, was 'unfathomable'.[13] Miss Smith, Visitor and member of the Bedford College's Council of Management, agreed with her questioner that parents were apt to attach 'an undue importance to accomplishments as distinguished from more solid instruction'. Expressing a taste for English literature clearly came, for her, under the heading of 'accomplishments'. She maintained, with belief in the importance of training the mind lying behind her statement, that it was necessary to understand parts of speech and the workings of grammar before tackling texts.[14] Frances Buss, Principal of the North London Collegiate schools, also remarked on the extreme ignorance of the girls she admitted, and regretted that few of them had any inducement to carry on their learning without help or encouragement after they left school:

11,575. You think they leave school without any taste for reading?—I think so.

11,576. Owing partly to their very bad education?—Yes.

11,577. And therefore that they are glad to be rid of it, as a thing which is unreal?—Yes; and they get no encouragement at home. They can read in a loose desultory way, but serious study is considered unnecessary and unsociable.

11,579. From the want of cultivation of their parents, in many cases?—I think so.[15]

Nor, of course, was much encouragement frequently given at home to the girl who had left school to continue with her reading in any serious or organized manner. As Millicent Garrett Fawcett put it, in the context of a plea not just for better mental training in schools but for opportunities to be made open for women in higher education, the eighteen-year-old girl was far too frequently—unlike her brother—assumed to have finished her education, and 'probably finds it nearly impossible to secure her time against those who consider any sort of idleness better for a woman than mental culture'.[16]

Various inspectors commented on specific points relating to the study of English literature which they found taking place in schools, whilst noting the general, depressing tendency to reduce it to rules of grammar, and the learning

[12] Emily Davies, 'On Secondary Instruction as Relating to Girls' (1864), *Thoughts on Some Questions Relating to Women, 1860–1908* (Cambridge, 1910), 70–1.

[13] Reports from Commissioners to the Schools' Inquiry, PP. 1867, XXVIII, Part IV, v. 233.

[14] Ibid. 698.

[15] Ibid. 261.

[16] Millicent Garrett Fawcett, 'The Education of Women of the Middle and Upper Classes', *Macmillan's Magazine*, 17 (1868), 513.

by rote of Biblical passages and poetic selections. Mr Bryce, touring Lancashire, was disappointed that literature was not studied more. In a mercantile community, he observed, men are sent so early in life to business, and are absorbed so constantly by it, that they can have little or no time for reading or thought, and must rely on their wives and daughters to keep them in touch with cultural and imaginative matters. But since girls' 'imagination is more susceptible than that of boys' in any case:

they are affected far more than young men are by the books they read. It is, therefore, a matter of the first importance to form their taste, to show them the books that are best worth reading, to give them some notions of the canons whereby literary productions should be tried, and in fine to make it their habit and their pleasure to exercise their minds upon what they read, whether it be a history, a poem, or a novel.[17]

Mr Hammond, visiting both Northumberland and Norfolk, found that girls' schools certainly studied English literature more than boys' counterparts, but regretted how much teaching was done via poetical extracts, with works seldom being considered in their entirety. Moreover, he observed notable differences between girls' and boys' responses as a result of the overall quality of their education, even when they came from similar social backgrounds. In respect of the typical young lady:

Within certain limits her general intelligence and her imaginative faculty would be more nimble and active in their play than a man's would be; she would take a more lively view of familiar and domestic incidents, and would extract more pleasure from light and elegant literature. But the study of solid and weighty writers and the discussion of matters of first-rate importance would be uninteresting to her owing to her lack of real comprehensive knowledge, and consequently of speculative power. Or if she attempted to interest herself in such matters, the want of a trained judgment and the imperfect development of her critical and reasoning faculties would oblige her to rely with blind credulity upon the dogmatic assertions of those about her.[18]

Notably, it was the system, rather than women's innate abilities, which was found wanting.

The Royal Commission on Secondary Education of 1894–5 commented on the great improvement in girls' education resulting from the growth in endowed and propriety schools. Beale, again, was called to give evidence. Asked whether she had seen great changes come about in the education of women during the last thirty years, she agreed that she had, although there was still room for very considerable improvement.[19] Even by the end of the period, by no means all middle-class girls were receiving all or most of their education away from home. In many middle-class households, particularly provincial ones, the pattern

---

[17] Mr Bryce, in Dorothea Beale, *Reports Issued by the Schools' Inquiry Commission on the Education of Girls* (1869), 59, 81.

[18] Mr Hammond, quoted ibid. 153–154.

[19] Royal Commission on Secondary Education (1894–1895), Minutes of Evidence, ii. 158.

seems to have been for the girls to be taught at home, often alongside their brothers, until they were about ten; then to attend a local day-school for two or three years, and, finally, to be sent to a 'select' boarding-school until they were about seventeen, at which time they would either come home, or spend a year abroad at a 'finishing' school. In the lower middle-classes, girls were likely to receive their basic education at home, from their nurse-maid and their mother, and then to attend local day-schools for about four to five years from the age of ten. The pressure on them to stay at home and play a central part in running the household—including imparting elementary educational instruction to their younger sisters and brothers—was strong.[20] Some girls, however, especially in the upper classes, never left home at all, and the implications of this fact for their reading practices were remarked upon. In the *Englishwoman's* education debate of 1896, Sir James Crichton-Brown, in a metaphor which uncomfortably and revealingly compares their intellectual nurturing with that of a beast for market, claimed that:

It will not be denied that home-reared girls read much more widely than do high-school girls. 'They browse unconfined,' to quote Mrs. Gaskell, 'on the wholesome pasturage of English literature,' while high-school girls are stall-fed on condensed primers; and the result is that there is often a breezy freshness and interesting diversity about those home-reared girls that contrasts not unfavourably with the dry precision and monotonous uniformity of their more systematically educated sisters.[21]

Answering him, Maud Venables Vernon queried his assumptions, reminding readers of the still prevalent belief 'that reading is a waste of time for women, and an amusement only to be indulged in when household and social duties leave a moment of leisure'. Such a moment is most likely to be filled with 'desultory reading', whilst a high-school girl is likely to be better organized, her formal education enabling her to plan 'systematic work' in her own time. Such a superior combination of content and method, Vernon adds, will enable her either to become 'a more intelligent and truly efficient mother', or, if remaining single, to combine thoughtfulness, culture, and practicality.[22] Other women educationists acknowledged that parents could do a great deal to organize and monitor their daughters' reading habits when they were at home, whether or not they attended school as well. Dorothea Beale, for example, in an early number of the *Women's Education Union Journal*, organ of the National Union for the Improvement of the Education of Women of All Classes (founded 1871),[23] recommends that half an hour after dinner be set aside for reading in

[20] See Dyhouse, 'Schooling, College and Femininity: Some Experiences of Middle-Class Girls', in *Girls Growing up*, 40–78.
[21] *Englishwoman*, 2 (1896), 458.
[22] Ibid. 3 (1896), 178.
[23] For the foundation of the Women's Education Union and of the Girls' Public Day School Company which it initiated, see Edward W. Ellsworth, *Liberators of the Female Mind: The Shirreff Sisters, Educational Reform, and the Women's Movement* (1979), 174–202.

the home: a means of consolidating family bonds, and also of promoting relaxation. However, the reading material must be carefully chosen. She advises strongly against sensation literature, making the point that while the adult reader can recognize the repetition of conventions at work, and can be sure that the hero will come out of the labyrinth and the minotaur be baulked of his prey, the young reader, not so familiar with the tricks of the genre, is far more liable to be affected by the effects of excitement. Indeed, she used the symptoms such over-stimulating reading matter might give rise to as a means of countering one of the favourite arguments of those who spoke apprehensively about the effects of sustained education on women, claiming that it would be well: 'if headaches and nervous exhaustion were always traced up to the true cause, instead of being hastily attributed to over-work. Some doctors would then prescribe abstinence from novels, instead of lessons.'[24]

The issues raised by Crichton-Brown are significant, however, not solely for the commentary which they offer on reading in the home. They serve to indicate the shift that took place in *how* English literature was regarded as a subject within women's education, for in the mid- and later nineteenth century, the greater part of educational theorizing about the place of reading within education related to teaching in the classroom.

From one point of view, literature could be said to build on and develop faculties which were already considered to be present within women, and to be a natural and valuable part of their being. Matthew Arnold, above all, made large claims for the civilizing influence of literary culture, thus formulating the terms which enabled the educational profession to propagate these claims, especially at a time when scientific and technical instruction were taking a growing place on curricula. English literature fulfilled the demand, as Chris Baldick has put it, for: 'a humane, moralizing subject which could harmonize an otherwise anarchic profusion of "dry facts" . . . since it could be offered as a substitute for Classics, acting as a liberal counterweight to technical learning without taking up so much time in basic linguistic drilling or teaching resources.'[25] It was in this atmosphere of cultural humanism that great powers were alleged for the centrality of English literature within girls' schools. 'Much that is claimed for the effect of classics on boys as a humanising influence is found by experience to be provided for girls through the humanities in English', maintained Burstall, without, however, noting that concurrent attempts were being made to establish English literature on the masculine curriculum, especially for the less academically able or for those from backgrounds with

[24] Beale, 'Rocks and Quicksands. No. II: Home Difficulties', *Journal of the Women's Education Union*, 1 (1873), 87.

[25] Chris Baldick, *The Social Mission of English Criticism 1848–1932* (Oxford, 1983; new edn., 1987), 62. Ch. 3, 'A Civilizing Subject', is especially illuminating in the context of my argument. See also D. J. Palmer, *The Rise of English Studies* (1965); Brian Doyle, 'The Hidden History of English Studies', in Peter Widdowson (ed.), *Re-Reading English* (1982); and id., *English & Englishness* (1989).

little or no access to high culture.[26] Dorothea Beale suggested to the
Commissioners to the Schools' Inquiry that, in contrast to the imagination-
numbing way in which the classics were habitually taught to boys, girls'
education had the advantage that it did not require additional stimuli to
encourage pupils to read texts which in any case were intrinsically more
interesting than Caesar's Commentaries.[27] By the twentieth century, this
revision of emphasis in the teaching of literature to girls was seen as having
spread to all types of education: 'it is possible that girls' schools have
strengthened the fight against allowing the teaching of literature to be degraded
into a memorising of notes'.[28] Beale led the campaign against annotating
literature texts with critical notes and parallel passages. A certain amount of
formal dissection is inevitable, she wrote, but while a botany student must pull a
flower to pieces and examine the calyx, the petal and the stamens, the true
naturalist should also consider the exquisite beauties of form and colouring in
the flower as it grows in its own habitat. So, by analogy, the schoolgirl is led to
consider literature, ultimately, as something inspiring, beautiful, and, in its
whole, transcending rational explanation.[29] School libraries, advised Burstall,
should not just contain standard, and necessary reference works, whether
dictionaries or volumes of a historical, geographical, and scientific nature, but
some French books—history as well as literature—and a good collection of the
classics: Thackeray, Scott, Jane Austen, and Stevenson are recommended by
name. Older girls should be allowed to work in the library, with open-shelf
access, during school hours, and to take books home. Younger ones should
have their reading material more closely monitored through consulting the
school librarian at fixed hours.[30] Bearing in mind the need for access to books,
she also recommended that one should not go along with the idealistic view that
there should be no prizes. These should be given to all who reached a required
standard (as had happened in her own schoolday experience) and they would
thus form a permanent library of standard texts in the home.[31]

Among the earliest people to comment at any length on the part which
English literature might play within the systematic education of the older girl

[26] Burstall, *English High Schools for Girls*, 108.

[27] Reports from Commissioners to the Schools' Inquiry, v. 739. Dorothea Beale went on to add
that boys were often turned away from their studies by the fact that their school placed overmuch
emphasis on sport: 'If a girl takes to croquet or novel-reading the result is the same'.

[28] R. L. Archer, *Secondary Education in the Nineteenth Century* (Cambridge, 1921), 257.

[29] Beale, preface to *Reports Issued by the Schools' Inquiry Commission*, p. xxvi. For a later
description of the pernicious effects of over-annotated texts, see Rosalind M. Haig Brown,
'English', in Sara A. Burstall and M. A. Douglas (eds.), *Public Schools for Girls: A Series of Papers on
their History, Aims, and Schemes of Study* (1911), 63.

[30] Burstall, *Retrospect & Prospect: Sixty Years of Women's Education* (1933), 127–8. Histories of
individual schools give some idea of the growth of their libraries. For example, Colston's Girls'
School (founded 1891) had as its auditor a Mr Ryland, who, impressed by his visits to 6th-form
Reading Club meetings, left his library of nearly 10,000 books to the school on his death in 1909 (E.
Clutton, *Colston's Girls' School Jubilee 1891–1941* (Bristol, 1941), 4).

[31] Burstall, *Retrospect and Prospect*, 58.

was Charles Kingsley. He taught English Literature at Queen's College, Harley Street, when it opened in 1848, founded by Kingsley's friend Frederick Denison Maurice with the aim of raising the professional standards of governesses. Its courses of lectures were soon open to other interested young women.[32] In his introductory lecture on the subject, Kingsley proclaimed that the aim of the college's literature teaching was to help prepare the English woman of the nineteenth century to play her full part in a century which looked likely to become the most glorious which Christendom had yet beheld. In order to lead her into the fulfilment of her personal and national heritage, it was imperative that she should not be cut off from her roots, and nourished solely on 'Elegant Extracts' and 'Beauties of British Poetry'. There is a foretaste of Crichton-Browne's unpleasant image of force-feeding the marketable beast when Kingsley claims that the young woman, presented with texts in this form, does not receive them 'fresh and whole, but cut up into the very driest hay'.

But Kingsley's stress on the desirability of establishing stability and continuity was not just projected at a national level, but at a domestic one too. For he notes:

a general complaint that the minds of young women are outgrowing their mothers' guidance, that they are reading books which their mothers never dreamt of reading, of many of which they never heard, many at least whose good and evil they have had no means of investigating; that the authors which really interest and influence the minds of the young are just the ones which have formed no part of their education, and therefore those for judging of which they have received no adequate rules; that, in short, in literature as in many things, education in England is far behind the wants of the age.

Now this is all wrong and ruinous. The mother's mind should be the lodestar of the daughter's.[33]

So how, according to Kingsley, could the teaching of literature best function as a substitute for, or consolidation of, maternal guidance? In broad terms, it should offer the pupil 'something to worship', the craving for which is 'a woman's highest grace'. More precisely, it should take her through from the legends and poetry of the Middle Ages 'to the latest of our modern authors'. If one does not approach literature chronologically, the reader is liable to fling herself from one emotional extreme to another: from the 'dry class-drudgery' of Pope and Johnson to the 'forbidden fruit' of Byron, Shelley, and sentimental fiction writers; from their 'morbid self-consciousness' to the light relief offered by ballad literature; from this to 'deep draughts of Wordsworth's celestial and pure sympathy', yet, craving once more something more exciting, and rich in facts and passions, she will pick up Shakespeare. Just as it would be ill-advised

[32] For the history of Queen's College, see Rosalie Glynn Grylls, *Queen's College 1848–1948* (1948), and Elaine Kaye, *A History of Queen's College, London, 1848–1972* (1972). The college admitted girls of 14 or over: a school for the under-14s was founded in 1860.

[33] Charles Kingsley, 'On English Literature': Introductory Lecture given at Queen's College London, 1848, *The Works of Charles Kingsley*, xx. *Literary and General Lectures and Essays* (1880), 246–7.

for a young woman to develop socially according to this system of contrast and rebound, so, Kingsley advises, English should be studied step by step, from its infancy (writing before Shakespeare is characterized as being 'more simple, more childlike, more girlish as it were') through to the present day. Such a pattern would encourage, he believed, reverence to our forefathers and, indeed, foremothers: he specifically mentions Elizabeth Fry, Felicia Hemans, and Hannah More as worthy role models. The key to understanding the present lies, he claims, without elucidating precisely why, in the past. But at the same time, it is necessary to teach students about the writings of the present day: for, without the aid of people like himself, the voices to whom the young woman is most likely to listen will, as probably as not, be bad voices—not because of any innate corruption in her, but because her 'honest disgust at the follies of the day' is likely to be stirred by those who rail against society. Without guidance, she will not know whether she is reading the work of a man who is a 'bungler and a charlatan', or one whom, even if he is said to be 'dangerous and unchristian, somehow makes them more dutiful, more earnest, more industrious, more loving to the poor'. 'I speak of actual cases', claims Kingsley.[34] Regrettably, he is not more specific: however, it is clear that for him, the moral state of the writer who forms the object of study is as important as the content of the text itself, and, indeed, is the force which ultimately is most likely to touch the young and susceptible reader.

Many of Kingsley's remarks would be applicable to the male, as well as to the female student of literature. However, he is emphatic that women are particularly adept and sympathetic readers because of their intuitive capacity to feel and imagine themselves living through others' lives. He did not see this reading merely as feeding back into the domestic economy. Delivering his lecture in a year of European political instability,[35] he spoke of how a knowledge of English literature would lead 'to the spread of healthy historic views among us. The literature of every nation is its autobiography',[36] presenting not a set of notable personages or of remarkable events:

but of the living human souls of English men and English women. And therefore one most adapted to the minds of woman; one which will call into fullest exercise her blessed faculty of sympathy, that pure and tender heart of flesh, which teaches her always to find her highest interest in mankind, simply as mankind; to see the Divine most completely in the human; to prefer the incarnate to the disembodied, the personal to the abstract, the pathetic to the intellectual; to see, and truly, in the most common tale of village love or sorrow, a mystery deeper and more divine than lies in all the theories of the politicians or the fixed ideas of the sage.[37]

[34] Ibid. 256.
[35] It was perhaps in this context that Kingsley expressed himself far from happy with the reading of too much Continental literature, although he acknowledged that it would be absurd to adopt a John Bull attitude and forbid it completely.
[36] Kingsley, 'On English Literature', 257.
[37] Ibid. 258.

This, Kingsley claimed, was the way God intended woman to look instinctively at the world: 'Would to God that she would teach us men to look at it thus likewise!'[38] In his conclusion to the lecture, he combines patriotic with familial reasons in his final flourish on the subject of how women should be encouraged to read literature:

Our teaching must be no sexless, heartless abstraction. We must try to make all which we tell them bear on the great purpose of unfolding to woman her own calling in all ages—her especial calling in this one. We must incite them to realise the chivalrous belief of our old forefathers among their Saxon forests, that something Divine dwelt in the counsels of woman; but, on the other hand, we must continually remind them that they will attain that divine instinct, not by renouncing their sex, but by fulfilling it; by becoming true women, and not bad imitations of men; by educating their heads for the sake of their hearts, not their hearts for the sake of their heads; by claiming woman's divine vocation, as the priestess of purity, of beauty, and of love; by educating them to become, with God's blessing, worthy wives and mothers of a mighty nation of workers, in an age when the voice of the ever-working God is proclaiming through the thunder of falling dynasties, and crumbling idols: 'He that will not work, neither shall he eat.'[39]

Exactly when literature was encountered within schools, however, was a matter for debate. How far down the school should literature be taught? Lucy Soulsby, headmistress of Oxford High School, indicates that literature was kept in her establishment as a subject for special study for the two upper forms, extra history being taught further down the school 'as being almost equally humanising, and yet more exact'. English lessons carried the capacity to stretch a girl's interests, and to inculcate the lesson—at the point of leaving school—of in fact how little she knows.[40] To some extent, external factors affected the nature of literature lessons. Cecily Steadman, looking back to the early years of Dorothea Beale at Cheltenham Ladies' College, reminds one that English teaching was then seriously hampered by the almost complete non-existence of school editions—indeed, of cheap editions of any kind. Beale had some texts privately printed for her own lessons, 'but in general it was impossible to place texts freely in the pupils' hands, because, for instance, to study *The Ancient Mariner*, one had to buy the complete works of Coleridge'.[41] This was a limitation which gradually eased during the latter years of the century.

As the material cited so far in this section indicates, much Victorian theory concerning the reading of literature within education was based, like the material in the previous section, upon dominant assumptions about the social role of women, constructed and phrased in relatively generalized terms. Similarly, schools of all types used issues surrounding reading as a means of confirming not just social values, but the standards of behaviour and

---

[38]   Kingsley, 'On English Literature'.
[39]   Ibid. 265.
[40]   Soulsby, *School Work* (1890), 14–15.
[41]   F. Cecily Steadman, *In the Days of Miss Beale: A Study of her Work and Influence* (1931), 43.

'innocence' which they believed to be appropriate for young women. Some autobiographical writers recall the manœuvres to which certain teachers resorted in order to ensure the purity of their reading material. Pupils at Queen's College remembered the puritanical standards imposed by Owen Breden, English and Elocution Professor there in the 1890s. L. V. Hodson notes that when reading Sheridan in his classes, they first had to take a pencil and cross out all the expletives, and Lady Dilke records:

reading the sleep-walking scene in Macbeth when the Professor held up his hand:
    'Ladies, before proceeding further we will turn to the next page. We will count one, two, three lines from the top. We will count one, two words in this line. We will erase or cross out the second word and substitute the word 'thou'. This line will then read 'Out thou spot. Out I say.'[42]

Even within higher education, strict standards could prevail in relation to what it was, or was not, considered suitable for young women to read. Thus E. Terry, at Newnham College, Cambridge in 1902, recalls being coached in Middle High German Lyrics by a Dr Breul: they came to 'a love-song that I thought particularly charming and wanted to say so, but Dr Breul turned the page very firmly and said, "Er ist nicht erbaulich" (not edifying)';[43] W. Gascoigne, also at Newnham, remembers trouble with disapproving authorities when John Galsworthy was asked to come and speak to the Literary Society in 1911.

It was not just literary texts which fell under strict scrutiny. Katharine Chorley, at a private school in Folkestone at the end of the century, noted that 'we were discouraged from discussing politics at all and no newspapers were allowed to us'.[44] But the prohibition may have had resonances which went beyond the political. This is clarified by Vera Brittain, who, attending her aunt's school in Surrey shortly before the First World War, glossed her practice of allowing them to read extracts from newspapers:

We were never, of course, allowed to have the papers themselves—our innocent eyes might have strayed from foreign affairs to the evidence being taken by the Royal Commission on Marriage and Divorce or the Report of the International Paris Conference for the suppression of the White Slave Traffic—and the carefully selected cuttings invariably came from The Times or the Observer unmodified by contrary political opinions, but the fact that we had them at all testified to a recognition of the importance of current events far from customary at a time when politics and economics were still thought by most headmistresses to be no part of the education of marriageable young females.[45]

On other occasions, it was not so much the reading material itself which formed the crucial grounds for comment, as the set of moral expectations

---

[42] Grylls, Queen's College, 66.
[43] E. Terry, in Ann Phillips (ed.), A Newnham Anthology (Cambridge, 1979), 55.
[44] Katharine Chorley, Manchester Made Them (1950), 205.
[45] Vera Brittain, Testament of Youth (1933), 39.

surrounding the act of reading. This was particularly prevalent in those private boarding-schools where education in social propriety was as important—or more important—a part of the curriculum as more academic learning. An especially chilling anecdote is recounted by Mary Crawford Fraser, who had been a pupil at her aunt Elizabeth Sewell's small boarding-school on the Isle of Wight. Reading aloud from *Cranford* one evening, her aunt came to a sudden full stop at the beginning of the episode 'where the nephew plays a practical joke—something connected with a baby—on the old ladies'. She skipped a little, and took up the story later on. The copy of *Cranford* was left on the table in the drawing-room that evening, a silently teasing presence to the girls who came to do their piano practice there, although not, Fraser believes, a deliberate test. One girl, however, could not resist the temptation, and nearly coaxed Fraser into sharing her discovery, but the narrator went off and informed her aunts. They showed no mercy, blaming themselves for having admitted, for the first time, a girl from the wrong kind of background. 'Poor Rosie, with her bar sinister of Trade, had had no opportunity of learning what honour meant.' Despite the protestations of all the girls that Rosie had merely carried into action the promptings of their own curiosity, she was expelled. As Fraser recalls it, the departing girl seemed like a scapegoat for their shared desire to read forbidden material.[46]

As one might anticipate, anecdotes can be found within autobiographies which show the gap between theory and practice: there is plenty of evidence of girls responding to the presence of books in ways which undercut the pedagogic theory which surrounded reading within schools. This demonstrates the absurd lengths to which the authorities went in order to ensure that rules were applied, and the anxiety that they were capable of manifesting when the reading of their charges looked as though it was taking a dangerously independent path. Another former Queen's College student, Mimi Bartick-Baker, was a friend of Katherine Mansfield Beauchamp's, a boarder at the school from 1893, and they had 'long discussions over Tolstoy, Maeterlinck and Ibsen, in the lower corridor. We came in an hour earlier for this, and were suspected of immorality', although whether because of their choice of literary subject-matter or their personal intimacy is not made clear.[47] Margaret Cole, sent to the girls' school Roedean in 1907, recalls that their reading was censored: 'unsuitable story-books were confiscated and not returned till the end of term—if necessary with a note of warning to the parents.' But it was not just fiction which was deemed unsuitable: the right text at the right time was a matter of protocol. Girls in the top forms were allowed to read, she recollects, in a small school library at the end of the assembly hall, but she forfeited that privilege when a sub-prefect reported her for reading Macaulay's *Essays* during preparation time, despite the fact that she had finished her allocated French task. Macaulay,

---

[46] Mrs Hugh Fraser, *A Diplomat's Wife in Many Lands* (1910), 227–8.
[47] Grylls, *Queen's College*, 68.

Hazlitt, Kipling, Browning, and others had to be smuggled up into Cole's bedroom in a large embroidery bag, 'since reading—though not sewing—in one's bedroom except on Sunday morning was prohibited and rated a discipline mark if one was caught'.[48] The other side to Dorothea Beale's literary enthusiasms is given by Janet Courtney, remembering her time at Cheltenham Ladies' College in the early 1890s, and the headmistress's 'persistence in holding up as ideals the women of Chaucer and Spenser, whose pictured presentiments filled the stained-glass college windows. How tired we used to get of Britomart and Una!'[49] One also imagines that Beale would have been less than delighted at Annabel Huth Jackson's memory of the impact which a copy of Swinburne's *Poems and Ballads* made at Cheltenham: 'half the house went mad over it and we copied out most of the book because we could not afford to buy it.'[50] What is notable about all these examples is that the writers are presenting their chosen reading material as more serious and stimulating than the official texts selected for them.

In the early years of the twentieth century, developments in pedagogical theory led to the formulation of various ideas about what happens in reading and learning processes in terms which overtly placed less emphasis on inculcating social propriety, but demonstrated concern with the workings of the young person's mind in terms which remain familiar today. The role played by reading in imitative role-playing, for example, was taken up by Professor Edgar, from the University of St Andrews, in *Child-Study* (1908). He claimed that it was time that psychology recognize the Platonic value of imitation, and continued, with no reference, admittedly, to girls:[51]

The heroes of legend and story—especially the simpler types of the distant past—find entrance into their hearts and minds. Because Plato knew this, he began the child's education with stories about gods and heroes—deeds worthy of being emulated, characters and lives worthy of being imitated, and he banished from his ideal state all stories or legends which 'imitated' or 'represented' actions or lives unworthy of being models for a boy.

Imitation, he points out, does not operate upon a *tabula rasa*, but reveals both a child's 'natural' tendencies, and its capacities.[52] Later the same year, H. Davy, president of the British Medical Association, built on this theory by claiming that it is 'necessary to choose children's literature having in view the "ideals" we

---

[48] Margaret Cole, *Growing up into Revolution* (1949), 27–32.

[49] Janet E. Courtney, *Recollected in Tranquillity* (1926), 114.

[50] Annabel Huth Jackson, *A Victorian Childhood* (1932), 160.

[51] By the turn of the century, it became noticeable that educational theory—particularly that concerning the younger child—was far less likely to take gender as a factor into consideration than had been the case throughout the nineteenth century. This is especially true of work emanating, as so much of it did, from the United States.

[52] J. Edgar, 'Individuality and Imitation in Children', *Child-Study: The Journal of the Child-Study Society*, 1 (1908), 16–17. Edgar appears to be drawing on G. Stanley Hall's stress, in *Adolescence* (1904), on the importance of reviving 'the ancestral experiences and occupations of the race' through introducing children to tales of the heroic (I. xi).

wish them to form from their reading'.[53] The importance of such views does not particularly lie in their contents. These replicate the principles of much nineteenth-century educational practice, and of the wider belief, which we have amply seen already, in the affective power of literature. One could instance such biographical compilations like John Maw Darton's *Famous Girls, who have become Illustrious Women* or Catherine Mary MacSorley's *A Few Good Women, and what they teach us*, which were discussed in the introduction. And to look back to just one earlier educational commentator: Robert Johnson, director of Education at the Belsize College for Ladies, in a conservative *Lecture on Female Education* of 1860, in which his belief in women's inferior intellectual power came across strongly, nevertheless advocated a balanced, systematic programme of education for girls, in which the reading of biography had a particularly important part to play:

For our purpose it should be very full in its accounts of Eminent Women, honourably distinguished for the faithful and intelligent discharge of their duties, not only under extraordinary circumstances of difficulty and danger, but in the unusual vocations of common life. I specifically mention the latter object, because it meets a prejudice that the young are very apt to imbibe, that high attainments are wanted chiefly for 'great actions.' Truly great actions are duties properly fulfilled, however insignificant and trivial they may individually appear; and I believe it will be found, on trial, to be much easier, under the influence of powerful excitement, to enact for a moment the brilliant part of a heroine, than for a long series of years, and with the ordinary vicissitudes of fortune, to discharge with dignity and grace the unobtrusive, and perhaps unappreciated, duties of a Wife and a Mother.[54]

But what was new about Edgar's work was that ideas linking reading with identificatory practice were being put across in a new educational journal, supposedly building on the latest theories in the field. However, as Carol Dyhouse has shown, both *Child-Study* and the *Paidologist* were heavily dependent on G. Stanley Hall's views on adolescence.[55] And here, we should note that in *Adolescence* (1904), Hall had some specific comments to make about women's reading. In part, these relate to its content. He claims that the fact that girls, past the age of ten, pick masculine heroes in their literature is indicative that they are not being provided with 'adequate womanly ideals in history or literature'.[56] None the less, he gives no reasons, other than an unsupported belief in instinct, why girls should prefer to read about the Virgin Mary or Beatrice Clotilda de Vaux, or the 'rich anthology of noble mothers' who have preceded them, so that one is left to presume that he values such role-models because of the degree to which they re-enforce the social desirability of

---

[53] H. Davy, 'The Cultivation of the Mind in Children', *Child-Study*, 1 (1908), 51.

[54] Robert Johnson, *A Lecture on Female Education* (1860), 24.

[55] Dyhouse, *Girls Growing up*, 129.

[56] G. Stanley Hall, *Adolescence: Its Psychology and its Relation to Physiology, Anthropology, Sociology, Sex, Crime, Religion, and Education* (New York, 1904), 619.

maternity.[57] This tallies with the fact that Hall also advises methods of education which 'keep the purely mental back' and use 'every method to bring the intuitions to the fore'.

Bookishness is probably a bad sign in a girl; it suggests artificiality, pedantry, the lugging of dead knowledge. Mere learning is not the ideal, and prodigies of scholarship are always morbid. The rule should be to keep nothing that is not to become practical; to open no brain tracts which are not to be highways for the daily traffic of thought and conduct; not to overburden the soul with the impedimenta of libraries and records of what is far off in time or zest, and always to follow truly the guidance of *normal and spontaneous* interests widely interpreted.[58]

So far as she is taught psychology, for example, it should be on the 'genetic basis of animals and children': so far as philosophy goes, 'if a woman Descartes ever arises, she will put life before theory', valuing sentiments and feelings in everything above intellect.[59] Such theories, however much they might apparently partake in a spirit of newness and social change (articles on reading in *Child-Study*, for example, appear side by side with some fascinating material about the early cinema) ultimately reinscribe women into an educational system which sets them up for their presumed role as mothers at home and within the Empire.[60] Not that there was anything new about this, as Kingsley's 1848 lecture showed.

It is in the light of this last point that one can see a communality of interest among educationists who based their premisses about a girl's education on assumptions about her physical make-up and consequent social role, and those who were concerned with the relationship between her education and the facts which she absorbed. For English literature was not just valued within girls' education because of the humanist influences which it might impart, or the heroic models which it might offer. It could also be studied in conjunction with the history of the language, which not only linked it, with some methodological rigour, to the formal teaching of grammar, but which, more notably, could be used to impart a sense of both national identity and continuity. At the broadest level, we find this belief voiced by Miss Kennedy in her inaugural speech as Headmistress of Leeds Girls' High School: 'no course of education would be complete which did not impart to the pupil a sufficient familiarity with the earlier structure of our language, to enable them to read with facility such monuments of English literature as the "Canterbury Tales" or the "Vision of Piers Plowman".'[61] A series of articles in the *Journal of the Women's Education*

---

[57] Ibid. 635.
[58] Ibid. 640, emphasis added.
[59] Ibid. 644.
[60] For connections between the eugenics movement and progressive thought, see Michael Freeden, 'Eugenics and Progressive Thought: A Study in Ideological Affinity', *Historical Journal*, 22 (1979), 645–71.
[61] Miss Kennedy, quoted in an unsigned article, 'The Leeds Girls' High School', *Journal of the Women's Education Union*, 4 (1876), 144.

Union, where this speech was reported, took English teachers through a rapid summary of earlier authors and works, on the premiss that

if the present daylight world of literature appears to us with a background only of blank darkness for its past; if all these full-grown creations of the mind are, apparently, without beginning or growth—effects without a cause—we may be sure that they cannot be rightly valued or understood.

The writer goes on to praise the "Gleeman's Song", the *Battle of Finnisburgh*, and *Beowulf*, before singling out Cædmon for special commendation as the first genuine English poet, setting him up in thought, imagery, and style as a worthy compatriot of Milton.[62]

These comments help one understand, in part, why school syllabuses could place a great deal of importance on formal questions to do with the history of the language. But less idealistic reasoning doubtless informed the construction of syllabuses: the preparation of schoolgirls for the examinations which they would have to take. Success in examinations was, for many schools, a means of advertising their own worth, and attracting and keeping their pupils in an expanding competitive field. Whilst educationists paid lip service to the humanist qualities which could be transmitted through reading and studying English literature, the translation of such ideals into the setting of examination questions did not seem possible for the Victorians or Edwardians. Discursive essays were rarely invited. Thus a two-hour paper for the Senior Local Examinations, taken by girls leaving school at eighteen, might pose five grammatical questions ('What is meant by "phonetic decay"?'; 'What is the force of the English prefix *for*? What of the prefix *um*?'); and require the identification of the author and a brief description of a list of ten works, from 'The White Doe of Rylstone' to *The Fable of the Bees*. The girl who was asked to give 'some account' of 'the fourth period of Shakespeare's career as a dramatist' and of 'Addison's periodical essays'; to locate ten quotations from poems (which can all be found in Palgrave's *Golden Treasury*); to 'Give as accurate an account as you can of "Il Pensoroso," or "The Passions," or the two poems in which Wordsworth's "Matthew" appears'; to answer three contextual questions on *The Merchant of Venice* and *Hamlet*; to write textual notes on ten brief quotations (from 'We have done but greenly | In *hugger-mugger* to inter him' to 'Some men there are love not a *gaping pig*', and finally, to give the substance of Belial's speech 'in the infernal consultation', and to 'exhibit your acquaintance with some lyrical passage of "Comus".'[63] In the light of this, it is hardly surprising that a significant proportion of autobiographers claim that they were kept so busy at school that there was scarcely any time for recreational reading.

[62] 'On Early English Language and Literature, with reference to the Cambridge Local Examinations', ibid. 74, 76.

[63] This examination paper is given in full by Pascoe, in *Schools for Girls*, 126–8: he cites it approvingly as an example of the standards which can be reached by schools, advocating competitive public examinations 'as affording the only satisfactory guarantee to parents that their children are being properly educated' (p. 88).

This anxious over-filling of a timetable could, understandably, have counter-productive effects. An article on 'Boarding-Schools for Girls', in the *Victoria Magazine* in 1877, lamented that: 'for our own part, we think, there is some excuse for the young lady who, after "cramming" for a year or two at her final school, puts her books on an upper shelf with a sigh of relief, and determines to read nothing in future but three-volume novels.' Recognizing a need for escapism, but not acknowledging any lasting value in it, Lucy Soulsby, writing twenty years later, used a fondness for light fiction as a stick with which to beat over-demanding methods of education. Speaking to mothers at a drawing-room meeting, and subsequently publishing her address, she complained against the current tendency for a girl's 'faculties and vitality' to be completely absorbed by her lessons: 'We can hardly blame her if, in her leisure moments, she craves complete relaxation, and turns entirely to tennis and to novels—very trashy novels, too—never having intellectual vigour to spare for the old-fashioned hobbies. Overwork means frivolity.'[64]

As differing pressures mounted during the remainder of the century—the pressures to be seen to be giving value for money; to be protecting girls from the thoughts and habits which might develop if they had too much unregulated free time; to be achieving good results in public examinations—so did such anxieties. It is around this context that positions in the debate about literature and girls' education became established. On the one hand, to study literature was, as we have seen, conceived of as a means of training the imagination and developing sympathy: 'womanly' characteristics, as they were commonly described. At the same time, it was considered capable of stimulating thought, understanding, and deepening social commitment in fields which reached far beyond the domestic—something which necessarily had both conservative and radical implications. On the other, the regulation of study which accompanied such reading could be envisaged as stifling the very impulses which acquaintance with literary texts was designed to foster. Whereas the 1869 commissioners found little evidence of formal grammar being taught in schools, with girls 'never invited to study a poem critically, to examine its archaic words, to hunt out all its allusions, or exhaust its meaning',[65] by 1904 the novelist Flora Annie Steel was complaining that her daughter, at a high school, 'wrote criticisms on the literary work of the Early Victorian era and would have learnt to parse on Milton's sonnets had I not struck at the sacrilege'.[66] Moreover, the risk was perceived of a whiplash effect, with too much formal analysis leading the young reader straight back to seeking escapist solace in non-demanding fiction.

[64] Soulsby, *Home Rule, or Daughters of To-Day* (Oxford, 1894), 30–1.
[65] Mr Fitch, giving evidence concerning Yorkshire schools, in Beale, *Reports Issued by the Schools' Inquiry Commission*, 38.
[66] Letter from F. A. Steel, 'The Reading of Upper-Class Girls', *Saturday Review* (5 Nov. 1904), 578.

The degree to which scholarly specialization and formal methodology should be encouraged in the study of literature; the timing, in educational terms, of the introduction of formal questions into such study; the issue of whether literature should be envisaged as a broad-based humanist discipline, or whether such an attitude encourages the unquestioning acceptance of dominant ideological standpoints: these are unresolved, and unresolvable problems which remain with us. What we can see here is how these issues have their origins in the ways in which literature was approached in girls' schools in the nineteenth century. This shows, above all, how scholarly practices in reading literature were seen, where girls were concerned, as de-feminizing the subject of study.[67] Yet to be placed against this was the fact that using literature to cultivate both the imagination, and the powers of subjective response to emotional and aesthetic factors, meant encouraging precisely those non-critical reading practices which induced concern in both protective and feminist commentators alike.

[67] Simultaneously, however, studying English literature could still, in traditional circles, be thought of as an effeminate thing for a man to do. Vera Brittain records that at Oxford, where the Final Honours School in English Language and Literature was established in 1893, the subject was popularly known as 'pink sunsets' until after the First World War (*The Women at Oxford* (1960), 40).

7   Reading in the Periodical Press

All the contexts in which the woman reader has been considered thus far have been, broadly speaking, prescriptive. Moreover, they have inscribed the issue of women and reading within larger institutional and cultural frameworks. But one also encounters this issue in less overtly prescriptive contexts. In the final chapter of Part II, I shall examine the ways in which reviews and articles served to consolidate Victorian and Edwardian assumptions about women as readers. On the one hand, they drew on the ideas developed in the texts which I have already cited. On the other, particularly in the later part of the period, they attempted to establish for themselves evidence which confirmed or challenged generalized perceptions of the subject.

In the case of magazine articles—apart from those which offered practical advice about methods of reading, and which were considered in Chapter 5—the woman reader was encountered in a number of guises. First, understandably, she formed a frequent category of reference or appeal in book reviews. Occasionally the focus of the review was itself a text about reading; more frequently, the terms of the criticism indicate that gender distinction was adopted by many critics as a means of classification, and that attributes commonly associated with woman readers (usually unflatteringly, and especially regarding their intellect or discrimination) proved a useful shorthand for judging the literary merits of a work. Second, types of the woman reader appear in many chatty, conversational articles: often couched in terms of heavy-handed humour which quickly betray the masculine perch of superiority from which they were written. Third, and most immediately interesting from a socio-historical point of view, are those articles, growing in number towards the end of the century and into the Edwardian period, which claimed to investigate precisely what girls or women were reading. Additionally, if woman was 'other', a topic for investigation and prescription for quite a few of these journalistic correspondents, so, in her turn, the working-class woman reader was doubly 'other', and formed a separate area for study. And finally, the question of access to suitable reading material for working-class women, particularly in cities, leads into the way in which women's reading practices were considered as part of the whole debate about how best to set up facilities in public libraries. In all of this, the different audiences for periodical publications are presented with a variety of assumptions about the woman reader, deriving from, and in their turn serving different social and ideological stances. Necessarily, this is particularly apparent when one examines the periodicals which appeared from within the growing ranks of the women's movement.

Women Readers and the Reviewers

Consider the central picture in Augustus Egg's triptych, *Past and Present* (1858) (Fig. 12). In the foreground lies, prostrate, the wife and mother whose adultery has been disclosed, one presumes, by the correspondence which her devastated husband is reading. Behind her, her daughters look up in shocked surprise, the card castle which they had been building collapsing to the floor. This castle had as its foundation a yellow-covered volume, on the spine of which one can clearly read the name 'Balzac'.[1] Corruption has entered the home through French fiction, eating into its basis as surely as the worm is rotting the apple which also, symbolically, lies split open on the floor. The implications of reading this particular author had been made clear in a number of articles and reviews. G. H. Lewes wrote, emphatically, that: 'By dwelling on the myriad affectations (usually characterized by him as adorable) of the *dame comme il faut*; by his very talent for penetrating into the secret springs of vanity and display, he corrupts the taste of his admiring reader. He should be strictly forbidden to young women.'[2] Such resonances were readily taken up by those critics able to decode Egg's picture, notably Tom Taylor in *The Times*, who called the French novel 'a Hogarthian indication of the source of [the] mother's perversion',[3] and John Ruskin, who in a private letter amplified the implications of the woman's probable reading habits. For him, Balzac would not be to blame if properly read, but a superficial reading, based on expectations raised by English fiction, would have been likely to have contributed to her downfall:

The picture does not pretend to represent a very pretty story—but a piece of very commonplace vice—an ordinary husband—employed at some house in the city—an ordinary wife—who can't read French well enough to understand the least bit of de Balzac's subtlety or Sand's nobleness but who reads Bulwer, or James, and Harrison Ainsworth; who has been seduced by a sham count, with a moustache—and who has mixed his lost letter with unexpected Christmas bills.[4]

The French Novel was a topos familiar in Victorian reviews and other cultural forms, carrying with it, despite Ruskin's qualification, the generic assumptions of its power to corrupt. Commentators found themselves unable to be precise in print, however, about what exactly they regarded as unacceptable about this foreign fiction. Although able to refer in generalized terms to 'its vile

[1] For the reception of Balzac's novels in England, see Clarence R. Decker, 'Balzac's Literary Reputation in Victorian Society', *PMLA* 47/2 (1932), 1150–7. Egg's triptych has been widely discussed. See esp. Teri J. Edelstein, 'Augustus Egg's Triptych: A Narrative of Victorian Adultery', *Burlington Magazine*, 125 (1983), 202–10; Lynda Nead, *Myths of Sexuality: Representations of Women in Victorian Britain* (Oxford, 1988), 71–8.

[2] [G. H. Lewes] 'Balzac and George Sand', *Foreign Quarterly Review*, (1844), 273.

[3] *The Times* (22 May 1858), 9.

[4] John Ruskin, quoted by John Lewis Bradley, 'An Unpublished Ruskin Letter', *Burlington Magazine*, 100 (1958), 25.

12. Augustus Leopold Egg, 'August the 4th. Have just heard that B—— has been dead more than a fortnight, so his poor children have now lost both parents. I hear she was seen on Friday last near the Strand, evidently without a place to lay her head. What a fall hers has been! known as Past and Present, No. 1 (1858)

morality and its vitiated taste', W. R. Greg, for example, writing in the *National Review*, defines it, as though it itself partakes of the discourse surrounding contemporary womanhood, through incorporating the terms both of medical science and of formal legislature in his attack. But he is unable to speak of what most repels:

We shall have to analyse its elements and its sources without being able adequately to exemplify or prove the correctness of our diagnosis by the most flagrant and conclusive specimens. We shall have to use the strongest language and to pronounce the most unmeasured condemnation, while we are precluded by the very nature of the case from justifying the sentence by adducing and detailing before our readers the most heinous of the offences which have called it forth.[5]

Moreover, whilst the subject-matter of French fiction was often condemned in its own right, its reputation also suffered through contiguity, since France was the customary source of imported pornography. Hence, as well as corrupting, French fiction could also, it was presumed, excite. Indeed, its potential for excitement made corruption the more likely. Nor was this stimulation solely linked with private enjoyment of a text, but had its social implications. In the late 1880s, the *Saturday Review* summed up the allure of the music-halls and restaurants which are frequented by the *demi-monde* by claiming that there is the same attraction in going to these places as there is in reading French novels 'of more than doubtful morality', and continues: 'Let it be known that there is a book out that is hardly decent, and the rush for it is immense among our young married ladies, and even among some of the elder spinsters. Indeed, not to have read any book that is more indecent than usual is to be out of the fashion.'[6] The quintessential work of French fiction in the mid-century was not in fact taken to be by Balzac, despite, as we have seen, the fact that he could provoke disapproving reactions, but a novel which appeared the year before Egg's picture: Gustave Flaubert's *Madame Bovary* (1857). Fitzjames Stephen commented, before going on to discuss the book at length in the *Saturday Review*, that it 'is not a work which we can recommend any man, far less any woman, to read': an opinion based both on the representation of Madame Bovary herself as a woman apparently deficient in any sense of duty or responsibility, and on the yet more damaging fact that Flaubert does not seem to have presumed that his readers possess any capacity for making moral distinctions themselves.[7] Stephen omits to mention, however, the fact that Flaubert himself suggests that one of the prime reasons for Madame Bovary's imagination taking the direction it does is the romance-reading in which she indulged at her convent school. For six months, 'Emma se graissa donc les mains' with the stories smuggled into the school in a maid's apron. She absorbed the historical melodrama of Walter Scott, and feasted on the

[5] [W. R. Greg] 'French Fiction: The Lowest Deep', *National Review*, 11 (1860), 402–3.
[6] 'Young Married Women', *Saturday Review* (23 July 1887), 113.
[7] [Fitzjames Stephen] 'Madame Bovary', *Saturday Review* (11 July 1857), 40–1.

sentimentalism of keepsake volumes. The fictional images which she ingested at that time feed into her self-image when she becomes fatally involved with Rodolphe: 'elle se rappela les héroïnes des livres qu'elle avait lus, et la légion lyrique de ces femmes adultères se mit à chanter dans sa mémoire avec des voix de sœurs qui la charmaient.'[8]

There were, however, other ways in which the practice of alluding to French fiction could be employed beyond incorporating it as a signifier of the presence of sexuality within a text. Above all, it could be turned into a means of celebrating English superiority in bringing up girls, the presence of certain texts within the home provoking the same anxieties about undesirable influences within the domestic circle as might be excited by a foreign governess. Parents should be on their guard against the latter, Shirreff states openly in *Intellectual Education*, 'lest instead of repressing she should rather cultivate sensibility as something interesting, and encourage the exhibition of emotion'.[9] An article on 'French Novels' in Mary Braddon's magazine, *Belgravia*, in 1867, makes clear the variations in domestic styles which facilitate the assumption of this cultural difference. 'While advising every prudent mother to prevent her girls from dipping indiscriminately into the perennial spring of French literature', the writer none the less repudiates the idea that the moral practices of France and England are in fact radically different. What is different is the relative amount of freedom afforded to young women. In France they are strait-jacketed by convention, shackled to chaperones: marriage is seen as 'the only outlet to her prison walls'. The name of 'wife', it is argued, brings with it relative freedom, rather than suggesting, as it does for the English girl, 'a weight of duty which rather damps than elates her young hopes'. Under such circumstances, a French girl is hardly likely to be presented as an interesting heroine if unmarried, since the foreign writer is unlikely to show her as capable of experiencing passion, uncertainty, liberty. Such characteristics must be postponed until after marriage: however, 'it is revolting to the true English sense of delicacy to see matrons, mothers, and wives exposed to declarations and protestations which degrade them'.[10]

---

[8] Gustave Flaubert, *Madame Bovary* (Paris, 1857; édn. déf., 1875), 39. For a valuable discussion of the importance of Emma Bovary's reading, see Carla L. Peterson, *The Determined Reader: Gender and Culture in the Novel from Napoleon to Victoria* (New Brunswick, 1986), 161–75.

[9] Emily Shirreff, *Intellectual Education and its Influence on the Character and Happiness of Women*, (1858) 142.

[10] 'M', 'French Novels', *Belgravia*, 3 (1867), 78–9. Robert Lee Wolff, in his biography *Sensational Victorian: The Life and Fiction of Mary Elizabeth Braddon* (1979) points out that most of *Belgravia*'s articles were in fact written by Braddon herself. He implicitly alerts one, too, to a certain two-facedness in this article, since Braddon was borrowing from Balzac in her current novel, *Dead Sea Fruit*, and had adapted *Madame Bovary* itself in order to provide the plot of *The Doctor's Wife* (1864). Access to over-stimulating reading material may not have been as difficult for young French women as Braddon imagines, however, considering the number of contemporary warnings to be found in French advice manuals and studies of womanhood at the time: see e.g. Auguste Debay, *Physiologie descriptive des trente beautés de la femme* (6th edn., 1877), 224–5, 253–4; Mgr. Dupauloup, *La Femme studieuse* (1869), 36–55; Madame Romieu, *La Femme au XIXe siècle* (1858), 38–9; Evaniste Thévenin, *Le Mariage au XIXe siècle: ce qu'il est—ce qu'il doit être* (1862), 157–72.

In general, throughout the whole period, the claim that a volume was unsuitable for girls, even for women, primarily acted as reviewers' shorthand for the fact that it contained material which, by the standards of the time, was sexually explicit, even faintly bawdy, and should be kept from 'our tender young girls, the margin of ignorance, and, if you will, ignorance, which we are all heartily glad to believe in'.[11] Thus—to take a couple of random examples from the very many which would be possible—the *Eclectic Review* complained that *Pickwick Papers* contained 'some jokes, incidents, and allusions, which could hardly be read by a modest woman without blushing'.[12] Such views prompted Dickens, when publishing the novel in book form, to write in his preface that 'throughout this book, no incident or expression occurs which could call a blush into the most delicate cheek'.[13] But by 1840, he was warning John Overs, preparing material for *Evenings of a Working Man* (1844) that writers should beware of putting anything into print which could not be said 'anywhere': 'Mrs. Scutfidge may have stripped in public—I have no doubt she did—but I should be sorry to have to tell young ladies so in the nineteenth century, for all that.'[14] A few years later, Charles Kingsley, writing in *Fraser's Magazine*, noted the 'coarseness' of *The Tenant of Wildfell Hall* 'which will be the stumbling block of most readers, and which makes it utterly unfit to be put into the hands of girls'.[15] As we shall see in chapter 10, the sensation novels of the 1860s were especially liable to call forth apprehension about their effects on young women readers. The *London Review*'s critic, for example, used language suggestive of sexual assault to condemn Charles Reade's *Griffith Gaunt* (appearing simultaneously in England in the *Argosy* and in America in the *Atlantic Monthly*): 'the publishers have no right to use their magazine to insult young girls and virtuous women by thrusting upon them what no modest woman can read without a blush.'[16] This remark helped ensure both that the book was regarded as controversial, and established the terms of this controversy. Thus the *Spectator* affirmed that, in fact, 'there is not throughout the book one scene the most pure-minded woman might hesitate to read';[17] Edwin Arnold, after praising the novel in the *Daily Telegraph* wrote directly to Reade to add further personalized testimony, stating

---

[11] [Margaret Oliphant] 'The Condition of Women', *Blackwood's Edinburgh Magazine*, 83 (1858), 151.

[12] 'Posthumous Papers of the Pickwick Club', *Eclectic Review*, NS 1 (1837), 353.

[13] Charles Dickens, preface to *The Pickwick Papers* (1837; repr. Oxford, 1986). Dickens is here deliberately recalling, it would seem, the vocabulary of Thomas Bowdler, who in his Preface to *The Family Shakespeare* (4 vols. (1807), i, p. vi), wrote: 'it is hoped that the present publication will be approved by those who wish to make the young reader acquainted with the various beauties of this writer, unmixed with any thing that can raise a blush on the cheek of modesty.'

[14] Charles Dickens to John Overs (30 Dec. 1840), Madeline House and Graham Storey (eds.), *Letters of Charles Dickens*, ii. *1840–1841* (Oxford, 1969), 177.

[15] [Charles Kingsley] 'Recent Novels', *Fraser's Magazine*, 39 (1849), 424.

[16] *London Review* (11 Aug. 1866), 167, quoting the New York *Round Table*.

[17] 'Griffith Gaunt', *Spectator* (27 Oct. 1866), 1198.

that although 'in morals they call me a Puritan . . . I lent the book to my sister when I had read it'.[18] In a different controversy of the same year, Richard Grant White, reviewing Swinburne's *Poems and Ballads* (1866) in the *Galaxy* claimed that 'the woman who cannot read any of these herself without harm, is already long past mental contamination',[19] a view expressed by English as well as American critics. Alfred Austin, in a long piece for the *Temple Bar* in 1869 on the state of English poetry, also mentions, in passing, that no one would dream of pretending that Swinburne's 'lyrics and ballads are fit for the sole or even for part of the diet of girls'.[20] But his major concern is to repudiate Swinburne's claim that in some way his poetry may be thought of as 'masculine', and to launch, in his turn, an attack on what he sees as the whole tendency towards effeminacy in contemporary poetry—as exemplified especially by Swinburne and, before him, by Tennyson. In showing that literature may have the power to undermine manliness as well as to corrupt the feminine, he provides a reminder that the issue of gendered suitability in reading contributed directly towards the maintenance of a doctrine of separate spheres.

Where the figure of the woman reader was not directly called upon in a review, tropes of femininity could make her silent presence act with censorious force. Peter Bayne, reviewing the 1850 edition of *Wuthering Heights*, claimed that the effect of this and analogous 'spectacles is brutalizing', as though the reader is forced to watch a shamefully public display of cruelty; the general effect of the work of Ellis Bell or Edgar Poe 'is to produce a mental state alien to the calm energy and quiet homely feelings of real life'. They make the 'soul the slave of stimulants', and, temporarily fostering 'morbid irritability', they have a patently de-womanizing effect, since they 'shrivel and dry up those sympathies which are the most tender, delicate, and precious'.[21] Additionally, the belittling assumption that women read for escape, rather than for intellectual or political stimulation, fed into comments such as George Gissing's claim (admittedly not publicly communicated) for his novel *Workers in the Dawn*: 'It is *not* a book for women and children, but for thinking and struggling *men*.'[22] Thomas Hardy suffered from the same limiting belief that women read largely for wholesome entertainment when he submitted 'The Withered Arm' to *Longman's Magazine* in 1887, to be told that it was much too grim and unrelieved for a magazine mostly read by girls.[23] By contrast, a book could prove easy for a reviewer to

[18] Edwin Arnold, quoted in Charles L. Reade and the Revd. Compton Reade, *Charles Reade, Dramatist, Novelist, Journalist: A Memoir*, 2 vols. (1887), ii. 181–2.

[19] Richard Grant White, 'Mr Swinburne's Poems', *Galaxy*, 2 (1866), 639.

[20] [Alfred Austin] 'The Poetry of the Period (No. III): Mr Swinburne', *Temple Bar*, 26 (1869), 457.

[21] Peter Bayne, *Essays in Biography and Criticism*, 1st ser. (1857), quoted in Miriam Allott (ed.), *The Brontës: The Critical Heritage* (1974), 325.

[22] George Gissing, *Letters of George Gissing to Members of his Family*, collected and arranged by Algernon and Ellen Gissing (1927), 74.

[23] C. J. Longman to Hardy, 27 Sept. 1887, cited by Michael Millgate, *Thomas Hardy: A Biography* (Oxford, 1982), 288.

categorize as suitable, potentially popular women's reading if its style and subject-matter itself adhered to prevalent views about what was most desirable in womanhood. Thus a critic in the *National Magazine*, in 1858, commended Margaret Oliphant's *Orphans* for its 'delicacy' of handling, and for exuding 'an atmosphere of goodness and holiness, and that cheerfulness which is only attainable through sorrow . . . a book that only a woman would have written, and that no woman will read without feeling her heart warm to the author.'[24]

The general moral respectability of the novel as a genre became well established by the 1880s.[25] But the figure of the woman or, more frequently, the adolescent girl, in need of protection from the corrupting possibilities of print was so well established that it remained in force until the First World War. It provided, of course, the standard which George Moore attacked so scathingly in his assault on the stranglehold which Mudie in particular, and the circulating library system in general, exercised on what might and might not profitably be published. As Guinevere Griest has recorded, Mudie prided himself on the wholesome moral tone of the volumes on his shelves, and this fact was picked up repeatedly by contemporary commentators. These same commentators took as axiomatic, and in their turn reinforced, the assumption that women principally consumed fiction. Hain Friswell, for example, writing in 1871, noted that about a third of Mudie's stock consisted of novels, but that these, although they may be romantic, are 'noble and pure', and reminded the readers of *London Society* that one should not grudge their consumption, since fiction provided possibly the only sort of education which many middle- and 'higher' class women could be said to have.[26] It was, however, the precise nature of this education which gave rise to debate. Two 'ladies from the country', for example, wrote to Mudie complaining against the type of education which his

---

[24] 'Women's Novels', *National Magazine*, 3 (1858), 277.

[25] Kenneth Graham, *English Criticism of the Novel 1865–1900* (Oxford, 1965).

[26] Hain Friswell, 'Circulating Libraries: Their Contents and their Readers', *London Society*, 20 (1871), 523. Whilst Mudie has received most attention because of his attempt to legislate moral standards through his provision, or his refusal to provide, certain texts, it also seems that he saw the question of suitability of reading material in class terms, as is implied by his choice of the adjective 'select' in the full title of his library. It was his stated belief that he had erected 'a barrier of some kind' between his subscribers 'and the lower floods of literature' (Charles Edward Mudie, quoted in an unsigned article, 'Mr. Mudie's Library', *Athenaeum* (6 Oct. 1860), 451). Whilst the specific system which Mudie did so much to establish collapsed with the rapid demise of the three-decker novel after 1894, the idea, at least, that circulating libraries might act as guardians of public morality lasted into the twentieth century. In 1909, the 'Circulating Libraries Association' was formed, which brought together Mudie, W. H. Smiths, Boots, Day's, Cawthorn and Hutt, and the Times Book Club, their object being the classification of books offered them into three categories: satisfactory, doubtful, and objectionable. The first two lists which they in fact compiled were of books they would not handle—including George Moore's *Memoirs of My Dead Life*—and those whose issue they would restrict. The latter included Mrs Havelock Ellis, *Kit's Woman*; Ernest Thurston, *Sally Bishop*; Netta Syrett, *Child of Promise*; H. G. Wells, *Ann Veronica*; Henry Handel Richardsons' *Maurice Guest*; Dion Calthorpe, *Everybody's Secret*, and Stanley Hyatt, *Black Sheep* (Janet Courtney, *Recollected in Tranquillity* (1926), 194–7).

readers might receive from the scene in Moore's *A Modern Lover* (1883) in which Gwynne sits to her penniless artist friend as a model for Venus.[27]

In his preface to the English translation of Zola's *Pot Bouille* (*Piping Hot!*) (1885), written after he had felt the effects of Mudie banning his novel *A Mummer's Wife* (1885), Moore complained that 'Literature and young girls are irreconcilable elements, and the sooner we leave off trying to reconcile them the better'. 'Would you or would you not give that book to your sister of sixteen to read?' was, he felt, a ridiculous standard by which to judge all literature.[28] Such a comment depended, of course, on retaining intact the figure of the pure young girl. But Moore developed his critique on the ridiculous degree of private censorship operative on English fiction in a further pamphlet of the same year, *Literature at Nurse, or Circulating Morals*, when he questioned the viability even of this stereotype. For, whilst reiterating many of his earlier points, he simultaneously maintained that a young girl is in many ways less likely to be corrupted by work which an experienced adult might regard as unsuitable, since close analysis of the passions will be of little interest to her, whilst the avowedly 'pure' work may well lead her, far more damagingly, into believing in delusive idealism:

A pair of lovers—such as Paul and Virginie—separated by cruel fate, whose lives are apparently nothing but a long cry of yearning and fidelity, who seem to live, as it were, independent of the struggle for life, is the book that more often than any other leads to sin; it teaches the reader to look to a false ideal, and gives her—for men have ceased to read in England—erroneous and superficial notions of the value of life and love.[29]

Even writers commonly thought of as conservative were soon to follow Moore in stating openly that they found the litmus paper of the imaginary young female person far too constricting, preventing them from writing openly about the complexity of relations among adults. Eliza Lynn Linton, for example, in the *New Review*'s famous symposium of 1890 on 'Candour in English Fiction', also regretted that if such a standard for novel writing was invoked, books would not 'go beyond the schoolgirl standard'. Her suggestion that 'all well-ordered houses' should contain a 'locked bookcase' for the volumes aimed at mature readers seems guaranteed, however, to raise intense curiosity precisely among those whom she would most seek to protect.[30] Although 'the British daughter' remained as a presence to be invoked into the twentieth century, the widening scope of women's lives meant that this figure was employed to stir up anxieties

[27] See George Moore, 'A New Censorship of Literature', *Pall Mall Gazette* (10 Dec. 1884), 2. It is worth noting that whilst George Gissing privately supported Moore's point of view, in subsequent correspondence in the newspaper he made the point that difficulties lay far deeper than with the means of book distribution itself: 'If you abolish the library system tomorrow, you are no nearer persuading the "two ladies in the country" (typical beings!) to let this or that work lie on their drawing room tables' (*Pall Mall Gazette* (15 Dec. 1884), 2).

[28] George Moore, preface to Émile Zola, *Piping Hot!* (1885), pp. xiv–xv.

[29] Id., *Literature at Nurse, or Circulating Morals* (1885), 22.

[30] Mrs E. Lynn Linton, 'Candour in English Fiction', *New Review*, 2 (1890), 13.

not just about sexuality, but concerning social change. H. G. Wells's *Ann Veronica* (1909) was certainly not a popular book among feminists. 'There never was such a woman as Ann Veronica, and we hope there never will be such a woman', sneered the suffragette reviewer in the *Vote*,[31] resenting the way in which Wells's character became, eventually, yet another suburban housewife. But John O'London, writing in *T.P.'s Weekly*, believed that 'the British daughter' would need a clear head to see the dangers inherent in a sympathetically portrayed heroine who finds self-fulfilment through severing her home ties without tears or remorse, and finds happiness with an adulterer.[32]

Yet it would be falsely simplistic to suggest that reviewers only constructed women readers as innocent minds in need of protection, or that suitability was judged on the contents of works alone, even in the early and mid-Victorian periods. As we shall see in the next section, *Adam Bede* was a novel which was frequently forbidden within individual homes, but which was rarely castigated for the fact or manner of the depiction of Hetty Sorel in the major reviews. This may partly have been because Hetty was perceived to be at a social distance from the probable readers: 'every one knows that every sin under heaven is committed freely in agricultural villages', commented the *Saturday Review*, for example, before going on to complain, most surprisingly to a modern reader, that Eliot is at fault in giving so much detail in the stages preceding the birth of the child, making 'the account of her misfortunes read like the rough notes of a man-midwife's conversations with a bride'.[33] The attacks on the novel's supposed immorality appeared after Eliot's pseudonymic veil was lifted, and thus can be related to the author's gender, even to her particular circumstances, rather than to what had previously been regarded as a tactful treatment of error and repentance.

Moreover *Ruth* (1853), featuring an unmarried mother even more centrally than *Adam Bede*, and with Gaskell herself showing considerable sensitivity towards its subject-matter, was warmly welcomed in some quarters. G. H. Lewes, writing in the *Westminster Review*, for example, even went so far as to suggest that the novel might have a special appeal for those who found themselves in the heroine's position:

If women are to have their lives rehabilitated, it must be through the means of women, who, noble and pure in their own lives, can speak with authority, and tell them that in this world no action is final; and that, to set the seal of despair and reprobation upon any individual during any one point of his career, is to blot out the inner life by which we live.[34]

---

[31] 'E.T.', *Vote* (23 Dec. 1909), 103.

[32] John O'London [Wilfred Whitten] *T.P.'s Weekly* (22 Oct. 1909), 537.

[33] 'Adam Bede', *Saturday Review* (26 Feb. 1859), 251. The reviewer also condemns the explicitness of Charles Reade, *White Lies* (1857), and Holme Lee (Harriet Parr), *Sylvan Holt's Daughter* (1858).

[34] [G. H. Lewes] 'Ruth and Villette', *Westminster Review*, 59 (1853), 483.

In general, critics were readier to condemn the fact that Ruth was presented as preternaturally innocent, and over-pious than that she was presented at all. They thus failed to recognize that, of course, the novel operates as a critique of the very concept of the desirability of a young woman being kept in sexual ignorance, a topic which was to recur much more explicitly in later 'New Woman' fiction. They failed to pick up, also, on the hints of barely understood passion on Ruth's part which are suggested by Gaskell through the girl's responses to nature. Critical objections were raised, too, since Ruth dies at the end of the novel, bemoaning—as Dinah Mulock, for example, complained of the ending of *The Mill on the Floss*—that such a premature removal of the heroine from the text fails to provide readers with an exemplum of the importance of continuing endurance, forebearance, and altruism as a woman grows into and through middle age.[35] Elsewhere Mulock, indeed, wrote of the inadvisability of 'tenderly reared young ladies' reading only Jane Austen or Maria Edgeworth. Far better that they be brought face to face with 'lost women' in fiction (and that they are not led to believe that the redemption of such women is an easy affair) 'than be swaddled up for ever in the folds of a silken falsehood'.[36]

In other words, even in the mid-century, the susceptibility and moral fragility of the woman reader was not nearly so frequently assumed, or commented on, in the 'quality' reviews as in more popular periodicals, or, of course, in religious journalism. This is not to say that women as writers, or the portrayal of women within fiction were not recurrent topics of concern: many of the assumptions concerning their suitability to present domestic scenes, or their sentimentalism, or their tender sympathy, drew on, and reinforced, precisely the same sets of assumptions that fed into archetypes of the woman reader. But relative silence concerning the gender of the reader may be taken as indicative of the fact that the dominant critical standard was tacitly assumed to be male, and hence the reader, except when it was convenient to invoke a woman because of the rhetorical resonances connected with her reading practices, was habitually thought to be male as well.

There were, however, exceptions to this. One was the tendency of some women reviewers (such as Dinah Mulock and Margaret Oliphant) to consider the hypothesis of a reader of their own sex. The second was the slant often taken in religious, particularly evangelical publications; and the third was the reviewing practices of feminist journals, including and following the appearance of the *English-Woman's Journal* in 1858. Such critical appraisals as Mulock's were once again based, at least rhetorically, on the assumption that women would be passive consumers, automatically influenced by what they read. Other reviewers acknowledged that women may read in an active search for exampla and role models. 'Women instinctively resort to fiction as a source of

[35] [Dinah Mulock] 'To Novelists—and a Novelist', *Macmillan's Magazine*, 3 (1861), 441–8.
[36] Mulock, *A Woman's Thoughts About Women* (1858), 290.

consolation and help' claimed the *Eclectic and Congregational Review* in 1868. They may find within it comfort and hope in their loneliness and difficulties; may, through it, find it easier to trace the Divine Finger of Providence at work in their own lives. Such an argument is turned into a plea for women who have both the necessary depth of experience and 'the genius of sympathetic insight' to turn it to the consolation and enlightenment of their sisters. George Eliot and George Sand are advanced as the supreme examples of those who have utilized their knowledge of human nature in this way.[37] Reviews of Eliot's work by women further confirm her appeal as providing worthy exempla. Anne Mozley commended the power with which domestic values are conveyed in *Adam Bede*: 'proving . . . that it is the peaceful pleasures that wind the closest round the heart, which form the habits, mould the mind, satisfy the unconscious desires and needs of our nature';[38] Edith Simcox praised the 'instructive truthfulness' of the portrayal of Dorothea and her benevolent self-sacrifice.[39]

But it certainly could not be presumed that a reader would readily identify with the interests of the morally good characters. This point is made emphatically by Mulock in the same review of *The Mill on the Floss*. Having expressed her doubt as to this novel's capacity to teach any good at all, she enquired:

What reader will not confess, with a vague sense of uneasy surprise, to have taken far less interest in all the good injured persons of the story, than in this mad *Stephen* and treacherous *Maggie*? Who that is capable of understanding—as a thing which has been or is, or one day may be—the master-passion that furnishes the key to so many lives, will not start to find how vividly this book revives it, or wakens it, or places it before him as a future possibility? Who does not think with a horribly delicious feeling, of such a crisis, when right and wrong, bliss and bale, justice and conscience, seem swept from their boundaries, and a whole existence of *Dodsons*, *Lucys*, and *Tom Tullivers*, appears worth nothing compared to the ecstasy of that 'one kiss—the last' between *Stephen* and *Maggie* in the lane.

Is this right? The spell once broken—broken with the closing of the book—every high and pure and religious instinct within us answers unhesitatingly—'No.'

Or so Mulock hopes, for the enthusiastic tones in which she describes the effects of the novel's sexual content betray her own susceptibility.[40]

Sustained opposition to women as readers, above all of fiction, was a common feature of evangelical periodicals. Especially in the early and mid-decades of the period, these were aimed at the skilled working classes and at tradespeople;

---

[37] 'Lady Novelists', *Eclectic and Congregational Review*, 15 (1868), 301–2.

[38] [Anne Mozley] *Bentley's Quarterly Review*, 1 (1859), 436.

[39] H. Lawrenny [Edith Simcox] *Academy*, 4 (1873), 2.

[40] [Mulock] 'To Novelists—and a Novelist', *Macmillan's Magazine*, 3 (1861), 447. Whilst Mulock uses the male pronoun in this passage, she makes it clear earlier in the review that she is consciously doing so throughout—even in respect to Eliot herself: 'we use the superior pronoun in a general sense, even as an author should be dealt with as a neutral being, to be judged solely by "its" work' ibid. 442.

after 1870, the factory girl and shop assistant were increasingly targeted by them. What is particularly noteworthy about this opposition, repetitive in its stress on the power of novels to engender false standards and expectations and to promote frivolity, are the sensational anecdotes which are incorporated with the design of illustrating the appalling consequences of such reading. They turn the consequences of reading fiction into a narrative itself, as inevitable in its gloomy conclusion as the romantic ending was predictable in those novelettes which were supposedly causing the corruption in the first place. 'T.C.', for example, writing in *The Christian's Penny Magazine and Friend of the People* in 1859, painted a dismal vignette:

A whole family, brought to destitution, has lately had all its misfortunes clearly traced by the authorities to an ungovernable passion for novel-reading entertained by the wife and mother. The husband was sober and industrious, but his wife was indolent, and addicted to reading everything procurable in the shape of a romance. This led her to utterly neglect her husband, herself, and her eight children. One daughter, in despair, fled the parental home and threw herself into the haunts of vice. Another was found by the police chained by the legs, to prevent her from following her sister's example. The house exhibited the most offensive appearance of filth and indigence. In the midst of this pollution, privation, and poverty, the cause of it sat reading the latest 'sensation work' of the season, and refused to allow herself to be disturbed in her entertainment.[41]

This woman, at least, had achieved the respectability of marriage before her addictive habit ruined her. Not so the protagonist of another piece of journalistic sermonizing printed in the *Wesleyan-Methodist Magazine* of 1855, in response to the question 'What is the Harm of Novel-Reading?'. The writer here places responsibility in the hands of the parent, setting up the figure of a profligate merchant who mocks the strict Presbyterian notions of his brother, and is determined that his own daughter should be brought up without the hampering restrictions which have hemmed in his nephews and nieces. So she is left at liberty to choose her own books, and soon, with narrative inexorability:

wandered in the paths of the tempter. The love-tales of her favourite authors inflamed her imagination. She dreamed and spoke of splendid matches, till she became quite unfitted for the matter-of-fact world in which her lot was cast. As for domestic duties, they were too common-place for so gay a young lady. These she would leave to the home-spun Marthas, whose genius was formed to superintend them. She possessed no fortune, but was fully prepared to spend one, should it ever come into her possession. Her course downward was fearfully rapid. Erelong she told a confidant that she would rather become the mistress of a gentleman than the wife of a tradesman!—words, alas! but premonitory. A 'gentleman' appeared as a suitor, promised marriage, abused her credulity, kept her in suspense, and then abandoned her. She was forsaken of all her friends. Misery stared her in the face. Golden dreams of sinful pleasure—the creation of novel-reading—ended in disgrace, ruin, disease, a broken heart, and an untimely grave!

[41] 'T.C.', 'Novel Reading: A Letter to a Young Lady', *Christian's Penny Magazine and Friend of the People*, 14 (1859), 155.

She passed into eternity without hope, in what might have been the very bloom of her days, leaving behind her two unhappy infants, to perpetuate her shame.[42]

In what might be termed a more specialist publication, the *Magdalen's Friend and Female Homes Intelligencer*, reading is specifically referred to as a source of immorality, producing an 'erroneous view of life in general, and of *love*, courtship, and marriage in particular'.[43] As these examples suggest, the bulk of religious-oriented criticism which dealt with the subject of women and reading concentrated on the problems posed by fiction, thus reflecting wider trends. Evangelical criticism, with its well-estabished tendency to regard fiction with suspicion, was the most outspoken in its fears about women's vulnerability.

At the other end of the spectrum of critical opinion, feminist periodicals, as one would expect, constructed their model of the woman reader in a different mould from those publications which were dedicated, overtly or implicitly, to maintaining the predominance of the domestic ethos.[44] Suffragette publications will be considered in more detail in Part III: they built on a set of emphases and expectations put forward by earlier editors, from the *Englishwoman's Review* (1866–1910) onwards. This journal, which bore the subtitle 'of Social and Industrial Questions' chose to review books which concentrated on political economy and questions of welfare, as well as works which ostensibly focused on women's issues. It thus emphasized, of course, that the condition of women was not one which could be considered in isolation from these other factors. Since most of the notices were descriptive, making great use of quotation, rather than analytical, there are very few comments which draw attention to notions of difference between women and men as either writers or readers It is notable, however, that among the many biographies it covered, some were particularly commended for the role models which they offered. Thus of W. H. Davenport Adams's *Celebrated Women Travellers of the Nineteenth Century* it was said that 'if the book serves as an encouragement to ladies to undertake independent and varied expeditions, it will have served its purpose'.[45] Very little fiction was mentioned: that which received attention, such as Mrs Eiloart's *Some of Our Girls* (1875), was pressed to serve the magazine's overall ethos, celebrating the necessity for hard work and social responsibility. Thus Eiloart is praised for her straightforward delineation of a variety of worthy types: Millicent, who cures herself of a disappointment by draining and rebuilding her village, establishing

---

[42] 'S', 'What is the Harm of Novel-reading?', *Wesleyan-Methodist Magazine*, 78 (1855), 933.

[43] 'The Great Social Evil: Mr. Harding's Second Lecture', *Magdalen's Friend and Female Homes Intelligencer*, 2 (1861), 340.

[44] For consideration of Victorian feminist periodicals, see Philippa Levine, ' "The Humanising Influences of Five O'Clock Tea": Victorian Feminist Periodicals', *Victorian Studies*, 33 (1990), 293–306. A list of such periodicals is provided by David Doughan and Denise Sanchez, *Feminist Periodicals 1855–1984: An Annotated Critical Bibliography of British, Irish, Commonwealth and International Titles* (Brighton, 1987).

[45] *Englishwoman's Review*, 14 (1883), 257.

a children's reformatory, and taking an interest in women's rights; Polly, who has not had enough professional training to carry on her father's chemist's business after his death, and must instead become a governess and companion; and Madge, the product of the workhouse system, whose sympathies are awakened when she tries herself to help some destitute children. But the *Englishwoman's Review* did not move with the times, being far less sympathetic towards late-century fiction which drew polemical attention to the politics of the home and family rather than concerning itself with more publically visible vocational and employment questions. Sarah Grand's *The Heavenly Twins* (1893) was cautioned against: 'not healthy reading for the growing youth or maiden', although 'for the fathers and mothers of growing youths and maidens it may be revelation of thoughts working unsuspected in their children's minds, a warning of dangers they were wholly careless of.'[46]

Despite these relatively isolated examples, the predominant impression given by the *Englishwoman's Review* is that a woman should not confine her reading to those topics which were generally held to concern her sex only, still less to those which, like botany or needlework, were frequently culturally assumed to be women's special province. The same is true of reviews in Emily Faithfull's *Victoria Magazine* (1863–78), which presumed an extremely wide range of interests among its readers, from glaciers to the anti-slavery cause, and from ethnology to fish-hatching. It gave, none the less, a noticeable amount of space to such works as Jessie Boucherett's *Hints on Self-Help* and Frances Power Cobbe's *Essays on the Pursuits of Women*. Moreover it did pause to warn against potentially misleading fiction, such as *Margaret Stourton; or, A Year of Governess Life*, which idealizes the occupation. Not only is the accomplished, attractive heroine fortunate enough to have her charges fall in love with her at first sight, but the family for whom she works introduces Margaret to her future husband, a local landowner and model English gentleman: 'Half-educated girls engaged in or preparing for governess life, on whom alone this book can be supposed to have any influence, may find in it materials for castle-building. They certainly will not learn from it to respect their work, or to accommodate themselves cheerfully to the real exigencies of their position.'[47]

Similar tendencies to those found in the *Englishwoman's Review* and the *Victoria Magazine* apply generally to most of the other Victorian feminist periodicals which carried book reviews: a stress on serious non-fictional reading, especially dealing with public issues, and a willingness to regard as important those publications which dealt with what was conveniently known as 'the woman question', although not emphasizing them to the exclusion of all others. Not until the appearance of the liberal-feminist *Shafts* (1892–9) does one find literary criticism which both selects particular books relevant to the interests of forward-thinking women, such as the Letters of Geraldine

[46] Ibid. 24 (1893), 198.
[47] *Victoria Magazine*, 1 (1863), 478.

Jewsbury to Jane Welsh Carlyle, or, indeed, *The Heavenly Twins*, and which
suggests that women may have different priorities from men in their methods of
reading and in the aspects of texts which they stress. Thus George Meredith's
work is praised for his capacity to portray 'the *sisterly* feeling of women',
something rarely found in fiction but exerting a powerful force for good.[48]

Conventional literary judgements and habits of linguistic usage are
challenged in the pages of *Shafts*. For example, we are asked to consider the
logic behind the idea that there must be a clear connection between literary
quality and the state of society. What, if this is the case, should we make of the
Elizabethan period, when men were dominant on the literary scene, and bloody
heads were stuck up on Temple Bar, religious free-thinkers were burnt alive,
and women were legally regarded as the chattels of their husbands, possessing
neither property nor rights regarding their children?[49] Women are encouraged
to become alert to the deployment of language: 'the word effeminate ought to
be banished from the pages of our literature as an insult to women.'[50] In 'An
Appeal to Girls' Teachers' we find a strong plea against sexist language in
education:

Do teachers not see that the idea that a girl is inferior to a boy is being fostered by such
apparently trifling causes as the use of the masculine pronoun in the prefaces to books,
'The student . . . if *he* should not succeed,' etc. etc.; by having sums badly worded—for
instance, 'If the work be done by a man, a woman, and a boy be in proportion of 3, 2, 1
etc . . . ;' by being told in French and other languages that, given a whole string of
feminine nouns, one masculine noun alone is sufficient to alter the agreement of an
adjective, etc., etc., etc.[51]

Corrective action is recommended in the classroom. Additionally, readers have
their attention drawn to the unconscious acceptance of the masculine norm by
writers of the books reviewed in *Shafts*. Thus it is asked of Edith Carrington's
Workers Without Wage, concerning the activities of ants, beetles, and spiders,
whether it is 'absolutely necessary always to use the masculine pronoun in
describing living creatures, even when the sexes work equally, even where the
workers are neuters?'[52] Even the *Children's League of Pity Paper* is castigated for
publishing pictures in which boys occupy the front seats on a trip to see the
Queen, and girls take the rear ones:

The writer of this notice will never forget . . . how she wept over a large engraving given
her by a lady, who had not even noticed the cruel defect. It was a picture of Christ
blessing little children. When asked why she wept so sorely, she sobbed out, 'Oh, there is
not *even one* little girl among them all.'[53]

---

[48] 'Mr George Meredith on Women's Status', *Shafts* 1 (1892), 9.
[49] 'Mr Buchanan's Appeals for "Literary Freedom"', *Shafts*, 3 (1894), 206.
[50] *Shafts*, 1 (1892), 72.
[51] T.C.L., 'An Appeal to Girls' Teachers', *Shafts*, 2 (1893), 96–7.
[52] 'Reviews', ibid. 117.
[53] Ibid. 119.

'Our object is to encourage thought', announced the editor of *Shafts*, Margaret Sibthorp, in the first issue.[54] This extended beyond awakening readers to the gender biases which lurk within the habitual employment of language and images. Rational analysis of social facts was promoted. It is on these grounds that writers like Eliza Lynn Linton, determined to construct stereotypes of 'political wild women', were castigated, since they fail to look around them and perceive that such 'wild women' have hardly the leisure to spend on superficial pursuits, on face-painting and cigarette smoking, which Linton conflates with the political activists attempting to improve women's lot.[55] Women were explicitly encouraged to read critically, not putting ' "ourselves into our author's hands," as Sterne says',[56] but considering their own point of view with relation to the principles at stake, and comparing the information given in a text, fictional or otherwise, with their own knowledge of facts.

One set of facts which *Shafts* was particularly keen should be imparted were those relating to sexual relationships, something which linked the editorial policy to such 'New Woman' novelists as Sarah Grand, as well as with contemporary campaigners who pointed out that 'innocence' was merely another word for 'ignorance', a state which rendered a girl vulnerable rather than sacrosanct: 'teach children the truth about themselves, and the beauty and power of purity, and they will be armed against all wrong. As they grow older teach them that there is danger; give them a large idea of it, *without the sickening details*, they will soon learn to discern what is pure and true from what is impure and false.'[57] This was the line taken by Sibthorp in the interventions which she made to the long-running debate in the correspondence column about the degree of supervision that should be exercised over a child's reading. Whilst agreeing with the view that 'a girl's mother ought to be the best judge whether a girl should have knowledge of vice or not', she was in complete accord with the woman who claimed that terror and loathing of sexual malpractices were a far better preserver of chastity than strict vestal vows.[58] It is with this in mind that she could put her full support behind Grand's *The Heavenly Twins*, with its highlighting of the existence of double standards with regard to sexual purity, and the concomitant dangers of sexually active men infecting their innocent, ignorant brides and offspring with venereal disease:

> 'Once in a lifetime is uttered a word
> That is not forgotten as soon as 'tis heard'?

These words and deeds so rare, so full of living energy, gather, gather like stars in the firmament of time as the ages roll along, and make the lights and the worlds of future generations. This book will take its place among that deathless company; it will

---

[54] 'What the Editor Means', *Shafts*, 1 (1892), 8.
[55] F. E. French, 'Mrs Lynn Linton on Modern Manners', ibid. 68.
[56] 'Reviews', *Shafts*, 3 (1894), 309.
[57] 'Reviews', *Shafts*, 2 (1893), 92.
[58] 'Choosing Books', ibid. 253.

accomplish the work for which it has been sent forth; those who read it have themselves to blame if they do not become wiser and gladder.[59]

The contrast between this notice and that in the *Englishwoman's Review* highlights the rapidity of change, the growth in openness, taking place between generations of feminist readers.

Women Readers Surveyed

The considerable interest paid in the pages of *Shafts* to what women and girls should be reading, and were actually reading, was part of a far broader attempt in the latter decades of the Victorian period to classify and determine the practices of the female reader. Notably, it was *girls* rather than women who formed the centre of attention, something which emphasizes, once again, the presumed vulnerability of adolescence. It indicates, too, the fascination exercised by the concept of the woman emerging into adulthood. These articles manifest a concern with both the content and style of the literature which was specifically targeted at a female market, and with the degree to which this corresponded with girls' actual preferences. In both cases, the concept of reading is brought into play as a marker of sexual differentiation, mirroring the assumptions of publishing itself.[60]

Believing that complimentary emphases are desirable, these articles often open the issue of why girls' books are not 'as palatable to girls as boys' books are to boys'[61]—and, on many occasions, as boys' books were to girls.[62] Charlotte M. Yonge went so far as to doubt that boys were in fact the major consumers of

---

[59] 'Reviews', ibid. 268.

[60] Elizabeth Segal, in ' "As the Twig Is Bent . . . ": Gender and Childhood Reading', Elizabeth A. Flynn and Patrocinio P. Schweickart (eds.), *Gender in Reading: Essays on Readers, Texts, and Contexts* (Baltimore and London, 1986), 165–86 indicates how, whilst English children's books are generally regarded as dating from the 1740s, with the exception of early school stories, there was little or no gender division in publication, marketing, and reception in the late eighteenth and early nineteenth centuries. Segal invokes in support Elizabeth Rigby's long article 'Children's Books' in the *Quarterly Review*, 74 (1844), 1–26, which makes no mention of girls' books or boys' books in the essay itself or in the list of recommended reading which follows. However, within a few years, adventure stories came to be thought of as 'boys' literature' and domestic tales as 'girls' books'. Segal plausibly argues that this division took place only when the market had grown large enough to support such separation—indeed, as F. J. Harvey Darton has argued, subdivision became an economic inevitability. F. J. Harvey Darton, *Children's Books in England: Five Centuries of Social Life* (3rd edn. rev. Brian Alderson (Cambridge, 1958), 217.

[61] Edward G. Salmon, 'What Girls Read', *Nineteenth Century*, 20 (1886), 515. Salmon gives comprehensive lists of what he considers to be 'boys'' authors: Reid, Henty, Verne, Kingston, Aimard, Hughes, Hopes, Hodgetts, Ballantyne, Frith, Fenn, Reed, Stables, Blake, Hutcheson, and Edgar; and 'girls'' authors: Alcott, Dodge, Marshall, Banks, Browne, Beale, Symington, Owen, Sewell, Wetherell, Holmes, Meade, and Yonge.

[62] Agnes Blackie, in her history of Blackie & Sons, one of the foremost publishers of story-books, school readers, and 'reward books' in the late nineteenth and early twentieth centuries, notes that Henty's fan-mail shows how popular boys' books were among girls. Agnes A. C. Blackie, *Blackie & Son 1809–1959* (Glasgow, 1959), 39–40.

'boys" books, believing them to be 'more read by mothers, sisters, and little boys longing to be at school, than by the boys themselves'.[63] Boys, she claims, are far more likely to be interested in some branch of natural history, physical science, or mechanics, and to be reading manuals on these subjects, or to take up volumes of real travels, by Franklin, Kane, Livingstone, Erskine, or members of the Alpine Club, than they are to be consuming, say, Mayne Reid. Edward G. Salmon, in 'What Girls Read' (1886) noted the same tendency, blaming the off-putting 'goody-goody' quality and preaching which characterized books for girls for making them turn to their brothers' bookshelves instead. Moreover, although the triumph of virtue might be a fictional resolution which lacks realism, he deplores the tendency of too many novelists making their reformed heroines meet an early death: another off-putting characteristic of girls' literature. He cites, in this context, Elfrida in Emma Marshall's *Court and Cottage* (1883), Marion in Sarah Doudney's *Marion's Three Crowns* (1873), and Lady Blanche in Elizabeth Sewell's *The Earl's Daughter* (1850). Didactic writing, he sensibly emphasizes, must at least offer a path and a reward which the reader herself would wish to follow, or else a clear warning. It is in such terms that he recommends, in language which indicates that it was no longer considered to be the scandalous novel of twenty years previously, that *East Lynne* 'ought to be placed in every girl's hands as soon as she has arrived at an age when she may find that life has for her unsuspected dangers. The work teaches many lessons valuable to young ladies, especially those of a jealous or impulsive disposition.'[64] Moreover, the inevitable textual sermons found in much feminine didactic fiction have the effect of holding up the action, of which he considered, in any case, there was too little:

Girl-life does not lend itself to vigorous and stirring treatment in the manner that boy-life does. It is far more difficult to enlist the reader's interest in domestic *contretemps* and daily affairs than in fierce combats between nations, or in the accidents of all kinds into which boys and men, by the very nature of their callings, are for ever being led.[65]

The unmistakably masculine assumptions here blatantly exemplify the point that Virginia Woolf was to make in *A Room of One's Own* (1929) that:

the values of women differ very often from the values . . . [of men] . . . naturally this is so. Yet it is the masculine values which prevail. Speaking crudely, football and sport are 'important', the worship of fashion, the buying of clothes 'trivial'. And these values are inevitably transferred from life to fiction. This is an important book, the critic assumes, because it deals with war. This is an insignificant book because it deals with the feelings of women in a drawing-room.[66]

[63] Miss Yonge, 'Children's Literature, Part III: Class Literature of the Last Thirty Years', *Macmillan's Magazine*, 20 (1869), 453.

[64] Salmon, 'What Girls Read', 524.

[65] Ibid. 516.

[66] Virginia Woolf, *A Room of One's Own* (1929; repr. Harmondsworth, 1973), 74.

Although Salmon commends Louisa M. Alcott for being able to make even something as prosaic as the boiling of a plum pudding interesting, he attributes this to the fact that she, like many of her countrywomen, had her sights widened by the violent activity she witnessed during the American Civil War. He failed to consider that the popularity, notwithstanding his reservations, of such writers as Charlotte M. Yonge and Elizabeth Sewell, or for that matter Antony Trollope, may have rested to a considerable extent on their ability to structure their plots so as to turn the domestic arena into a site of suspense and speculation.

The female reader postulated by Salmon's text might well have need of such imaginary excitement in the life he envisages for her. For what emerges from this article is that the subject is being considered not in terms of her individual development, but in relation to the presumed eventual effects of reading upon her as representative of both gender and race. His terms are those used by certain late nineteenth-century educational theorists, as described in the last chapter. He addresses parents about their responsibility not just to their particular offspring, but, sharing the priorities of current psychological and educational theory, he bids them to think in nationalistic terms. Reading is enlisted to play its part in the eugenicist movement:

Boys' literature of a sound kind ought to help to build up men. Girls' literature ought to help to build up women. If in choosing the books that boys shall read it is necessary to remember that we are choosing mental food for the future chiefs of a great race, it is equally important not to forget that in choosing books for girls that we are choosing mental food for the wives and mothers of that race. When Mr. Ruskin says that man's work is public and woman's private, he seems for the moment insensible to the public work of women as exercised through their influence on their husbands, brothers and fathers. Woman's work in the ordering, beautifying, and elevating of the commonweal is hardly second to man's; and it is this which ought to be borne in mind in rearing girls.[67]

A sustained debate on the topic of what girls should read took place in the *Saturday Review* towards the end of 1904. Here, too, there was considerable overlap with the discussions already outlined about the role and nature of literary study within girls' school education. It was occasioned by 'John Oliver Hobbes' (Pearl Craigie) having claimed that *Tom Jones* and *Amelia* should be given to every girl on her eighteenth birthday, on the grounds that currently 'trashy, neurotic and erotic novels are being produced by the hundreds, and read by the thousands'. 'Half the books now eagerly gloated over, and followed

---

[67] Salmon, 'What Girls Read', 526. For discussion on eugenicism and woman's role in the late nineteenth and early twentieth centuries, see 64 n. 41, and, additionally, Carol Dyhouse, 'Social Darwinistic Ideas and the Development of Women's Education in England, 1880–1920', *History of Education*, 5 (1976), 41–58; B. Semmel, *Imperialism and Social Reform: English Social Imperialist Thought 1895–1914* (1960), esp. 29–52. An excellent survey of the way in which boys' literature in the later part of the nineteenth century was geared to inspiring imperial ideals in their readers is given by Joseph Bristow, *Empire Boys: Adventures in a Man's World* (1991); of particular relevance is ch. 1: 'Reading for the Empire'.

as exemplars of life as it should be, are utterly unfit to be read by girls', Craigie had told a reviewer. Esther Longhurst was quick to condemn her choice of antidote, however: '*Tom Jones* is the last book to be read, understood or appreciated by the English girl of normal, healthy instincts.' She laments that now, in 1904, girls 'of the upper middle-class' lack the literary grounding of some fifteen or twenty years earlier, when the reading of Thackeray, George Eliot, Mrs Oliphant, Trollope, Mrs Gaskell, and often Charlotte Brontë and Jane Austen, gave young women a standard by which to judge modern productions. Longhurst blamed the changed state of affairs on a shift in educational emphasis: today a girl is schooled in a way which fits her to pass examinations successfully, 'but which fails to make her love and appreciate what is beautiful in her own language'.[68]

In reply, the novelist F. A. Steel disagreed with Longhurst in protesting against *Tom Jones*. Quite apart from any intrinsic merit possessed by the work, she believed that a good education, whether at school or home, should make the specific giving or withholding of any text unnecessary, 'a confession of ineptitude on the part of those responsible for their education, the primary object of which was the unconscious formation of taste and habits which would serve their acquirer in good stead when mere pupilage was over'. But, as we saw in the last chapter, she expresses sympathy with current criticism about how literature is taught within formal education. Schools, in her opinion, fail in their task to instil into girls 'that unconscious taste for pure literature which the less cultivated parents of the past held it in their duty to cultivate in themselves'. The effect is that 'the trash of the bookstalls' now lies on study tables, and 'pure literature' has become a subject for joyless academic dissection.[69]

Dorothea Beale responded with a long letter. She claimed that she, and other experienced teachers, had found that girls most frequently read magazines in their leisure time. 'Poetry she never touches, and solid prose of any kind she finds too difficult. When a girl does really care for reading, it is because the atmosphere of the home is favourable to it.' Indeed, she maintained that it is the responsibility of parents to inculcate a taste for reading into their daughters, particularly if they are at day-school, and parental advice is certainly necessary: 'we do not leave our children to choose without guidance their own food.' She recommends the revival of the habit, familiar from her own childhood, of reading aloud in the evenings. Schools, of course, will continue to do the best they can: at Cheltenham, they have house libraries, suggest books for the holidays, inquire of the pupils on their return what books they have chosen for themselves, and spend time in discussing these. Beale commends publishers for bringing out cheap editions of good books, but maintains that more could be done by volunteers in lending libraries giving advice to girls about what is worth reading. She applauds the recent setting up of an association for opening

[68] Letter from Esther Longhurst, *Saturday Review* (29 Oct. 1904), 548.
[69] Letter from F. A. Steel, ibid. (5 Nov. 1904), 578.

bookshops, where books should be sold solely by educated women, and draws attention to the value of the National Home Reading Union, which she constantly commends to girls leaving Cheltenham.[70]

Beale's letter is more remarkable for its tone of moral crusading than for its specific contents. But its idealism functioned as a catalyst, provoking two subsequent letters which credibly suggest the actual heterogeneity of reading practices. 'A Mother' records the books consumed since July by her sixteen-year-old daughter, characterized in her modernity by the fact that she plays hockey and cricket in gymnasium costume and is on the point of going in for the 'Senior Cambridge'. Established nineteenth-century classics appear alongside school stories in the list, which reads:

'Old Mortality', 'The Farringdons', 'By Mutual Consent' (L. T. Meade), 'To Call Her Mine', 'Katherine Regina', and 'Self or Bearer' (Besant); 'Christmas Carol', 'The Cricket on the Hearth', 'Hypatia', 'Concerning Isabel Carnaby', 'The Virginians', 'The Adventures of Tom Sawyer', 'The Head of the House' (E. Everett-Green), 'A Double Thread', 'The Heir-Presumptive and the Heir-Apparent', 'Sesame and Lilies', 'A Tale of Two Cities'.[71]

The following week, 'A Parent' of 'two very modern girls' who actually attended Cheltenham Ladies' College reminded readers that:

Miss Beale must not rely too much on the returns of books read in the holidays sent in by girls, as they are 'faked', books being omitted if likely to displease her. They have always liked travel and boys' books. Girls' books and papers they scorn. 'Chums' and 'Scraps' are great favourites; and they fight over 'Home Chat' and many other things.

'Far Off', 'Near Home', 'Esperanza', 'The Coral Islands' and 'The Captain of Waterloo' have been read more than once. They also delight in 'The Fairchild Family'.[72]

The problem of obtaining accurate information from a wide sample of girls or women about what they actually read was bedevilled by returns suspiciously appearing to give 'suitable' rather than accurate responses: perhaps an indication in itself of how those questioned had internalized assumptions about the 'correct' at the level of reading. Salmon quotes from a survey of a thousand girls conducted by Charles Welsh, in which the ten favourite authors emerge as Dickens (330), Scott (226), Kingsley (91), Yonge (91), Shakespeare (73), Wetherell (54), Mrs H. Wood (51), Eliot (41), Lord Lytton (41), and Longfellow (31). Salmon finds it impossible to imagine that Carlyle (6) is more popular than Elizabeth Sewell or Maggie Symington, who receive no mentions at all; the *Saturday Review*, commenting somewhat sceptically on Salmon's whole piece, regards it as a sign of untrustworthiness that there is no mention of Robert Louis Stevenson or Rider Haggard, of Ouida, Rhoda Broughton, Helen

[70] Letter from Dorothea Beale, ibid. (12 Nov. 1904), 609.
[71] Letter from 'A Mother', ibid. (19 Nov. 1904), 643.
[72] Letter from 'A Parent', ibid. (26 Nov. 1904), 666.

Mathers, or Florence Marryat. In this writer's eyes, these were the truly popular writers among girls.[73]

Twenty years after Salmon's investigations, in 1906, two articles in the *Nineteenth Century* set out to determine 'The Reading of the Modern Girl' and 'The Reading of the Colonial Girl'. Florence Low launched her research for the first of these from the assumption that 'many of our girls are reading to-day books of an inferior nature, and are in many cases neglecting the standard novels which, if not read in youth, are so seldom read later in life'.[74] She sent a survey round to two hundred schoolgirls between fifteen and eighteen years old in different parts of England, stressing the fact that replies would be anonymous and the results not revealed to teachers, and found a degree of uniformity in the answers which bore out her suspicions.[75] Thus the majority of girls claimed that Edna Lyall's free-thinking *Donovan* and *We Two* were their favourite novels, followed by Merriman's fiction, and *The Prisoner of Zenda*. Marie Corelli, L. T. Meade and E. E. Green scored a good number of votes, and no more than 3 per cent of the elder girls mentioned *David Copperfield*: Dickens was, indeed, the only 'standard novelist' to find a place among the favourite novels. When it came to questions on specific authors, Thackeray and Jane Austen were 'only known to a select few'; Elizabeth Gaskell's *Cranford* was the only book of hers which had been read, and that only by six respondants, and Charlotte M. Yonge and Miss Mulock's novels, whilst known, were mentioned, without much enthusiasm, as writers for girls in their early teens. On the other hand, over a hundred papers named three magazines as read regularly, with between fifty and sixty girls writing down the names of five periodicals. Thus, Low deduces, 'the habit of desultory, miscellaneous reading has, alas! taken firm root in our midst'.[76] Such writers as Margaret Oliphant, Juliana Ewing, and Louisa Alcott, whom Low recollects with acute nostalgia, have sunk out of sight: 'too serious, too uneventfully written' for today's girls.[77]

Low takes some heart from the fact that the reading of the modern girl is in no way 'vicious'. But what, she asks, has caused this deterioration in taste? Various hypotheses are advanced. Mothers do not exercise as strict a supervision over their daughters' reading as formerly: thus they borrow books from school friends, and from Low's *bête noir*, the public library, which in her

[73] Salmon, 'What Girls Read', 527–9; 'Books for Girls', *Saturday Review* (9 Oct. 1886), 477.

[74] Florence B. Low, 'The Reading of the Modern Girl', *Nineteenth Century*, 59 (1906), 278.

[75] 'The following questions were asked: (1) Which are your favourite novels? (2) Which of Scott's novels have you read? (3) Which of Thackeray's novels have you read? (4) Which of Dickens's novels have you read? (5) Which of Jane Austen's novels have you read? (6) Which of Mrs. Gaskell's novels have you read? (7) Do you like C. Yonge's stories? (8) Do you like Miss Muloch's stories? (9) Do you like Miss Thackeray's stories? (10) Do you read magazines? If so, which? (11) Which are your favourite poets? (12) Name six poems you are very fond of' (ibid. 279).

[76] Low, 'The Reading of the Modern Girl', 280.

[77] Concerning poetry, there was again unanimity, Tennyson being the clear favourite (especially *Idylls of the King*) followed by Longfellow, Robert Browning, and Scott. Low comments, however, on the very narrow range of poets referred to, regarding this as reflecting a narrow range being taught in schools.

opinion encourages scrappy, indiscriminate browsing. Moreover, not only does the average parent encourage a magazine-reading habit by bringing them home themselves, but their diminished surveillance of pocket-money is responsible for the current fashion for reading 'trashy' papers on school-bound trains. Nor is a love of literature encouraged by the way in which it is now taught in girls' schools, pupils learning philological details and, more recently, character studies off by heart in order to pass examinations, rather than concentrating on aesthetic and moral priorities. Additionally, examination requirements lead to a narrow range of texts being taught: 'The ordinary girl of eighteen leaves school with a knowledge of probably two or three Shakespeare plays, a Chaucer story, one book of the Faerie Queen, perhaps a volume of Burke, and some of Scott's poems.'[78] Little or no nineteenth-century literature is studied.

Where, for Low, lies the remedy? She would like parents to ban the reading of more than one magazine a month (she never considers that the 'snippets', the 'lightest of literature', and the 'superficial knowledge' which she condemns girl readers as absorbing through magazines may be in part a reaction against the dull, concentrated study of texts in school). Reading aloud in the family circle should be encouraged, and schools should cease to regard literature as an examination subject. Throughout all of her criticism and advice lies a deep desire to turn back the clock, and to restore as the ideal prototype of well-read girlhood the image of herself when young. Her own notion of correct or desirable taste is encapsulated in the pre-selection of the writers she names. What passes as a sociological investigation at first sight is indeed, as Constance N. Barnicoat put it in the *Nineteenth Century* later that year, a 'jeremiad'.

Barnicoat herself focused on 'The Reading of the Colonial Girl', canvassing, again, girls between fifteen and eighteen. She employed, however, a different questionnaire, which gave more scope for acknowledging individual taste, and for judging, Barnicoat believed, a girl's overall intelligence.[79] At the same time as sending this questionnaire abroad, she circulated it to some hundreds of girls in British high schools, and arrived at a set of conclusions far more optimistic than those of Low. Various general points emerge. First, she notes how girls 'evidently tend to follow one another rather like sheep', in that one particular book or author will enjoy a notable vogue within an individual school. Second, although Colonial girls are frequently very widely read, the bright climates and

---

[78] Low, 'Reading of the Modern Girl', 285.

[79] 'The following were the questions sent out: 1. What books do you read for recreation? 2. Which novels have you read of the following writers:—Scott, Thackeray, Dickens, Kingsley? 3. Of the following living novelists: Meredith, Kipling, Rider Haggard, Gilbert Parker, Conan Doyle, Barrie? 4. Name any novels you have read by the following women writers: George Eliot, Jane Austen, Charlotte Brontë. 5. Name any novels that interest you by other writers than these. 6. Which English classics do you like best? 7. Which poets? 8. What are your favourite poems? 9. What is your favourite study? What books do you read in connection with it? 10. What is your favourite hobby? What books do you read in connection with it? 11. Do the daily or weekly newspapers interest you? If so, what parts? 12. Which of the monthly magazines do you read?' Constance A. Barnicoat, 'The Reading of the Colonial Girl', *Nineteenth Century*, 60 (1906), 939–40.

open-air life in which they are brought up often means that they are not initially accustomed to 'literary culture', but become especially interested in history and historical fiction, and in works which deal with their own Colony: Ethel Turner, Rolf Boldrewood, and Guy Boothby are remarked on as being especially popular in Australia, for example, although, interestingly, she finds that '*The Story of a South African Farm* . . . is rarely, if ever, cited in replies from that country.'[80] 'The Colonial girl is also devoted to adventure books, often of the hair-breadth escape, somewhat bloodcurdling order. This tendency is especially noticeable in the South Africans, and it is a problem for students of the influence of the environment whether the veldt may not have something to do with this.'[81] She includes a list of favourite novelists:

British Girls	*Colonial and Indian Girls*
1. Edna Lyall	1. Edna Lyall
2. Henry Seton Merriman	2. Louisa M. Alcott
3. R.L. Stevenson	3. Mrs. Henry Wood
4. Stanley Weyman	4. Rosa Nouchette Carey
5. Anthony Hope	5. L. T. Meade
6. F. Marion Crawford	6. Charlotte M. Yonge
7. Mrs. Gaskell (nearly always *Cranford*)	7. Marie Corelli
8. Lytton	8. Stanley Weyman
9. Marie Corelli	9. Farrar
10. Allen Raine	= 10. Lytton
	Henty[82]

but also notes a commendable amount of reading 'classic' authors: among the names she offers the recipients of her questionnaire, Dickens and George Eliot fare best. Certainly, she acknowledges the influence of school literature teaching on many choices, but does not find grounds for as much pessimism as Low when it comes to magazine-reading, except among Indian girls. The average Colonial girl claims to read three to three and a half magazines a month (preferring the *Strand*, way in front of all others, followed by the *Windsor*, and, a long way behind, *Pearson's*, the *Royal*, and *Pall Mall*), as against the British girls' two and a half. What she takes pains to emphasize is the degree to which girls claim to read newspapers ('though a few girls, notably some Australians, say they are not allowed to read the papers').[83] Colonials are most interested in war news, she finds; the British pay more attention to politics and Parliamentary news. Both mention book reviews; hardly any the women's page.

Unlike Low, Barnicoat superficially has no social or educational axe to grind, unless it is to convey an impression of alert, usually discriminating and intelligent young women readers proliferating at home and abroad. But at a

---

80 Ibid. 944.   81 Ibid. 943.
82 Ibid. 950.   83 Ibid. 949.

time when the Suffrage Movement was becoming increasingly active and prominent within Britain, the importance of transmitting this message was, in itself, not a negligible one.[84]

Working-class Reading

As I mentioned in the introduction to this chapter, for the majority of social investigators, the working-class woman was doubly other, distanced by class as well as by sex. But as with the middle-class woman, discussion of working-class reading habits was dominated by anxieties about influence and corruption. This was as true of concern about boys' reading material as it was of girls'. In the case of the young male, it was frequently presumed, the results might be more dramatic than in the case of the young woman, but less insidious. Thus in 'What Girls Read', Salmon commented: 'Boys may be driven to sea or to break into houses by the stories they read; their actions are at once recorded in the columns of the daily papers. With girls the injury is more invidious and subtle. It is almost exclusively domestic.'[85] Salmon makes his point appear the more dramatic by entirely failing to take into account further social influences, such as the acquaintances these supposed boys keep, for example, or the boredom and frustrations in the girls' lives, remarking, as he does, that 'we should probably find that the high-flown conceits and pretensions of the poorer girls of the period, their dislike of manual work and love of freedom, spring largely from notions imbibed in the course of a perusal of their penny fictions'.[86] Others even blamed girls' reading for male juvenile crime. Lily Montagu, in 1904, condemned their 'craving for nervous excitement' and their irresponsibility:

Can we be surprised that, having had no experience of pure enjoyment, she soothes her feeling of unrest in the contemplation of crudities, whether revealed in the newspaper column of police news, in the halfpenny novelette, or on the music-hall stage? Girls living in rough districts are often inspired by 'these studies' to instigate and encourage fights among their boys by rewarding the victors with their favour.[87]

In another of Salmon's articles for the *Nineteenth Century*, 'What the Working Classes Read', published in July 1886, Salmon runs through the newspapers most frequently bought and read by the working *man*, before moving to castigate, again, the penny novelettes, which 'find their chief supporters among

---

[84] For another, far more chatty and anecdotal repudiation of the conclusions reached in Low's article, see Margarita Yates, 'Do Our Girls Take an Interest in Literature?', *Monthly Review*, 23 (1906), 120–32.

[85] Salmon, 'What Girls Read', 523. See also Salmon's 'What Boys Read', *Fortnightly Review*, NS 39 (1886), 248–59.

[86] Salmon, 'What Girls Read', 523.

[87] Lily H. Montagu, 'The Girl in the Background' in E. J. Urwick (ed.), *Studies of Boy Life in Our Cities* (1904), 238, 244.

shop-girls, seamstresses and domestic servants . . . Crime and love are the essential ingredients, and the influence exercised over the feminine reader, often unenlightened by any close contact with the classes whom the novelist pretends to portray, crystallises into an irremovable dislike of the upper classes of society.'[88] They find their counterpart in the derision 'of the aristocracy, the plutocracy, and sometimes even the monarchy itself'[89] to be found in such Sunday papers as *Lloyd's*, the *Weekly Dispatch*, and Salmon's particular *bête noire*, *Reynolds' Newspaper*. Whilst, as we shall see in Chapter 10, one of the complaints frequently made against women of the middle classes reading sensation fiction was that it broke down the desirable status quo in terms of the ways in which social stratification could be gauged through cultural taste, here Salmon seems to be complaining against the tendency of working-class reading to consolidate class strata.

But how familiar was Salmon with the material which he condemned? Not all journalism which addressed itself to the reading of working-class woman was as sensationalist as his, particularly if it took the trouble to examine the novelettes and magazine stories themselves. The author of a piece on 'Penny Novels' in the *Spectator* of 1863 had looked at a number of fictions, and concluded by disproving the commonly held notions that their tone was immoral, and that they fostered depraved taste. The latter belief, the writer claimed, was founded 'on a total misapprehension of the relation which exists between writer and reader'.[90] There was a habitual requirement that the plot should be exciting, and that at least some of the characters should come from 'high life', a point picked up by various other commentators. It was only the comfortably off who could afford to make a tailor like Alton Locke their hero, pointed out Margaret Oliphant: 'he is no hero for the sempstress, who makes her romance out of quite different materials.' The working-class woman none the less enjoys reading, Oliphant tells us, about the domestic settings in *Mary Barton*. Perhaps, one might wishfully surmise, such a reader might also have enjoyed the fact that the happy ending, in romantic if not in socio-economic terms, is brought about by female enterprise and activity, and that it is a novel in which 'feminine' values of compassion and empathy, visibly located in men as well as in women, prevail. But usually, 'even poor superior high-minded governesses, and refined poverty in elegant distress, those staple commodities of fiction, do not flourish in the penny periodicals', continues Oliphant; '*that* public does not care to know how careful gentility makes ends meet.'[91]

If there was to be a working-class heroine with whom the reader might identify herself, and not all commentators saw this as a crucial factor, she must,

---

[88] Salmon, 'What the Working Classes Read', *Nineteenth Century*, 20 (1886), 112–13.

[89] Ibid. 114.

[90] 'Penny Novels', *Spectator* (28 Mar. 1863), 1807.

[91] [Margaret Oliphant] 'The Byways of Literature: Reading for the Million', *Blackwood's Edinburgh Magazine*, 84 (1858), 206, 208.

in some way or another, possess particular, innate qualities. 'Servants—ladies' maids especially—must be on terms of familiarity with their mistresses, the depositaries of their most dangerous secrets, and the chief sharers of their confidence . . . it is no unusual thing to find the lady of title in these stories consulting her maid as to her future husband.'[92] The poor, in these fictions, always get the better of the rich; emotional outpourings, whether partings or proposals, are always conducted in exaggerated language; murders are commonly introduced into the plots for sensational effect, and each number necessarily ends on a cliff-hanger. Writers are well aware that these fictions are read for escape. Their consumers:

like to be taken amid scenes which are wholly different from those which they encounter in their own daily experience. The poor factory girl likes to withdraw in her dinner hour to the saloons of the great, as they are supposed to be by persons whose acquaintance does not rise higher than the footman.[93]

However improbable the novelettes may be, they none the less contrast advantageously, in this critic's view, with most French fiction. The same conclusion was reached by James Payn in 1881, finding penny fiction, to his disappointment, as pure as 'milk and water', vapid, dull, and devoid of humour. The only explanation he claimed to be able to advance for its popularity rests more in its language, interestingly enough, than in its content, for it could clothe 'very conventional thoughts in rather high-faluting English', giving each reader a sense of power in being able to articulate their own thoughts and feelings in more impressive-sounding terms than they could arrive at independently.[94] A writer in *Macmillan's* in 1866, whilst noting that penny fictions are now 'well washed with moral sentiment', suggests that this development is of relatively recent date,[95] but Sally Mitchell's study of popular fictions in the late 1840s and early 1850s, concentrating on periodicals aimed at upwardly mobile skilled artisans and their families (such as the *London Journal* and the *Family Herald*) indicates that the shift towards conventional moral values may be dated earlier.[96]

Later in the century, Agnes Repplier confirms the relative propriety of a number of penny novelettes which she had examined, taking them as a type of 'English railway fiction' read by 'the clerks and artisans, shopgirls, dressmakers, and milliners, who pour into London every morning by the early trains'.[97] She claims that their 'wonderful dullness' is not really due to the absence of incidents, vice, or dramatic situations, but to the placidity with which the incidents and situations are presented. A complacency on her own part reveals

---

[92] 'Penny Novels', *Spectator*, 1807.
[93] Ibid. 1808.
[94] James Payn, 'Penny Fiction', *Nineteenth Century*, 9 (1881), 149, 154.
[95] 'Penny Novels', *Macmillan's Magazine*, 4 (1866), 101.
[96] Mitchell, *The Fallen Angel*, 7–18.
[97] Agnes Repplier, *Points of View* (1893), 209.

itself through the faintly condescending tones in which she recounts the improbable plots and stilted dialogue of tales entitled 'Elfrida's Wooing' and 'Golden Chains'. Repplier chides other commentators, such as Payn and Wright, with being far too solemn in their analysis of Penny Literature (she contrasts them with Wilkie Collins's interest in the subject) and seems determined to make up herself for their deficiencies in flippancy. More specifically, however, she challenges Salmon's reading, or rather lack of it. Were he familiar with the genre at first hand, she claims, he would recognize that the aristocrat of penny fiction was always fair, never dark; nor had she herself found any socialistic tendencies whatsoever in these tales. Indeed, she cites the contents of two of the most popular of fiction-bearing magazines, *Dorothy, a Home Journal for Ladies*, and *The Princess*, to show how publishers juxtaposed the long stories with items of society and court gossip, as well as answers to correspondents and hints to dressmakers. Whilst *Bow Bells, A Magazine of Short Stories*, and the *Book for All* (divided into separate compartments for women, girls, men, boys, and children) were less preoccupied with the upper classes, and more given to providing encyclopaedic information on a far-reaching range of topics, they could not in any way be thought of as seditious.

Helen Bosanquet, writing in 1901, also had examined working-class periodicals closely. She noted how girls' publications could usually be differentiated from those intended for boys by their covers alone, which made an attempt to be ornamental, suggesting aesthetic refinement, often including a wreath of flowers or a sentimental head or figure. Unusually among popular fiction's investigators, she took the trouble to look at the illustrations inside the volumes, too, remarking on the conventions by which the aristocratic nature of the characters is indicated: 'The men are long and thin, with wonderful pointed feet and lofty brows; the women are simply lay figures in appropriate attitudes, carrying the hats and gowns from the latest fashion plates. But you see at once that they are people with a wardrobe at their disposal, and to readers who have none that suggests a great deal.'[98] In the text, she finds material to support her view that reading such fiction inevitably involves an identificatory process: 'the shop-girl soothes away the irritation of the long day's toil by soaring with a heroine (in whom she finds a glorified self) into a heaven of luxury and sentimentality.' Almost invariably, they contain 'the old, old story of meeting, parting, and the church-door in the last chapter. As if making a brief claim for their literary respectability, she notes that since girls' stories seem to require less sensationalism and fewer hair's-breadth escapes than those aimed at boys, there is more room for at least rudimentary characterization in them—particularly in the minor characters, for the heroines' lot is invariably

[98] Helen Bosanquet, 'Cheap Literature', *Contemporary Review*, 79 (1901), 678. Bosanquet also indicates that the precise details of luxurious ball-gowns given in the text 'could hardly fail to stir the feminine longings of the girl reader' (p. 677).

predetermined. Here Bosanquet becomes more critical of the limiting social implications of the texts. 'Their role is to be injured and misunderstood, loving and faithful through all affliction, and it is clear that any outbreak of originality would be very disturbing.' She regrets that the inevitable result of the fact that the heroine appears to exist only 'to love and be beloved' is the narrowing one of 'the constant suggestion that the whole point and interest of a woman's life is contained in the few months occupied by her love story'.[99]

Many of these novelettes did indeed offer easy points of entry for their readers. Francis Hitchman, looking at the genre in 1890, remarked on the tendency of stories in both *The Illustrated Family Novelist* and *The Princess's Novelettes* to show romances developing from chance encounters in the street. In one, the heroine is rescued by a gentleman from a gang of working men who are harassing her on an underground station; in another, she falls in love with a handsome actor whom she meets accidentally in the street.[100] *The Princess's Novelettes* and the *Dorothy Novelette* series are unmistakably formula fiction, juxtaposed with fashion supplements and advice on etiquette. Most of the stories are set in England, often in a rural or small-town setting: a small number take place in Ireland, making use of League politics in the 1890s to provide a melodramatic backdrop. The majority of the heroines come from the affluent middle classes, a few from the aristocracy. Working women are very much relegated to minor, if implacably trustworthy roles. Thus Jane, the maid in the opening number of the *Dorothy Novelette* series, the plagiaristically entitled *Lady Ashley's Secret* (1889), tries to advise her mistress to send away Harold Tremaine, a house-guest whom we already know is an adventurer and are beginning to suspect has also been an American train robber. Lady Ashley pays dearly for ignoring this counsel. What is often crucial about the heroines, however, is their attitude towards material wealth and towards fashionable society. Kathleen, in *Kindred Spirits* (*Princess's Novelettes* (1893)), complains against the depersonalizing effort involved in her daily life now that she has 'come out':

I never have a moment to myself—not a moment in which to think or read, or really enjoy myself in my own way. I am always rushing from one place to another, without breathing space between. I could not be so tired if I were a working man's wife, and scrubbed the house from top to bottom every day. I would exchange thankfully with any poor labourer's wife or daughter, if some good fairy would give me the offer. But such luck is not for me.[101]

Two more specific, marital offers, do, however, come her way: one from an amiable, gentlemanly, rich, boring man in his mid-forties, the other from Dunbar, a poet living in a Chelsea garret, with frayed shirt cuffs and a coat

[99] Helen Bosanquet, 'Cheap Literature', 676, 680.
[100] [Francis Hitchman] 'Penny Fiction', *Quarterly Review*, 171 (1890), 166–7.
[101] *Kindred Spirits*, *Princess's Novelettes*, 14 (1893), 34.

threadbare at the elbows. Needless to say, and after a brief series of misunderstandings, she chooses the latter, in no doubt that they will be 'happy poor'. The plot, however, eventually provides neatly for them, not through the fruits of literary success, but through Dunbar's hard labouring in the California goldfields.

Honor, in *Wedded by Treachery* (1893), is likewise defined as a sympathetic character through her compassion as she walks out one winter's morning with Norman Sergison, a young barrister who has just come into an inheritance:

Frosty weather is delightful for walking in, I know, but while I am walking, and feeling nice and warm, I am thinking of the thousands of people who are not free to follow my example, and of those who cannot afford big fires, and plenty of banquets, and warm clothing. It is so little one can do, individually, to relieve distress, and cold is the worst distress I can think of . . . oh! why do not all the rich people in England amalgamate to prevent their poorer brethren suffering in the long, bitter winters? So little from each rich person would do so much.[102]

Such charitable musings prompt Sergison's proposal: 'I have twice as much money as I can spend. Will you take charge of it—and of me, and do what you will with both.' It is some considerable time later—following a dreadful deception practised by a local doctor who is also in love with Honor, and is driven to desperate measures by the hereditary mental disease from which he suffers—before, however, their union can at last come about.

The women journalists cited above appear to have approached their subjects with sympathy as well as insight into their motives for reading. They reveal no concealed agenda that attempts to connect reading practices with broader social trends. In this, they differ from, say, James Haslam's *The Press and the People: An Estimate of Reading in Working-Class Districts* (1906). These pieces, reprinted from the *Manchester City News*, discuss the reading habits of women and men in some detail, although Haslam's presentation is as illuminating about his sociological assumptions as it is about the actual content of his findings. From women newsagents and their customers in Ancoats he learns that sensational papers dealing with violent crime, suicides, divorces, seduction, sporting papers, and penny novelettes sell best. The last especially interest him: his impression of the escape which they offer is used to highlight his dramatization of the human and aesthetic poverty of Ancoats life. The tale he buys is commended to him for its portrayal of 'proper love, no slobberin' an' kissin all the time', a typical example of the fiction bought to read both at home and in the factory.

It was a love story. The scenes were those of old baronial houses, country roads, wealthy mansions, floral parks, old and stately trees, delicious glens, limpid streams, hunting expeditions, billiard rooms, and continental pleasure places. The characters were rich men and beautiful women; titled men such as earls and knights, and ladies of

---

[102] *Wedded by Treachery*, ibid. 164.

refinement, wealth, education; real British pride, and charms irresistible; women who spurned work, treated low life ignominiously, and spoke in terms of contempt of people, however rich and good, who had made money by industry; women who could only appreciate a man born to wealth, title, idleness, comfort, influence, and the joy of life.

Well, I fancied there must be some fascination, some momentary pleasure, some enchanting reflection in the mind of the Ancoats woman reading such stories, meant to amuse and not to reform—reading such stories in a sunless, flowerless, and airless court.

'It is the chief pleasure of my life,' said a hard-working woman to me, who was buying one of these stories, 'to read these tales—they're lovely!'[103]

He also records the reading of another stereotypical form of romantic fiction, in which the factory girl marries a millionaire, with all ending happily after many protestations from the millionaire's relatives. In both cases, his interest in what these forms of fiction contain is sanctimoniously coloured by the expression of a wish that the slum residents would do more than engage in imaginative wandering in a brighter, wealthier clime: he wishes them to realize the need for self-effort and social regeneration, which should replace their escapist reading of exaggerated novels. His thesis is based to some extent on an assumed correlation of environment, quality of culture, and human worth: 'better surroundings, better people, better reading'—so he is pleased to find women and girls who live in the leafier, more prosperous suburb of Harpuphey, and work in warehouses, offices, and shops, buying penny 'fashion' periodicals in order to transfer their guidance to their own dressmaking. On the other hand, he still finds a certain number of women resorting to romance reading, and the social-Darwinist assumptions with which he approaches society surface: 'Whatever must be uppermost in the minds of females fed on this weekly trash cannot be for the good of the race. No wonder we have careless mothers, improperly fed children, and high infant mortality in crowded districts of towns and cities.'[104]

The following year, Lady Bell, in *At the Works*, a study of life in Middlesborough based on observations which she had spent thirty years gathering, devoted an entire chapter to the issue of reading. She notes that the workman reads, on average, more than his wife, 'not only because his interest on the whole is more likely to be stimulated by intercourse with his fellows, widening his horizon, but because he has more definite times of leisure in which he feels he is amply justified in "sitting down with a book".'[105] The prevailing impression is, unsurprisingly, of a population who read for relaxation

---

[103] James Haslam, *The Press and the People: An Estimate of Reading in Working-class Districts* (Manchester, 1906), 6–7.

[104] Ibid. 15. The sources of Haslam's psychological and sociological beliefs are clarified by his comment regarding a Salford newsagent: 'I . . . felt that a delineation of some of the old lady's customers, from Gall, Lavater, Spurzheim, Broca, Lombroso, or Mantegazza, would have been interesting' ibid. 11.

[105] Lady Bell, *At the Works* (1907), 145.

and escape, but with many of the women feeling guilty unless they are primarily engaged upon household tasks. Bell looks in detail at the reading patterns of 200 houses, and, whilst acknowledging that this is hardly a high enough number to give a fair sample, draws the following statistical conclusions:

17 women who cannot read.
 8 men who cannot read.
28 houses where no one cares to read.
 8 men who actually dislike reading.
 3 women who actually dislike reading.
 7 women who say they 'have no time for it.'
50 houses where they only read novels.
58 houses where they read the newspapers only.
37 houses where they are 'fond of reading' or 'great readers.'
25 houses where they read books that are absolutely worth reading (this includes the men who read books about their work)[106]

and also, one may add, the woman who 'revels in "Hamlet".' The detailed description of households reveals, too, the woman who, when asked what she liked reading, replied 'Something that will take one away from oneself'; the husband who 'does not like his wife to read—thinks she might "get hold of wrong notions"',[107] and the popularity of Mrs Henry Wood's writing among the women. She is by far the most frequently cited of all novelists, and Bell, considering why this should be so, thinks that her popularity is probably due in the first instance to:

the admirable compound of the goody and the sensational: the skill in handling which enables her to present her material in the most telling form, and a certain directness and obvious sentiment that they can understand, while at the same time it is just enough above their usual standard of possibilities to give an agreeable sense of stimulus. 'East Lynne' is perhaps the book whose name one most often hears from men and women both. A poor woman, the widow of a workman, who had gone away to a distant part of the country, and was being supported by the parish, wrote to someone in her former town to say that she thought that if she had 'that beautiful book "East Lynne" it would be a comfort to her'.[108]

Otherwise, she notes, women tend to read penny novelettes, which are morally irreproachable, invariably contain some love interest, with the addition of a mild dose of religious sentiment. She notes as particularly prevalent a plot pattern in which the poor and virtuous young man turns out to be a long-lost son, thus becoming rich and powerful.

For Bell, as for Salmon before her, the key to encouraging more profitable reading lies in the better provision of books. People, she observes with as much an eye on the 'drawing-room reader' as on the working classes, tend to read

[106] Ibid. 162.
[107] Ibid. 160, 159.
[108] Ibid. 166.

whatever is closest to hand: in the women's case, on sale in corner shops. Some enterprising retailers of penny novelettes set up near mill gates, in order to cater for the mill's employees.[109] Whilst the Free Library exists, and is much used by the 'better class' of workman, she suggests that it may be intimidating for women to use:

A woman who lives in a distant part of the town, whose outer garment is probably a ragged shawl fastened with a pin, may not like going up an imposing flight of stairs, getting a ticket, giving a name, looking through a catalogue, having the book entered, etc.; whereas many of these would read the book if it were actually put into their hands. Women, at any rate, of all classes know how often our actions are governed by our clothes, and how the fact of being unsuitably clad for a given course of conduct may be enough to prevent us from embarking on it.[110]

One solution may, Bell suggests, lie in the provision of less intimidating reading and borrowing environments, perhaps attached to work-places. Another, perhaps potentially more popular possibility, would be an enterprising hawker or two setting up door-to-door lending service in the poorer streets: 'He would certainly find customers; for . . . the working man's wife, as a rule, is ready to hire anything that is offered to her.'[111]

Other commentators, however, pointed out that it was not just the difficulty of gaining access to books which meant that working-class girls and women read even less than their male counterparts. 'A Working Woman', writing in *Chambers' Journal* in 1899, who herself left school and went to work in a large factory when she was thirteen, claimed that the free public library movement had been instrumental in developing her own taste in reading. Generally, however, she notes that either girls were expected to devote most of their time to domestic duties at home in the evening, or else they were too tired, jaded, and worn to enjoy reading. The working conditions of the servant, the factory girl, and the seamstress will have to change, she writes, before any alteration in reading habits may be anticipated.[112]

[109] Bosanquet, 'Cheap Literature', 672.
[110] Bell, *At the Works*, 163. As Bell here indicates in passing, open access to books was not the norm in public libraries in the Victorian period: the customary, laborious method of book-borrowing was to look up a title in the catalogue, then look it up again on a card index which indicated which books were in and which out, then request it from a librarian and have it entered in the borrowing register. This system could lead to some mistaken choices. The Aberdeen Free Library Annual Report in 1888/9 recorded that 'The fact that a small devotional work, entitled "The Best Match," was called for (and quickly returned) sixty-five times by readers, chiefly of the female sex, is hardly to be taken as a proof of the popularity of that particular book or of the exceptionally devotional character of the library readers. Rather it is to be taken as one of the many cases where, the substance of the book not realising the hopes raised by the title, it is with all possible speed returned to the library' (*Library*, 1 (1889), 345–6).
[111] Bell, *At the Works*, 169.
[112] 'A Working Woman', 'Do Public Libraries Foster a Love of Literature Among the Masses?', *Chambers' Journal*, 6th ser., 3 (1899), 134–5.

Public Libraries and Women Readers

As Lady Bell's comments indicate, the question of the availability of books was a further issue which occupied magazine and periodical writers. The Ewart Act, providing for the foundation of free public libraries in England, received Royal Assent on 14 August 1850.[113] Although the spread of these libraries was relatively slow, apart from the initial enthusiasm shown by large cities such as Manchester and Liverpool,[114] their growth did not just offer women new opportunities of access to books: it gave them prospects of working with them. England lagged behind America in this respect. The Conference of Librarians in 1877 heard various representatives of the American library system comment with surprise how few women library assistants were employed in England, whereas in Boston Public Library, for example, they had their pick of graduates from Vassar and Wellesley: women with a fair knowledge of Latin, Greek, Italian and Spanish, who—significantly—'for the money they cost . . . are infinitely better than equivalent salaries will produce of the other sex'.[115] By 1882, however, it could be reported that women were gradually making their way into libraries, and that it was no longer necessary to give reasons why they should not be employed. Henry Tedder, librarian of the Athenaeum, outlined some of the reasons which had previously been offered:

They are said to be wanting in intelligence or physical strength; they are reported to distract the attention of male readers; and the duties of a librarian are considered inappropriate to their sex. Some people object to the presence of young women as assistants in a library on the ground that such a proceeding savours of novelty, and therefore ought to be opposed.

But in fact, Tedder claimed: 'It is easy to find young women fully qualified, both by education and natural aptness, and they are generally more refined and more teachable than the young men of their own class.'[116] Manchester libraries were the first in England to engage women, finding their assistance particularly useful in calming the more boisterous elements in boys' reading-rooms, where they were always put in charge. In general, they were recruited from the daughters of tradesmen and shopkeepers, and paid between 10*s.* per week to

[113] For the establishment and growth of public libraries in the UK, see Richard D. Altick, *The English Common Reader* (1957; repr. 1963), 213–39.

[114] Altick (ibid. 227) records that in town after town, proposals to 'adopt the acts' were repeatedly defeated. By 1896, only 334 districts, many of them small, had levied the library rate: 46 districts with populations of over 20,000 had refused to do so, opposition being particularly strong in London. The peak period for the foundation of British libraries (225 were established in England and Wales between 1897 and 1913) was largely the result of the generosity of Andrew Carnegie.

[115] Prof. Justin Winsor, addressing the Conference of Librarians, Oct. 1977, reported in the *Library Journal*, 2 (Jan.–Feb. 1878), 280.

[116] Henry R. Tedder, 'Librarianship as a Profession', *Transactions and Proceedings of the Fifth Annual Meeting of the Library Association of the United Kingdom* (Cambridge, 1882), 171.

£80 per annum, depending on ability and experience.[117] Clerkenwell, in 1889, was among the earliest London rate-supported libraries to employ female assistants: four years later, a spokesman was glad to report that the work of the library had not suffered 'from the frivolity said to be inseparable from the female character'.[118] In Bristol, indeed, the library committee were 'great believers in the humanizing power of the gentler sex in library work'.[119] None the less, some libraries remained slow to employ women. Both Bolton and Croydon, for example, waited for the shortage of men which the 1914–18 war brought about before they did so.

Women librarians could be deployed throughout a library: almost invariably, they were to be found in women's reading-rooms. The establishment of such reading-rooms, where newspapers and periodicals, and in some cases reference books, could be made readily available to women alone was frequently debated at a local level. So far as I am aware, Sheffield was the first Public Library to install such a room, in 1860, followed by Derby, in 1871, recording that the library committee believed 'that such a room would be a boon to many young persons employed in shops and elsewhere, who might be induced thus profitably to employ their leisure hours in the evening'.[120] Greenwood, by the fourth edition of his book on Public Libraries, despite having earlier encouraged the establishment of Ladies' Rooms, argued against them on the grounds that they encouraged gossip, and that fashion sheets and plates occasionally went missing from the tables. Not only would their abolition (and replacement by separate tables for women in reading-rooms) lead to an economizing of supervisory staff, but the renewed presence of women is conceived of by him in favourable decorative terms: 'their presence in a large room aids the general decorum, and gives an appearance of cheerfulness and brightness to a news and reading-room.'[121] Minute-books and records of various libraries suggest other problems which could arise in segregated rooms. In both 1906 and 1909 complaints were received that the Ladies' Room in Horbury Free Library, in West Yorkshire, 'was being used as a nursery . . . [and] is little better than a playground for little girls'.[122] But in a long defence of their existence in the *Library*, Butler Wood believed that the advantages of such reading-rooms—properly supervised—far outweighed such problems as Greenwood mentioned, even if—which he doubted—these allegations of

[117] [Harry Rawson] 'The Public Free Libraries of Manchester: Their History, Organisation and Work', *Library*, 4 (1892), 292.
[118] J. D. Brown, 'The Working of Clerkenwell Public Library', *Library*, 5 (1893), 116.
[119] Thomas Greenwood, *Public Libraries: A History of the Movement and a Manual for the Organization, and Management of Rate-Supported Libraries* (4th edn., 1894), 224.
[120] *Derby Free Public Library Annual Report*, 1 (1872), 11. The room was, however, temporarily closed the following year, due to 'some unprincipled individuals purloining, &c., newspapers and periodicals' (ibid. 2 (1873), 4).
[121] Greenwood, *Public Libraries*, 386.
[122] *Minute Book of the Carnegie Free Library, Horbury, Sept. 1905—July 1909*, 31 July 1906, 107; Chairman's Annual Report, Apr. 1909, 279.

misconduct could be seriously substantiated. Above all, separate reading-rooms would encourage women readers to visit the library, and he cites his own experience in Bradford: 'Before opening the separate room it was an uncommon thing to see a woman enter the general Reading-room, and whenever one did so, it was with the air of an intruder who felt her position, and who would very soon beat a retreat from what appeared to be an embarrassing situation.' The daily average of visitors was now, he claimed, over 260: the room (which had accommodation for 50) was over half full during the day, and almost fully occupied in the evenings.[123] Moreover, Wood came out, in the same article, in favour of establishing separate counters for women and men borrowers. On the face of it, he said, this might seem to be 'carrying the fad of separation too far', but statistics proved otherwise. Before Bradford installed separate counters, in both the Lending and Reference sections, women did not constitute more than 10 per cent of the whole; but of 10,806 borrowers installed in 1890, 4,540 were women. Moreover, the existence of separate counters allowed separate tallies to be made of book issues. During 1890, the figures were: 'Reference Department: Men, 69,313; Women, 2,157; Lending Department: Men, 95,978; Women, 77,430.'[124]Wood believed that at the time of writing, twenty-two other towns had opened separate women's reading-rooms.[125]

From Wood's evidence, and from the readiness with which many libraries provided separate rooms, separate tables within reading-rooms—sometimes, even, separate entrances for women—it would appear that such moves could be effective in attracting women into public libraries. That such a move should be necessary becomes clear when one considers the class and occupational background of public library users. Until after the First World War, at least, public libraries primarily served the skilled working classes and tradespeople, the middle classes continuing to patronize circulating and subscription libraries.

[123] Butler Wood, 'Three Special Features of Free Library Work—Open Shelves, Women Readers, and Juvenile Departments', *Library*, 4 (1892), 108. Wood includes a list of the publications laid on the table in the women's reading-room: London Daily Newspapers: *Daily News, Daily Graphic, Standard, Telegraph, The Times*; Provincial Daily Newspapers: *Bradford Observer* (2 copies), *Bradford Telegraph* (2 copies), *Leeds Mercury, Liverpool Mercury, Manchester Guardian, Yorkshire Post*; Weekly Publications: *Bazaar* (thrice weekly), *Bradford Weekly Telegraph, Bradford Observer Budget, Bradford Weekly Mercury, Girl's Own Paper* (2 copies), *Graphic, Illustrated London News, Ladies' Pictorial, Punch, Queen, Schoolmaster, Tit Bits, The Lady, Yorkshireman, Young Ladies' Journal*; Monthly Periodicals: *Atlanta, All the Year Round, Argosy, British Workman, Cassell's Magazine, Century Magazine, Chambers' Journal, Good Words, Harper's Magazine, Ladies' Treasury, Leisure Hour, Longman's Magazine, Mother's Friend, Mrs. Leach's Dressmaker, Myra's Journal, Quiver, Sunday at Home, Sunday Magazine, Sylvia's Journal, Weldon's Journal, The Women's Review*.

[124] Ibid. 111.

[125] The list he gives is: Belfast, Bradford, Cardiff, Chelsea, Darlington, Doncaster, Dunfermline, Edinburgh, Gateshead, Grangemouth, Halifax, Hanley, Leicester, Newark, Norwich, Nottingham, Plymouth, Portsmouth, Rochdale, Rotherham, St Helen's, and Sunderland. This does not, of course, include branch libraries. Birmingham had also tried the experiment, but it was not successful, apparently because of insuffient supervision: however, separate tables for women had now been installed in the main reading-room.

The exception, in many cases, was formed by teachers and governesses.[126]
Since libraries were also, as Richard Altick has pointed out, the haunts of
vagrants, the unemployed, eccentrics, and those searching after betting
news,[127] they not only put off potential women users—and doubtless some
men—but did not fit in with their administrators' impression about what
formed a suitable environment for the female sex. Thus the librarian of
Wolverhampton library, contributing to the discussion in the *Library* about
whether or not betting news should be removed from the columns of the
newspapers in reading-rooms, recorded the conditions which had led to his
institution adopting this decision:

great difficulty was experienced in removing hordes of loungers round the doors,
spitting, smoking, and discussing the merits and demerits of horses in language unfit for
quotation; to these evils was added another hitherto unheard of, viz., that timid ladies
were deterred from entering the building and using the library, on account of the roughs
assembling near the entrance.[128]

Thomas Kelly, in his history of public libraries, *Books For the People* (1977)
claims that the reading-room was usually the lowest of all parts of the library in
social estimation,[129] and contemporary descriptions bear this out. One woman,
for example, wrote to the *Bolton Evening News* complaining against the thirty or
forty 'unwashed gentlemen either of the tramping or loafing fraternity' whom
she found seated around the tables 'either having a doze or gazing apparently
into futurity . . . or more or less busy killing time'.[130] Although most of the men

[126] This information can be gathered from the individual records of public libraries, usually
found in their annual reports. These can be extremely detailed: the reports of Wimbledon Public
Library from the late 1880s and 1890s, for example, include not only lists which classify the
borrowers by occupations, but which trace the borrowing records of certain chosen books
throughout the year, so that it is possible to find out the occupations and ages of those who took
them out. The reports for Aberdeen Public Library at the turn of the century are similarly
informative: that for 1900–1, for example, giving 26 examples of individual reading patterns
throughout the year, choosing those practising occupations as diverse as law clerk and fish curer.
Thus we learn that 'A Young Lady (No occupation stated)' borrowed Adeline Sergeant, *This body of
death*; Mary E. Wilkins, *Understudies*; H. Rider Haggard, *Lysbeth*; C. J. S. Thompson, *Poison
Romance and Poison Mysteries*; W. Le Queux, *Of Royal Blood*; Frances Harrod, *The Hidden Model*; E.
M. Nicholl, *Observations of a Ranchwoman*; and 'Rita', *The Sin of Jasper Standish*. 'A teacher.
(Female.)' borrowed Florence Marryat, *An Angel of Pity*; E. Bain, *Merchant and Craft Guilds*, S. R.
Crockett, *Ione March*; Rudyard Kipling, *The Day's Work*, W. Le Queux, *The Bond of Black*; Florence
Marryat, *Heart of Jane Warner*; Lucas Cleeve, *What a Woman will Do*; and Adeline Sergeant,
Daunay's Tower. (Aberdeen Public Library, *Report for 1900–1901*, 20, 25).
[127] Altick, *English Common Reader*, 238.
[128] J. Elliot, 'The Extinction of the Betting Evil in Public News Rooms', *Library*, 5 (1893), 193.
Elliot notes, incidentally, that women were themselves among those who followed racing form.
[129] Thomas Kelly, *Books for the People* (1977), 168.
[130] *Bolton Evening News* (25 Apr. 1911). Not all the reasons which were advanced for women not
making as full use as they might of public libraries focused on the issue of social propriety, however.
Greenwood noted with surprise that Yorkshire ladies do not represent a large proportion of those
who made use of the reference section of Leeds Public Library, and surmised that this may be due
to the large number of steps which they had to climb before reaching this room. (*Public Libraries*
(4th edn.), 114).

in an illustration by E. F. Brewtnall, 'In the Reading-Room of a London Free Library' (*Graphic* (15 Oct. 1892)) look respectable enough (Fig. 13), the plate represents clearly the cramped proximity to which some objected. On occasion, those who provided facilities for women worked to establish surroundings radically different in atmosphere. When Hull Central Library moved to its new premises in 1901, a contemporary account noted that the Ladies' reading-room on the left-hand side of the front hall was:

25 feet long by 14 feet 6 inches wide, furnished in walnut with comfortable tables and chairs, while in the chimney piece is a fine piece of beautifully figured onyx, which enhances the appearance and cosiness of the room. The ladies who are to use this room have evidently been consulted, as the overmantel contains a fine mirror, which may give rise to 'fair reflections' when literature fails to charm.[131]

Bury Library opened a women's reading-room in 1902, following a gift of £1,000 from a Mrs Davies: Mr Sparke, the librarian, 'fitted up the room with £125 worth of furniture over and above the ordinary equipment of a reading-room, and obtained gifts of lovely pictures for the walls. Plants and settees give the apartment a special air of coolness and repose.'[132] At Southend, where a Ladies' Room was opened in 1906, the programme of the official opening noted that this room was particularly attractive, with red distempered and frieze-decorated walls.[133]

Not all women, however, welcomed the idea of separate reading-rooms, perhaps on the grounds suggested by a cartoon (from an unidentifiable source) pasted into the scrapbook of the Guildhall Library (Fig. 14); and by the comments of feature writers. The popular stereotype of women using public libraries as places in which to giggle and gossip and pick up fashion hints is borne out by a page of sketches from the *Lady's Pictorial* of 20 April 1895 (Fig. 15). Perhaps such a view was not always unfounded: the annual report of Kidderminster Public Library in 1909 noted that 'The popularity of the Ladies Table has grown so much that it has become a frequent source of inconvenience to readers in our Reference Library.' The following year, a Ladies' Room having been established, it was remarked that 'The reference Room has also been more largely used by Students since the removal of the Ladies' Table, the increased quiet, so essential to study, being greatly enjoyed.'[134] The verbatim report of the Middlesborough Free Library Committee gives a good idea of the combination of seriousness and irreverence with which women's social issues could be treated. At its May meeting:

[131] This information comes from an unmarked cutting kindly sent to me by the Librarian of Hull Public Library.

[132] *Daily Dispatch* (29 July 1902), 7.

[133] Programme of the official opening of Southend Library, 24 July 1906: information supplied by the County Librarian, Essex County Council.

[134] Borough of Kidderminster, *Public Library: Twenty-ninth Annual Report* (1909–10), 4; *Public Library: Thirtieth Annual Report* (1910–11), 2.

13. E. G. Brewtnall, *In the Reading Room of a London Free Library*, *Graphic*, 15 October 1892

15. *Some Women at the Free Library, Lady's Pictorial*, 20 April 1895

14. *In the Library*, unidentified newspaper clipping

a petition signed by ladies was received, asking the committee to again consider the question of providing better accommodation for the ladies visiting the Reading Room. Ald. Hugh Bell said it appeared to him that the petition was not quite so weighty as at first it seemed to be. Someone had struck out the word 'again' and put over it 'not'; while another person had placed a query after 'ladies'. Someone had written, 'A good many of the females are not half so well behaved as the men,' to which was added, in another hand, 'Hear, hear.' A person who did not give any indication of his or her name wrote, 'What ridiculous nonsense,' and one lady went so far to opine 'It is tommy rot.' Though he could not cap 'tommy rot,' another inscription ran 'Please do no such thing.' Ald. Sanderson said that could be easily accounted for, because there were a number of young girls who, if they had their own way, would prefer to have an opportunity of looking at the men, and being looked at by them. The matter was adjourned.[135]

Women were frequent users of the British Museum Reading-Room, in the course of employment as much as for leisure. In 1881, Percy Fitzgerald noted the number who worked there as copying-clerks 'for some literary man who has cash and position'.[136] But, on occasion, men evidently felt jealous of a territory which they considered their own. The *Saturday Review*, in August 1886, reported a current spate of letters to newspapers complaining that the presence of women in this Reading-Room made it a place where study was impossible. The rustling of dresses was frowned on:

They also grumble that they cannot slake the dust of the floor by scattering ink from their pens thereon, as seems to be their habit, for fear of blotting the skirts of the ladies. They also report—we fear with some truth—that woman talks and whispers and giggles beneath the stately dome, nay, that she flirts, and eats strawberries behind folios, in the society of some happy student of the opposite sex. When she does read, she is accused of reading novels and newspapers, which she might better procure elsewhere. Certainly novel-readers in the crowded Museum Library are sitting where they ought not, and are occupying room more needed than their company, unless they are very pretty indeed.

The *Saturday Review*—notwithstanding its own would-be humorous bias displayed in the last sentence—ostensibly came out in favour of women's presence in the Reading-Room, however, claiming that 'the natives of our Oriental dependencies' who have come there because it is thought to be the warmest place in London, and boys reading cribs, are equally to blame. Women can be as industrious and quiet as any men, and tend to be less disturbed by masculine presence than men are by women. The writer claims that attempts to keep a portion of the seats aside for women have not been very successful, but

[135] 'Library Notes and News', *Library*, 5 (1893), 140. According to information supplied by Middlesborough Library, a Ladies' Room was indeed established in 1894 (there had been 'Ladies' tables in the Central Reading-Room since 1887), moving with the library in 1912 and continuing in use until 1964–5.

[136] Percy Fitzgerald, 'A Day at the Museum Reading Room', *Belgravia*, 46 (1881), 161. A subsequent short story (Edward Kersey, 'A Romance of a Public Library', ibid. 68 (1889), 35–49) deals bitterly with the way in which (male) library assistants are very much at the mercy of those female scribes and researchers who choose to compensate for their inferior positions by expecting the library staff to work for *them*.

concludes, tellingly: 'Perhaps some other room may be set apart for men whose names and business prove that they were very serious and important students indeed.'[137] Whilst no such a room was provided, such complaints may have fuelled the debates about overcrowding, which led to the formation of a rule of 1889 that readers might not be supplied with novels within five years of their publication, unless they satisfactorily stated their reasons in writing.[138]

As Altick notes, arguments about the establishment and use of public libraries in the nineteenth century tended to focus on their presumed social value: the knowledge acquired through learning would, it was argued, defuse radical tendencies; library facilities presented an answer to the drink problem; and a more settled, sober, and law-abiding population would aid the progress of the English economy. Greenwood tells an affecting little tale which exemplifies this viewpoint, and gives public libraries a conventionally feminine redemptive role to play. To him, they:

are centres of light, and not only feed, but create a taste for reading, and, unquestionably, whatever does this is a benefit to the whole community, and aids materially in the repressing and taming of the rougher and baser parts of human nature. The writer, who formerly held the position of librarian, is well aware how often wives and children come for books, and make the request, 'Please pick me a nice one, sir, for if I take home an interesting book, my husband (or father, as the case may be) will stop in during the evening and read it aloud.'[139]

The particular benefits which reading might bring to an individual were hardly, if ever, mentioned. Indeed, 'the old religious and utilitarian prejudices against reading for entertainment still persisted; if the nation were to subsidize the reading habit, it should only do so for serious purposes'.[140] Hence it was not just in relation to the British Museum's library that fiction was a contentious matter. Certain libraries, such as that of Newcastle upon Tyne, banned modern novels entirely, fearing that if they were to admit them 'their library would be flooded with unmitigated trash'.[141] Partial censorship, too, was regularly practised, right into this century, with the aim of exercising a kind of quality control. Acton Free Library Committee in 1894 excluded the work of Ouida, Fielding, and Smollett;[142] Marie Corelli was banished from the shelves of Ealing Public Library in 1893, although *Thelma* and *A Romance of Two Worlds*

---

[137] 'Ladies in Libraries', *Saturday Review* (14 Aug. 1886), 213. Fitzgerald had noted that the non-occupancy of these seats was a standing joke. The special labels specifically reserving certain tables for ladies were removed when the Reading-Room was redecorated in 1907, at a time when the numbers of women readers in the Library were rapidly expanding: the daily average was 1 : 5 in 1906, rising to 1 : 3 by 1913. G. F. Barwick, *The Reading Room of the British Museum* (1929), 137, 144.

[138] *Library*, 1 (1889), 110.

[139] Greenwood, *Public Libraries*, 35.

[140] Altick, *English Common Reader*, 231.

[141] Report of the annual meeting of the Newcastle-upon-Tyne Literary and Philosophical Society, *Library*, 1 (1889), 178.

[142] 'Library Notes and News', *Library*, 6 (1894), 252.

were reinstated after it was said, during a heated debate on the author's merits, that the Queen enjoyed reading her.[143]

Whilst records of meetings show that a certain amount of the debate as to whether or not lighter forms of fiction should be available for public borrowing centered on the belief that office boys and clerks wasted their own and their employers' time through devouring 'trivial literary trash', the familiar complaints that 'many a home is neglected and uncared for owing to the all-absorbed novel-reading wife' were also put forward.[144]

But notwithstanding the instances cited above, the role of library officials as moral literary police officers declined by the end of the century. By 1889, when the Library Association held a symposium on the issue of the availability, or otherwise, of fiction in public libraries, earlier evangelical objections had faded away, and it was virtually unanimous that libraries should provide novels as a route to relaxation, as well as supplying texts with a more conspicuous claim to cultivate knowledge.[145]

Taste in books, whether read for relaxation or for self-improvement, provided an instant means by which Victorian and Edwardian women could be classified. The mere mention of certain titles was enough to stimulate sets of expectations about social attitudes. Thus a portrayal of 'The Glorified Spinster' in *Macmillan's Magazine* has her living in economical lodgings: abstemious, tidy if Bohemian-Newnham in her decorative tastes, with well-filled bookshelves over the mantelpiece: 'in which may be noted Mill's Logic, two volumes of Mr. Browning's poems, one of Walt Whitman's, Mr. Herbert Spencer's "Study of Sociology", and several French and German novels. The Spinster is an omniverous reader, and would sooner forego her breakfast than her newspaper.'[146] 'The Modern Young Person' is instantly recognizable through another set of props: 'On a table beside her, lay a box of cigarettes, the current number of the "New Review," and the last novel of Zola's. On her lap was a copy of the "Heavenly Twins".'[147] Both these women have been placed within a distinctive 'habitus', to use Pierre Bourdieu's term: a social space, in other words, which has been constructed according to a 'generative formula which makes it possible to account both for the classifiable practices and products and for the judgements, themselves classified, which make these practices and works into a system of distinctive signs'.[148]

Nowhere is such pigeon-holing so obvious as in contexts with an ostensibly humorous end. Written to entertain rather than to inform and instruct,

---

[143] 'Jottings', *Library*, 5 (1893), 49.
[144] Altick, *English Common Reader*, 232.
[145] See 'Fiction in Libraries', *Library*, 1 (1889), 386–90.
[146] Frances Martin, 'The Glorified Spinster', *Macmillan's Magazine*, 58 (1888), 372–3.
[147] 'Rita' [Eliza Margaret Humphreys] 'The Modern Young Person', *Belgravia*, 86 (1895), 61.
[148] Pierre Bourdieu, *Distinction: A Social Critique of the Judgement of Taste* (*La Distinction: critique sociale du jugement* (1979)), trans. Richard Nice (1984), 170.

'humorous' pieces helped, on occasion, to reinforce the prevalent images of the 'woman reader'. These pieces were not invariably by men, even when they adopted a masculine persona. Early in her career, Mary Braddon published an essay entitled 'My Daughters' in the *Welcome Guest*. In this, the purported writer complains against the way in which his grown-up daughters are completely taken up with whatever happens to be the fashionable text of the moment, which infects their attitudes, their vocabulary. They form their ideas of suitable husbands around Sidney Carton or John Halifax, Gentleman. Reading Tennyson, Juliana, Augustina, and Fredericka complain, should their father refuse them a new silk dress or a box at the opera, that their lives are 'weary' and that, on the whole, they would find it agreeable to be dead; when they come fresh from *Friedrich the Second*: 'Oh, the abusive names I have been called, on venturing to remonstrate on the subject of milliners' bills! Dryasdusts, phosphorescent blockheads, putrefied spectralities, and all sorts of insulting epithets have rained down on this devoted head.' All this mimicking of writers' tones is sadly empty, however, if they indicate that reading has been merely a means in itself, not an end. Braddon, retreating, one is tempted to think, to her 'own' voice at the end of the article, concludes with a solemn warning: 'if these books do not teach them better things than to lie on the sofa all day reading them, and to spend all the rest of the day talking of them, they do not read those books aright'.[149]

This is a more daring article than it appears at first sight, under its guise of anxious, harassed paternalism. For it suggests that somehow any girl who recognizes an exaggerated version of herself must take responsibility for her own reading and life. The self-indulgent mock lamentations of the father provide little guidance: indeed, they serve to preserve the daughters in an atmosphere of belittlement which, the writer suggests at the close, they could use their reading to transcend.

There is far less subtlety, far less ultimate sympathy with the woman's position to be found in most of the male 'humourists'. In 'Our Audience' (1863), Charles Collins complained against the lack of attention paid by many readers (especially women) to literary productions. In tacit opposition to the topical complaint that sensation fiction absorbed their concentration to the exclusion of all else, Collins, in a pompous effort at humour, sets up a number of stereotypes of inattentive women readers. First, there are those who use a book as a prop, sulking behind it as a 'literary rampart' when they wish to withdraw from an argument, or pretending preoccupation whilst actually observing and chastising their children's misbehaviour—and 'what sort of reverence will they feel in after life for a volume which they look upon as a kind of domestic ambush?' Alternatively, reading, he maintains, cannot be taken seriously when combined with other activities: knitting, for example, or sitting at

---

[149] M. E. Braddon, 'My Daughters', *Welcome Guest*, 3 (1861), 79–82.

the dressing-table: 'I must protest against the introduction of a nail-brush into my strong passages. I really cannot sit down tamely under the thought that a hair-pin may be at this moment blasting one of my tender speeches.'[150]

In 1897, the *Academy* ran a series of sketches entitled 'What the People Read'. Couched as dialogues, the 'people' who were talked to included a solicitor, a bookstall keeper, a constable, an 'ambassador of commerce', and various women. In this popularization of an earlier nineteenth-century form of descriptive sociology, there is no guarantee (such as Mayhew offers) that these are more or less authentic interviews: what does, however, emerge clearly is a range of preconceptions concerning the reading of particular social groupings. Thus 'A Waitress', whose favourite words of commendation are 'lovely' and 'nice', recognizes her preferred books—*East Lynne*, *The Sorrows of Satan*, and *We Two*—by title alone, the names of Wood, Corelli, and Lyall counting for nothing, and prefers love stories about those of her own 'rank' or higher.[151] 'A Wife' listlessly condemns novels about cavaliers, the future (though she admits that one has to read Bellamy and Wells, 'because everyone talks about them'), foreigners, and Jews, preferring novels about 'the sort of people one meets every day, only—you know—put into strange situations';[152] whilst 'An Aunt' values Tennyson, Dickens, and the sweetness of Rhoda Broughton.[153] Later the same year, 'He, She and the Library List', somewhat more seriously, tried to identify the characteristics which distinguished men's fiction from women's fiction: why should men return repeatedly to Kipling and Conan Doyle, women to Anthony Hope and Mr Merriman? Tentatively, the writer suggests 'that man takes his novel as a stimulant, woman as a sedative'. Man prefers story, action, power; woman minute analysis of character and motive, descriptions of scenery, and 'irrelevant chatter'.[154] Such 'passion for detail', incidentally, was increasingly identified with the novel 'written by women for women'.[155]

In medical and psychoanalytic texts, the consideration of reading was generally an incidental issue, subordinated to the writer's broader arguments regarding systems of perception and assimilation, intuition, and maturation. As we have seen, this incorporation of the topic of reading not only had the dual effect of consolidating physiological and psychoanalytic theory through the provision of empirical detail, and of confirming assumptions about reading through offering them the support of 'scientific' discourse; it also simultaneously drew on and reinforced certain dominant social attitudes. Many of these attitudes were more blatantly instilled in books of advice, in which reading often appeared as a central point of reference, being an activity common to many young girls, and a

[150]   Charles Allston Collins, 'Our Audience', *Macmillan's Magazine*, 8 (1863), 162–3.
[151]   'What the People Read. II. A Waitress', *Academy*, 52 (1897), 303.
[152]   'What the People Read. XI. A Wife', *Academy*, 53 (1898), 293–4.
[153]   'What the People Read. XII. An Aunt', ibid. 377–8.
[154]   'He, She, and the Library List', *Academy*, 54 (1898), 553.
[155]   See W. L. Cortney, *The Feminine Note in Fiction* (1904), pp. x–xiv.

convenient site for the legislation of private thoughts and responses. The very terms of its occurrence in these self-help manuals, with their strong emphasis on the capacity of print to influence, necessarily worked, of course, to legitimize the existence of such volumes in the first place. In educational writing, as in medical texts, the issue of reading tends to be subordinated to broader discussions of child development and the learning process, although since reading is intrinsic to education, it invariably occupied a far more centralized position. What the material drawn upon in this final section has shown is how readily these social attitudes were employed in order sometimes to formulate and legitimize critical opinion and sometimes, in the case of feminist writers, to challenge it. We have seen, too, how dominant attitudes fed into public social policy, particularly in the case of the provision of public library facilities, and how they could be used to categorize women without troubling to consider too deeply the reality which might lie underneath the stereotype. But at the same time, there was considerable curiosity, sometimes disquiet, about these stereotypes. We find this reflected in the growing number of social surveys designed to find out what women and girls actually were reading. It comes as no surprise that a huge variety of actual practices start to emerge from these surveys, and it is on the implications of this variety that I shall be concentrating in Part III. It is this variety that serves, in the long run, to undermine prevalent Victorian assumptions that women could be relied on to respond to their reading material in predictable ways.

Part III

8   Reading Practices

The previous chapter introduced a range of material which addressed itself to the issue of the 'woman reader'. It bore witness to the prevalent stereotypes, to the reiteration of preoccupations and anxieties concerning the desires and susceptibilities of woman readers, particularly, if not exclusively, those who were young and came from the middle classes. Additionally, it indicated that attempts were made to investigate and categorize the reality behind the stereotypes and assumptions. Now, however, we turn to the accounts not of those who comment as outside observers, but of those who have something to relate concerning their own reading practices.

Evidence of what individual women were actually reading throughout the period, and the ways in which they incorporated references to their reading activities into autobiographies, letters, and journals considerably complicates our view of the Victorian woman reader, challenging many of the generalizations advanced by contemporary commentators. It emphasizes the extreme heterogeneity of readers and their texts throughout the period and provides a set of examples and narratives through which we may examine the relationship between theory and practice. Simultaneously, it reminds us of the specificities of circumstance, the variables of parental occupation and family affluence, of urban or rural lives, of religious affiliations, enthusiastic relatives, and modes of education which militate against establishing neat patterns of generalization, whether contemporaneous or retrospective.

One needs, necessarily, to exercise a certain amount of caution when using autobiographical material. The very fact of each of these authors committing themselves to paper apparently indicates the degree of importance they placed on the value of the written word: they were, perhaps, atypical in this literary self-awareness. Moreover, each will have had her own reasons for wishing to foreground certain aspects of herself through those texts which she chose to present as having been crucial to the development of her personality. At the time that one is experiencing an event or epoch in one's life, one generally remains uncertain about patterns of cause and effect as they relate to oneself: it is only retrospectively that the autobiographer, to quote William Howarth, 'artfully defines, restricts, or shapes that life into a self-portrait—one far removed from his original model, resembling life but actually composed and framed as an artful invention'. The character must be carefully distinguished from the author, since 'it performs as a double persona: telling the story as a narrator, enacting it as a protagonist'.[1] Autobiography, in other words, involves

---

[1] William L. Howarth, 'Some Principles of Autobiography', in *Autobiography: Essays Theoretical and Critical*, ed. James Olney (Princeton, NJ, 1980), 86–7.

self-fashioning through selectivity and arrangement. This fact was well recognized in the nineteenth century: Edith Simcox, for example, writing that 'no autobiographies are intentional impostures throughout . . . but there are varieties of falsehood and degrees of truth. Facts and intentions admit equally of misstatement; real actions may be explained erroneously, and imaginary conduct accounted for by real motives.'[2] In more formal terms, we might say that the autobiographical text becomes, as Sidonie Smith puts it, 'a narrative artifice, privileging a presence, or identity, that does not exist outside language. Given the very nature of language, embedded in the text lie alternative or deferred identities that constantly subvert any pretensions of truthfulness.'[3] In this way, autobiography may be seen to partake, to some extent, of the nature of fiction. Indeed, it has been argued that so unwieldy was the masculine autobiographical form with which women had to contend in the nineteenth century that it was in fact easier for them to couch their experiences, their frustrations, and desires in fiction, maybe thus rewriting them. One might think of Charlotte Brontë's *The Professor* or *Villette* at one end of the period; of Sarah Grand's *The Beth Book* at the other.[4]

Many, though not all, of the women who thought it valuable to publish their autobiographies were to some degree unusual in that they were in the public eye, whether as writers, educationists, activists in the women's movement, or administrators. As Jane Marcus has pointed out, the writing of autobiography may be understood, for such women, as a resignation from public discourse into private discourse, a re/signing of their names in women's history. The reassertion of the domestic sphere which in part, at least, results, represents a dynamic flowing against the direction which most feminist historians have opted to study, the move from private to public spheres. What, almost inevitably, these women came to address, Marcus claims, was a 'private collective world of women readers'.[5] This stress on the domestic, is, as Jelinek indicated, something which tends to differentiate the autobiographies of publicly successful women from those of their male counterparts:[6] it offers, evidently enough, a means whereby women may present their lives in a way which does not come across as remote, inaccessible, and unachievable by contrast to the circumstances of their readers.

None the less, the emphasis which may be placed in such autobiographies on the home and family and the support that they may offer (or the restrictive

---

[2] [Edith Simcox] 'Autobiographies', *North British Review*, 101 (1869), 392.

[3] Sidonie Smith, *A Poetics of Women's Autobiography: Marginality and the Fictions of Self-Representation* (Bloomington, Ind., and Indianapolis, 1987), 5.

[4] See e.g. Deborah Epstein Nord, *The Apprenticeship of Beatrice Webb* (Amherst, 1985), 58–9. This generalization seems more valid when one considers the autobiographies of women in public life than when one considers spiritual or confessional forms.

[5] Jane Marcus, 'Invincible Mediocrity: The Private Selves of Public Women', in Shari Benstock (ed.), *The Private Self: Theory and Practice of Women's Autobiographical Writings* (1988), 114.

[6] Estelle C. Jelinek, 'Introduction: Women's Autobiography and the Male Tradition', in ead. (ed.) *Women's Autobiography: Essays in Cr'''iticism* (Bloomington, Ind., and London, 1980), 8–10.

atmosphere which they may create) should not be confused with an apparently revelatory account of the subject's inner life. Indeed, as Regenia Gagnier has noted in her important work *Subjectivities: A History of Self-Representation in Britain, 1832–1920* (1991), 'women's anxiety concerning self-representation decreases in proportion to women's participation in other discourse, such as that of religion, family, or human rights, and increases in proportion to women's desire to participate in the male romantic tradition of autonomous genius'.[7] In other words, to write of one's own powers, without reference to others, may be a particularly difficult task for a woman. In its turn, this fact increases the degree to which the history of women's autobiography in the nineteenth century may be interpreted in terms of histories of shared subjectivities.

It is useful in this context to distinguish between two distinct types of autobiography, drawing on different types of discourse. On the one hand there are the self-presentations of women who have forged a public role and name for themselves: not easy texts to compose, for as various commentators have pointed out, their models tend, from St Augustine to John Stuart Mill, to be male ones: autobiographies which (despite the internal conflicts experienced by the protagonists) 'rest upon the Western ideal of an essential and inviolable self, which, like its fictional equivalent, character, unifies and propels the narrative'.[8] Such models adapt uneasily to the presentation of a woman who, by going against the cultural norms of her time, frequently has difficulty in expressing her success without apology, embarrassment, or as though destiny or chance, rather than her own effort, has placed her in the position which she now occupies. On the other are those autobiographies which present childhood and adolescence by way of an act of reminiscence, and which attempt to assert or create the permanence and significance of some of the most private and transitory moments which have gone into the formation of their subjects' sense of self. These memoirs are, at least at first sight, of a different nature to those where the author regarded the communication of personal experience not just as an act of notation or arrangement performed for self-gratification, but as playing a part in a wider didactic or political enterprise. The emphasis placed by many of the writers on childhood may plausibly be thought of as another trait particularly associated with women's writing of autobiography. For many women, Patricia Meyer Spacks has suggested, 'adulthood—marriage or spinsterhood—implied relative loss of self. Unlike men, therefore, they looked back fondly to the relative freedom and power of childhood and youth.'[9] This remark is especially suggestive in view of the number of women who wrote

[7] Regenia Gagnier, *Subjectivities: A History of Self-Representation in Britain* (New York and Oxford, 1991), 217.

[8] Bella Brodzski and Celeste Schenck, 'Introduction', *Life/Lines: Theorizing Women's Autobiography* (Ithaca, NY, and London, 1988), 5.

[9] Patricia Meyer Spacks, 'Stages of Self: Notes on Autobiography and the Life Cycle' in Albert E. Stone (ed.), *The American Autobiography: A Collection of Critical Essays* (Englewood Cliffs, NJ, 1981), 48.

Jugenderinnerungen, the term set up by Richard Coe to signify the recording of the experiences and sensations of childhood, as distinct from the *Bildungsroman*, the recounting of one's life story.[10] In women's writing particularly, these two categories may, of course, be valued differently. Jelinek makes the point that the irregularity and disconnected patterning of women's lives in contrast to the chronological, progressive model offered by the careers of many men means that such diffusion and diversity frequently spills into women's self-presentations, 'so by established critical standards, their life studies are excluded from the genre and cast into the "non-artistic" categories of memoir, reminiscence, and other disjunctive forms'.[11] Alternatively, there is a strong argument for viewing many of the most intimate and apparently unstructured memoirs as being linked to women's perception of their social role, for a significant number are explicitly addressed to the writer's children, particularly her daughters: an attempt to forge some kind of bond with them through a recognition of both temporal distance and—although this would be hard to reconstruct with certitude in any individual case—a sense of shared enjoyment of the natural world, of pet cats and goats, of games and fantasy worlds.

Although the experiences and reactions recounted by the autobiographers considered in this section are continually, and crucially, determined by gender, and although the way in which women's autobiography may be structured frequently distinguishes it from that written by men, it none the less is the case that the way in which women's autobiography may be seen to work on its *readers* does not differ as greatly from men's writing as many recent commentators would have us believe. Bella Brodzski and Celeste Schenck have claimed that the very authority of masculine autobiography derives from an assumption held by both author and reader that the life being written or read is in some way an exemplary one, and they use this as a pointer, a distinguishing mark to set against women's writing.[12] Yet such a model for autobiographical writing was also followed by a substantial number of Victorian and Edwardian women writers, themselves doubtless influenced by the broader exemplary genre and the belief that 'good biographies are very improving books'.[13] Just as biographies of famous women set out to show that desirable traits of character could be recognized and copied across generations, across classes, so allusions to texts and past reading experiences played an important part in emphasizing the link between the autobiographer and reader in the present, and in suggesting that a 'community of readers' existed at the level of potential activity, not merely passive receptivity. Like certain forms of fiction, autobiography provides a reader with a vicarious means of experiencing empowerment. In this

[10] Richard Coe, *When the Grass Was Taller: Autobiography and the Experience of Childhood* (New Haven, Conn., 1984), 1–40.

[11] Jelinek, *Women's Autobiography*, 17.

[12] Brodzski and Schenck, 'Introduction', *Life/Lines*, 2–3.

[13] C. M. Sedgwick, *Means and Ends; or, Self-Training* (1839), 239.

case, however, the reader takes on board the knowledge that actual, not fictitious barriers have been overcome.

However, it would be misleading to suggest that the differences between female and male autobiography were negligible in other respects. For, as many commentators have noted, the domestic and public spheres are notoriously hard to bridge in male autobiography. This fact, in its turn frequently contributes to the establishment of a sense of distance and division between these spheres. But the ready incorporation of allusions to the private experience of reading, and the situating of such experience within broader familial and social contexts offered a means whereby woman autobiographers could portray a sense of integration between these different domains. Indeed, reading about reading in autobiography throws into question the absolute nature of any distinction between the subjective and the social.

Leslie Stephen, writing in 1881, claimed that the autobiographer 'has *ex officio* two qualifications of supreme importance in all literary work. He is writing about a topic in which he is keenly interested, and about the topic on which he is the highest living authority.'[14] Whatever challenges women faced in finding a form which suited the shapes of their lives, it is possible to see that autobiography may be an area in which women can, legitimately, claim the right to compose with authority. The central issue to be addressed in this chapter deals with the transmission of this authority. What does it mean for a woman to employ references to reading when constructing and presenting an identity through autobiography? To what extent does she use them to confirm and consolidate her position—and by implication, that of her reader—within a set of predetermined social beliefs, or to oppose or question them? How far does she present reading as a private activity which has fed into her sense of what it means to be a unique individual, differentiating her from, say, her parents, or how far does she perceive it as an act which binds her to others? At the same time, autobiographies, by their very nature, rarely can claim the same transformational powers that a novel, even an advice manual may offer. When we read these retrospective accounts, we are dealing not just with the personal and specific memories of an individual, but with their construction of a historical period. What frequently comes across strongly, however, is not so much a sense of nostalgic difference and loss, nor yet a gratitude for things that have changed, but the recognition, passed on to the reader, of the need for active self-analysis and definition to go hand in hand with one's social practices.

Reading and the Family

Autobiographical material provides us with a great deal of circumstantial information about women's access to reading material. Again and again, the

[14] [Leslie Stephen] 'Autobiography', *Cornhill Magazine*, 43 (1881), 410.

family circle is presented as crucial, and accounts of domestic practices show clearly that the dominant strands of advice and anxiety which I recorded in Part II were both the reflection and the determinants of attitudes within particular homes. Throughout the period, a certain amount of supervision was commonly exercised over the reading material of childhood and adolescence, although prescriptive strictness, particularly with regards to the separation of Sunday and weekday reading, diminished somewhat by the late Victorian and Edwardian decades. There is plenty of first-hand evidence, too, of the prevalent assumption that different types of books were considered desirable and suitable for girls and for boys. The amount of support which girls received in relation to their reading varied enormously, as did the amount of time available for it. As we shall see later, this was especially the case in working-class households. 'Cultivation of the mind? How is it possible? Reading?' asked the tailor and suffrage organizer Ada Nield. 'Those of us who are determined to live like human beings and require food for mind as well as body, are obliged to take time from sleep to gratify this desire.'[15]

But even within those middle-class homes where one might expect to find a degree of respect for cultural pursuits, encouragement for reading could not be counted on. Janet Courtney (b. 1865), a vicar's daughter and early student at Lady Margaret Hall, Oxford, recollects that 'Reading, even in my mother's eyes, was a recreation, not an occupation. We were often asked . . . if we had no sewing to do when we were seen with a book.'[16] She was subsequently delighted to find that Harriet Martineau had had the same experience. For Martineau (b. 1802) wrote critically of this aspect of her upbringing in her *Autobiography* (written 1855, published 1877), stating that when she was young, it was not thought proper for young ladies to study conspicuously, and certainly not with pen in hand. 'Young ladies (at least in provincial towns) were expected to sit down in the parlour to sew,—during which reading aloud was permitted,—or to practise their music; but so as to be fit to receive callers, without any signs of blue-stockingism which could be repeated abroad.'[17] Yet in other families, as we shall shortly see, recreational reading was not only carefully encouraged, but actively planned. Charlotte M. Yonge (b.1823) recalled how, after her daily constitutional in the late afternoon, she was set to read twenty pages of history, from a work like Goldsmith's *Rome*; one chapter of Walter Scott, and then whatever she liked among chosen story-books, books of travels (such as Franklin's *Voyages*), Bowdler's Shakespeare, and Potter's

[15] Ada Nield, *Crewe Chronicle* (5 May 1894), quoted in Jill Liddington and Jill Norris, *One Hand Tied Behind Us: The Rise of the Women's Suffrage Movement* (1978), 112.

[16] Janet E. Courtney, *Recollected in Tranquillity* (1926), 8.

[17] Harriet Martineau, *Harriet Martineau's Autobiography*, ed. Maria Weston Chapman, 2 vols. (Boston, 1877), i. 77. For Martineau's autobiography, which presents the history of her own mind as an exemplum for other women seekers after truth and social amelioration, see Mitzi Myers, 'Harriet Martineau's Autobiography: The Making of a Female Philosopher', in Jelinek, *Women's Autobiography*, 53–70.

translations of the Greek tragedies. This reading was supplementary, incidentally, to her formal lessons.[18]

But many women who were taught at home did not—or, perhaps, could not—distinguish so neatly between which reading material formed part of their formal lessons, and which was consumed in their leisure time. The predictable exceptions to this are the frequent complaints, especially from those born in the 1840s, 1850s, and early 1860s, against the fatuous aridity of the information which they were expected to memorize from question-and-answer books. They were taught elementary historical information from Mrs Markham's *History of England*, geography from *Near Home* and *Far Off*, science from *The Child's Guide to Knowledge*, *Stepping Stones to Knowledge* (the advice given in these that the best course of action in a thunderstorm is to get into one's bed in the middle of a room and pray attracted wry comment from more than one reader), and *Brewer's Guide to Science*. General knowledge came from *Mangnall's Questions*. Such texts were the customary, and probably often desperate tools of governesses who were themselves somewhat skimpily educated. It was not just the contents of such cribs, incidentally, which a governess might impart to her charges. Annabel Huth Jackson, for example, claimed that it took her some time to extricate herself from the 'terrible taste' in literature produced by her governess's fondness for Mrs Henry Wood and Margaret Hungerford, author of *Molly Bawn* (1878).[19]

Even if the reliance of governesses, mothers, and schoolteachers on these tedious methods of imparting knowledge divorced from context appears to have been depressingly frequent, the authors and titles of more stimulating works recur continually. Throughout the period, Shakespeare, Scott, and Dickens are cited as favourite family reading. Story-books such as *The Wide Wide World*, *Holiday House*, *Misunderstood*, *Henry and his Bearer*, and *Sandford and Merton* are, likewise, often mentioned. Many recall Felicia Hemans, Tennyson, especially the *Idylls of the King*, and Longfellow, although the canon of frequently named poets is far smaller than that of novelists. Few had relatives as enterprising as Winifred Peck's stepmother, who introduced her to poets as diverse as Traherne and Emily Dickinson.[20] Specific forms of reading could be fondly associated with certain family rituals. Sybil Lubbock remembers the excitement of Christmas annuals, with their eclectic contents, as well as the reading which prefaced Christmas: as she and her sister embroidered their father's slippers, or prepared things for the Hospital Box, 'our mother read aloud to us from Mrs Ewing or Miss Yonge, from *The Talisman* or *Quentin Durward*'.[21] On Sundays, besides the Bible, collects, hymns, and the catechism, there were Cowper's poems, the *Pilgrim's Progress* and the *Fairchild Family*, *Line Upon Line*, *The Peep of Day* and Mrs Gatty's *Parables from Nature*.

[18] C. M. Yonge, 'A Real Childhood', *Mothers in Council*, 3 (1893), 19.
[19] Annabel Huth Jackson, *A Victorian Childhood* (1932), 107.
[20] Winifred Peck, *A Little Learning or A Victorian Childhood* (1952), 94.
[21] Sybil Lubbock, *The Child in the Crystal* (1939), 38.

With the exception of autobiographers who are clearly setting out to present their reading as exemplary within a Christian context, there is a tendency for recollections of Sunday reading to be characterized by the memory of tedium, constraint, and the enforcement of texts—excepting the Bible and Bunyan—which were decidedly inferior in literary or narrative interest to those read during the rest of the week. Jean Curtis Brown, daughter of a Presbyterian minister in a northern seaport, was not alone in her complaint against the special shelf of books kept for Sundays: 'missionary stories of hardship and heroism in appalling English, "Being and Doing", several volumes of Bible stories "retold" (and why?) with badly drawn pictures of bearded men in dressing-gowns.'[22] The future Vice-Principal of Lady Margaret Hall and Principal of Westfield College, London, Eleanor Lodge (b. 1869), daughter of a Hanley manufacturer, while having no objection to the more instructional books which she and her brothers were expected to read on Sundays, complained about stories which were broken into by chapters on collects or epistles.[23] The novelist Ada Cambridge recollected that memoirs were marginally more attractive than sermons to read, since at least human interest was supplied: once at the beginning, by the portrait, and then at the end, when one found what the worthy subject died from. Far more alluring, as religious reading, was the missionary magazine which a servant used to smuggle in to her, 'full of pictures of black men swinging on hooks thrust through their backs, widows burning alive on pyres, missionaries being horribly tortured, cooked and eaten—all sorts of interesting things'.[24] Ethel Smyth's memory of how 'on Sundays, all the Mudie books were swept into a cupboard and replaced by various well-bound serious works', was typical: she adds how sometimes they would surreptitiously retrieve the immured library books, 'and were driven to the conclusion that one or two novels must surely be upstairs in my mother's bedroom'.[25]

Women frequently express their gratitude to one or both parents, or to other relatives, for introducing them to specific authors or for encouraging their reading generally. A number of reminiscences confirm the prevalent assumption made in advice manuals and in many reviews: that a girl's reading was primarily dependent on her mother's choice and guidance.[26] In the early period of childhood, her influence, predictably enough, commonly took the form of reading aloud to her children: a potentially comforting, bonding practice. Leonora Eyles was taught Felicia Hemans' poem 'A Dear Little Girl Sat Under a Tree' by her mother in the 1890s. Remembering her, in 1953, as an aura,

[22] Jean Curtis Brown, *To Tell My Daughter* (1948), 35.
[23] Eleanor C. Lodge, *Terms and Vacations* (1938), 11.
[24] Ada Cambridge, *The Retrospect* (1912), 157.
[25] Ethel Smyth, *Impressions that Remained*, 2 vols. (1919) i. 23–24.
[26] On this point, the comment made by Jelinek (*Women's Autobiography* 12) that women are less likely to focus on mothers when writing their autobiographies than men are would seem to be founded on insufficient evidence.

'safe and warm and eternally kind and gentle', she notes that she could not read this particular poem 'even now without a feeling of enwrapt protection'.[27] But maternal involvement could also involve more disciplined supervision. The social reformer Josephine Butler (b. 1828) wrote of the debt which she and her siblings owed to their mother:

who was very firm in requiring from us that whatever we did should be thoroughly done, and that in taking up any study we should aim at becoming as perfect as we could in it without external aid. This was a moral discipline which perhaps compensated in value for the lack of a great store of knowledge. She would assemble us daily for the reading aloud of some solid book, and by a kind of examination following the reading aloud assured herself that we had mastered the subject. She urged us to aim at excellence, if not perfection, in at least one thing.[28]

'Vernon Lee' (Violet Paget, b. 1856), had a vexed relationship with her mother, partly because of her ostensible emotional favouring of Violet's half-brother Eugene; partly, one might surmise, because she held very definite ambitions for her daughter, determining that she should become 'at the very least, another De Staël'. She gave her philosophical training in the works of George Coombe and Henry Thomas Buckle, and taught her to write out of Blair's *Rhetoric* and Cobbett's *Grammar*:

I disagreed with all her criticisms, trembled before them; smarted and secretly rebelled under her teaching; and in my heart adored it, like her. And when I now look into my literary preferences I find that I care for a good deal of what I have read, and even for some of what I myself have written, because in some indirect manner it is associated with her indescribable, incomparable person.[29]

A mother's involvement could bring to life practices of self-help which seem dry and depersonalized when suggested through the medium of an advice manual. This is something which reinforces the idea that such texts themselves partly functioned as substitutes for an inventive parent. One of the daughters of Florence Barclay, a writer of popular fiction redolent with sentimental spirituality, recounts how her mother used, in the 1880s, to read aloud to them a great deal: Hans Andersen's Fairy Tales, children's books like *Little Lord Fauntleroy* and *The Little Duke*:

and later on, Scott. At one time, when reading Scott, she told us to stop her every time we came on a word of which we did not know the meaning. This was then written down on a piece of paper, and the next day part of our schoolroom lessons was to find out the meanings of all these words with the help of our governess and a dictionary. It was characteristic of my mother that we never looked at this plan as a dull schooly thing, or as

---

[27] Leonora Eyles, *The Ram Escapes* (1953), 43.

[28] Josephine E. Butler, *An Autobiographical Memoir*, ed. George W. Johnson and Lucy A. Johnson (Bristol and London, 1909), 12–13.

[29] 'Vernon Lee', *The Handling of Words, and Other Studies in Literary Psychology* (New York, 1923), 301.

a tedious interruption to the story; rather, the reading became doubly thrilling, because there was the added excitement of the hunt after unknown words. It was just my mother's own enthusiasm for language that prompted the plan, and she herself always did everything as if it was an exciting game.[30]

The task of teaching a child to read was, of course, one area in which a mother's authority could legitimately be exercised. This is dramatized particularly clearly by Lady Aberdeen (b. 1857), looking back at her early childhood in London in the late 1850s. She learnt to read from the under-butler, sitting with him in the front hall where he waited to open the door to visitors. But when the discovery of her new-found ability was made, the fairy-story books which had first excited her curiosity were banished to a top shelf in the schoolroom, and she was 'furnished with a "Mavor's spelling book" and made to start in the proper fashion'—letter by letter, rather than by recognizing words—'under my mother's personal superintendence'.[31]

Reading with one's mother at home was not without its distractions, however, particularly in the form of interventions deriving from the mother's role as domestic manager. Writing an addendum entitled 'The Interruptions' to the copious journal which she kept in the early 1830s, Emily Shore gave a wry picture of the difficulties attendant on reading Sir Joshua Reynolds' *Discourses* together with her mother one morning. First they were interrupted by the housemaid saying that a man had come round selling baskets, and then entering with the baskets themselves; then by a man servant, answering a bell which had not been rung by them; then by the cook, complaining that the butcher had not sent the scrag of mutton; by the nursemaid, asking about frocks to mend; by a maid, enquiring about a lost thimble; by Emily's younger brother, wanting some paper, and finally by the man-servant announcing a visitor.[32] Nor, incidentally, was it always easy to find a quiet space within the home for independent reading. Frances Buss, founder of the North London Collegiate School, grew up in a house full of younger brothers: she was forced to hide under a sofa on the second floor of the house lived in by her family, in the room of a Government clerk who was out all day.[33] Zoë Procter (b. 1867) describes how, during the 1870s, when her father was governor of the County Gaol at Bury St Edmunds, she 'could not gain sufficient solitude for reading my little story books and was obliged to use the only secure retreat—the long, narrow W.C.'.[34]

---

[30] One of Her Daughters, *The Life of Florence L. Barclay: A Study in Personality* (1921), 103. Florence Barclay's best-known book was *The Rosary* (1909); her aim, quoted by her daughter: 'Never to write a line which could introduce the taint of sin, or the shadow of shame, into any home' (*Life*, 240).

[31] Lord and Lady Aberdeen, *'We Twa': Reminiscences of Lord and Lady Aberdeen* (1925), 104.

[32] Emily Shore, *The Journal of Emily Shore* (rev. edn., 1898), 356.

[33] K. Anderson, 'Frances Mary Buss, the Founder as Headmistress, 1850–94', in R. M. Scrimgeour (ed.), *The North London Collegiate School 1850–1950: A Hundred Years of Girls' Education* (1950), 27.

[34] Zoë Procter, *Life and Yesterday* (1960), 6.

But it would be misleading to believe, along with hopeful Victorian commentators, that the practice of shared reading automatically strengthened the bond between mother and child. Accounts given by daughters can be more revelatory of their mothers' frustration than helping to build up any picture of a nurturing relationship. Margaret Campbell (b. 1888, and better known as the novelist Marjorie Bowen) tells of how she was 'too stupid' for her mother's patience, attempts to teach her to read and write inevitably ending in punishment, with her shut up in a room with bread and water, or beaten on the back of the hands with a hairbrush, although she does not present herself as harbouring resentment at this treatment, claiming that such things were considered part of 'the normal discipline' for a 'sullen child'.[35] Whilst reading could confirm continuity from generation to generation, it could also lead to the recognition of both age difference and a gap in taste and values between daughter and mother. The autobiography of the historian and political analyst Margaret Cole (b. 1893) contains a great deal of information about her reading as a child and adolescent in the 1890s and early twentieth century. Her father taught at Trinity College, Cambridge: she was brought up with plenty of books around, from Dickens, Thackeray, and Kipling to Lewis Carroll, Beatrix Potter, and Juliana Ewing, and read 'with enormous voracity . . . while eating, minding the baby, washing, or lacing my boots for skating'.[36] Yet reading her mother's early volumes of the *Girl's Own Paper*, with illustrations of girls in 'ridiculous clothes', and 'highly moral stories about girls who insisted on higher education and neglected their little brothers so that they fell downstairs on their heads and became idiots for life' indicates how quickly dated such material became to its consumers.[37] Amy Barlow, writing of the late 1890s, recalls how her mother seemed to have a vivid memory of her childhood reading, and would recommend enthusiastically to her daughters books which had meant much to her, but which 'we were inclined to regard with suspicion and levity'. Their titles included *Aunt Jane's Hero*, *Stepping Heavenward*, and a particular object of derision, *The Old Helmet*:

I had heard so much about this book that, when it came my way when I was about sixteen, I pounced on it eagerly. The story, as I remember it, was of a young lady of fashion, elegant and proud, who habitually wore velvet and a picture hat adorned with sweeping ostrich feathers, and galloped about on a spirited chestnut horse. The proud beauty found herself, to her surprise and indignation, attracted by a poor young missionary dedicated to converting the heathen in Patagonia. After a very moving scene in a hut to which they had both repaired to shelter from a storm—I don't know what happened to the horse—the lovely lady capitulated, deciding that she would willingly give up the velvet habit and ostrich plumes to help the young missionary in Patagonia. I

---

[35] Margaret Campbell, 'Margaret Campbell (Marjorie Bowen), 1873', in *Myself When Young: By Famous Women of Today*, ed. Margot Asquith (1938), 46.

[36] Margaret Cole, *Growing up into Revolution* (1949), 10.

[37] Ibid. 12. Cole identifies the story as Rosa Nouchette Cary, *Decima's Promise*.

don't remember much more about it except that the heroine subsequently made red flannel petticoats for the heathen in Patagonia. A moving story, indeed, but wasted on us.[38]

The awareness that changing reading patterns could signify a distance between generations was not limited to daughters, however. Phyllis Bentley (b. 1894) grew up with no supervision being exercised on her reading whatsoever, something which she retrospectively records with surprise. 'My mother did once mildly demur about *Jane Eyre*, which had been forbidden reading to her in her teens, but after a moment she yielded with a smile, probably enjoying the sensation of being more advanced than her own parents.'[39]

Nor were daughters invariably the true primary beneficiaries of a mother's ostensibly altruistically, educationally, and morally motivated acts. Understandably, it appears that mothers used the socially sanctioned activity of reading aloud to their children as a means of sustaining their own interests, as well as of stimulating the imagination and curiosity of their offspring. Elizabeth Sewell (b. 1815), for example, remembered her mother in the 1820s reading aloud Anson's *Voyages*, Lemprière's *Tour to Morocco*, and the *History of Montezuma*.[40] Lillian Faithfull (b. *c.*1860) recalls her mother reading widely and thoroughly, making careful annotations, no day being considered satisfactory without its quota of what was known as 'solid reading'. Carpenter's *Mental Physiology*, H. T. Buckle's *History of Civilisation*, and John Seeley's *Ecce Homo* remained in Faithfull's memory as being among the books with which they battled together,[41] whereas Mary Cholmondeley recollects that her mother's turn of mind was scientific: 'She read and was deeply interested in books on hydraulics, astronomy, anything that had a law behind it, and was bitterly disappointed that her children refused to be interested in these—to her—entrancing subjects.'[42] The issue of reading could be incorporated into reminiscences which establish further contexts accentuating the distance between mother and child. In her autobiography, significantly entitled *A Lady's Child*, Enid Starkie writes with a certain amount of bitterness about how her Irish mother habitually insisted on 'proper' behaviour and appearance from her children, befitting her own consciousness of her social status. Reading became an imaginative and symbolic, rather than an actual means of effecting a bridge between mother and daughter:

When we were small we were somewhat shy of my mother, for we were always cleaned and tidied to be taken down to the drawing-room to see her and did not associate her with our everyday life, since she did not play with us or romp with us. I do not believe

[38] Amy Barlow, *Seventh Child: The Autobiography of a Schoolmistress* (1969), 20–1.
[39] Phyllis Bentley, *'O Dreams, O Destinations': An Autobiography* (1962), 42–3.
[40] Elizabeth Sewell, *The Autobiography of Elizabeth Sewell*, ed. by her niece, Eleanor L. Sewell (1907), 9.
[41] Lillian M. Faithfull, *In the House of my Pilgrimage* (1924), 17, 25.
[42] Mary Cholmondeley, *Under One Roof: A Family Record* (1918), 48.

that she approved of external manifestations of affection or emotion. As a small child I often longed for the animal warmth of simple maternal love. I longed for someone to take me in her arms, to kiss me and to hug me, to rock me to sleep in her lap. Later, when I began to read French stories, those to which I returned most frequently were those which described close family life and the deep instinctive love of parents for their children.[43]

Notwithstanding the crucial part played by maternal influence, a large number of autobiographical texts stress not so much the mother's role in the development of literary taste and reading practices as the important part played by the father, especially once the girl was out of the nursery. This is hardly surprising, although it was a topic rarely considered in advice literature. A clergyman, academic, or businessman, with his own study or small library containing the largest concentration of books in a household, acted as custodian, censor, facilitator of access to the printed word. His own education very probably gave him access to, or the promise of access to, knowledge which reached beyond the immediate domestic sphere.

Reading could be an area in which the father could reinforce his authority and influence. At its most pronounced, paternal power became fused with spiritual jurisdiction. Thus the Reverend Samuel Charlesworth passed on to his daughter, Florence Barclay:

a most profound reverence for the Bible, as being the inspired word of God. Apart from the *mind's* veneration, he insisted on outward reverence being paid to the book. He would allow no other book—not even a prayer-book—to be placed upon a copy of the Bible. This lesson of outward reverence had a vital effect, for it brought home to the child's mind the reality and meaning of the *inspiration* of the Scriptures. Her faith in this became the dominant idea in her mind, and greatly affected her life and future activities.[44]

Charlotte M. Yonge's father clearly believed in books as rewards for virtue. His daughter perhaps had it in mind to provide an edifying account for the 'upper classes' of the Mothers' Union to pass on in their own relations with girls when she narrates a tale demonstrating not only the intrinsic merit of conscientious-ness and self-knowledge, but also the fact that their manifestation does not go unrewarded. Simultaneously, the anecdote presents herself, editor of the journal as well as highly popular author, as one who knows what it is like both to experience moral fallibility, and scrupulous honesty:

Tea used to come in at eight o'clock, and at the crucial moment of an interesting employment Grandmamma bade me go and call my father. I rose unwillingly, giving what my mother called my black look, and used to say was like Cain. She reproved me sharply, for she had a horror of any disrespect to her mother. Immediately after, on going into the dining-room, my father presented me with two beautifully bound volumes of

---

[43] Enid Starkie, *A Lady's Child* (1941), 45.
[44] *The Life of Florence Barclay*, 46.

Mrs Jameson's *Female Characters of Shakespeare*, as a reward for diligence and good conduct.

I burst into tears, and sobbed out that I did not deserve the book as I had just been very naughty to grandmamma.

He said that it should wait for another time, and so it did, till I was recovering from a feverish attack in the winter, and was said to have shown much patience and good humour.[45]

But authority could be wielded decisively without employing such ostentatiously symbolic means. This is exemplified in Mary Carbery's *Happy World: The Story of a Victorian Childhood* (1941) where she tells not only how her father taught her to handle a book—how to take it down from a shelf, how to replace it without squeezing it, how to turn the pages slowly and with respect—but how he gave her books, some of which (Schliemann's *Troy*, Wilkinson's *Ancient Egyptians*, Guizot's *History of France*, Cobbett's *Rural Rides*, Strickland's *Queens of England*) were to be read only in his library, although others (*Tales of a Grandfather*, *Passes of the Alps*, a book of ballads) could be taken away and read elsewhere.[46] Jean Curtis Brown's minister father also kept a shelf of books for her in his study—Mrs Molesworth, all the Andrew Lang Fairy Books, *The Water Babies*, and volumes of reproductions of Italian paintings. He allowed her the free run of his library, knowing that she would find no 'trash' in it (and she notes that it contained very few novels), and flattered her, as she sat reading on his sofa, by asking her to look up references for him. This 'filled me with pride and I tried to pick out the right book quickly and accurately'.[47] Her mother, she remarks in passing, was not much of a reader. Whilst not having such a clearly defined task, Dora Montefiore (b.1851) describes, in a less academic sphere, learning from her father's literary habits. She recalls her father's reliance on Shakespeare, and his practice of looking up Shakespeare's views on any topic which came up in conversation in a Concordance, so that she had a fair working knowledge of the plays and sonnets by the time she was twelve.[48] The explorer, Mary Kingsley (b. 1862) presents herself as having been exceptionally strongly influenced by her father: first by the language of his letters home from the South Sea Islands in 1867, and then by the contents of his library. They shared an interest in chemistry, physics, zoology, medicine, and the history of African exploration, often both wanting to read a new book—such as Lockyer's *Solar Physics*—simultaneously. In all these texts, however, commented Mary Kingsley, she was able to find no female role models, other than occasional mentions of the wives of explorers, government officials, and missionaries.[49] Other readers who were allowed open access to their father's, or household's, formal library tend to express gratitude for the experience, and

[45] Yonge, 'A Real Childhood', 19–20.
[46] Mary Carbery, *Happy World: The Story of a Victorian Childhood* (1941), 86.
[47] Brown, *To Tell My Daughter*, 45–6.
[48] Dora B. Montefiore, *From a Victorian to a Modern* (1927), 19.
[49] *Mainly About People* (20 May 1899), 469.

also indirectly almost invariably confirm the belief that a child's innate powers of self-censorship, abandoning that which does not seem relevant to itself, render the practice of unrestrained browsing a harmless one. Beryl Lee Booker recollects the dark, comfortable study in Cambridge Square, where she passed her childhood, and comments: 'I think children take no harm whatever from reading any decent library. I can certainly remember trying *Tom Jones*, but abandoning it for *What Katy Did*.'[50] Fathers doubtless communicated a desire for companionship with their daughters by the practice of reading to them, but, yet more frequently than seems to have been the case in mother and child relations, the subject-matter chosen did not necessarily contribute easily towards building up the personal connection. This is noted by C. B. Firth in her biography of Constance Maynard, the Mistress of Westfield College. When she was thirteen or fourteen, Maynard's businessman father used to read Monier Williams on the religions of the East, William Law, and Jacob Boehme aloud to her. Her most intimate contact with reading, however, took place away from his influence and outside the domestic interior, in a secluded corner of the garden, where she haphazardly consumed Milton's sonnets, Cowper, Irving's Orations, and Tennyson, feeling particularly attuned to 'Fatima':

> O Love! O fire! once he drew
> In one long long kiss my whole soul through
> My lips, as sunlight drinketh dew.[51]

In other cases, fathers attempted themselves to discipline the random nature of their daughters' leisure reading. Lucy Masterman, in her edition of Mary Gladstone's Diaries and Letters (which in themselves constitute a record of the extremely heterogeneous nature of a leisured woman's reading in the 1860s and 1870s) claims that Gladstone's father became anxious that she was reading for emotional stimulus rather than intellectual aim, and 'tried to press for a male University standard of study . . . it was obviously under his influence that she read Butler's *Analogy*'.[52]

If paternal interest in a daughter's reading is a recurrent feature in these records, support from other male members of the family was not always so forthcoming. Girls could meet with discouragement which, whilst possible to interpret in terms of family tensions, may also be understood as the working through of gender assumptions. Elizabeth Sewell's brother William, seeing *her* reading Butler's *Analogy*, exclaimed 'You can't understand that', which made her reticent for years about the comfort and strength this book had given her during adolescent depression.[53] Ella Hepworth Dixon (b. 1857), daughter of the editor of the *Athenaeum*, and subsequently a journalist, short-story writer,

[50] Beryl Lee Booker, *Yesterday's Child 1890–1909* (1937), 31.
[51] C. B. Firth, *Constance Louisa Maynard: Mistress of Westfield College* (1949), 44, 49, 75.
[52] Lucy Masterman, introd. to 1864 section, Mary Gladstone, *Letters*, 12.
[53] Elizabeth Sewell, *Autobiography*, 53.

and author of *The Story of a Modern Woman* (1894), recalled how George Moore called round at one of her family's Sunday At Homes, with a letter of introduction from a friend in Paris, and a copy of *Pagan Poems*, which he presented to her as the youngest of the company. However, a vigilant elder brother got hold of the volume and promptly hid it at the back of the bookcase. This may have been the same elder brother who, when Hepworth Dixon enquired a few years later if she should read Herbert Spencer, replied 'Certainly; if you will promise me not to talk about it!'[54] Male relatives, too, could impose their taste through pointed teasing. Ethel Voynich's *The Gadfly* (1897), about political events in Italy leading up to 1848, was a popular novel in its time: its stammering, shabbily treated hero affecting, among others, the young Amy Barlow. But when her brother-in-law caught her sniffing over it, he began to weep in sympathy. 'He sobbed violently, blew his nose, mopped his eyes, wrung out imaginary tears from his handkerchief, staggered to and fro and knocked his head against the wall. *The Gadfly* was hidden from that hour.'[55]

On the other hand, plenty of girls shared Leonora Eyles's experience in discovering that male tastes in reading material opened up a sense of the imaginative possibilities to be found for travel and action in the world. She was particularly grateful to her uncle for leaving a number of Rider Haggard's books in their house;[56] and sharing books with brothers, too, provided ample evidence for the general observation that girls often preferred books about boys. Octavia Hill found *Tom Brown's Schooldays* 'one of the noblest works I have read', delighting not just in 'the enobling influence of having someone depending on one' but in the athletic games.[57] Faithfull was delighted when she could lay her hands on a smuggling story or *Children of the New Forest*.[58] Dorothy McCall regularly identified with Henty's heroes, especially admiring the physical mobility and resourcefulness shown by Godfrey in *Condemned as a Nihilist*, fleeing from Siberia on foot over the Arctic circle, or by the Young Carthaginian escaping in a boat through the underground sewers of Carthage.[59] Eleanor Farjeon (b. 1881), who expounds at length on the part her father played in introducing her to writing from Shakespeare to the *Arcadia*, from Dickens to Dumas, recreates her identificatory enthusiasm as she read *The Three Musketeers*, which enabled her to step outside the bounds even of male, let alone female, notions of propriety:

Oh, which *which* of these wonderful men will I be? I cannot ever hope to be D'Artagnan. I am Porthos. I love him more than anyone I am. I love boasting like him, and being vain like him, and stupid like him, and making love like him, and having an enormous

---

[54] Ella Hepworth Dixon, *As I Knew Them* (1930), 54, 162.
[55] Barlow, *The Seventh Child*, 31.
[56] Eyles, *The Ram Escapes*, 100.
[57] Letter of Octavia Hill to Mary Harris (Oct. 1856), quoted in C. Edmund Maurice, *Life of Octavia Hill: As Told in her Letters* (1913), 89–90.
[58] Faithfull, *In the House of my Pilgrimage*, 34.
[59] Dorothy McCall, *When That I Was* (1952), 116.

appetite like him, and being the third-best fencer in the world, and the very strongest man.[60]

Margaret Cole shared with her brothers copies of *Puck*, *Sexton Blake*, and the *Magnet*, as well as boys' school stories, remarking:

In no other country will you ever find females, old and young, interesting themselves passionately in the prefects, the (invariably large and unruly) Shell or Remove, the inky fags, and the final dramas of cricket match or rugger match—never by any chance soccer—in which Old Boys of the school go behind the pavilion and weep because 'Caesar held the ball safely in his lean brown hands'.[61]

Whilst Cole claims that this phenomenon 'as yet awaits explanation', some of the attractions now seem obvious. Not just was the girl reader offered, in some cases, an apparent glimpse of the world of her own brothers, and, of course, as already suggested, an imaginative means of entering an active environment with a more exciting atmosphere than that of a girls' school, but she was also presented with an idealized, thoroughly reassuring image of patriarchal society. Despite the inner tensions, at times, between its members, its clubbish unity is seen to operate according to clear principles of honour, loyalty, and attachment to institutions beyond self. Moreover, and this is true from *Tom Brown's Schooldays* onwards, men are comfortingly shown to have tender emotions, even if these have to be expressed discretely, behind the pavilion. Highly conservative in class terms, as Cole's sardonic reference to soccer shows, these fictions control threats to what they make the reader believe is the firmly established order: neither the working classes nor women figure except in an extremely periferal manner, and war is still capable of being turned into an excuse to magnify schoolboy heroism into a grander perspective. The hero of *The Hill* (1905), Cole remembers, was just one of the gallant fictional soldiers who 'perished nobly on the Veld'.[62]

In many cases, of course, a combination of domestic influences acted on the young woman reader. Two cases in point are provided by Phyllis Browne, who presents paternal authority and maternal sympathetic understanding as being in conflict, and by the more harmonious encouragement of reading recorded in Elizabeth Raikes's 1908 biography of Dorothea Beale, the pioneering and influential headmistress of Cheltenham Ladies' College. In *What Girls Can Do*, Phyllis Browne recounts her own experience in a way designed to convince her audience of the pitfalls of being too strict in the matter of exercising control over their daughters' reading. She acknowledges that great judgement is required in selecting stories for the young, but points out that too much caution may kill off enjoyment in reading altogether. There is an implicit warning, too,

---

[60] Eleanor Farjeon, *A Nursery in the Nineties* (1935; repr. 1960), 331.

[61] Cole, *Growing up into Revolution*, 12–13. She identifies the last incident as occurring in H. A. Vatchell's novel of intense relationships between Harrow schoolboys, *The Hill* (1905).

[62] Cole, *Growing up Into Revolution*, 20.

in her tale, against allowing paternal authority rather than maternal sympathy to direct the path taken:

When I was a girl I was passionately fond of reading. On one occasion I went to stay for a few weeks with a friend in the country, who had by some means or other become possessed of a number of three-volume novels of a questionable character. These were stored away in a box in a garret, 'out of the way,' as it was thought, but I discovered them. I was at once in clover. I used to go into the garret, sit on the ground, and read all day long books of all kinds, until I was almost dazed. I have looked at some of these books since, and I have wondered how I could get through them, but then they were most delightful to me. My friend wrote to tell my mother that she was so pleased to have me staying with her, for I was no trouble, which was, I should imagine, perfectly true.

At last my excellent father came upon the scene. He discovered how I had been employed, and his dismay was beyond expression. He expostulated with me at some length, though I had been unconscious of a fault in what I had done, and at last made me promise that I would not for twelve months open any book that he had not placed in my hands.

As I was eager to continue my literary studies, I begged him at once to give me something to read. He handed to me Dr. Dick's 'Christian Philosopher,' which he had just read himself and enjoyed exceedingly. I found this most excellent work a very decided change from my delightful novels. I tried hard to read it, but it was beyond me, and 'Othello's occupation was gone.' The unreal world in which I had been living had spoiled for me the every-day world in which I found myself, and the book to which I turned for solace was not written for such as I.

I became very miserable, but my mother rescued me. On my return home she discovered my unhappiness and its cause. She talked to my father, and persuaded him to be merciful towards me. The 'Christian Philosopher' was put on one side for a time, and if I remember rightly, 'Bracebridge Hall' was given to me instead. I was still held to my promise not to read any book that my parents had not sanctioned, but my father had learnt a lesson as well as I, and books were chosen for me, which, whilst they contained a good moral lesson (and usually plenty of it), were suited to the capacity of a girl. Meantime a taste for reading was confirmed in me. For many long years now books have been dear friends to me, and their companionship has saved me from many long hours of dreariness and repining.[63]

Raikes's book draws considerably on Beale's first-hand reminiscences, and provides a very clear example of how literature came to hold a central position in the life of an individual, and how early reading practices formed the foundation of later educational policy. Beale's values were rooted in the family circle, where she learnt to love Shakespeare through her father reading it aloud, and looked up to him as one who expected people to care for literature and public events. Though she also read history and general literature with her mother, the memory of the father as arbiter in both morals and taste lingered. ' "Blessed are the pure in heart"—poor Swift,' he said one day as he handled a volume of the great satirist. 'That', said Dorothea long after, 'was the best

---

[63] Browne, *What Girls Can Do*, 104–5.

literature lesson I ever received.'[64] This home teaching contrasted dramatically with her experience when she went to school, around 1841, where literature lessons consisted of repeating the Lamentations of King Hezekiah, Cowper's 'Mother's Picture', and some doggerel verses on the solar system. Ill health causing her to leave at thirteen, she continued her education herself, benefiting from access to two London libraries: those of the London Institution and of Crosby Hall, in addition to the Medical Book Club. She read far more history than fiction, plus the major reviews of the time—the *Edinburgh*, *Quarterly*, and *Blackwood's*; and foreign literature. Pascal's *Life and Provincial Letters* inspired a spirit of emulation in her: she borrowed a Euclid and worked her own way through the first six books, and taught herself algebra. In all her reading she received help and sympathy from her aunt, Elizabeth Complin, who knew Latin, Greek, and Hebrew, had a strong taste for mathematics and philosophy, and was one of the first subscribers to Mudie's. What all this gave to Beale, in addition to factual knowledge, was an understanding of the value of effort and search when acquiring such knowledge, and she attempted to incorporate this into her subsequent pedagogic practice. Method joined with her belief in education as 'the drawing out of the powers, of the right sympathies, of the judgement, to guide and strengthen the will'.[65] This can be seen, for example, in her admiration for St Hilda, notable for her piety, her charity, her teaching of the strict importance of justice, her activities as a patron (suitable for one who maintained at least a public belief in the importance of women's education to enable them to be better, more informed wives), and 'who so loved order that she immediately began to reduce all things to a regular system'.[66] A system of practical moral didacticism underlay her literature lessons, which stressed the importance of knowledge of character, especially when it came to marriage and choosing a husband. She annually read and lectured upon one of Shakespeare's plays to the first class, with very little variation on her main theme:

Ophelia, to take an instance, was for all the generations of girls who read *Hamlet* at Cheltenham the woman who failed a man because she could not dare to be true. A matter like this was vital to Miss Beale . . . Desdemona, again, was always marked as the wife who not unnaturally roused the suspicions of a jealous-minded husband, because he knew that in marrying him she had deceived her father. The misery that may follow a secret wilful marriage was always hinted at when this story was told.[67]

Beale's belief in the capacity of literature to inculcate correct conduct was such that she even approved of controversial modern fiction, writing that though 'of course' she disliked much of Sarah Grand's writing, the conclusion of *The Heavenly Twins* is effective in keeping the horrors of a mercenary marriage before readers.[68]

[64] Elizabeth Raikes, *Dorothea Beale of Cheltenham* (1908), 7.
[65] 'A Utopian' [Dorothea Beale] 'On the Education of Girls', *Fraser's Magazine*, 74 (1866), 512.
[66] Raikes, *Dorothea Beale*, 226.
[67] Ibid. 262.
[68] Ibid. 308.

Beale's concerns alert one to the way in which autobiographies are invaluable for the details which they give of actual access to books outside the immediate circle of home, and of the interaction, or lack of it, between domestic habits of reading and those which schools attempted to instigate. Sara Burstall, attending Camden High School and North London Collegiate School in the 1870s, lamented the absence of a free public library, and the ensuing difficulty in getting hold of books, even textbooks needed for school. On the other hand, Evelyn Hopkinson, attending Ellerslie College in Manchester, recorded that after hearing Arthur Symonds lecture on logic and moral philosophy, she was able to obtain such writers as John Stuart Mill through the Free Library, whilst her family's financial circumstances would otherwise have rendered them unobtainable.[69]

Almost all chroniclers of reading shared the central belief of those who commented on the practice: that it could play a formative, influential role. As George Eliot put it in an early letter, men and women alike are:

imitative beings. We cannot, at least those who ever read to any purpose at all, we cannot I say help being modified by the ideas that pass through our minds. We hardly wish to lay claim to such elasticity as retains no impress. We are active beings too. We are each one of the Dramatis personae in some play on the stage of life—hence our actions have their share in the effects of our reading.[70]

Mention of books of advice themselves are relatively rare, however. George Eliot herself was in fact unusual in this respect. In another letter to Maria Lewis, of September 1840, she enthusiastically advised her to 'recommend to all your married friends "Woman's Mission" a 3/6d book and one you would like to read; the most philosophical and masterly on the subject I ever read or glanced over', commenting a month later, moreover, how preferable is the original French version of Aimé Martin's work, *L'Education des mères*.[71] The future doctor, Sophia Jex-Blake (b. 1840), provides another of the rare examples of a woman later becoming active in a secular sphere and who records seeking help and solace in advice literature. She mentions in her diary when she was seventeen that she thought she had better take heed of the recommendations offered regarding happy and unhappy women in *Woman's Thoughts*, and dedicate herself to a life of usefulness and activity.[72]

Both Jex-Blake's and Eliot's comments are made within a private form of communication, rather than in published memoirs. Many other autobiographers picked out certain books which, whilst not belonging to the advice

[69] Evelyn Hopkinson, *The Story of a Mid-Victorian Girl* (1928), 30.
[70] Mary Ann Evans to Maria Lewis (16 Mar. 1839), *The George Eliot Letters*, ed. Gordon Haight, 9 vols. (1954–1978), i. 23.
[71] Letters of Mary Ann Evans to Maria Lewis, 17 Sept. and 27 Oct. 1840, *George Eliot Letters*, i. 66, 72. For a discussion of the possible influence of Martin's work on Eliot's writing, see Bonnie Zimmerman, '*Felix Holt* and the True Power of Womanhood', *English Literary History* 46 (1979), 432–51.
[72] Margaret Todd, *The Life of Sophia Jex-Blake* (1918), 55.

genre, they wished to demonstrate as having been crucial to the shaping of their inner lives, their domestic practices, their careers. Florence White, for example, chose to present herself as an exemplary figure characterizing aspects of dominant prescriptive views concerning reading. As a child in the late 1860s and 1870s, the books she used to read were *The Wide, Wide World*, *Queechy*, and *Ministering Children*: 'I tried to imitate their heroines.'[73] In the case of Susan Warner's *The Wide, Wide World*, this meant practising the submission of the self: not, however, by submission towards husband or father, but by means of conquering one's own passions. This may, as Jane Tompkins has argued, thus be seen as an assertion of autonomy, rather than capitulation to an external authority—or capitulating to external authority as it is put forward as the will of God, which means that by 'conquering herself in the name of the highest possible authority, the dutiful woman merges her own authority with God's'.[74] Such a point is easily linked with the way in which the most significant reading material alluded to in Warner's novel, the Bible, is employed as a gift from mother to daughter: a reminder of a mother's love and teachings; a transmission of spiritual power, and an acknowledgement of a shared recognition that woman's earthly submission is ultimately what will lead her to a position of celestial power. Part of this submission, indeed, involves being prepared to practise self-censorship on one's reading material. Ellen Montgomery, the heroine, was forbidden to read *Blackwood's Magazine* since it contained fiction, and when her future husband embarks on several years' absence she submits to his desire that she should read no novels during this time. The protagonists of Maria Charlesworth's *Ministering Children* (1854), too, are deeply given to reading the Bible: the ministrations of the Clifford family largely consist of helping the poor gather in their firewood and taking them soup. White, however, was not beyond recognizing, unquestioningly, the superiority of masculine cultural domination in her own life. She recounts her gratitude to her brother, Herbert, for ensuring that she was brought up 'decently':

> I remember once when I was dusting his room, he brought home one of Rhoda Broughton's novels and put it on his writing-table with the remark:
> 'I don't want you to read this book. It is not a bad book or I shouldn't read it myself, but you can't read everything, and I want you to read only the best books until your taste is planned.'
> But he left it on the table, thereby showing that he trusted me.[75]

She gives no hint that she betrayed this trust, nor that she disobeyed his parting advice when he left for India, which was not to read any books that were not

---

[73] Florence White, *A Fire in the Kitchen: The Autobiography of a Cook* (1938), 45.

[74] Jane P. Tompkins, *Sensational Designs: The Cultural Work of American Fiction, 1790–1860* (New York, 1985), 162–3. For the novel's appeal to English girls, see also J. S. Bratton, *The Impact of Victorian Children's Fiction* (1975), 153–6.

[75] White, *A Fire in the Kitchen*, 55–6.

well reviewed in the *Spectator*. After his departure, she applied herself hard to her lessons, taking inspiration, she claimed, from Todd's *Student's Manual* and Samuel Smiles's *Self-Help*: 'I used to practise the exercise of my will-power under Smiles's guidance, saying "I *will* do it, I *will* do it," until I conquered myself.'[76] Although she had ambitions to go to Girton College, Cambridge, her stepmother insisted that she leave school at fourteen and a half to teach her stepbrothers and sister and take on the work of a general servant:

> Fleda in *Queechy* was my inspiration as far as cooking was concerned as she also was terribly poor and had to make meals out of nothing. It was because I learnt so much from the everyday details put down in books of all kinds that I am putting down some of the everyday details of my own life in the hope they may help some other girl or woman.[77]

Despite the unabashed didacticism in her desire that her own writing should have social usefulness, however, it is impossible not to read strategies of self-protection covering early disappointments into White's chronicling of her dutifulness in the matter of reading.

Most of this section has so far been concerned with books consumed during childhood, adolescence, and young womanhood. With the exception of women who read material which had direct bearing on their professional careers, records of reading after marriage are scarce in autobiographies, if more frequently encountered in diaries. Lucy Lyttelton, for example, continued reading as avidly as ever after her marriage to Lord Frederick Cavendish, although she seems to have been happy that he should choose the books for their honeymoon: *Westward Ho!*, Carlyle's *French Revolution*, and Butler's *Analogy*—'rather an odd trio!'. A month after they left for their travels, they were still on *Westward Ho!*.[78] The paucity of accounts of married women's reading is indicative of the way a preponderance of autobiographers who dealt with adult life felt domestic details which did not focus on their role as wife and mother to be irrelevant. It may also be a reflection of the small amount of leisure time which they in fact had; and, most worryingly of all, suggests that they may, indeed, have seen or wished to represent their marriage as stamping a seal on their own personality, curtailing the development of their private, unshared consciousness. None the less, a small number of testimonies reveal that marriage, even in a non-Catholic country, could be perceived as a watershed when it came to assessing the suitability of texts. The suffragette Viscountess Rhondda (b. 1883) makes mention of a friend of hers who married at twenty-

---

[76] White, *A Fire in the Kitchen*, 60.

[77] Ibid. 69.

[78] *The Diary of Lady Frederick Cavendish*, ed. John Bailey, 2 vols. (1927), i. 222, 228. Lucy Cavendish's diary, kept both before and after her marriage, provides one of the fullest accounts we have of the day-to-day reading of a Victorian girl and woman. It ranges from gift books—'Aunt Wenlock gave me a delightful book: "Half-hours with the Best Authors"'(26 Jan. 1855 (i. 25))—bowdlerized Shakespeare, Longfellow, and Scott when she was still in the schoolroom, to the combination of religious debate, historical studies, and modern novels which characterized the literary consumption of her adult life.

five 'and looked forward to the wedding for that, among other liberties, she would after marriage be allowed to read Conan Doyle's "The White Company"'.[79] Beryl Lee Booker, looking back at herself in the early 1900s, presents herself as 'a girl who loathed clothes, loved animals, machines, games, and messing about in backyards over bicycles and hen-coops': an image of a mildly rebellious stand against an over-feminine image which she fixes by remembering how amused she was by Elinor Glyn's *The Visits of Elizabeth* (1900), with its immaculate heroine, who never became hot and dishevelled, and whose entire life, stage-managed by her mother, was directed in pursuit of the elegible male. But none the less, the concluding page of Booker's autobiography shows how the symbolism of reading serves to define the relative orthodoxy of her attitudes when she entered her own marriage. The institution is presented as more liberating than constricting, perhaps since she is linking her life with that of her good-humoured cousin, Arthur. The couple, due to leave for India where he was posted, went off in different directions immediately after their wedding and reception to finish their shopping:

At Marshal and Snelgrove's I ran into one of the wedding guests who looked rather shocked—I don't know why—and then I took a hansom and drove to Hatchards and bought a hitherto forbidden novel, and then I walked up and down the Burlington Arcade.

I was a married woman.[80]

Reading, Prohibition and Transgression

Not all accounts of reading are as overtly untroubled as those outlined in the previous section. Numerous narratives of prohibitions, warnings, and censorship are told, which amount to a substantial body of evidence about the control exercised within some families, particularly concerning the ideas and emotions which were considered suitable for girls to encounter. Such accounts of transgression provide sites for the writer's own assertion of individuality, measures of the distance she has travelled from her family background and the ideological assumptions of her parents, even siblings. Julia Kristeva may claim that the adolescent is one of those mythic figures which has the function of distancing us from certain of our faults by reifying them in the form of someone who has not yet grown up,[81] but the role of the figure of the adolescent reader in many of these writings is to problematize the idea of fault. A symbolic action against family or against dominant social beliefs is not so much distanced from the time of writing as highlighted; presented as an incident which helps form

[79] The Viscountess Rhondda, *This Was My World* (1933), 101.
[80] Beryl Lee Booker, *Yesterday's Child 1890–1909* (1937), 197, 256.
[81] Julia Kristeva, 'The Adolescent Novel', in John Fletcher and Andrew Benjamin (eds.), *Abjection, Melancholia and Love: The Work of Julia Kristeva* (1990), 8.

the recognition and assertion of individual identity which leads directly towards the self-confidence necessary for the writing of published autobiography.

Sometimes, these instances of rebellious reading took place in carefully chosen social contexts, like Marie Corelli (b. 1855) deliberately startling her governess with quotations from *Don Juan*,[82] or Mrs Benson, wife of the Headmaster of Wellington College, scandalizing his friends by letting her children read George Eliot, and thrusting *Adam Bede* into the hands of clergymen's wives telling them not to mind being seen reading it.[83] Sometimes they were private ones, like Jean Curtis Brown and her friend Lucy consuming the forbidden magazine *Home Chat*, borrowed from the kitchen on the cook's night out.[84] But the impact of the transgressive act was not necessarily dependent on breaching obvious moral imperatives or crossing class boundaries. It could signify a different form of assertion: access into the domain of parental property. Joan Evans, later to become a historian of medieval art and a well-known Ruskin scholar, was brought up in the 1890s in a house full of books, most of them dating from the early and mid-century: she could claim that she was more familiar with life in England between 1810 and 1850 than with anything happening in her own time. Yet despite the freedom of her access to the fiction of Scott and Thackeray, she was aware that she lacked poetry, of which there was little in the house other than the well-bound wedding presents, belonging to her mother, kept in a glass-fronted bookcase in the drawing room:

One of my few conscious naughtinesses after I had attained the age of perception was to steal into the drawing-room, when I knew my parents were safe in London, open the case, and take deep delicious draughts of verse. Tennyson and Matthew Arnold are all the sweeter for being read in secret.[85]

Controls over what was, or was not, considered suitable reading focused, as we saw in more general terms in the last chapter, around certain specific issues. Some of these controls were generically determined, demonstrating, especially, the distrust of novels. 'Lucas Malet', daughter of Charles Kingsley (b. 1852), told a reporter that 'novels were practically forbidden at Eversley Rectory', and that she was not allowed to read even so safe a writer as Charlotte Yonge until she was twenty. Despite the fact that she had the run of Kingsley's library, where she read history, philosophy, and the poets, 'novels were not within my reach', and she never recollects having seen her father open a novel.[86] This is perhaps not entirely surprising, given the attitudes towards women as readers of fiction which her father professed outside the home. In 'Nausicaa in London: Or, The Lower Education of Woman', written in 1879, for example, he paints a

[82] Bertha Vyver, *Memoirs of Marie Corelli* (1930), 19–20.
[83] Amy Cruse, *The Victorians and their Books* (1935), 278.
[84] Brown, *To Tell My Daughter*, 67.
[85] Joan Evans, *Prelude and Fugue: An Autobiography* (1964), 17.
[86] 'Lucas Malet' (Mary St Leger Harrison), interviewed by Sarah A. Tooley, 'Some Women Novelists', *Woman at Home*, 5 (1897), 187.

particularly dismal picture of the unhealthy modern girl, stunted, pallid, subsisting on tea and bread and taking a novel from the library as her stimulus.[87] On the other hand, Kingsley was not entirely consistent, recognizing elsewhere that women may have needs in their reading which can be met through fiction. He defended his habit of inserting pieces of information into his own novels on the ground that many readers enjoyed them, especially intelligent women who were starved of opportunities for serious discussion.[88] Kingsley's novels themselves, incidentally, were not immune from censure: Edward Pusey considered *Hypatia* 'a work not fit to be read by our wives and our sisters'.[89]

There are plentiful further examples of fiction being regarded with qualified disapproval. Mary Paley Marshall, for example, one of Newnham's first students, recalls her father in the 1860s reading aloud *The Arabian Nights*, *Gulliver's Travels*, the *Iliad* and *Odyssey*, Shakespeare, and, above all, Scott's novels, but she never understood why—unless it was the more pronounced 'religious tone' in Scott—which meant that his novels were allowed whilst Dickens's were forbidden: 'I was grown up before I read *David Copperfield* and then it had to be in secret.'[90] But it is impossible to arrive at any sound generalizations. Dorothy McCall (b. *c*.1884) recalls that *The Heart of Midlothian* was the one book in her father's library which she and her siblings were forbidden to read: 'he immured it in his dressing room, where we took our baths at night. It was a gentleman's agreement, and we behaved like gentlemen, and never looked inside it.'[91] On the other hand, Julia Grant, leaving for boarding-school for the first time in 1877, was bought a copy of the same novel by her father at the railway station, for reading on the journey.[92] And Anne Thackeray's (b.1837) memories serve to remind us that what an adult might find unsuitable was in any case often unintelligible to a child: she could not 'imagine how little Em'ly ever was so stupid as to run away from Peggotty's enchanted houseboat'.[93]

The combination, here, of reference to Scott's aura of religiosity on the one hand, and on the other to *David Copperfield*, the novel of Dickens's most commonly considered *risqué*, points to the two most common areas in which familial control was exercised: sexuality and religion. First, sexuality. Like McCall's family, Maurice Baring's sisters were not allowed to read *The Heart of Midlothian* 'which was not, as they said, for the J.P. (jeune personne)'.[94]

[87] Charles Kingsley, 'Nausicaa in London: Or, The Lower Education of Woman', *Health and Education* (1879), 82.

[88] See Brenda Colloms, *Charles Kingsley: The Lion of Eversley* (1975), 130.

[89] Quoted by Cruse, *The Victorians and their Books*, 275.

[90] Mary Paley Marshall, *What I Remember* (1947), 7.

[91] Dorothy McCall, *When That I Was* (1952), 118.

[92] Julia M. Grant, Katherine H. McCutcheon, and Ethel F. Sanders, *St Leonards School 1877–1927* (1927), 164.

[93] Anne Thackeray Ritchie, *Chapters from Some Memoirs* (1894), 78.

[94] Maurice Baring, *The Puppet Show of Memory* (1922), 49.

Frequently forbidden, too, was George Eliot's *Adam Bede*. Whilst Lucy Caroline Lyttelton's grandmother only left out one chapter of this new novel about which 'the world raves . . . a heart-rending book, with its stern true moral of the irrevocableness of sin' when she was reading it aloud to her grandchildren,[95] as late as the 1890s, Harriet Shaw Weaver's mother was shocked when she came upon her adolescent daughter reading *Adam Bede*: the story in part of a girl who had given birth to and disposed of an illegitimate child, written by a woman who herself lived unmarried, with a man. Weaver was sent immediately to her room, and the local vicar was asked to call in order to explain the book's unsuitability. This incident was to remain painful to her for fifty years, since it epitomized, for her, the forthcoming conflict between loyalty to her family and her championing of individual liberties.[96] Slightly less surprisingly, given its content, Yeats forbade his sisters to read George Moore's *A Mummer's Wife*: a proscription which led Susan Mitchell, who lived with the family, to 'gulp . . . guilty pages of it' as she went to bed.[97] Mary Butts's (b. 1890) mother warned her solemnly against the cupboard in her father's room:

I was not to look at the books in the cupboard. It was full of dreadful books. Books, she went on to explain, that only men read, and she wished indeed that my father would not read them. But I was always to remember that men were different. Also it seemed that even God would have to try specially hard to forgive Daddy for reading some of the books that were in there.

These works included books by Ronsard, Guy de Maupassant, Defoe, Balzac, and Stendhal. On her father's death, Butts's mother ceremoniously burnt the offending texts on a funeral pyre, paying no concern to their potential financial, let alone literary value, so shocked was she by what she knew, or presumed, of their contents: 'Little square old books, the noble pages of Burton in their gold and black, their delicate engravings of fabulous princesses. French memoirs, with their portraits of Ninon and the Dubarry and the great Pompadour.'[98]

   It was not only the young who could be presumed to be corrupted, or to think themselves corrupted, by what they read. A letter from Elizabeth Barrett Browning to Arabel Barrett tells of a sixty-year-old woman who believed that her morals had been injured by reading *Aurora Leigh* and that her character would be in danger if it were to become known that she had looked at the poem.[99] Josephine Butler recalled the publication of Elizabeth Gaskell's *Ruth* in

---

[95] *Diary of Lady Frederick Cavendish*, i. 83.

[96] Jane Lidderdale and Mary Nicholson, *Dear Miss Weaver: Harriet Shaw Weaver 1876–1961* (1970), 33.

[97] Susan L. Mitchell, *George Moore* (Dublin, 1916), 43.

[98] Mary Butts, *The Crystal Cabinet: My Childhood at Salterns* (1937), 102, 111. For Butts and her treatment of the past, see Patrick Wright, *On Living in an Old Country: The National Past in Contemporary Britain* (1985), 93–134.

[99] Elizabeth Barrett Browning to Arabel Barrett (19 Feb. 1857), Berg collection, New York Public Library.

1853 and the voicing of double standards to which it gave rise in Oxford University circles:

A moral lapse in a woman was spoken of as an immensely worse thing than in a man; there was no comparison to be formed between them. A pure woman, it was reiterated, should be absolutely ignorant of a certain class of evils in the world, albeit those evils bore with murderous cruelty on other women. One young man seriously declared that he would not allow his own mother to read such a book as that under discussion—a book which seemed to me to have a very wholesome tendency, though dealing with a painful subject. Silence was thought to be the great duty of all on such subjects.

This formed one among a growing list of iniquities which led Butler into 'revolt against certain accepted theories in Society'.[100] Gaskell herself recorded how one close Chapel associate of her family 'has forbidden his wife to read it',[101] and expressed to Anna Jameson her sorrow and surprise 'how very many people—good kind people—and *women* infinitely more than men, really & earnestly disapprove of what I have said & express that disapproval at considerable pain to themselves, rather than allow a "demoralizing laxity" to go unchecked.'[102]

Readers more willing to confess to their assertions of independence explicitly indicate how prohibition and censorship in themselves, unsurprisingly, led to inquisitiveness and transgression. These were presented as crucial acts in the development of their consciousness which they could look back to, in some cases, with gratitude. Lady Frances Balfour, for example, was brought up in a highly literary environment: her father and mother both read poetry aloud (she particularly recollected her mother repeating 'How well Horatius kept the bridge in the brave days of old') and at home she listened to Gladstone reading Latin and Italian. The book 'on which my youth was nourished', however, was *Uncle Tom's Cabin*, the plot of which served as an analogy for the liberation of her own bonds of thought and experience. She was forbidden to read the second volume of this 'but human nature cannot be denied, and of course I read it . . . It did its work! A woman's pen, under Divine inspiration touched the iron fetters, the rivets fell apart and "the slave where'er he cowers" went free.'[103] Netta Syrett recalls how when a pupil at North London Collegiate School, aged about thirteen, Miss Buss confiscated Lemprière's *Classical Dictionary* on the grounds that it was a 'clumsy book' which she did not wish her to read:

Up to that moment in perfect innocence (if anyone had been so unwise as to set it) I could have passed an examination in the stories of the gods and goddesses, sexual vagaries and all, for I looked upon these as part of the general incomprehensiblity of

[100] Josephine E. Butler, *Recollections of George Butler* (Bristol and London, 1893), 96.
[101] Elizabeth Gaskell, letter to Eliza Fox (?early Feb. 1853), *The Letters of Mrs Gaskell*, ed. J. A. V. Chapple and Arthur Pollard (Manchester, 1966), 223.
[102] Elizabeth Gaskell, letter to Anna Jameson (7 Mar. 1853), *Letters*, 226.
[103] Lady Frances Balfour, *Ne Obliviscaris: Dinna Forget*, 2 vols. (1930), i. 89.

grown-up people. But when the book was removed I never rested till I knew, at least dimly, why I was not allowed to keep it in my possession.[104]

Autobiographies and letters certainly show that many girls picked up what they knew about sex from what they read, and the patchiness of this knowledge is a vindication in itself for the campaign that greater straightforward information about sex should be given to girls, whether directly by their mothers or, if this proved too intimate and embarrassing, through the written word. H. M. Swanwick, in the late 1870s, absorbed what she could from any available scientific books and medical journals, and puzzled over the Bible, Shakespeare, Chaucer, La Fontaine. Forbidden *David Copperfield*, *Bleak House*, *The Heart of Midlothian*, and *The Vicar of Wakefield*, she read them none the less, 'and my attention was sharpened by the prohibition'. She:

must have been still a child when I rebelled against the common morality of the day in regard to responsibility in sex relations. These little Em'lys and Hetties and Olivias and Effies—by what divine law was it decreed that they must for ever live a life of abject penitence or, better still, die?[105]

When she was lent Dante Gabriel Rossetti's poems by a friend, 'Jenny', which takes a prostitute for its subject-matter, came as a welcome antidote.

The degree to which girls could be protected from 'unsuitable' material could be taken to ridiculous lengths. Mary Stocks (b. 1891) recorded how her Aunt Tiddy made great efforts to preserve her and her siblings from 'indelicacy':

In Tennyson's poem, 'The Revenge', which was among those she read to us, occurs the line: 'Bearing in her womb that which left her ill-content'. Over the word 'womb' Aunt Tiddy stuck a narrow strip of paper. My family still cherishes the tattered volume of Tennyson showing the marks from which the strip was surreptitiously removed by us to satisfy a curiosity very natural in the young.[106]

Dora Russell, at Sutton High School during the first decade of the twentieth century, knew 'nothing whatever about sex': she was not aided in any attempt at self-instruction by the fact that books on anatomy and physiology in the school library had 'certain dangerous pages stuck fast together'.[107]

In her biography of Marie Stopes, Ruth Hall indicates that prior to the birth-control reformer's marriage, her only sexual knowledge came from reading Browning, Swinburne, and—ignoring her mother's advice—Shakespeare's sonnets and 'Venus and Adonis', with the addition of novels, and 'the only book on sex that she had read before her marriage', Edward Carpenter's *Love's*

---

[104] Netta Syrett, *The Sheltering Tree* (1939), 20. Syrett's *The Victorians* (1915), a novel which draws considerably on her own childhood, gives considerable space to the importance played by reading in an adolescent girl's life.

[105] H. M. Swanwick, *I Have Been Young* (1935), 83–4.

[106] Mary Stocks, *My Commonplace Book* (1970), 12.

[107] Dora Russell, *The Tamarisk Tree: My Quest for Liberty and Love* (1975), 24.

Coming of Age. This last figures frequently in her letters. Certainly Carpenter believes that young people should be informed about sex, should be told how 'intoxicating, indeed, how penetrating—like a most precious wine—is that love which is the sexual transformed by the magic of the will into the emotional and spiritual', and that the young of both sexes should not be kept 'in ignorance and darkness and seclusion from each other'[108] but he includes virtually no physiological detail to support his rhapsody.

Some girls obtained straightforward practical information about sexual matters from standard household reference books. Vera Brittain's far from bookish home contained, in addition to the yellow-back novels which formed the main staple of her early reading, a volume entitled *Household Medicine*: 'the treatment of infectious diseases left me cold, but I was secretly excited at the prospect of menstruation; I also found the details of confinement quite enthralling.' She added the knowledge thus gained to other sources, recalling 'that intensive searching for obstetrical details through the Bible and such school-library novels as *David Copperfield* and *Adam Bede* which appears to have been customary almost everywhere among the adolescents of my generation'. None the less, she went into wartime nursing a relative innocent, only learning the details of venereal disease—the 'hidden plague' of newspaper reports—when she had to nurse a case in 1917; her knowledge of Army doctors and nurses, 'derived entirely from the more idealistic poems of Kipling', in no way helping her to understand her colleagues' suggestive language and furtive manœuvrings.[109] Other women add a small number of further texts to this catalogue of sources. The Viscountess Rhondda mentions *Midshipman Easy* as an enabling text, presumably because of the presence of the illegitimate child of Jack Easy's wet-nurse, and the general post-Fielding-and-Smollett stress on physical functions. Cicely Hamilton, the suffragette and actress, claimed that she learnt 'what are sometimes called "the facts of life" . . . fairly early from the Bible'.[110] Hamilton's autobiography also indicates how it was possible to come across potentially controversial material and read it undetected—even under the guise of approval—when she tells how she found a dusty copy of Eugene Sue's *Juif Errant* in a cupboard and, with the aid of a dictionary, read it from cover to cover. The fact that 'it contained episodes which those in authority would probably consider unsuitable for juvenile reading' only adding to her enjoyment, for, in this educational context, 'there were only smiles of approval when I was seen with a French book in my hand . . .'.[111]

Despite the considerable furore in the press concerning both sensation and the so-called 'New Woman' fiction, and the undesirable degree of explicitness on sexual matters which these genres were criticized for offering, and despite,

---

[108] Edward Carpenter, *Love's Coming of Age* (Manchester, 1896), 11, 102.
[109] Vera Brittain, *Testament of Youth* (1933, repr. 1983), 26, 48, 49.
[110] Cicely Hamilton, *Life Errant* (1935), 4.
[111] Ibid. 17.

too, the number of copies of such novels in circulation, few women noted that they made much of an impact. An exception is provided by Dr Elizabeth Chesser, recollecting Glasgow in the 1890s, at a time when the onerous duties of the daughters of professional men stretched to dusting the drawing-room and washing the aspidistras. She contrasts the atrophy inherent in this lifestyle with reading 'extraordinary "modern" sexual novels . . . in open drawers which were shut on the approach of adult footsteps', or hidden under the mattresses.[112] Maud Churton Braby recalls the excitement Grant Allen's *The Woman Who Did* aroused when she was a schoolgirl, 'and my acute disappointment when it was forcibly commandeered from me by an irate governess who apparently took no interest in these enthralling subjects'. But she claims that despite the temporary enthusiasm kindled by this and other fictions in precocious and impressionable girls, that the eventual lure of 'the Ring, the Trousseau, and the House of My Own' almost inevitably won out.[113]

It is worth while bearing in mind, despite all the testimony to the furtive but fascinated searches for sexual information entered into by many of the women who look back at their adolescence, that others of them remained unenlightened, despite the breadth of their reading. Nor did they necessarily resent this fact: they represent themselves as having had other priorities. Mary Hamilton (b. 1884), looking back at her time at Newnham, recalls that during her second year, Matthew Arnold was left open on the mantelpiece, to remind her of the vanity of human wishes and the essential loneliness of the heart. Even being in love, for her, 'expressed itself almost exclusively in highly spiritual and mental terms; although I had always been allowed, nay encouraged, to read omniverously, I remained blankly ignorant about sex and its manifestations, even the most normal ones'. She refers here to the lesbian relationships within her college which, looking retrospectively, she could recognize, but which, she said, she would not remotely have been able to comprehend at the time. An intense concern for politics, she said, made up for ignorance about sex.[114] There is a clear sense, here, of a young woman, proud of her educational achievements and intellectual interests, separating herself off—unconsciously at the time, consciously in later life—from the concerns of those whom she did not regard as privileged enough to share the same exalted mental space.

As this memory hints, not all prohibitions were based around preserving the 'innocence' of the young woman in relation to sexual matters, nor was sexuality the area with which the young woman's mind was necessarily the most consciously concerned. A variety of anxieties centred around the reading of religious works, or works which might cause the young woman to query important Christian tenets, or to find religion disturbing rather than affirmative.

---

[112] Elizabeth Sloan Chesser, MD, in Countess of Oxford and Asquith (ed.), *Myself When Young, by Famous Women of To-Day* (1938), 81.

[113] Maud Churton Braby, *Modern Marriage and How to Bear It* (1909), 6, 8.

[114] Mary Agnes Hamilton, *Remembering My Good Friends* (1944), 46–7.

Elizabeth Sewell and her sister were given a volume of Cardinal Newman's sermons by an Oxford friend of their brother William, 'but it was with the caution that there were two sermons which it was better for us not to read'. Whilst the prohibition was ultimately lifted, this was only when the friend had made up his mind that the girls were not likely to have their minds disturbed by the new teaching.[115] Laura Knight, in 1899, was mystified by being forbidden Foxe's *Book of Martyrs*: 'Just the sort of horrors I would love to read about—or so I imagined', having been used to enjoying Edgar Allen Poe, the more gruesome parts of *The Ingoldsby Legends*, and the *Boy's Own Paper*, bought with her weekly penny for helping with the housework.[116] And older women, too, could be disturbed by the tone and content of works which queried their religious beliefs. Fanny Kemble (b. 1809), for example, recalled how 'extremely disagreeable' Chambers's *Vestiges of the Natural History of Creation* was to her, although the knowledge that it dealt with facts, not fiction, gave it 'a thousand times more interest than the best of novels for me'.[117] Mary Howitt wrote to her daughter concerning Harriet Martineau and Henry Atkinson's 'new *infidel book*' *Letters on the Laws on Man's Social Nature and Development* (1851): first telling her that the volume was making such an excitement that it was always out from the London Library when she sent for it, and then, with disgust, noting that 'It is to my mind the most awful book that was ever written by a woman. It made me sick and ill to hear them talk of Jesus as a mere clever mesmerist.'[118]

But such disquiet and revulsion are predictable enough. More interesting, from the point of view of the individual's development, are those writers who, when they remember being frightened or unsettled by what they read, frequently indicate that a girl's perception of what texts might or might not be advisable differed from that of adults: troubling effects could not invariably be guarded against. Margaret Cole claimed that the only reading which was forbidden her was Bram Stoker's *Dracula*, Poe's *Tales of Mystery and Imagination*, and *What a Young Mother Ought to Know*, plus 'trashy magazines', but maintained that she read 'all that was forbidden' anyway. Whilst the motherhood manual was an obvious target for prohibition because of the explicitly sexual material it concerned, the more deliberately frightening material is introduced by her in the context of what *actually* disturbed her. Thus Cole writes that she was scared by Uncle Remus, by a series of American picture stories called the Golliwog books, and by a book of noble deeds,

[115] Sewell, *Autobiography*, 65.
[116] Laura Knight, *Oil Paint and Grease Paint* (1936), 7; ead., *The Magic of a Line* (1965), 56. Angela Brazil, on the other hand, was considerably disturbed by the pictures in the work, especially the final one which showed a half-charred body falling out of lurid flames. The disturbance worked at two levels, stimulating both physical revulsion and self-doubt: 'At night when I lay awake in the dark I saw those fearful pictures, and not the least of their horror was the persuasion that I had not the stuff in me to make a martyr'. *My Own Schooldays* (1925), 164.
[117] Frances Anne Kemble, *Records of Later Life*, 3 vols. (1882), iii. 242.
[118] Margaret Howitt (ed.), *Mary Howitt: An Autobiography* (1889), 67, 69.

principally rescues from shipwrecks and burning houses: 'Even today I cannot read the words "blind alley" without a faint reminiscent shudder born of a story, whose details I have entirely forgotten, of people fleeing from a burning building into a blind alley with the flames at their heels.'[119] On occasion, the experience of disturbance could derive from texts disapproved of by parents. For example, in the early 1870s, the ten-year-old Annabel Huth Jackson 'was terribly frightened by the episode of the mad woman tearing the wedding veil' in *Jane Eyre*, although the existence of this incident alone was doubtless insufficient to explain Jackson's mother's horror when she learnt her daughter had read the book.[120] But as many reminiscences, including Cole's, show, the reading which frightened rarely involved the reading material about which parents expressed direct apprehension. Margaret Campbell ('Marjorie Bowen'), for example, was particularly scared by a book—she believes one of Thackeray's novels—which 'had a yellow paper cover of a howling negro running along in terror while a man shot at him', and by Wordsworth's 'Lucy Gray';[121] Winifred Peck claims to have been 'terrified' by a book routinely figuring as a Sunday School prize, Wood's *Natural History*;[122] Janet Courtney remembers 'as a special terror' Scott's White Lady of Avenel in *The Monastery*,[123] and Cicely Hamilton, who had read all of Scott by the time she was eleven, wrote that one of his short stories, 'The Tapestry Chamber':

was a disturber of my rest for years. So too was an illustrated version of *The Ingoldsby Legends*; I remember the peculiar horror inspired by a devil, arrayed in Elizabethan garb, who danced up the room with a lady and *never came down again*! And the even greater horror inspired by the Dun Horse ridden by Exciseman Gill, with hell-fire streaming from its nostrils![124]

These instances act as reminders, too, that not all disturbing effects were necessarily linked to gender expectations, nor, in any explicit way, to the gendered experiences of the reader.

Reading and Influence

As well as these accounts which consolidate the assumed importance of domestic circumstances in determining reading habits, some autobiographers chose to present themselves as having, indeed, been influenced by what they

[119] Cole, *Growing up into Revolution*, 11.
[120] Jackson, *A Victorian Childhood*, 58.
[121] Margaret Campbell, in Oxford and Asquith, *Myself When Young, by Famous Women of To-Day*, (1938), 44, 48.
[122] Peck, *A Little Learning*, 34. John George Wood published a large number of volumes on natural history: most probably she refers to his *Natural History Book for Children*, 3 vols. (1861–3).
[123] Courtney, *Recollected in Tranquillity*, 25.
[124] Hamilton, *Life Errant*, 4.

read in a manner that justifies and confirms the repeated anxieties expressed in advice writing. Autobiographers, letter writers, and diarists put forward their experiences in a way that functions as a warning, or as an indication of the representative naïveté of their upbringing. Evidence for this is found throughout the period.

In a long letter of 1839 in which she considers the merits and demerits of novel-reading, Mary Ann Evans was doubtless writing under the evangelical influence of her teacher when she claimed that 'I shall carry to my grave the mental diseases with which (novels) have contaminated me'. Nor does she believe her case to be unique, maintaining that 'the same causes which exist in my own breast to render novels and romances pernicious have their counterpart in that of every fellow-creature'.[125] Again, the ten-year-old Beatrice Potter was probably parroting an older authority in her first diary fragment, of 1868, when she complains that reading too many novels leads a growing mind to be continually making up love scenes or building castles in the air, writing that she has found this 'a serious stumbling block to myself'. Six years later, she reprimands herself in much the same terms for thinking too much about men in a positively indecent manner, and deliberately adopts an authoritative voice to address the wayward, imaginative aspect of her personality: 'Do try and build no more castles in the air; do try to think purely and seriously about Love. I often think you are something like Rosamund in *Middlemarch*.'[126] Later still, the Viscountess Rhondda confirmed, in her autobiography, some of the strongest prejudices against romantic fiction. She explains how she gave up being an Oxford student for what was to prove an entirely unsuitable marriage with a foxhunting landowner:

I was prepared to believe that one deep and lasting love could make anyone completely happy, could even fill all the interstices caused by complete lack of any useful occupation or purpose in life. All the novels I read told me that—most novels did tell one that in those days—and I supposed it must be true.[127]

The same writer introduces a reminder, also, that individuation could take place not just through sampling forbidden texts, but simply through the assertion of one's own preferences. She felt the understandable suspicion that 'people read and enthused over good literature not because they liked it, but because they ought to like it': thus she doubted her enthusiasm for the language

[125] Mary Ann Evans to Maria Lewis (16 Mar. 1839), *George Eliot Letters*, i. 22.
[126] *The Diary of Beatrice Webb, i. 1873–1892*, ed. Norman MacKenzie and Jeanne MacKenzie (1982), 11, 17. For Webb's autobiography, see Nord, *The Apprenticeship of Beatrice Webb*. This is especially interesting, in the context of the Victorian woman reader, in its discussion of Webb's own reading of autobiographies (such as John Stuart Mill's *Autobiography*, Harriet Martineau's *Autobiography*, George Sand's *Histoire de ma vie*, and Wordsworth's *Prelude*, and the influences which they exerted on her formulation of her own life, 20. Nord reminds one (258 n 3) that many of Webb's reading notes have been left out of the typescript version of her Diaries, although they may be read in the original manuscript.
[127] Rhondda, *This Was My World*, 102.

of both Shakespeare and the Bible since it was the 'correct thing' to admire these.[128]

In some cases, significant reading moments in an individual's autobiography are presented with such a belief in their influential importance that it is hard not to read the autobiography concerned as an exemplary work in itself, putting forward the author's life as a path fit to be followed by others. Reading as political revelation is a topic to which I will revert in the section on reading and the women's movement: here I wish to examine some examples of those who claimed its importance to their spiritual development.

The issue of reading could be woven, almost incidentally, into the whole picture given of personal growth. Thus Elizabeth Sewell's consumption of 'modern' works in the late 1820s and the 1830s, she records, specifically mentioning Scott and Byron, led to worry and 'hysteria' based on the feeling that it would be pleasant to have someone caring for *her*. She had not yet learnt, she claimed, the joy that comes through caring for others.[129] Other autobiographies foreground reading more obviously, thereby, of course, underscoring their own potential didactic power as exemplary texts. Marianne Farningham looked back to her early life to find an incident which illustrates 'the awakening of the soul of a child', implicitly encouraging her Christian reader to make sure that suitable reading material exists in her own home for her own children. Rocking her brother in his cradle, she was reading from the *Sailor's Magazine* and came across 'two poems, which had a marvellous effect on me'. The first was about a family Bible, the last line of each stanza being 'The old-fashioned Bible that lay on the stand'; the second was Felicia Hemans's 'The Better Land', which overcame her with 'sweet, strange emotions' to the point of fainting.[130] Moreover, she hints at the origins of some of her own later writings, and at her belief in learning through example, when she records her childhood disappointment, when reading the Sunday School Union's magazines, at the incessant stories of poor boys who had risen to be rich and great men: 'Every month I hoped to find the story of some poor ignorant *girl*, who, beginning life as handicapped as I, had yet been able by her own efforts and the blessing of God upon them to live a life of usefulness, if not of greatness.' Such an absence of role-models, she claimed, fuelled her own later writing.[131] The popular religious poet Frances Ridley Havergal claimed 'I do not think I was eight when I hit upon Cowper's lines, ending "My Father made them all!" That was what I wanted above all to be able to say; and, after once seeing the words, I never saw a lovely scene again without being *teased* by them.'[132] And although her ambition did not persist, Enid Starkie claimed that

---

[128] Rhondda, *This Was My World*, 54–5.

[129] Sewell, *Autobiography*, 43.

[130] Marianne Farningham, *A Working Woman's Life: An Autobiography* (1907), 20–1.

[131] Ibid. 44. See e.g. Farningham's *Women and their Work: Wives and Daughters of the Old Testament* (1906).

[132] *Memorials of Frances Ridley Havergal* by her sister, M.V.G.H. (1880), 15.

reading Francis Thompson's 'The Hound of Heaven' when she was ten made her feel as though she had also been taken hold of and mastered, and determined that she should become a nun when she grew up.[133] Nor did didactic writers necessarily restrict themselves to their own past when it came to considering the formative effects of reading. They could also recycle the memories of others to their own ends. Charlotte M. Yonge, apprehensive that mothers in the 1890s were paying insufficient attention to what their daughters got up to on Sundays, regretted that children were not encouraged to become as passionately fond of their Bibles as Lady Augustus Stanley had revealed herself to be, devoted to a great Bagster's Bible, almost as large as herself, running after her sister to read it with her, and especially delighting in the Gospel of St John.[134]

Whilst, understandably, most of the spiritual effects of literature were reported as being for the good, Margaret Cole indicates how responses which probably would have gladdened certain writers' hearts were rapidly squashed by her family. She was discouraged from becoming a 'Golden Sunbeam'—a subscriber to a cheap religious periodical which she had come across whilst attending a Sunday Children's Service. Such a role would have entailed her bringing 'the word of God' into the life of a poor child. She was likewise dissuaded when attempting to emulate the pious heroine of *Bruey: A Little Worker for Christ*.[135] Alternatively, the imaginative stimulus bestowed by religious literature might not lead in a spiritual direction. Thus Beryl Lee Hooker was inspired by the Sunday book of the moment, *Pilgrim's Progress*, to attempt to make a suit of shining armour out of the silvery fish-skins from the roach and chub she and her brothers caught: a smelly and messy affair.[136] Moreover, stories which apparently were designed to suggest the importance of the mere display of goodness, dressed up in a way which linked girlhood innocence with power, could fail to convince. Sybil Lubbock could not *quite* believe in the message of Mrs Hodgson Burnett's *Editha's Burglar*, 'that the evil intentions of even the roughest miscreant could be instantly defeated by the appearance of a little girl in a white nightgown who would offer her toys in place of her parents' valuables'.[137] Lillian Faithfull, whilst highly enthusiastic about the ease with which it was possible to integrate oneself imaginatively into Charlotte M. Yonge's large families—'people of like passions, emotions, hopes and fears' to her fifteen-year-old self, going through similar periods of religious doubt and difficulty—found the 'stories of little philanthropists, baby missionaries and children's death-bed scenes' in such books as *Jessica's First Prayer* and *Ministering Children* heavy going, since 'the authors were more

[133] Starkie, *A Lady's Child*, 145.
[134] C. M. Yonge, 'Mothers to the Front', *Mothers in Council*, 3 (1893), 69. See [Elizabeth Charles] *Lady Augusta Stanley: Reminiscences* (1892), 30–1.
[135] Cole, *Growing up Into Revolution*, 21–2.
[136] Beryl Lee Booker, *Yesterday's Child 1890–1909* (1937), 40.
[137] Lubbock, *The Child in the Crystal*, 26.

anxious to point a moral than to tell the tale'.[138] (She may be contrasted with the future novelist and writer of domestic handbooks, Leonora Eyles, a child in the 1890s, remembering *Jessica's First Prayer*, *Christie's Old Organ*, and *A Peep Behind the Scenes* for the power of their sentimental, heart-rending portrayals of 'barefoot children, hungry children, poor old starving people'. She made the 'rather nauseating children' of *Ministering Children* her example, she claims; none the less, the spirited nature of *Little Women* came as a welcome relief.[139]) Nor was it necessarily the overtly pietistic, dutiful moments in didactic fiction which made the greatest impact on readers. Christine Longford, having read *The Wide, Wide World* in the first decade of the twentieth century, recalled that she had been especially impressed by the passage 'where the heroine, a schoolgirl, followed a difficult conversation in French among grown-ups, and when one of them forgot the name of an obscure battle, supplied it modestly and unobtrusively. I longed for that kind of triumph.'[140] Others reacted even more strongly against the moral attitudes which their designated literature attempted to inculcate in them. The reading diary of Hester Cholmondeley, which she kept in the 1880s when aged thirteen and fourteen, is full of such fulminations, especially, in her case, against Yonge: 'All Miss Yonge's books very young-lady-like, too good, too dull, and too high church. All so exclusively written for schoolroom girls. I hate them.'[141] Thomas Carlyle and Dante were much more to her taste.[142]

A particular form of autobiographical didacticism can be found in the information offered in features and books which claimed to give insights into the working lives and methods of writers, and which functioned as a form of self-publicity. These include such texts as George Bainton's *The Art of Authorship: Literary Reminiscences, Methods of Work, and Advice to Young Beginners* (1890), and Helen C. Black's *Notable Woman Authors of the Day: Biographical Sketches* (1893). Many of the authors whom Bainton cites are at pains to point out (whatever their own stylistic modes) the difference between 'good' and 'bad' writing, as though they are asserting their own claims to cultural legitimacy through emphasizing their acquaintance with the former. Thus Marie Corelli maintained that by choice and free will, she had studied Homer and the Classics, 'the best French,

---

[138] Faithfull, *In the House of my Pilgrimage*, 32–3. Faithfull, a student at Somerville College, went on to be Vice-Principal of the Ladies' Department of King's College, and in 1907 became Principal of Cheltenham Ladies' College.

[139] Eyles, *The Ram Escapes*, 43.

[140] Christine Longford, 'Early Snobberies', in *Little Innocents: Childhood Reminiscences*, with preface by Alan Pryce-Jones (1932), 117.

[141] Cholmondeley, *Under One Roof*, 82.

[142] Cholmondeley's forceful attitude is indicative both of the changing popularity of Yonge during the later decades of the century, and also of the fact that the greatest enthusiasm shown for her fiction tended to be in and around High Church circles—as exemplified by Mrs. Wilson, wife of John Keble's curate, who declared that when she had finished the book that she felt as though she had lost a close friend. This is recounted by Amy Cruse (p. 51) who includes a useful chapter in *The Victorians and their Books* on the reception of Yonge, especially among women readers.

German and Italian authors, together with all the finest works in the English language—particularly the poets, such as Byron, Keats, Shelley, and the king of them all, Shakespeare'. On the other hand, 'I have systematically and persistently avoided reading the penny newspapers, detesting their morbidness, vulgarity, and triviality.'[143] Shakespeare, Spenser and Scott are the writers most frequently cited as formative reading by other contributors. In a slightly different vein, 'John Strange Winter' (the nom-de-plume of Henrietta Stannard, author of the popular *Bootle's Baby*) was determined to dissociate herself from certain contemporaries. Her early preferences, she claimed, were for men's fiction—the Kingsleys, Charles Reade, Whyte Melville, and Wilkie Collins—yet once she began to write, she found herself gradually 'slipping into the Rhoda Broughton school'. Only the influence of Ruskin's prose rescued her from what she represents as the pernicious influence of Broughton's first-person, present-tense style. Novelist Louisa Parr emerges as the sole contributor to Bainton's book who does not betray anxiety about what her early reading habits may indicate about her literary standing, commenting that to expect young people 'to enjoy the books which more mature tastes regard as masterpieces of fiction is, I think, a mistake we elders often fall into. I remember when it was a penance to me to read Jane Austen.'[144]

The serious reading of Black's women writers stands out in even sharper relief since all the participants in his volume are carefully feminized through the details of the domestic circumstances in which they live and work, presented alongside their home decoration, personal memorabilia, children and pets. They tend to emphasize their omniverous reading, and the quality of its range not just in their childhoods, but currently. Thus Mrs Betham-Edwards claims rereading Goethe annually is, for her, 'a necessary mental pabulum'; she admires Spinoza and Plato, whilst finding Tolstoy, Ibsen, and Zola 'repulsive in the extreme'; Adeline Sergeant (b. 1851), novelist and member of the Fabian Society, and an active supporter of women's suffrage, claims for her part to enjoy not just Tolstoy and Dostoevsky, Flaubert and Henry James, but economics and theological speculation.[145]

Reading and Scholarship

So far, this chapter has largely concerned itself with recreational reading. But the reminiscences of a number of nineteenth-century women indicate impressive schemes of reading—historical, classical, scriptural, mathematical,

[143] Marie Corelli, cited in George Bainton, *The Art of Authorship: Literary Reminiscences, Methods of Work, and Advice to Young Beginners, Personally Contributed by Leading Authors of the Day* (1890), 7.
[144] Ibid. 96.
[145] Matilda Betham-Edwards, cited in Helen C. Black, *Notable Woman Authors of the Day: Biographical Sketches* (Glasgow, 1893), 124; Adeline Sergeant, cited ibid. 167–8.

scientific—which many set themselves in the absence of formal serious education. Whilst conservative fiction, such as Charlotte M. Yonge's *The Daisy Chain*, presented the abandonment of an attempt to keep pace with one's brother's learning (for such was the light in which Yonge chose to depict an interest in the classics) as a necessary sacrifice to one's less selfish duties within home and community, there are plenty of examples of women who persisted with a self-imposed rigorous intellectual discipline in the face of familial and social suspicion and disapproval.

Many of the women who set themselves such formidable programmes were, consciously or otherwise, preparing themselves to enter into public debate, frequently in print, with men who had been through rigorous systems at school and university. Frances Power Cobbe's (b. 1822) scheme of self-education provides an excellent example of this. As a young child, in Ireland, she had been allowed the free range of her parent's library, which awakened, she claimed, a 'genuine appetite' for reading in her. A French governess introduced her to 'a good deal of solid history', such as Rollin, Plutarch, and Gibbon. But it was whilst at a frivolous, rote-learning girls' school in Brighton that she developed her determined, methodical approach, reading, by herself, 'as many of the great books of the world as I could reach'. She made it a rule, whether bored or not, to finish each, following Gibbon's advice that before beginning a book, one should take a walk and rehearse all that one knows in one's mind of its subject, and then, on its completion, take another book, and register 'how much has been added to a store of ideas'. She read all the *Faerie Queene*, all of Milton's poetry, the *Divina Commedia* and *Gerusalemme Liberata* in the originals, and in translation the *Iliad, Odyssey, Aeneid, Pharsalia*, and all, or nearly all, of Aeschylus, Sophocles, Euripides, Ovid, Tacitus, Xenophon, Herodotus, and Thucydides. Moreover, she took up various hobbies from time to time, such as astronomy, architecture, and heraldry, and read, in what translations were then accessible, in Eastern sacred philosophy, such as Anquetil du Perron's *Zend Avesta*, and Sir William Jones's *Institutes of Menu*, and found out as much as she could about the Greek and Alexandrian philosophers from Diogenes Laertius and the old translators, as well as from a large Biographical Dictionary. Having, she claimed:

always a passion for Synopses, I constructed somewhere about 1840, a Table, big enough to cover a sheet of double-elephant paper, wherein the principal Greek philosophers were ranged,—their lives, ethics, cosmogonies and special doctrines,—in separate columns. After this I made a similar Table of the early Gnostics and other heresiarchs, with the aid of Moshem, Sozomen, and Eusebius.[146]

When she was seven, her interest in religious subjects had been activated by hearing Bunyan being read aloud to her brothers, and as a young woman, she

[146] Frances Power Cobbe, *Life of Frances Power Cobbe: as told by herself* (1904), 71.

extended her knowledge into the area of theology, especially concentrating on Deist writing—Gibbon, Hume, Tindal, Collins, and Voltaire—and 'heathens': Marcus Aurelius, Seneca, Epictetus, Plutarch's *Moralia*, Xenophon's *Memorabilia*, and a little Plato. Among modern works, she wrote with enthusiasm of Blanco White's *Life*, F. W. Newman's *Soul*, whilst 'the epoch-making book for me' was Theodore Parker's *Discourse of Religion*.[147]

At one level, it would be possible to argue that Cobbe was developing her sense of self in relation to her brothers, attempting to equal, or surpass, the formal education which they as individuals received, and which could be seen as representative of men of their class: her reading acting as both personal and symbolic protest at women's second-rate educational treatment (something which she treats most scathingly in her autobiography), and hence social devaluation. Moreover, her detailed delineation of the authors she studied thus acts as a rhetorical gesturing towards a need to be taken seriously—that is, judged according to male educational standards, and regarded as mind, not body—within the self-presentation of her autobiography. However, to support this line of interpretation exclusively is also to run into the danger of ourselves taking male education as the ideal, or at least the norm against which to judge other formal attempts to gather information and opinions. Cobbe's account is also a description of delight taken in ideas for their own sake, and for the sense her reading gave her of increasing what she describes as her 'natural' mental powers. This is foregrounded in a brief passage when she characterizes her pleasure:

When the summer morning sun rose over the trees and shone as it often did into my bedroom finding me still over my books from the evening before, and when I then sauntered out to take a sleep on one of the garden seats in the shrubbery, the sense of having learnt something, or cleared up some hitherto doubted point, or added a store of fresh ideas to my mental riches, was one of deepest satisfaction.[148]

Cobbe chooses to present herself retrospectively as almost continually motivated, organized, and cheerful: an example to others. The evidence of Anne Jemima Clough's Journal, however, is somewhat different. Clough, like Cobbe, had a brother whom she greatly admired, especially for his capacity to engage in debate on current literature as well as for his poetry. She, too, went on into public life, becoming the first Principal of Newnham. We see her in May 1840 aged twenty, embarked on an ambitious course of study which could be directed towards no quantifiable end:

This month I want to do over one book of Euclid, as far as the 80th page in the Greek grammar, translate book ii of Virgil from the German, read 2nd and 3rd volumes of Milman's *History of the Jews*, Milton over again, and the second volume of Wordsworth.

[147] Ibid. 97.   [148] Ibid. 74.

Working hard at these things may perhaps be of no particular use to me so far as knowing these things goes, but I may at least hope to acquire industrious habits and strength of mind, which I lack terribly.

But by July, she claims that she is getting tired, and expresses doubt about the point of it all; by August, after admitting to doing 'one bad thing' (which turns out to be reading Byron's 'The Corsair') she notes, rather desperately, that 'I am bothered a good deal about learning; I don't know whether there is any good seeking after it. I am discouraged about these things. I feel a great want of companions of my own age . . . '.[149] However, she remained fundamentally undiscouraged, and one finds her own depressing experiences as a young woman underlying her later energetic efforts on behalf of women's education.

But it was not always the case that wide-ranging intellectual reading functioned as preparation for public life. Take the 'self-improvement' of Louisa Martindale, as her daughter, the factory inspector Hilda Martindale, called it. At home, after leaving school in 1857, her reading was, at first, chiefly the Bible. On 16 September she started to take *Fraser's Magazine*, and her diary becomes full of references to this, and to articles in *The Times* on subjects as diverse as Fortification and The War in New Zealand. She read, and was 'charmed by', Coleridge's translation of Schiller's *Wallenstein*. She read Symington on architecture, sculpture and painting, and as a result of this decided to put up in her room engravings of Raphael's *Self-Portrait*, Rubens's *Descent from the Cross*, and Vandyck's *Dead Saviour* and *His Mother*. Further books which she read included Froude's *History of England* (then in course of publication), *The Bible and Modern Thought*, Butler's *Analogy*, *Memorials of Fox*, Bancroft's *American Revolution*, Rollin's *Ancient History*, Waddington's *Church History*, the Works of Paley, *Locke on the Human Understanding*, and Mrs Jameson's *Characteristics of Women*: 'not a bad list for a young woman of 24 years of age, whose boarding-school education had not helped her in her choice of books', laconically comments her daughter.[150] Hilda Martindale goes on to describe her mother's specific interest in writing dealing with the condition of women, from Mary Wollstonecraft, to Caroline Norton's struggle for her rights over her children,[151] to Emily Davies and Elizabeth Garrett Anderson's efforts in the spheres of education and medical training, to the emphasis on women's employment to be found in the *Englishwomen's Journal*. Whilst the attraction of the latter material may, from our own perspective, be obvious—here is a woman assessing her own domestic situation against the wider lot of women in recent and contemporary English society—our understanding of her reading practice

[149] Blanche Athena Clough, *A Memoir of Anne Jemima Clough* (1897), 23, 28, 29.
[150] Hilda Martindale, *From One Generation to Another 1839–1944* (1944), 18–22.
[151] For an interesting discussion of the ideological implications of Caroline Norton's public protestations against her domestic wrongs, see Mary Poovey, 'Covered but Not Bound: Caroline Norton and the 1857 Matrimonial Causes Act', *Uneven Developments: The Ideological Work of Gender in Mid-Victorian England* (Chicago, 1988), 51–88.

is problematized by the heterogeneous collection of print which she consumed when taken as a whole. Since Louisa Martindale appears to have turned her acquired knowledge and understanding to no use measurable by external standards of involvement with public affairs, or with the development of woman's formal education, one is left with the hypothesis that she found the accumulation of such knowledge an enjoyable, self-sustaining process in its own right: the antithesis of the popular image of the woman at home seeking solace for her boredom in escapist fiction.

Other women record programmes of self-education which were less schematic. Mrs Humphry Ward came, as Mark Pattison put it when he met her as a girl of sixteen, 'of a literary stock': she was familiar with the writing of her uncle, Matthew Arnold, with certain pieces of Ruskin's *Modern Painters*, which she had copied out and carried round with her, and with Scott. But he advised more rigorous training for her literary ambitions: ' "Get to the bottom of something," he would say. "Choose a subject, and know *everything* about it!" I eagerly followed his advice, and began to work at early Spanish in the Bodleian.' She was made free of its 'Spanish room', and confesses to much undisciplined wandering from shelf to shelf, which at least instilled in her the sense of the vastness of history '—almost, one might say, a training, of a kind'.[152] But a final example in this section is provided by Joan Evans, a woman who found that the pursuit of her adolescent interests and inquiries fuelled the direction that she subsequently took in her academic career.

Like Cobbe and Ward, Evans had plenty of exposure to varied types of writing as a child. Her mother had been a pupil of the classicist, Jane Harrison, went up to Oxford, aged thirty, to study classics, and then, for a brief period before her marriage, lectured on classical archaeology. Her father, whose income derived from his ownership of a paper mill, was also an amateur archaeologist, President of the Society of Antiquaries and Treasurer of the Royal Society. But interestingly, although she shared the same fundamental areas of interest as her parents, Evans differentiated herself from them—particularly from her mother—through the early methodological preferences which she indicated. Her mother, in fact, did provide the initial questioning impetus, giving Evans, in 1909, Salomon Reinach's *Orpheus: A History of Religions*: 'she was, I think, quite unconscious that it was an odd and unsettling book to give to a girl who had just been confirmed'.[153] For it indicated that there were other codes and points of view other than those held by Anglican headmistresses; that morals and organized religion were not inextricably bound together; taboos not sacrosanct; legends not binding. The second book which made a crucial impression on Evans was Jane Harrison's *Prolegomena to the Study of Greek Religion*: achieving its impact, even if she could not have put it in so many words at the time, from the method which it

---

[152] Mrs Humphry Ward, *A Writer's Recollections*, 2 vols. (1918), i. 141–2, 151.
[153] Evans, *Prelude and Fugue*, 57.

suggested: 'the creation of synthesis out of many details, the finding of a pattern in scattered shreds, the discovery of cause and effect in things of the mind.'[154] Despite the fact that it was by her mother's old tutor, it differed entirely from the analytical catalogues of facts towards which her mother directed her: books like Farnell's *Cults of the Greek States* and Frazer's *The Golden Bough*. Evans presents the influence of this relatively early reading as crucial to all her subsequent intellectual development.

At university, or away from home and working, the woman reader was at last free from the supervisory restrictions which governed reading in many families, and most schools. At this point, many autobiographers become far less gender-specific in what they record, except in the pride which they express at being educational pioneers, or unless, as we shall see later, the women concerned were particularly alert to the relations between their cultural consumption and the women's movement as a whole. As they move into adulthood, recording the development of a distinct sense of themselves in the public sphere, or as having a prominent position within a household; as many of them acknowledge and reconstruct the personal romances which they have known, reading tends to play a greatly diminished part in their recorded perception of their lives. Various reasons can be put forward: their own sense that they have, in reaching adulthood, achieved full subject-hood and that they are no longer watching their past selves undergo a process of formation; their belief that what they do in their leisure time is unimportant, or should be regarded as such; the possibility that they did not have any considerable portions of leisure time to spend at all, on a pursuit which might be thought frivolous, whether by themselves or by others. This last point is, of course, in no way intended to suggest that the adult woman did not read: the evidence in the rest of this book conspicuously contradicts that. It is rather a comment on my sources, since so many writers of autobiographies which go beyond the genre of the *Jugenderinnerungen* have tended to regard their lives as worthy of record because of their exceptionally active commitment to public life, to the production of literature, or to the public sphere of their husband. At this point, their method becomes far closer to that of their male counterparts, and details of their private lives are bland, rather than emphasizing interiority.

University, however, was for many adult women in the latter half of our period, a time of decision about the direction, public or otherwise, in which they would go. Clearly, the reading (as well as the personalities) connected with their specific subjects of study played a major role in this, although one which largely falls outside the sphere of this book. But other reading, often discussed within a sympathetic environment, was recollected as important for other reasons. Many of the books themselves were provided by individuals, rather than by the

---

[154] Evans, *Prelude and Fugue*, 57.

institution. According to Sara Burstall, when she went up to Girton in 1878, there was no library, hardly any books, besides various departmental libraries in lecture rooms, 'and there was an old beloved bookcase in the reception room full of *belles lettres*, including a complete Browning, George Eliot and Jane Austen'.[155] Revisiting Royal Holloway College in 1898, on the other hand, a former student wrote rapturously of the many books in the library, commenting, incidentally, that there were no novels in it other than those of Eliot, Scott, Dickens, and Thackeray: there was a library of 'frivols'—'our lighter literature'—in the Lower East Common Room.[156] Eliot was enormously popular, too, at Cambridge. Jane Harrison, who went up to Newnham in 1874, recalls that 'we used to wait outside Macmillan's shop to seize the new instalments of *Daniel Deronda*'. When Eliot came to Newnham in person, and visited Harrison's room for a few minutes, Harrison became 'almost senseless with excitement'; she describes the 'ecstasy' as sending her into oblivion.[157] But Harrison's autobiography serves not only to recognize the cult of adoration which was the cumulative response to Eliot from many young women;[158] it also implicitly cautions one against assuming that all Eliot's women readers would automatically identify with Maggie's independent wilfulness, or Dorothea's desire for self-fulfilment through altruism, or even Gwendolen's painfully slow enlightenment as to her own egoism. For, claimed Harrison, proud of her Yorkshire lineage:

Until I met Aunt Glegg in the *Mill on the Floss*, I never knew myself. I *am* Aunt Glegg; with all reverence I say it. I wear before the world a mask of bland cosmopolitan courtesy and culture; I am advanced in my views, eager to be in touch with all modern movements, but beneath all that lies Aunt Glegg, rigidly, irrationally conservative, fibrous with prejudice, deep-rooted in her native soil.[159]

In their different ways, these accounts of reading suggest that the practices of many middle-class homes were carried over into University recreational times. Inevitably, however, many students were exposed to reading material which they would not have met with at home, and which considerably influenced the subsequent course of their lives. The freedom could be of various kinds. A. Maude Royden, whilst at Lady Margaret Hall, became immersed in Tractarianism, and she read her way through the five volumes of the life of Edward Bouverie Pusey.[160] Margaret Cole, on the other hand, gives an impression of how her reading at Girton in the early twentieth century influenced her development as a Socialist. She indicates this at the level of

[155] Sara A. Burstall, *Retrospect and Prospect: Sixty Years of Women's Education* (1933), 64.
[156] 'An Old Student', 'A Short Visit to the Royal Holloway College', *Englishwoman*, 8 (1898), 109.
[157] Jane Ellen Harrison, *Reminiscences of a Student's Life* (1925), 45–6.
[158] See Gordon S. Haight, *George Eliot: A Biography* (Oxford, 1968), 452.
[159] Harrison, *Reminiscences*, 11–12.
[160] A. Maude Royden, *Myself When Young*, 370.

personal discovery: she was shocked by a comment in J. A. Hobson's *The Science of Wealth* to the effect that a certain number of wageless unemployed was a necessary condition of capitalist industry. This added to her childhood familiarity with *Oliver Twist* and Mrs Henry Wood, and: 'In this mood of altruistic indignation I picked up H. G. Wells's *New Worlds for Old*—under the misapprehension that it was another scientific romance like *The First Men in the Moon*, which had fascinated me years before—and tumbled straight into Socialism overnight.' This fortunate fall was consolidated through the reading community in which she found herself: she conveys the combination of amusement and delight she and her companions experienced reading Shaw, who made fun of the moral and social precepts on which they had been brought up; recognized fathers, uncles, and schoolmasters in Butler's *The Way of All Flesh*; enjoyed Chesterton's attack on money power and his defence of strikers, as well as writers and essayists of the Liberal-Radical left like C. E. Montague and Lowes Dickinson; and appreciated E. M. Forster, 'whose *Howards End* (a bestseller in those undergraduate circles) probed more subtly than the Socialists the make-up of English class society'. 'Our major prophet', she claimed, was H. G. Wells, although (and this acts as a corrective to any easy assumption that at this time women must inevitably have been drawn to what most conspicuously concerned them) she claims that she did not, at this stage, feel any yearning for the sexual freedom demanded by Wells's *Ann Veronica*.[161] On the other hand, Dora Russell, at Newnham, claimed unequivocally that 'the book for us young women was Wells's *Ann Veronica*'.[162]

Taken together, these two recollections simultaneously prove the heterogeneity of reading practices even among women of similar class and intellectual interest, and indicate the degree to which women autobiographers have been keen to make their own experiences representative. They seek to link their circumstances, as they perceived and remembered them, to their interpretation of what was being experienced by their contemporaries.

Working-class Reading

In *Lark Rise* (1939), Flora Thompson (b. 1876) recreates her childhood in rural North Oxfordshire through a barely disguised persona. She herself read considerably at home, but this fact bore little relevance to the mechanical and ritualistic way in which she was taught in the village school. Although the standard class text, the *Royal Reader*, contained a variety of lively pieces of writing—from 'The Skater Chased by Wolves' from Scott's *Ivanhoe* and Fenimore Cooper's *Prairie on Fire*, to Byron's 'Shipwreck' and 'Young

[161] Cole, *Growing up Into Revolution*, 41–3.
[162] Russell, *The Tamarisk Tree*, 40.

Lochinvar', the majority of 'Laura's' classmates took no interest in any of these or other pieces of writing. But, she stresses, there were very few really stupid children in the school, and nearly all showed an intelligent interest in other things:

the boys in field work and crops and cattle and agricultural machinery; the girls in dress, other people's love affairs and domestic details . . . Their interest was not in books, but in life, and especially the life that lay immediately about them. At school they worked unwillingly, upon compulsion . . . [163]

Flora Thompson's observation serves as a paradigm not just for the experience of many working-class children, but for the part which reading plays in their reminiscences. Not brought up, or brought up only unwillingly, within a print culture, the number who write their autobiography in the first place is far smaller than among the middle and upper classes: those who saw fit to record their lives are in some ways conspicuously unrepresentative. For information about working-class women's reading, one often needs to examine oral records or recollections gathered by local history societies, and what one finds here bears out Thompson's impressions of the interests of her contemporaries: plenty of circumstantial domestic detail, but few indications of the printed word playing any important part in the childhood or adolescence of either sex. Moreover, there is little evidence of adult women's reading habits either, for, as Elizabeth Roberts put it after interviewing inhabitants of Barrow and Lancaster about their memories of the period 1890–1914: 'One of the saddest answers often received is to the question "What did your mother do in her spare time?" "She never had any".'[164]

There were, of course, exceptions. But what working-class reminiscences survive tend rather to supply general evidence about reading patterns, rather than offering specific commentaries on what was read. A minority of these readers were advantaged through having other family members interested in books: Ellen Wilkinson, brought up in Ardwick, Manchester, went with her father to lectures on theological and evolutionary subjects, and by the time she was fourteen was reading Haeckel, Huxley, and Darwin with him.[165] At a less scholarly level, Alice Foley's father was an often drunk, sometimes violent Irish factory worker in Bolton, but when 'in sober mood, he read aloud to the family the novels of Dickens and George Eliot'.[166] She became the chief book-borrower for the family, and describes the complicated, and relatively daunting business of obtaining books from the local library at a time when there was no access to browsing on open shelves, and one had to check first a catalogue for

---

[163] Flora Thompson, *Lark Rise* (1939), 207–8.
[164] Elizabeth Roberts, 'Learning and Living—Socialisation Outside School', *Oral History*, 3 (1975), 14.
[165] Ellen Wilkinson, *Myself When Young*, 404–5.
[166] Alice Foley, *A Bolton Childhood* (Manchester, 1973), 12.

names of authors and works, and then an in-out card index to see whether the book had already been borrowed.[167] Foley continued her education by attending night school after going to work full-time in the mill when she was thirteen. She recalls choosing *Jane Eyre* as a prize, attracted by its strange name: 'I read the book avidly for it was an enchanting experience in a new romantic world, and it aroused a girlish passionate yearning for the ultimate union of the demure, yet indomitable little heroine with her frenzied and strangely dark lover.'[168] By the age of fifteen, she was 'enthusiastically imbibing socialist doctrines arising out of family readings and discussion of the weekly *Clarion* and Robert Blatchford's publication of *Merry England* and *God and My Neighbour*.'[169] Not all women who were to become politically involved, however, traced, or chose to trace, their literary experience in such a clear-cut and exemplary fashion. The suffragette, Annie Kenney (b. 1879), looking back to her girlhood working in a Lancashire factory recalls, rather, going shares in a weekly girls' paper, 'full of wild romance, centred round titles, wealth, Mayfair, dukes, and factory girls. The one whose turn it was to pay had the first read.'[170] That to read such material was a form of gender-bonding with one's companions is brought home by the contrary case of Ellen Johnson, the working-class Scottish poet—and, unlike the autobiographers just cited, not a beneficiary of the 1870 Education Act. Becoming a power-loom weaver when she was about eleven, in the 1840s, she drew her models of heroines from Scott, her pictures of romance from Wilson's *Tales of the Scottish Border*, and became, she claimed, 'courted for my conversation and company by the most intelligent of the factory workers, who talked to me about poets and poetry, which the girls around me did not understand, consequently they wondered, became jealous, and told falsehoods of me.'[171]

Hannah Mitchell's biography, *The Hard Way Up*, is valuable for its first-hand indication that the assumption that girls were likely to have leisure time to fill was very much a middle-class one. Later a suffragette, she believed that her first reactions to feminism began over this issue within the family's farm in the Peak District, in the late 1870s: 'Sometimes the boys helped with rugmaking, or in cutting up wool or picking feathers for beds and pillows, but for them this was voluntary work; for the girls it was compulsory, and the fact that the boys could read if they wished filled my cup of bitterness to the brim.'[172] Mitchell's brothers went, on a kind of rota system, to school: Mitchell traded in the performance of odd jobs which they were meant to perform at weekends, such

---

[167] Alice Foley, *A Bolton Childhood*, 25.
[168] Ibid. 55.
[169] Ibid. 62.
[170] Annie Kenney, *Memoirs of a Militant* (1924), 16.
[171] Ellen Johnson, *Autobiography, Poems and Songs of Ellen Johnson, the 'Factory Girl'* (Glasgow, 1867), 7, 9.
[172] Hannah Mitchell, *The Hard Way Up: The Autobiography of Hannah Mitchell, Suffragette and Rebel*, ed. Geoffrey Mitchell (1968), 43.

as cleaning boots and gathering firewood, for their bringing home books for her to read. Her experience indicates the very haphazard way in which a rural working-class girl might extend her reading. As her love of books became known locally: 'I was made free of such libraries as the neighbours possessed, which led to my reading some curious and unsuitable matter, old-fashioned theological works, early Methodist magazines, cookery books and queer tales of murder and robbery. One such, entitled "The Castle of Otranto", haunted my dreams for many a night.'[173] One windfall came from a passing walker, who asked if the family liked reading poetry. Although only familiar with verse in the local paper, Mitchell quickly answered in the affirmative, knowing that it meant reading matter. The walker (whom years later Mitchell recognized as the model Manchester employer Hans Renold) left her his copy of Wordsworth's poems, which Mitchell read and memorized until her mother removed them since they 'wasted' her time.

Once working, Mitchell was still dependent, initially, on good fortune for her reading matter. In the first family in which she was in service, she was allowed to borrow what she liked from the bookcase; subsequently, working as a dressmaker's assistant, she used money really needed for food on membership of a small library. This reading was supplemented by books read at a well-stocked bookstall which she passed on the way to work, and the bookseller himself lent her the books which she could not afford to buy. In lodgings, another boarder familiarized her with Robert Blatchford's writings, a common way into Socialism for many women, as well as men, towards the end of the century. Annie Kenney, too, regarded Blatchford's *Clarion* articles as crucial in awakening her interest in Labour when she was twenty. Moreover Blatchford was, she claimed, 'our literary father and mother. He it was who introduced us to Walt Whitman, William Morris, Edward Carpenter, Ruskin, Omar Khayyám, the early English Poets, Emerson, Lamb.'[174]

Other writers indicate how dependent they were on the books around them when they were in service. The demarcation between childhood and adulthood tended to be far sharper than that of the middle-to-upper-class girl, but it is apparent how many women were in fact grateful for the access to books which came to them after their formal education was finished. Mary Smith, companion and help to the family of a Nonconformist minister, thus became acquainted with Thomas Brown's *Moral Philosophy*, Whately's *Logic*, and other conceptual works. In order to read Lyell's controversial *Vestiges of Creation* when it first came to the house, she had to sit up through the night whilst the family were asleep.[175] Such access, apparently encouraged, was not, however, necessarily to be taken for granted. Isabella Fyvie Mayo recalls how, in the

[173] Ibid. 44.
[174] Kenney, *Memoirs of a Militant*, 23.
[175] Mary Smith, *The Autobiography of Mary Smith Schoolmistress and Nonconformist* (1892), 94, 162.

1860s, a servant 'was sneered at if she showed inclination for any reading but the most elementary "goody" books, deportations from the parlor'.[176] And the episode recounted by Mrs Layton (b. 1855) is less happy. She remembers, when she was in service, and about sixteen, being lent some 'trashy books' by the servant next door: narratives which came out in weekly episodes and which created a compulsive desire in her: 'After a while I became so fascinated with the tales that when the day came for the book to come out I had no peace of mind until I had been to the shop to get it and had found some means to read it.' She broke the habit, probably, she believes, through envisaging her mother's disapproval: her brother had lost his job through reading when he should have been at work. Layton recognizes the power that books potentially held over her, and regrets the opportunities that never arose: 'I have often thought how different my life at that time might have been if I had had a good book lent me to read and that I could have read it openly.'[177] She was, however, more fortunate in her next job, where reading was not considered a waste of time, and where she became particularly keen on reading travel literature, becoming 'quite a traveller in my mind'.[178]

Reading and the Women's Movement

The reading of those who were involved in the Women's movement, and more specifically within the Suffrage campaign of the early twentieth century, makes a particularly significant study. In the relatively large amount of autobiographical writing and journals penned by these women, we see the overall emphasis which they place on the importance of serious reading, within and outside formal education. Moreover, many of them choose to locate crucial moments in their own development as occurring when they came into contact with a specific text. Rather than necessarily accept, or question, the absolute veracity of these testimonies, one should consider the way in which they came to be employed within autobiography: as endorsements for the ideas which the important texts incorporated, and as inducements for the reader to go and read these works, if she was not already familiar with them. If the reader *did* already know these books, she is offered the assurance that shared experience has already taken place between two or more similarly thinking women, albeit necessarily unrecognized by the protagonists themselves at the time. Furthermore, these reading experiences are employed as moments of transition, of revelation, in which the original participant obtained a shifted, wider perspective on her

---

[176] Isabella Fyvie Mayo, *Recollections of what I saw, what I lived through, and what I learned, during more than fifty years of Social and Literary Experience* (1910), 356.

[177] Mrs Layard, 'Memories of Seventy Years' in Margaret Llewelyn Davies (ed.), *Life as we have known it: By Co-operative Working Women* (1931), 27.

[178] Ibid. 29.

current society, when her own subjectivity was redefined within an unfamiliar context, or when she was given the words and analytic tools to recognize and objectify her personal situation, and hence to develop a sense of distance from it.

In the earlier period of Victorian feminist activity, such a revelatory moment could be found in Jessie Boucherett's life: a moment which became enshrined as an exemplary narrative in future feminist histories. Boucherett (b. 1825), living in Lincolnshire in the late 1850s, lacked a sense of solidarity in her efforts to help women to better economic conditions. But she:

one day . . . caught sight, on a railway bookstall, of a number of the *Englishwoman's Journal*. She bought it, attracted by the title, but expecting nothing better than the inanities commonly considered fit for women. To her surprise and joy she found her own unspoken aspirations reflected in its pages. She lost no time in repairing to the office of the journal, where she expected to find some rather dowdy old lady. But instead a handsome young woman, dressed in admirable taste, was seated at the table. It was Miss Parkes; in a few minutes another young lady, also beautifully dressed, came in, of radiant beauty, with masses of golden hair. Such is the description given by Jessie Boucherett, long years after, of her first meeting with Barbara Leigh Smith and Bessie Parkes. She began forthwith to plan the desire of her life, a Society for Promoting the Employment of Women.[179]

If direct feminist writing could be an inspiration, so, too, could myth. Another member of the Langham Place group, Barbara Bodichon, who had in any case been imaginatively brought up by a father with strongly progressive views about education and the equality of women and men, used to remember with delight the books which James Buchanan, their father's friend and their own teacher, used to read them:

the Bible, the *Arabian Nights* and Swedenborg. He believed all the stories in *The Hundred Nights* to be parables, and never, never can I forget the intense delight I had in his explanations . . . That story of Perizade, the Princess who did not mind the black stones when she was bent on getting the living water, the talking bird and the singing tree, has made an impression on my whole life. Wasn't I glad she got to the top of the hill! Wasn't I glad she could do it though her brothers failed![180]

These two strands of inspiration, the factual and the allegorical, recur throughout the accounts which suffragettes gave of their own reading, and in the advice they give to others about books.

In suffragette memoirs, some writers give the impression that reading played an enormously central role in their life. Some, however, like Lady Constance Lytton, who believed 'that knowledge acquired without books, direct, is the best

[179] Helen Blackburn, *Women's Suffrage: A Record of the Women's Suffrage Movement in the British Isles with Biographical Sketches of Miss Becker* (1902), 50.
[180] Hester Burton, *Barbara Bodichon 1827–1891* (1949), 8.

of all',[181] played it down, or were only prepared to emphasize the importance of circulating ideas through the dissemination of *Votes for Women* and other publications. *Votes for Women* itself, none the less, among all the suffrage newspapers and periodicals, placed, as I shall show, a great deal of importance on the importance of reading. The publication itself provided information with which to argue one's case; for gaining a historical awareness of the social and political contributions made by generations of earlier women; for reliving contemporary history with the knowledge that one is recording the struggles of the current movement as an inspiration for future generations of women readers; and which acknowledged that reading could provide relaxation. That *Votes for Women* should place such importance on textual influence was in large measure due to the trust placed in reading by Emmeline Pethick-Lawrence, the newspaper's co-editor (with her husband) until 1912.

Emmeline Pethick-Lawrence's autobiography, *My Part in a Changing World*, provides a particularly interesting case-study. Reading, as an activity, first struck her deeply, she claims, when she was about sixteen and went with her sister to stay in Germany, taking some English books, including Carlyle's *Sartor Resartus*. Without mentioning the content or delivery of its social critique, nor, for that matter, considering that unfamiliar surroundings may themselves have been a spur to read in an unfamiliar way, she describes her excitement in physical, almost sexual terms: 'For the first time in my life I tasted that wonderful experience, when the printed words leave the page and become an infusion in the blood, making the heart beat faster, and transporting the imagination to some other sphere of existence.'[182] Around this time, Pethick-Lawrence was becoming increasingly weighed down by her sense that as a woman, she was obliged to fill a certain dependent position, and that this was something which she should feel grateful for, not struggle against. At home, her social consciousness was appealed to when she was told that if she were to attempt to earn an independent livelihood, she would only be increasing competition in the job-market of the mid-1880s, taking the bread out of the mouths of women less fortunate than herself. 'At a critical juncture', as she put it, she read a novel which appealed directly to her combined desires for independence, purpose, and social usefulness: Walter Besant's *Children of Gibeon*:

Its plot concerned a young woman—an heiress—who for a time changed places with a penniless girl, and went to live in the East End of London and worked in a factory. Very poignantly were the conditions of life described, and the delineation of the character of the factory girls brought out their roughness, yet their heroism in the face of desperate privation. The difficulties of the disguised heiress, and the way she ultimately succeeded in identifying herself with the girls, and in forming satisfactory human relationships were so well portrayed that the book made a profound impression and lived in my mind

---

[181] Constance Lytton to Theresa Earle, 1896, *Letters of Constance Lytton*, selected and arranged by Betty Balfour (1925), 65.

[182] Emmeline Pethick-Lawrence, *My Part in a Changing World* (1938), 61.

continuously. It suggested to me that even if I could not see my way through the intricate mazes of economics and finance, yet it might be possible to share with girls of my own age, who had been deprived of all that meant delight to me, some of the things that I valued myself.[183]

Pethick-Lawrence's identification with Beatrice may well be fulfilling a strategy aimed by Besant to work on girls like herself who came from comfortable backgrounds. But her imaginary fulfilment is couched not in the conventional terms of the romance, seeing herself as one of the partners in a successful courtship, but suggests a different textual possibility. Friendship between women may lead not just to personal satisfaction, but to the breaking down of class barriers. Pethick-Lawrence's practical reaction to *Children of Gibeon*, as she represents it, was to go and work with Katherine Price Hughes in the Working Girls' Club which formed part of the West London Mission, formed in 1887 by Mrs Price Hughes's husband. Indeed, when writing her autobiography, Pethick-Lawrence claims that she found retrospectively that more than shared Christian social purpose bound her to Katherine Price Hughes: both had found a girlhood hero in Joseph Mazzini, and it was reading a Life of Mazzini, with its description of how he founded the 'Young Italy' society, in which each member was pledged to work for the liberation of the country, which led her to consider how 'the young women of the leisured classes with their youthful idealisms' might be brought together to work for human solidarity within England.[184]

Nor did reading cease to influence Pethick-Lawrence after this. Before she came into contact with Suffragism, through Annie Kenney and the Pankhursts, she felt her political outlook, and that of her generation, had been conditioned by reading Morris, Carpenter, and Whitman's poetry. Her enthusiasm for Whitman, incidentally, was widely echoed. The trade unionist Margaret Bondfield mentions no other literature in her autobiography, *A Life's Work*, beyond the fact that on her travels on behalf of the National Union of Shop Assistants, Warehousemen and Clerks she would repeat, reflecting the love for those she represented:

> Allons! After the Great Companions and to belong to them
> They too are on the road, they are the swift majestic
>   men, they are the greatest women . . . [185]

---

[183] Ibid. 66–7. The plot is not quite as related here. It revolves around two girls brought up by Lady Mildred Eldridge: one her own daughter, an heiress; the other is the adopted daughter of a London washerwoman. Neither knows which is which. At twenty, they are introduced to the impoverished London family from which one of them comes, and one of the girls (in fact the heiress) is convinced that she is their daughter and goes to live with them. The plot is decidedly artificial, but this does not diminish the impact of the scenes of London working-class life.

[184] Ibid. 72. Most probably this was Emilie Ashurst Venturi's *Joseph Mazzini; a memoir. With two essays by Mazzini: Thoughts on democracy, and The duties of man*, ed. P. A. Taylor (1875), reviewed favourably in the *Englishwoman's Review*, 6 (1875), 67–9.

[185] Margaret Bondfield, *A Life's Work* (1950), 37, quoting Walt Whitman, 'Song of the Open Road' (1856), ll. 149–50.

Harriet Shaw Weaver, as an adolescent, found *Leaves of Grass* 'a liberating influence and even could discreetly read it on Sundays as it wasn't a novel!'[186] As well as the Socialist writer, Pethick-Lawrence wrote how Sabatier's Life of St Francis[187] had influenced all her circle of friends to 'think and talk about simplicity of life and the sharing of all we possessed'.[188] However, as we shall see shortly, it was in her contributions to *Votes for Women*, which she co-founded with her husband in 1907, that Pethick-Lawrence was best able to carry into practical use her internalized belief that reading may have a crucial influence on individuals.

The circulation of this paper was central not just to the dissemination of suffrage demands, but to the formulation and establishment of many women's sense of a gender identity which was not dependent on the existence of men for its validation or expression. To this end, as well as reporting current events, it published articles on earlier women's history. *Votes for Women* concentrated, although not exclusively, on those nineteenth-century developments which paved the way for the current suffrage campaign. Regularly, it put forward the basic reasons for women deserving the vote, and arguments intended to combat a range of common objections, in terms designed both to convince new readers of the paper, and to provide ready formulated grounds whereby readers could attempt to convince others. Whereas national and local daily papers tended to concentrate on the sensational and militant aspects of the movement, the many small reports of local meetings, as well as coverage of nation-wide happenings, affirmed a sense of solidarity, of belonging: 'No woman, however lonely, who joins the English Suffrage Movement but has friends.'[189] A conversion narrative precisely illustrating such desired effects of reading in action is told by Margaret Smith, who sceptically bought a copy of *Votes for Women* around 1909, took it home, and read it straight through:

I had never been able to understand why women wanted a vote, still less why, in order to secure one, they did the outrageous things reported in the Press. When I had finished reading that paper I understood, and moreover, I realized that I had been a Feminist all my life without knowing it.[190]

Nor was it through sales alone that *Votes for Women* was distributed. Readers wrote in claiming that they had left around copies on their holidays in locations as diverse as the YWCA at Dovercourt, near Harwich, and at Finhaut in Switzerland; and they were exhorted to deposit copies in their local station

---

[186] Harriet Shaw Weaver to B. W. Huebsch (6 Jan. 1960), quoted *Dear Miss Weaver*, 26.
[187] Charles Paul M. Sabatier, *Life of St Francis of Assisi*, trans. L. S. Houghton (1894).
[188] Pethick-Lawrence, *My Part in a Changing World*, 145.
[189] Elizabeth Robins, 'The Feministe Movement in England', *Way Stations* (1913), 42. The article was first published in the American paper, *Collier's Weekly* (29 June 1907).
[190] Margaret Smith, *A Different Drummer* (1931), 138.

waiting-rooms. Moreover, the publication supplemented a broader diffusion of literature by the Women's Social and Political Union, the largest of the suffrage organizations. In the first number, in October 1907, it was claimed that already during that year the WSPU had effected the sale of 80,000 books, pamphlets, and other publications;[191] in March 1908 the literature department of the WSPU was converted to The Woman's Press, with a turnover that year of £2,000. In May 1910, the Woman's Press bookshop opened at 16 Charing Cross Road.[192]

Votes for Women reviewed books which its editors believed to be of especial interest to women—not romantic fiction and volumes of household advice, but biographies, histories, novels and polemical works which foregrounded women's independent capacity for taking action. Pethick-Lawrence wrote a large number of these reviews herself, and her opinions reached, potentially, a large number who were sympathetic towards, or at least curious about, both the suffrage itself and a broader spectrum of women's interests. By 1909, she stated, *Votes for Women* had a circulation of nearly 30,000.[193] Many of the books reviewed enthusiastically related directly to the suffrage, or the condition of women. These ranged from a notice of Josephine Butler's autobiography and memoir (28 May 1909, p. 720), which Pethick-Lawrence turned into two and a half columns praising her courageous work in connection with the repeal of the CD Acts, to a favourable review of R. Storry Deans, *The Trials of Five Queens* (30 July 1909, p. 1001: 'A most fascinating record of ill-fated women who, dispossessed of all else beside, remained possessed of the "unconquerable soul" ') to W. Lyon Blease's *The Emancipation of English Women* (25 Nov. 1910, p. 124), looking at the history of the movement from the 1750s to the present.

In her writing, Pethick-Lawrence showed an awareness of what general features were likely to cause a book to be popular with her readership, and also suggested that the suffrage struggle shared certain characteristics with popular forms of writing: what could be more fulfilling, therefore, than to read of the campaign itself? This is most directly stated in her review of Sylvia Pankhurst's *The History of the Women's Militant Suffrage Movement*:

To those who are outside the movement, and the mere spectator of the drama, what will this story mean? What will it mean to those who will read it a few years hence, when the ban of political outlawry has been removed from the womanhood of the nation? A romance, a thrilling tale to be read with deep interest and forthwith forgotten, or a living inspiration to prompt the women of a future day to great ideals and further attainment? A romance it most certainly is. No novel ever penned can outvie it for rapidity of incident,

---

[191] 'The Outlook', *Votes for Women*, 1 (1907), 1.
[192] Ibid. (31 Dec. 1908), 226. For further details of the WSPU bookshop and the establishment of the Woman's Press, see Ann Morley with Liz Stanley, *The Life and Death of Emily Wilding Davison* (1988), 87–92.
[193] Pethick-Lawrence, *My Place in a Changing World*, 213.

for perilous adventure, for miracle of human achievement, for depths of human trial and endurance. What is more than all, this is no work of a vivid imagination, no made-up fairy tale. Even children will love this story, because it is 'a true one'.[194]

The tactics of the WSPU made it desirable to praise books which showed, as Christabel Pankhurst put it, 'the effectiveness of a militant policy': on this occasion, Lord Eversley, long-standing chairman of the Commons and Footpaths Preservation Society's *Commons, Forests and Footpaths*, and a history of Welsh protestors against the introduction of toll-gates, Henry Tabit Evans's *Rebecca and her Daughters*.[195] The attributes of inspiring heroes were made relevant to the women's cause: thus Garibaldi showed 'the courage and the heart of a lioness with whelps: fierce, indomitable, and passionately tender'.[196] Of course, particular attention was devoted to the bravery of women, whether *en masse*, as in Russia, where women take 'the front line of danger' in revolutionary politics,[197] or individually: Matilda of Tuscany's refutation of 'the foolish argument that women cannot fight' is directly related to 'the spirit which we find reawakened in the women of the W.S.P.U. to-day'.[198]

Not all the books receiving favourable reviews in the suffrage press were by women. Philip Gibbs's *Intellectual Mansions, S.W.*, for example, was greeted particularly enthusiastically. Even visually, with its purple, green, and white cover, it had a function as a momento: moreover, its documentary features meant that it was perceived as a text for future women to read:

I can imagine in days to come a present member of the Union reading the description of the political meeting and the story of the deputation to the House of Commons, as told in this novel, to wondering children and to girls just entering upon their womanhood. 'That is what the fight for liberty meant to your mother. That is what it meant to the women who won this great gift for you,' she will say to them.[199]

The same summer, Pethick-Lawrence recommended *The Letters of John Stuart Mill*, whose life must, she claimed, be an inspiration to those who share his belief that 'the emancipation of women means the regeneration of humanity',[200] and T. Douglas Murray's translation (originally published in 1907) of original documents relating to the life, achievements, and death of Joan of Arc, together with Bernard Vaughan's new life of her, *The Matchless Maid*:

Women who are fighting their great battle for the emancipation of womanhood, women who realise that it is to God and not to man that they must yield their soul, could find no

---

[194] *Votes for Women* (16 June 1911), 610.

[195] Ibid. (13 Jan. 1911), 242.

[196] Pethick-Lawrence, review of G. M. Trevelyan's *Garibaldi and the Thousand*, ibid. (29 Oct. 1909), 70.

[197] Ead., review of Jaakoff Prelooker, *Heroes and Heroines of Russia*, ibid. (19 Nov. 1909), 118.

[198] Unsigned review of Nora Duff, *Matilda of Tuscany*, *Votes for Women*, 3 (3 Dec. 1909), 214.

[199] Ibid. (27 May 1910), 562.

[200] Ibid. (10 June 1910), 594.

inspiration more beautiful than the life of the warrior, the martyr, the saint and the woman whose life is set forth in the pages of 'The Matchless Maid'.[201]

Even books which might be likely to antagonize a committed suffragette were greeted with some tolerance, in terms which suggest less gender-awareness in literary criticism than the columns of *Shafts*. Reviews in the suffrage press on occasion demonstrated a strong affection for the security of the middle-class ideology of the Victorian family. This highlights the complex relations between those who regarded suffragism as an end in itself, and those who saw it as linked to a far wider overhaul of opportunities for, and conceptions concerning, women. Thus, for example, Pethick-Lawrence claims that she is not sure whether or not E. V. Lucas's *Mr. Ingleside* is pro- or anti-suffrage, but recommends it as escapism if one is 'on a railway journey which is going to end in a public meeting': surely, she says, suffragettes have taken serious blows enough not to be able to withstand 'a little elder-brotherly teasing'.[202] The next week, an unsigned review of *The Charms of Womanhood* acknowledged that 'In this dainty little anthology, women are still on the pedestal upon which writers of all ages have combined to place them', but adds that 'suffragettes should keep this dainty little book by them, for refreshment after the day's work.'[203] But other writers indicated to *Votes for Women*'s readership the difference which an alertness to women's issues made to their cultural understanding in general. S. Bullan, for example, wrote of the revival of Ibsen's *A Doll's House* in February 1911, and indicated how the play which she had first seen ten years previously had changed. No longer was it a problem play, but a rendering of an 'everyday story', and her interpretation was now differently focused:

The fearless exposure of evil which we thought morbid in one playwright is courage when we see it done by a united band of women; the demand of Nora "to her own life," which ten years ago we applauded with weak sympathy while agreeing that it was wholly impracticable, we now heartily commend. We come away from the play, not puzzled and depressed as in old days, but cheerful and energetic . . . We see the play in the light in which the Votes for Women movement has put into our souls.[204]

The same writer, in April 1911, favourably reviewing Charlotte Perkins Gillman's *What Diantha Did*, with its message that housework should be a skilled, paid profession, practised by those who enjoy it, again uses contrast of past and present to show the change in receptivity wrought by the women's movement. Fifteen years earlier, she claimed, she had had to 'read by stealth and with a sense of pleasurable wickedness' the poems of Mrs Perkins Stetson,

---

[201] Ibid. (22 July 1910), 708. For the importance of the figure of Joan of Arc to the suffragettes, emphasizing her function as a paradigm both for female militancy and for its persecution, see Lisa Tickner, *The Spectacle of Women: Imagery of the Suffrage Campaign 1907–14* (1987), 209–12.

[202] *Votes for Women*, 3 (28 Oct. 1910), 54.

[203] Ibid. (4 Nov. 1910), 70.

[204] Ibid. (17 Feb. 1911), 323.

who described, among other topics, the tragedy of the woman living entirely in 'the woman's sphere', neglecting her own soul:

> Six hours a day a woman spends on food!
> Six mortal hours a day . . .

Such protests, claims Bullan, can be far more openly voiced today.[205]

Of all writers who were referred to in *Votes for Women*, and indeed in suffragette memoirs more generally, Olive Schreiner's fiction and non-fiction was regularly drawn upon as a source of inspiration. On 13 May 1910, the paper printed a considerable extract from *The Story of an African Farm*.[206] Whilst a substantial number of readers would, one might presume, already be familiar with this, it acted as a confirmation of their ideas as well as providing an introduction to the novel for others.[207] At a reception for sixteen released prisoners on 21 January 1911, Nellie Sergeant gave a moving recitation of Schreiner's 'Dreams in the Desert',[208] a text popular, too, among suffragette prisoners in Holloway, and in March of that year Pethick-Lawrence gave Schreiner's polemical *Woman and Labour* an exceptionally enthusiastic review. It will become 'a scripture infinitely precious' to the women's movement, she writes, at once 'a prophecy and a gospel': a visionary book which takes woman's demand for full political power for granted, and whose inspirational qualities transfer directly into Pethick-Lawrence's own exalted prose, which freely uses a register familiar from more orthodox spiritual texts:

It is not a book to be borrowed from the circulating library, to be read once and then put aside. It is a book that everyone of us must have for our own, as a necessity of every day mental and moral life. It must be studied, marked, learned, and inwardly digested. It must be made the basis of thought and meditation until we have the vision of the great inheritance which is to be won as a result of our spiritual struggle.[209]

Autobiographical writings testify to the impact made by Schreiner's works. Annabel Huth Jackson, although herself a 'convinced feminist' after reading an article on the White Slave Trade in the *War Cry* when she was thirteen, remembers how at Cheltenham Ladies' College, 'when Hildegarde Muspratt smuggled in *The Story of an African Farm*, just out, the whole sky seemed aflame and many of us became violent feminists'.[210] 'I wonder if the words "The Story of an African Farm" have the same grip upon others that they always have upon

[205] *Votes for Women*, (7 Apr. 1911), 442.
[206] From 'Don't you wish you were a woman, Waldo?' to 'Then, but not now—', Ralph Iron [Olive Schreiner] *The Story of an African Farm*, 2 vols. (1883), ii. 35–58.
[207] *Votes for Women* (13 May 1910), 535. An indication of the probable familiarity of many suffragettes of Schreiner's writing at this time is given in the 'Local Notes' (4 Feb. 1909), 318: the Wimbledon branch of the WSPU had heard an address about and reading from Schreiner the previous week.
[208] Ibid. (27 Jan. 1911), 272.
[209] Ibid. (3 Mar. 1911), 354.
[210] Jackson, *A Victorian Childhood*, 138, 160–1.

me!', exclaimed Ethel Hill in a highly laudatory article on Schreiner in the *Vote*.[211] In *Testament of Youth*, Vera Brittain records three works which made an enormous impact on her between fifteen and eighteen: Shelley's 'Adonais', which taught her to recognize beauty in literature, and consolidated her ambition to become a writer; Mrs Humphry Ward's *Robert Elsmere*, which converted her 'from an unquestioning if somewhat indifferent church-goer into an anxiously interrogative agnostic', and *Women and Labour*. 'I can still tingle with the excitement', she wrote in 1933:

of the passage which reinforced me, brought up as were nearly all middle-class girls of that period to believe myself destined to a perpetual, distasteful but inescapable tutelage, in my determination to go to college and at least prepare for a type of life more independent than that of a Buxton young lady:

> '*We take all labour for our province!*'
> From the judge's seat to the legislator's chair; from the statesman's closet to the merchant's office; from the chemist's laboratory to the astronomer's tower, there is no post or form of toil for which it is not our intention to attempt to fit ourselves; and there is no closed door we do not intend to force open; and there is no fruit in the garden of knowledge it is not our determination to eat.[212]

Constance Lytton much admired *The Story of an African Farm*, and was delighted to have the opportunity to meet Schreiner in person when she visited Southern Africa in 1892.[213]

It is easy enough to see why *Women and Labour* should have had such a strong impact. What, however, was it about *The Story of an African Farm* that ensured it such influence? Set on a remote community in the veldt, it is a story of general human suffering. This results from individual greed, selfishness, and small-mindedness, and also, the passages of elevated natural description suggest, is necessarily linked to a sense of humanity's smallness and impotence under the vastness of the sky, with the loose red earth of the bare, cracked Southern African plain stretching wearily in all directions. Waldo, the young boy, experiences powerlessness, anger, frustration, as much as the ostensible heroine, Lyndall. It is he who has John Stuart Mill's *Political Economy*—a book which, together with the writings of Herbert Spencer, Buckle, Carl Vogt, and Darwin, had much influenced the young Olive Schreiner herself[214]—snatched away from him and burnt, just when access to print has enabled him to make the crucial discovery: that the thoughts in this book 'were his, they belonged to him. He had never thought them before, but they were his . . . So he was not alone, not alone.'[215] To Lyndall, on the other hand, is given a chapter in which she indicates that oppression is not just to be found in isolation, or in the limited

[211] Ethel Hill, 'Olive Schreiner (An Impression)', *Vote*, 1 (15 Jan. 1910), 136.
[212] Brittain, *Testament of Youth*, 41.
[213] *Letters of Constance Lytton*, 33, 65.
[214] See Ruth First and Ann Scott, *Olive Schreiner* (1980; repr. 1989), 60–1.
[215] [Schreiner] *The Story of an African Farm*, i. 180–1.

society of the uncomprehending, but within the wider world. She speaks bitterly to Waldo of her experiences when she went away to finishing school, a nicely adapted machine 'for experimenting on the question, "Into how little space a human soul can be crushed?"'.[216] She tells him of the restrictions which women must suffer in the name of their own protection; of the lack of culture which makes them do even that which they are expected to do—the task of motherhood—poorly; of the fact that the only way in which they can exert their power is by manipulating men; of the fact that although men may speak of the importance of chivalry to women, they treat the elderly and the unmarried with contempt.

Mary Brown, who first met Schreiner when the novelist was eighteen, wrote in her *Memories* that:

I asked a Lancashire working woman what she thought of *Story of an African Farm* and a strange expression came over her face as she said 'I read parts of it over and over.' 'What parts?' I asked, and her reply was 'About yon poor lass' (Lyndall), and with a far-off look in her eye added 'I think there is hundred of women what feels like that but can't speak it, but *she* could speak what we feel'.[217]

Despite the fact that Lyndall never recovers from the illness which follows her giving birth to an illegitimate child, and that Waldo, to all intents and purposes, dies on the novel's final page, and despite the frustration and anger which Lyndall articulates about the position of women, *African Farm* is not a pessimistic book; nor was it perceived as such. The reason for this, and the reason for its inspirational popularity in the late nineteenth century, I would argue, is that whilst painfully articulate on the subject of suffering, it presents this both as something which is shared—across genders, across (albeit only implicitly) races, across continents—and as something which can be transcended, to a certain extent, by recognizing that sufferers can be bound together by a wider vision of the beauty and grandeur of the natural world. This is the vision Waldo possesses at the end of the novel, which enables him to die in peace, and one which has been present throughout. It is not evasive, since it is bound in with so much specific protest against social cruelty during the course of the novel: rather, it conveys a spiritual, whilst non-doctrinal, optimism that there is, somewhere, a reachable ideal which lies outside both domestic and political structures, and, moreover, that one's struggle to attain this is tied in, at a more microcosmic level, with the feminist cause.

Emmeline Pethick-Lawrence has so far featured prominently in this section, both because of her firm belief in the power of reading to influence, and because of the degree to which this belief translated itself to the contents of many of the book reviews in the widely circulating *Votes for Women*. We should

---

[216] [Schreiner] *The Story of an African Farm*, ii. 32.
[217] Mrs John Brown, *Memories of a Friendship* (Cape Town, 1923), 5.

now look at the way in which the testimony of other late nineteenth- and early twentieth-century feminists reinforces Pethick-Lawrence's claims.

Emmeline Pankhurst (b. 1858) emphasized the value of her childhood reading in forming her guiding principles. *Uncle Tom's Cabin* fused with talk of bazaars, relief funds, and subscriptions in her Manchester home to awaken first an admiration for fighting spirit and heroic sacrifice, and then an appreciation of a gentler, restorative spirit. She consolidated the impression that reading can induce an inspired state of brave, idealistic action by listing her other favourite childhood books which remained a lifelong source of inspiration: *Pilgrim's Progress* and *The Holy War*, the *Odyssey*, and Carlyle's *French Revolution*.[218] Her interest in politics she traced to reading the paper aloud to her father.[219] In turn, her daughter Sylvia Pankhurst (b. 1882) singled out Dickens's novels as having made real for her 'the cause of the People and the Poor'.[220]

H. M. Swanwick claimed that it was John Stuart Mill and Shelley—reformers, but not pulpit-pounders like Kingsley, Ruskin, and Carlyle—who 'discovered to me the marvellous fact that they were feminists and that I too was a feminist, which the others were not'.[221] One should note, of course, that here, as in many cases, Mill's and Shelley's words did not fall on unprepared ground: Swanwick was already indignantly aware of the gap in her early teens between her brother's education and her own. The Viscountess Rhondda wrote at some length about the excitement she felt when introduced to the suffrage movement by her artist cousin Florence Haig, and her immediate emotional sympathy with its aims. Released into energy, she began, as many did, to educate herself, reading avidly in order to find out why she believed what she did, consuming every book, every pamphlet for and against suffrage. None the less

Of books that mattered dealing directly with feminism there were curiously few. Only three now stay in my mind: John Stuart Mill's 'Subjection of Women', Olive Schreiner's 'Woman and Labour', Cicely Hamilton's 'Marriage as a Trade'; and perhaps one should add a fourth, Shaw's 'Quintessence of Ibsenism'.[222]

There were some other influential stray passages—in Israel Zangwill's essays, for example—and some tangentially influential texts, such as *Mrs Warren's Profession*. Moreover, from feminist literature proper she was led into other disciplines, reading widely in political science, especially of the nineteenth century, economics, psychology, sociology, and anthropology, in order to understand and contextualize the position of women in society. She recounts

[218] Emmeline Pankhurst, *My Own Story* (1914; repr. 1979), 3. As Liddington and Norris point out (*One Hand Tied Behind Us*, 264), this autobiography was in fact ghosted by an American, Rheta Childe Door, as part of a campaign to raise money and support in America.
[219] Emmeline Pankhurst, *My Own Story*, 8.
[220] Sylvia Pankhurst, in Oxford and Asquith, *Myself When Young*, 262.
[221] Swanwick, *I Have Been Young*, 81.
[222] Rhondda, *This Was My World*, 125.

the difficulty she had in acquiring some of her reading material, particularly Havelock Ellis's *Psychology of Sex*: even her father was not able to go straight into a shop and buy the set of volumes for himself.

One had to produce some kind of signed certificate from a doctor or lawyer to the effect that one was a suitable person to read it. To his surprise he could not at first obtain it. I still remember his amused indignation that he was refused a book which his own daughter had already read,[223]

for the Viscountess had been able to obtain it from the Cavendish Bentinck Library, the membership of which was limited to women.

Finally, one should not forget the stress placed by suffragettes on what they read in prison—at least until they started to demand to be treated as political prisoners, and were forbidden access to prison libraries and gifts from outside as a result of their protests. Although later suffragettes, particularly in Holloway, clearly benefited from donations which had been made to the prison library by supporters of the cause, not all the reading material available to prisoners, particularly during the earliest periods of militant activity, was exactly of their own choosing. Some texts, indeed, could be alluded to in order to highlight the contradictions and ironies inherent in their situation. Dora Montefiore, sent to Holloway in October 1906, recalls the decor of her cell: 'On the shelf were a Bible, a wooden spoon, a salt cellar, and one other book whose name I forget, but I remember glancing into it and thinking it would appeal to the intelligence of a child of eight.'[224] It was in this context that the issue of reading could be used as a site of conflict: small in the provocative scale, but emphasizing, to anyone within reach, the pervasiveness of conventional gender roles. Florence Spong recounted in August 1909: 'As to breaking my cell window, I told them I only followed the advice given in the book, placed in my cell, entitled "A Healthy Home, and How to Keep It." In this book it stated that windows must be open both top and bottom, otherwise one laid oneself open to many dreadful diseases, including consumption.'[225] Margaret Smith recalled that when in Holloway, the chaplain asked, quite pleasantly, whether she had anything to read:

'Yes, thanks. There is a book here, *Lives of Great Men of the Seventeenth Century*. As it happens, however, I am much more interested in the lives of some great women in the twentieth century, so if you could let me have a copy of the paper, *Votes for Women*, I should be very grateful.'

The chaplain made no reply. He looked at me coldly and walked away. Moreover, he never returned.[226]

'General' Drummond, too, would have been glad of reading material which contained women role models. In Holloway, she read Jane Porter's *The Scottish*

---

[223] Rhondda, *This Was My World*, 127.

[224] Dora B. Montefiore, *From a Victorian to a Modern* (1927), 97.

[225] Florence Spong, 'My Mutiny and Hunger Strike', *Votes for Women* (13 Aug. 1909), 1055.

[226] Smith, *A Different Drummer*, 193.

Chiefs and Samuel Smiles's *Life and Labour*. Whereas in the first she learnt how 'Lady Wallace and Helen . . . had helped in the fight for freedom long ago', she was sorry to find that the latter 'only mentioned one woman, Mrs Somerville—a famous scientist—who wrote a great book on astronomy whilst looking after the babies in the nursery.'[227] By May 1909, however, Miss Broughton seemed to have fared better: she read the lives of great women reformers like Florence Nightingale and Miss Weston, and around the same time Mrs Reonold was 'especially cheered and encouraged' by reading a life of Joan of Arc. Suffragettes were aware, too, of the potential of prison to provide a space in which other inmates, not necessarily political ones, could receive an education, in personal and practical terms, through books. Thus Constance Lytton, finding that the prison chaplain did not know of Moore's *Esther Waters*, promised to send a copy: 'I thought that novel ought to be in every women's prison because of the heroic and triumphant struggle depicted in it of the mother of an illegitimate child.'[228] It seems that only retrospectively were suffragettes prepared to confess that not all their reading whilst in prison directly fed into their pursuit of the cause. Thus the Viscountess Rhondda eventually owns up to having turned to relatively conventional material. Whilst she had taken with her Morley's *Life of Gladstone* and a volume containing famous speeches of famous men, she resorted in preference to the Edna Lyall novels which she borrowed from the prison library, until the prison chaplain denied her this privilege as a consequence of her hunger strike.[229]

The very issue of access to books became an important one as the suffragettes campaigned for political status in prison. Sylvia Pankhurst pointed out that in 'despotic Russia' prisoners were, on the testimony of the just-released Tchaikovsky, allowed to receive books from outside, whilst no such 'privilege' was permitted in Holloway.[230] In 1908, Miss New reported on her release that no novels were allowed during the first month, but that the librarian had allowed her to have a volume of Shakespeare. As though having learnt from the style of the commonplace book, she records that she took 'Out of the nettle danger we pluck the flower safety' as her motto, and commends it to anyone feeling timorous.[231] In similar, but more bellicose vein, Emmeline Pethick-Lawrence wrote of having read Shakespeare's history plays whilst in prison, which appealed to her 'because of the courage and the calm with which the actors of the drama take the consequence of their risk and their action'. She singled out *Henry V*, and the King's consideration for the ordinary soldier, and on her release quoted, at length, his speeches before the battle of Agincourt:

[227] 'General' Drummond, 'The Story of My Third Imprisonment', *Votes for Women* (12 Nov. 1908), 108.
[228] Constance Lytton, *Prisons and Prisoners* (1914), 121.
[229] Rhondda, *This Was My World*, 159.
[230] Sylvia Pankhurst, 'The Treatment of Political Prisoners', *Votes for Women* (7 Jan. 1909), 251.
[231] 'The Release of Mrs. Leigh and Miss New', *Votes for Women* (27 Aug. 1908), 406.

Now, friends, that is the spirit that dwells in us. 'I would not lose so great an honour as one man more, methinks, would share from me'—that is what I want you to feel. Don't let one more go to prison without you being there. Don't wait until there are so many who go that your going will mean very little. Remember, the greater the risk, the greater the reward; the greater the opposition the more the honour. Let us love honour—love it better than we love anything else in the world, love it better than we love ourselves.[232]

As we saw at the beginning of this chapter, the difficulties faced by Victorian and Edwardian women in finding an appropriate autobiographical form have been recognized by various recent commentators. Carolyn Heilbrun (who perhaps overstates the paucity of autobiographies written by 'privileged' women in order to emphasize her point) claims that in writing their lives: 'the public and the private life cannot be linked, as in male narratives. These women are therefore unable to write exemplary lives: they do not dare to offer themselves as models, but only as exceptions chosen by destiny or chance.'[233] But the treatment of reading by Suffragette autobiographers suggest that she is mistaken, at least so far as they are concerned. For, writing at the time of the demand for the vote as well as retrospectively, they represent themselves as unexceptional, whatever leadership, courage, or transgression of customary social behaviour they might demonstrate. The very essence of their self-presentation lies in the degree to which they suggest that any reasonable woman would feel as they feel, if only she knew what they knew; had read what they read. Hence the emphasis placed by them on the giving out of information, in newspapers and pamphlets as well as in public addresses; and the emphasis, too, on the power of literature to move and inspire. Reading, for them, is one means of joining with other women, not of asserting their aberrant individuality.

This power of reading—to offer a bridge between the consciousness and experience of many women—may be extended to its employment in other autobiographical writings, making Heilbrun's claims look increasingly shaky. Certainly, it was not easy for a writer within the Victorian period (as opposed to one looking back after the social changes caused in part by one or two world wars) to express anger and frustration at her position in society and within the family, although to indicate the irrelevancy and time-wasting of many forms of education seems to have been easier. At the same time, however, one should not see the autobiographers of this time as cocooned within their self-fashioning, concerned only with the emergence of the individual. For the amount of emphasis which women tend to place on the domestic, and on childhood and adolescence, favours the incorporation of anecdotes about

---

[232] 'At the Criterion Restaurant', *Votes for Women* (23 Apr. 1909), 569. The paper printed the text of a speech delivered by Emmeline Pethick-Lawrence at a banquet given for her on her release from Holloway: a speech in which, incidentally, she thanked fellow suffragettes, among other things, for their gifts to the prison library.

[233] Carolyn G. Heilbrun, 'Non-Autobiographies of "Privileged" Women: England and America', in Brodzski and Schenck, *Life/Lines*, 71.

reading. But whereas people's family circumstances, and their perception of their immediate environments, are going to be unique, their reading material is not: the sheer frequency with which certain texts recur in women's memories as having been significant to them is testimony to this. To have responded to *Adam Bede*, to *The Story of an African Farm*, even to *The Wide, Wide World*, is to have shared a relationship with others: to have broken down some of the barriers which divide public and private worlds.

To argue this is to fall in line with the models of the formation of female selfhood proposed by certain feminist social historians and psychoanalytic theorists, such as Sheila Rowbotham and Nancy Chodorow, stressing the importance of identification, interdependence, and community to woman's development of her sense of identity.[234] Such allegiances were often hard to assert openly in nineteenth-century women's autobiography, although one can find them both in the writings of those overtly working within the women's movement, and in those who are explicitly, and intimately, addressing their own daughters. But the presentation and discussion of reading material and its effects provides a specific arena in which connections between women may be made. It highlights the degree to which women may share both subjectivity and socialization.

And yet, it would be wrong to end this section by suggesting that a sense of communality should be praised at the expense of difference. For the differences which remained *between* women (differences of class, of regionality, of sexual preference) were precisely those which many suffragettes played down or ignored in their political campaigning. Reading may offer some ways of bridging these gaps in imaginative terms, but not in practical ones. It may be easier for a woman to say 'I' if she is claiming to speak with a representative voice, but this may well be to the fatal cost of simultaneously suppressing the necessary recognition of heterogeneity.

[234] For a further discussion of these writers in relation to theories of autobiography, see esp. Susan Stanford Friedman's important essay, 'Women's Autobiographical Selves: Theory and Practice', in S. Benstock (ed.), *The Private Self: Theory and Practice of Women's Autobiographical Writings* (1988), 34–62.

Part IV

9   Fictional Reading

Alexander M. Rossi's *Forbidden Books* (1897) (Fig. 16) shows six girls loosely grouped together in a fashionable artistic interior. Two on a sofa have their heads close together over a book, whilst a third sits on the oriental rug in front of them, her hands clasped around her knees as she listens. A fourth, nearer to the bookcase, perches on the back of the sofa. Two more girls sit in the window, not reading, but scrutinizing the picture on the easel, which appears to be of a full-frontal female nude. The floor is littered with piles of books, either already leafed through, or waiting, promisingly, for the girls to pick them up. They are, however, about to be interrupted. An older woman is gently turning the doorknob and entering. Her identity is not clear: perhaps the mother of one or some of the girls (she wears a wedding ring): the fact that she is dressed in mourning tacitly alludes to the absence of male authority in the house. Certainly, she is about to interrupt their transgressive pleasures.

In its depiction of young women avidly reading 'forbidden' material, Rossi's work is close in spirit to Auguste Toulmouche's *Dans la Bibliothèque* (*Les fruits défendus*: Fig. 17), exhibited at the Paris Salon in 1868. Here, the positioning of the figures (two reading, one up a ladder reaching to the top shelves where the most scandalous books are likely to be kept, and one listening intently at the door) is tighter than in the Rossi painting, accentuating the sense of clandestine bonding between the protagonists. But one is invited to read the scenes in very similar ways. Both of them employ the convention that there are some books which are habitually kept well out of the reach of young women readers, but that, given half a chance, these same young women will fall enthusiastically upon these very volumes and become engrossed in their contents. The girls are shown as absorbed, oblivious to any audience one might postulate in terms of the artist or viewer of the picture.[1] Yet both Rossi and Toulemouche share an attitude of amusement, rather than prudery, at what these girls are getting up to. More unnervingly, the cultural inference that what they are reading about is sex in its turn sexualizes them, confirming that they do not just possess good looks, but adult knowledge. What, however, is hard to crack—assuming that one continues to postulate a male artist or observer—is the sense of solidarity which is created between the girls themselves, and which diminishes any sense of their vulnerability or accessibility.

This process of bonding which can be created through reading (whether the reading material be French fiction, John Stuart Mill, or a Rhoda Broughton

[1] For a discussion of absorption versus theatricality in painting, see Michael Fried, *Absorption and Theatricality: Painting and Beholder in the Age of Diderot* (Berkeley, Calif., 1980).

16. Alexander Rossi, *Forbidden Books* (1897)

17. Auguste Toulmouche, *Dans la Bibliotèque* (1869)

novel) was something which both fascinated men, as these paintings testify, and which was exploited, in differing ways, by novelists of both sexes throughout the period. In Part IV of this book, I shall specifically be considering the fictional representation of reading as an activity, concentrating on the ways in which authors recognize and manipulate the conventions which have already been considered in this book. In this chapter, I examine the varied uses to which references to reading are put within novels. The following two chapters, on sensation fiction and 'new woman' fiction, draw on existing scholarship which sets out to understand why such novels should have proved so controversial: the substance of this controversy, and the reasoning behind it, should come as no surprise, given the material already presented in this study. But my main point is to show that through incorporating references to reading—at times quite extensive references—these novelists were attempting to question dominant ideas about the relationship between women's reading practices and their responses to what they read. Polemic against the common expectation that women automatically and unreflectingly identified with central women charac- ters, or that they would be unfailingly corrupted by reading about matters concerning sexuality, was met head on within the pages of those very books which caused conservative commentators the greatest anxiety.

Reading about Reading

The incorporation of references to reading material and practices within novels can be seen to work in various ways. First, one encounters the direct quotation, either woven into the narrative, or standing separate, as the epigram to a title- page, part, or chapter. Second, authors employ references to specific texts. Sometimes these function in a manner related to Matthew Arnold's dictum in 'The Study of Poetry' (1880) that: 'There can be no more useful help for discovering what poetry belongs to the class of the truly excellent, and can therefore do us most good, than to have always in one's mind lines and expressions of the great masters, and to apply them as a touchstone to other poetry:'[2] although novelists draw upon these references not as part of an act of literary criticism, but in order to enhance the aesthetic value of the work in question. Or the naming of individual texts can function didactically, relying on the reader's prior acquaintance with character or plot development in an earlier work, hence suggesting specific narrative models to be adopted or shunned or to be used as a point of comparison.[3] Third, often the least self-conscious mode of incorporating references to reading, we find them functioning in a way which

[2] Matthew Arnold, 'The Study of Poetry', introd. to *The English Poets: Selections with Critical Introductions*, ed. Thomas Humphry Ward (1880), p. xxv.
[3] For a discussion of the incorporation of direct allusion in a range of Victorian novels, see Michael Wheeler, *The Art of Allusion in Victorian Fiction* (1979).

appears to heighten the mimetic realism of a fiction, encouraging the reader to believe that she is reading of a social and cultural environment with which she is, or could become, familiar. Accepting the 'naturalness' of the reading practices which are depicted is thus a device which consolidates the impression that narrator and reader share the same values. And fourth, the topos of reading can be used in a manner which is both more generalized and more self-referential. To draw attention to what is involved in certain types of reading (the reading of romantic fiction, in particular) acts as a comment on the status of the text in which such a reference is found. It thus emphasizes the compliance, or otherwise, of this text with established conventions concerning both fictional form and the response of readers, and alerts the reader to pay attention to the implications of her own practice and to be aware of her own expectations of a novel.

Necessarily, the distinctions between these practices are not as clear-cut as this summary sounds. Take, for example, Trollope's frequent allusions to women's reading in his fiction. In *Is He Popenjoy?* (1878), Mary Lovelace, 'so pretty, so pert, so gay, so good' marries Lord George Germain, 'so grim, so gaunt, so sombre, and so old'.[4] Quite apart from a general speculation about whether or not Trollope is incorporating any reference to Richardson's manipulative anti-hero (and recognizing as the novel progresses that even if Mary herself is exculpated, the name 'Lovelace' may function as a warning to expect a story concerned with sexual intrigues and uncertainties), it is hard to know how much weight to give to the specificity of detail of Mary and Lord Germain's first, awkward evening together in their new London house:

Of course there were books. Every proper preparation had been made for rendering the little house pleasant. In the evening she took from her shelf a delicate little volume of poetry, something exquisitely bound, pretty to look at, and sweet to handle, and settled herself down to be happy in her own drawing-room. But she soon looked up from the troubles of Aurora Leigh to see what her husband was doing. He was comfortable in his chair, but was busy with the columns of *The Brothershire Herald*.[5]

Clearly, what is announced here is incompatibility of taste. But how may one interpret Mary's choice of reading matter? It works on one level as a signifier of period detail: the novel was published in 1878, and this reference helps to locate the time of its action in 1857 or shortly afterwards, for Barrett Browning's volume is introduced as just one item in an entire houseful of new, unused objects. But to a reader familiar with the poem, the resonances are more unsettling, for to imagine Mary, having agreed to marry her humourless husband in order to please others rather than to please herself, coming upon Aurora condemning:

---

[4] Anthony Trollope, *Is He Popenjoy?*, 3 vols. (1878), i. 3.
[5] Ibid. 154.

a man,
Who sees a woman as the complement
Of his sex merely. You forget too much
That every creature, female as the male
Stands single in responsible act and thought
As also in birth and death   (ii. 434–9)

is to imagine the space, regretful or rebellious, into which her subjectivity may
have been led. We are not told Mary's reactions to the reading material, beyond
the fact that 'On that occasion she did not care very much for Aurora Leigh.
Her mind was hardly tuned to poetry of that sort. The things around her were
too important to allow her mind to indulge itself with foreign cares.'[6] It is left
unspecified whether what was especially uncongenial was reading anything at
all, since this was an activity which separated her from her husband, or whether
the topic of a woman asserting her right to self-determination seemed singularly
inappropriate, or whether a poem in which happiness is found within Italy is not
comforting reading material when her new husband's own elder brother, long
presumed a bachelor, was on his way back from that country with a new wife
and (although she does not yet know this) heir. Because we are not told the
details of her responses to Barrett Browning's poem, aspects of Mary's
reactions, and hence of her inner self are hidden from the reader, just as they
are to become increasingly concealed from Lord George. For that matter,
leaving these details open prevents alienating either camp of reader who was
familiar with, and had opinions about *Aurora Leigh*, either admiring it for its
feminist sentiments, or regarding its subject-matter as unduly disruptive or
risqué.

This example serves to show how reconstructing patterns of reception among
Victorian women readers cannot involve supplying or assuming a predictable set
of reactions with which one may confidently fill those spaces within texts which
open up with the incorporation of a book title or literary allusion. We are
reminded, rather, of the range of potential responses available both to fictional
character, and, by extension, to the contemporary reader.

The employment of direct quotation by Victorian and Edwardian writers
functioned in various ways. In the first place, 'Quotes are a proof if not a badge
of learning', as Stefan Morawski puts it in *Inquiries into the Fundamentals of
Aesthetics*.[7] So to employ a literary reference is to assert one's place within the
cultural assumptions of that society. Quotations could thus be a means for
women to claim, even if not consciously, their right to be considered on equal
terms with other, male writers. Alternatively, women writers could offer either
quotations taken from a different set of texts from those which tended to be
cited by men, suggesting, for example, women's readier familiarity with

---

[6] Ibid.
[7] Stefan Morawski, *Inquiries into the Fundamentals of Aesthetics* (Cambridge, Mass., 1974), 341.

romantic poets and Shakespeare rather than with allusions to Greek and Roman writings, or else they could offer a critical revision of the original implications of the texts themselves. Thus Charlotte Brontë can be seen to make one of the best known of all nineteenth-century fictional woman readers, Jane Eyre, adopt the broad narrative model of *Pilgrim's Progress* as she recounts her autobiography. But the female protagonist does not rely on Providence alone to direct her along a path of righteousness, but must make her own rational decisions and choices. Additionally, Brontë reworks Miltonic texts. Ushering in a sequence of references to *Paradise Lost*, the reference at the beginning of Chapter 23 to the orchard at Thornfield as 'Eden-like' may make the reader wary, but deceit, here, will be found to lie with the man rather than with the woman. When Jane leaves Thornfield 'weeping wildly as I walked along my solitary way',[8] she is virtuous, not a fallen Eve.[9]

Quotations had further functions. Writers could call on favourite writers in a way which suggests both an act of literary homage and the establishment of a community of taste between themselves and their readers. In this way, for example, Emilie Barrington resolutely employs quotations from both of the Brownings to act as epigrams to *Lena's Picture* (1892) in order to emphasize the intense emotional weight of its subtitle, a 'Story of Love'. Finally, and perhaps more surprisingly, writers of women's popular fiction very frequently incorporated literary quotations and references into their novelettes. Thus the opening number of the *Illustrated Family Novelist*, a tale entitled 'Living Forgotten—Loving Forlorn', introduces two girls on a train. One has 'luxuriant hair, golden as an aureole of Cimabue's angels', her younger sister a: 'wealth of raven hair, "crisped like a war-horse's encolure," as Robert Browning hath it. Very charming, in truth, was Lucy, and, gazing at her, no man would wonder that swart Cleopatra could "rule the heart of warrior or statesman, and live in the world's memory for evermore." '[10] Implicitly, allusions to 'high' culture increase the literary status of a romantic tale, enabling the reader to justify (to herself as much as to others) spending time on escapist literature. Moreover, for any reader, quotations similarly function to consolidate the sense of membership of a community sharing knowledge and expectations. In the case of texts like 'Living Forgotten—Loving Forlorn', they may also grant the reader the temporary illusion that she is part of a social and cultural milieu from which most of the heroines of such writing are drawn, and in which literary and artistic references are freely shared.

[8] Charlotte Brontë, *Jane Eyre* (1847; repr. Oxford, 1969), 410.

[9] The literary allusions in *Jane Eyre*, and the ways in which Charlotte Brontë uses her heroine's reading to structure her own novel, have been widely discussed. See Wheeler, *The Art of Allusion*, 27–43; Carla L. Peterson, *The Determined Reader: Gender and Culture in the Novel from Napoleon to Victoria* (New Brunswick, NJ, 1986), 82–102; Barry Qualls, *The Secular Pilgrims of Victorian Fiction* (1982), 43–69; Robert K. Martin, 'Jane Eyre and the World of Faery', *Mosaic*, 10 (1977), 85–95; Mark Hennelly, 'Jane Eyre's Reading Lesson', *English Literary History*, 51 (1984), 693–717.

[10] W.J.E.C., 'Living Forgotten—Loving Forlorn', *Illustrated Family Novelist*, 1 (24 July 1878), 2.

Julia Kristeva, in *Séméiotiké* (1969) argues that reading is a form of aggressive participation, with each reader attempting to incorporate quotations and allusions into a coherent semiotic unit. To do so necessarily is an act of appropriation, involving disrupting both literary chronology and the privileged authority of the original texts and those who inscribed them and positioned those words which are subsequently prised from their settings. Seen in this way, to encounter and recognize these quotations has implications which go beyond confirming one's confident membership of a cultural group. For to perceive that a quotation is something other than it was when found in its original context is to see it as metaphor, and as such has the potential to engage a reader in interpretative activity, ensuring that meaning and significance must be constructed, rather than passively, unthinkingly extracted.[11]

This understanding of the functioning of quotation and direct reference is particularly useful when it comes to considering the more controversial women's writing of this period. Especially significant is quotation consciously employed for a polemical end. Morawski coined the term 'para-quotation' to signify the use of a certain type of interpolation 'with a stimulatory-amplificatory function', such as Piscator's employment of captions or film sequences to anticipate actions on stage, or Manet's use of a Japanese print (which serves both amplificatory and ornamental ends) in his 1867 portrait of Zola[12]—or, one might add, Egg's use of a volume labelled 'Balzac' in *Past and Present I*. Not only, argues Morawski, is paraquotation a means adopted particularly by artists with theses to prove—like the 'New Woman' writers, say—but he claims that quotations habitually 'accumulate in art when the boundaries between it and other forms of social consciousness become vague'.[13] Quotations and allusions forge links between the private activity of reading and the social contexts within which this reading takes place. This serves to emphasize still further the claim which may be made for reading as an activity with the power to break down some of those distinctions which both contemporary and subsequent critical discourses have erected between the domestic and the public spheres of life. The remainder of this chapter moves away from a direct consideration of quotations taken from individual texts to examine some of the ways in which widely circulating notions about women's reading and their presumed responses were incorporated within contemporary fiction, demonstrating the different ways in which the concept of shared subjectivity was played upon.

Many of the numerous references to the reading of women and girls which one encounters in nineteenth- and early twentieth-century fiction are utterly predictable. They confirm the messages that are endlessly reiterated in advice

---

[11] For this understanding of the functioning of quotation, see further Michael Worton and Judith Still, 'Introduction', *Intertextuality: Theories and Practices* (Manchester and New York, 1990), 11–12.

[12] Morawski, *Fundamentals of Aesthetics*, 255–6.

[13] Ibid. 359.

books and magazine articles: that reading fiction itself is something only to be
indulged in moderation; that romantic novels, in particular, carry with them a
propensity to corrupt; that French publications are the worst of all.

In overtly Christian fiction in particular, reading methods are commented on
as readily as the nature of the reading material itself. This should come as no
surprise after the admonitory tones of advice literature. Self-restraint and self-
discipline in relation to books is used as a mark of moral virtue. For example, it
forms a touchstone by means of which the reader may discriminate between the
two sisters in Elizabeth Sewell's *Margaret Percival* (1847):

Agatha read books by stealth, which her mother did not approve; Margaret not only
refused to follow her example as a child, from a hatred of deception, but when left to the
choice of her own studies, closed instantly any volume, however interesting, with which
she would have blushed to be seen.[14]

Particularly in the early part of the period, novelists can be found introducing
laboured homilies on the topic of reading which mirror faithfully the tenor of
the less compromising manuals of guidance. Even when she was not herself a
Christian, as in the case of the Jewish writer Grace Aguilar, a fictional moralist
played upon the expectations of her readership when discussing a subject as
delicate, in some quarters, as the power of poetry. Aguilar, in *Home Influence; A
Tale for Mothers and Daughters* (1847) shows Emmeline, one of her heroines,
writing verses and singing them to the harp. Her mother speaks words of
caution to her: 'Poetry is a dangerous gift, my child; but as long as you bring it
to the common treasury of Home, and regard it merely as a recreation, only to
be enjoyed when less attractive duties and studies are completed, you have my
full permission to cultivate.' Emily, her cousin, has been listening attentively,
and asks 'Why is poetry a dangerous gift, dear Aunt?'

Because, my love, it is very apt to excite and encourage an over-excess of feeling; gives a
habit of seeing things other than they really are, and engenders a species of romantic
enthusiasm, most dangerous to the young, especially of our sex, whose feelings generally
require control and repression, even when not joined to poetry. To a well-regulated
mind and temper, the danger is not of the same serious kind, as to the irregulated, but
merely consists, in the powerful temptation it too often presents to neglect duties and
employments of more consequence for its indulgence.[15]

In other less heavy-handed didactic fiction, the narrator assumes that shared
responses towards certain types of reading will work as one of the grounds on
which to build up a bond between heroine and reader. Thus in Juliana Ewing's
Six to Sixteen (1876), there is a calculated attempt to enlist the reader on the side
of Margaret, the sympathetic narrator, through textual matters. In the
schoolroom, she and her sister Matilda dutifully read Mrs Markham's *England*

[14] Elizabeth Sewell, *Margaret Percival*, 2 vols. (1847), i. 150–1.
[15] Grace Aguilar, *Home Influence; A Tale for Mothers and Daughters*, 2 vols. (1847), ii. 273–4.

and Miss Trimmer's *Bible Lessons* aloud to the governess, who was as bored as they: however, the governess's solution, telling them stories about what she claimed had happened to herself is not condoned. Margaret believes many of these stories had their origins in the numerous books she borrowed from the circulating library: the governess 'was one of those strange characters who indulge in egotism and exaggeration', had difficulty in telling fact from fiction, 'and it was well for us that her reign was not a long one'.[16] The state of mind of the governess (or, indeed, of the reader who might be tempted to sympathize with this governess's frustration and boredom) is, unsurprisingly, left unconsidered.

Elsewhere, over-absorption in reading could be used to create a dramatic scenario illustrative of the dangers attendant on abnegating one's responsibility towards others in favour of self-satisfaction. Ethel May, in Charlotte M. Yonge's *The Daisy Chain* (1856), may indeed be perusing a story in a religious magazine, but her attention should not have wandered so far as to let her little brother Aubrey ignite his pinafore with a newspaper he had stuck in the fire.[17] Luckily he is hardly scorched, but Ethel's irresponsibility provokes Dr May to threaten to put an end to both her philanthropic and her scholarly activities, if she cannot cope with more immediate demands on her attention. His solemn warning is in no way challenged by the narrative commentary, although *The Daisy Chain*, like many of Yonge's fictions, carries within it the potential to provoke indignation, even anger, in the reader who identifies with Ethel's rebelliousness, impetuosity, and desire to keep up with her brothers in classical learning, but who does not go along with the values which Yonge places on female self-sacrifice performed in the interests of the family and one's immediate social sphere.[18] This can be seen more subtly in *The Clever Woman of the Family* (1865), where in the opening of the novel a certain amount of sympathy is demanded for Rachel, the attractive, healthy heroine. She complains against the fact that she is tied down by conventionalities and proprieties, not allowed out late, to choose her own friends, to put forward her own opinions:

I am five-and-twenty, and I will no longer be witheld from some path of usefulness! I will judge for myself, and when my mission has declared itself, I will not be witheld from it by any scruple that does not approve itself to my reason and conscience.[19]

---

[16] Juliana Horatia Ewing, *Six to Sixteen: A Story for Girls* (1876), 100.

[17] Charlotte M. Yonge, *The Daisy Chain* (1856; repr. 1988), 136–7.

[18] The earliest fiction of Mary Arnold (later to become Mrs Humphry Ward) was highly imitative of Yonge. This incident is transferred to an outdoor setting in 'Lansdale Manor', in which the narrative focuses on Edith being so absorbed in her reading that she allows her younger brother to fall over a cliff. Rescued by his father, the incident provokes a homily from him to attend to the 'duties to the home in which God has placed you. Learn to watch against the beginnings of evil my child, the neglect of some little duty . . . '. See John Sutherland, *Mrs Humphry Ward: Eminent Victorian. Pre-eminent Edwardian* (Oxford, 1990), 25.

[19] Yonge, *The Clever Woman of the Family* (1865; repr. 1985), 3.

The danger, for Yonge, is conveyed by the topical force of the word 'mission', fuelled by the wrong kind of reading, factual and theoretic, which led Rachel into discontent not just with the 'condition of the masses' in an abstract sense, but with her own immediate relations:

It was a homely neighbourhood, a society well born, but of circumscribed interests and habits, and little connected with the great progressive world, where, however, Rachel's sympathies all lay, necessarily fed, however, by periodical literature, instead of by conversation or commerce with living minds.[20]

The lesson which she learns is inevitable, from Yonge's fictional perspective: Rachel is not 'clever' enough in the ways of the real world to prevent the philanthropic society for local unemployed lacemakers which she sets up being embezzled by the crook Mauleverer/Maddox. Moreover, she falls in love and realizes that it is in caring for her family that her true vocation lies. Yet her reading is not condemned out of hand, but rather is seen as indicative of a sympathetic nature which has not been properly channelled. In addition, Yonge accepts that a certain amount of informative reading is desirable. Thus, when Rachel is sorting out her theological position and discussing her doubts with the country parson, Mr Clare, she is comforted, on asking him 'Do you object to my having read, and thought, and tried?' to be told 'Certainly not; those who have the ability should, if they feel disturbed, work out the argument. Nothing is gained while it is felt that both sides have not been heard.'[21] None the less, one is left in no doubt that this apparent freedom to read and choose one's own position, in religious as with other matters, is one from which Yonge assumes her readers will always make the correct choice. Nor, in Yonge's writings and in those of her close contemporaries, will reading take the place of more appropriate domestic duties. In Rosa Nouchette Carey's *Nellie's Memories* (1868), the hard-working heroine, bringing up her motherless brothers and sisters, is clearly inviting approval and emulation when she responds to a question from a more leisured neighbour:

'Alas, I rarely open a book; a leisure hour is a rare treat to me.'
'Why what on earth can you find to do?' was Miss Rivers' next question, arching her eyebrows inquisitively.
'We are a large family,' I said, 'and I am the oldest and the housekeeper, and I have many children to work for.'[22]

Yet it is not solely in edifying domestic fiction that reading appears in a didactic guise. Throughout the period, other novels echo and reinforce the many diverse ends and warnings concerning the activity which were meted out in advice literature. The fact that time spent reading could be a means of

[20] Yonge, *The Clever Woman of the Family*, 6.
[21] Ibid. 323.
[22] Rosa Nouchette Carey, *Nellie's Memories*, 3 vols. (1868), i. 204.

obtaining useful information could be brought home using exaggeratedly improbable means to catch the reader's attention. Thus, at its most extreme, the resourceful heroine of *Robina Crusoe, and her lonely island home*, serialized in the *Girl's Own Paper*, was extremely grateful to have spent hours reading books of travel and adventure, and learning from volumes dealing with botany, geology, chemistry, cookery, and medicine. Whilst few of her readers, she acknowledges, are likely themselves to be marooned for years on a desert island, she would strongly advise them to devote some portion of their time to similar study, for 'even the happiest and most guarded home will be incalculably benefited by the mistress of it having some knowledge of the laws of health—of the science of the common objects of everyday life'.[23]

But the most common lesson taught through the introduction of reading as a topos in non-religious, as well as within Christian fiction, was that the consumption of romance led to a narrow, and at worst self-delusory outlook. There was nothing new about this, as Chapter 2 illustrated. The tradition of presenting love stories as potentially arousing false ideals and expectations continued throughout this period, and can be found in fiction aimed at a broad variety of readers. J. Parsons Hall, for example, in 'The Reserved Husband', a short story in the *London Journal* of 1849, a magazine with a readership predominantly drawn from the skilled working classes, describes the dissatisfaction felt by the wife of a fitter in a locomotive department at her husband at the end of a day's work. He offers no conversation, and regularly falls asleep, snoring, in his chair. She allows feelings of dissatisfaction to grow from the unfavourable comparisons she makes: 'The ideal lover she had read of in the pages of fiction, with his glossy black locks, eagle eye, and elegant figure, bore no resemblance to the stalwart frame of her husband, with his herculean shoulders, brawny arms, and bronzed thick neck.'[24] She runs away with a clerk and ends her life penniless in a cheap lodging house. The blame is not made to lie entirely on the effects of romantic fiction, for the story also emphasizes the husband contemplating the fact that perhaps he could have put more effort into the marriage, but romance fiction is instrumental in creating the gap in communication which exists between the couple. Similarly, in a quite different type of novel, George Eliot makes it clear that the distance between Rosamond Vincy and Lydgate, in *Middlemarch* (1872), can to some extent be blamed on Rosamond's unrealistic appropriation of romantic expectations. We learn little directly about Rosamond's reading habits, other than that she is 'not without relish' for the Keepsake annual writers Lady Blessington and Letitia Elizabeth Landon,[25] but the literary register which Eliot employs to describe the scenario into which Rosamond's imagination inserts Lydgate ('Strangers, whether wrecked and clinging to a raft, or duly escorted and accompanied by

[23] 'Robina Crusoe, and her lonely island home', *Girl's Own Paper*, 4 (1883), 245.
[24] J. Parsons Hall, 'The Reserved Husband', *London Journal*, 9 (19 May 1849), 166.
[25] George Eliot, *Middlemarch* (1874 edn., repr. Norton, New York and London, 1977), 187.

portmanteaus, have always had a circumstancial fascination for the virgin mind .
. . And a stranger was absolutely necessary to Rosamond's social romance';[26]
'Rosamond had registered every look and word, and estimated them as the
opening incidents of a preconceived romance—incidents which gather value
from the foreseen development and climax'[27]) make it very easy for the mid-
Victorian reader to utilize her imbibed knowledge of reading practices. To
attempt to live one's life according to fictional criteria is to follow a dangerous
path.

Not only did the introduction of a heroine who bases her judgements on
assumptions derived from her reading material invariably tell the reader that the
character was about to make a potentially disastrous mistake. It established a
distance, characterized by sympathetic superiority, between reader and
protagonist. Thus the seventeen-year-old Phyllis, in Arabella Kenealy's *Dr
Janet of Harley Street* (1893), instantly appears vulnerable as she walks in the
garden on her wedding day, musing to herself, 'in a pleased reverie': 'How good
the Marquis is . . . and what a happy girl I am. He is just like the old French
marquises in books; he has such lovely manners, and makes such charming
compliments. He is like a dear stately old father'—a remark challenged by the
narrator a few pages later when this sextugenarian approaches her possessively,
kissing her 'fiercely' with 'the coarse, crude passion of which alone he was
capable'.[28] Understandably, Phyllis runs away from him before the marriage is
consummated, and learns to develop a combination of intuition and rationality
which leads, eventually, to her training for the medical profession.

Novels increasingly warned the reader that too concentrated a diet of
romantic fiction may not solely lead one into making errors in relation to one's
own circumstances, but may also mean that one misinterprets the lives of those
with whom one comes into contact. Shallowness of outlook can be exposed in
the process. Evelyn, in Lanoe Falconer's *Mademoiselle Ixe* (1890) assumes, when
her foreign governess sets eyes on a Russian count visiting the family and turns
pale, that only one possible reason can lie behind such behaviour. ' "There can
be no doubt about it," was the verdict of this experienced little novel-reader,
"she is in love with the Count." '[29] Even after Mademoiselle Ixe starts to tell
Evelyn something of her history—that back in her country, people lie crushed
beneath a monstrous tyranny—the English girl remains slow on the uptake, the
narrator commenting, pointedly:

Had the range of Evelyn's ideas and interests been a little less narrow, had she been in
the habit of reading anything else besides stories in the magazines or fashionable gossip
in the papers, had she been awake to the throes and pangs which now convulse the
national life of countries less happy than her own, this speech might have revealed to her

---

[26] George Eliot, *Middlemarch*, 80.
[27] Ibid. 114.
[28] Arabella Kenealy, *Dr Janet of Harley Street* (1893), 4, 8.
[29] 'Lanoe Falconer' [Mary Elizabeth Hawker] *Mademoiselle Ixe* (1890), 122.

the nationality and the character of the woman beside her. But Evelyn cared for none of these things. She classed them all under the name politics, which to her meant everything that was dry, lifeless, and prosaic.[30]

Only when the governess attempts to assassinate the Count, and reveals herself to be a Russian nihilist, does understanding, and fuller political understanding born out of personal sympathy, begin to dawn on Evelyn. Misleading fictional stereotypes did not, moreover, have to be confined to the direct domain of romance, and this theme was developed increasingly towards the end of the period, when women's fiction itself came to centre on romantic plots with less regularity. In Maud Churton Braby's *Downward: A 'Slice of Life'* (1910), for example, Dolly, the central character, works as a nurse, and Braby, through her, sets out to point to the truth behind what was already coming to be a novelistic convention: 'In fiction . . . the pretty nurse, same as the pretty typist, is a stock character, and all her male patients fall in love with her. In real life the majority of both classes are plain.'[31]

The common theme of romantic and other fiction fostering illusions repeatedly emphasizes the need for girls and women to be more self-aware, thinking for themselves rather than lazily allowing novelistic conventions to determine their expectations. But reading could be presented as having a more sinister capacity to corrupt. This can be seen in Caroline Grey's *Sybil Lennard* (1846), in which a wife and mother is lured away from home and husband by Hardress Fitz Hugh, a radical Irish MP. He sets to work to flatter, excite, and seduce Sybil by giving her to read Rousseau's *Eloisa* ('meat too strong for one so little experienced in such mental food'); Byron, with the more sentimental and passionate passages deliberately marked in the margin, and French novels. The governess who narrates the novel makes her position clear by repeatedly comparing Fitz Hugh to Milton's Satan, working on the innocence of a woman who is completely without defences but is susceptible to guileful charm. The seduction methods are turned into an occasion for solemn homily:

French novels—exciting poetry—questionable works of imagination—dread sounds!— How many a soul has been blighted by their poison—beneath their influence how many a heart, once pure and spotless, is 'tainted with festering sore disease.'

Oh, what do they merit, from whose pens works of evil tendency have proceeded—whose will has sent forth these noxious draughts to do their unrighteous deeds? On that day which will summon us all to the bar of eternal justice, will not the perverters of talent, equally with those who have misused wealth or power, 'call in vain on the mountains to fall on them, or the hills to cover them.'[32]

Corruption through unsuitable reading material could set in at any social level. H. G. Jebb's story of a reformed prostitute, *Out of the Depths* (1859)

---

[30] Ibid. 135–6.
[31] Maud Churton Braby, *Downward: A 'Slice of Life'* (1910), 77.
[32] [Caroline Grey] *Sybil Lennard*, 3 vols. (1846), ii. 122.

follows evangelical non-fiction in locating a crucial element in her fall within Mary Smith's passion for reading. Initially, the material itself could not so much be said to be to blame, as what are presented as being the innate workings of Mary's mind. This suggests that certain natures are, despite the interventions of those close to them, particularly over-disposed to a dangerously active imagination. Mary tells us that she was:

passionately fond of books of a certain sort; anything in the shape of a tale I used to devour; adding to and altering the original story as pleased my imagination, and afterwards putting myself into the position of the principal female character in the book . . . I was often scolded by mother for neglecting the little household duties which devolved on me at home, through this cause; and sometimes even my beloved sewing was made to give place to the 'Pilgrim's Progress,' or Mrs. Sherwood's 'Henry Milner'.[33]

Whilst there could be nothing wrong with these two examples on their own (to condemn the reading of all narratives would be to call into question the position of the reader of *Out of the Depths* itself, after all), the *habits* which Mary failed to check in herself combined with other influences to lead to disastrous effects. Aged fifteen, she becomes apprentice to a dressmaker in a local town—always an occupation, in Victorian fiction, with overtones of danger for young girls' morals. Moreover, her long walk there and back gave her ample opportunity for consuming stories. Retrospectively, she warns her readers to be careful about the company that they keep, and reminds them of the importance of bearing a mother's standards in mind:

It was during this period that I first read a novel, which one of my young companions in the workroom lent me, seeing that I was very fond of reading; and I soon procured others for myself, which I carefully concealed from my mother's eyes; for I had an instinct that she would disapprove of such books, though I had never so much as heard of a novel till then . . . I can see now that there was no character more certain to derive injury from novel-reading than mine as it was at that time; and the trash I devoured did its baneful work indeed.[34]

By the mid-nineteenth century, the trope of fiction as a fast route to corruption was so familiar that it could be used not just in its own right, for didactic purposes, but as a way of encouraging the reader to think critically about their own practices when consuming novels. The incorporation of the theme of romance reading into Charlotte Brontë's *Shirley* (1849) is somewhat troubling. Mrs Pryor and Caroline discuss the subject of love together. At the time, neither Caroline nor the reader know that this is, in fact, a conversation between mother and daughter, and hence that there is a particular poignancy underlying the acerbity of the older woman's remarks. Love, claims Caroline, is real: it is the sweetest, although also the bitterest experience that we know:

---

[33] [H. G. Jebb] *Out of the Depths* (1859), 8. I am indebted to Karen Avenoso for this reference.
[34] Ibid. 11–12.

'My dear—it is very bitter. It is said to be strong—strong as death! Most of the cheats of existence are strong. As to their sweetness—nothing is so transitory: its date is a moment,—the twinkling of an eye: the sting remains for ever: it may perish with the dawn of eternity, but it tortures through time into its deepest night.'

'Yes, it tortures through time,' agreed Caroline, 'except when it is mutual love.'

'Mutual love! My dear, romances are pernicious. You do not read them, I hope?'

'Sometimes—whenever I can get them, indeed; but romance-writers might know nothing of love, judging by the way in which they treat of it.'

'Nothing whatever, my dear!' assented Mrs Pryor, eagerly; 'nor of marriage; and the false pictures they give of those subjects cannot be too strongly condemned. They are not like reality: they show you only the green tempting surface of the marsh, and give not one faithful or truthful hint of the slough underneath.'[35]

How, ultimately, one interprets this depends on our own reading of the novel's conclusion. If one accepts the marriages of Caroline to the mill-owner Robert Moore, and of Shirley to his brother Louis as an entirely happy ending, a celebration of mutual love, then Mrs Pryor's comments can be read as an understandably bitter comment on her own life. But if one picks up on the formality of the newspaper wedding announcement (the closest we get to the nuptials) and the way in which it shows male identity to be commonly regarded as dependent on place and property ownership, whilst female identity is defined in relation only to male relatives; if one regrets, along with the narrator, the passing of the green and lone and wild Hollow, where Caroline and Shirley used to meet and talk together, and the more general disappearance of the countryside, together with local folklore, under the stone and brick and ashes of a manufacturer's daydreams; and if one recollects the implicit parallels which are drawn throughout the novel between the powerlessness of women and of workers, then one turns back to Mrs Pryor's remarks. Not only, after all, is Caroline's own fate perhaps less happy than the girl hopes it will be, but the way in which the reader has been led into following the momentum of a narrative based upon love interest is itself held open to questioning.

This incitement to consider fictional conventions, and to use this consideration to interrogate the relationship between novels and life, is a further use of references to reading within fiction. We see it operating again in *The Mill on the Floss* (1861) when Maggie Tulliver hands back *Corinne* unfinished to Philip, foreseeing, from previous reading experience, how the book will end: 'that light-complexioned girl would win away all the love from Corinne and make her miserable. I'm determined to read no more books where the blond-haired women carry away all the happiness.'[36] Here, the reader accepts a two-fold possibility. Either this, just for once, will be a story 'where the dark woman triumphs'; or Maggie, and hence the reader, is made to foresee something of

---

[35] Charlotte Brontë, *Shirley* (1849; repr. Oxford, 1979), 427.

[36] George Eliot, *The Mill on the Floss* (1861; repr. Oxford, 1980), 292. For discussion of Maggie Tulliver's reading, see Petersen, *The Determined Reader*, 182–207.

her own inevitable fate according to the established patterns of fictionality. The outcome, of course, is hardly as simple as this, for whilst the blonde Lucy is left alive, and eventually marries Stephen Guest, we finally encounter her visiting Maggie's grave, a figure of grief rather than happiness. She becomes a vehicle, given the sympathy Lucy had expressed earlier for Maggie, for the reader's mourning. Simultaneously, Maggie's death is presented in emotional, if not material terms, as a form of triumph rather than of misery. The convention is, whilst not overthrown, at least subverted: foregrounding it within the course of the story is one of the means by which the reader is led to consider the implications of fictional endings.

At the end of the century, a further example of a narrator manœuvring the reader to consider the implications of reading can be seen particularly clearly in George Gissing's *The Odd Women* (1893). Here it is not so much the consumer's own practice which is at stake, as her understanding of the motivations which lead others to books. Additionally, attitudes towards reading are used by Gissing to establish characterization, a means of defining his 'new woman', Rhoda Nunn. We see her rehearsing her beliefs after she learns that one of the former pupils of the establishment where she trained young women for office employment (and where they were supplied with a 'bookcase full of works on the Woman Question and allied topics' which 'served as a circulating library'[37]) had, after leaving suddenly, reappeared as the mistress of a married man. This was, Rhoda claims, no more than might be expected:

All her spare time was given to novel-reading. If every novelist could be strangled and thrown into the sea we should have some chance of reforming women. The girl's nature was corrupted with sentimentality, like that of all but every woman who is intelligent enough to read what is called the best fiction, but not intelligent enough to understand its vice. Love—love—love; a sickening sameness of vulgarity. What is more vulgar than the ideal of novelists? They won't represent the actual world; it would be too dull for their readers. In real life, how many men and women *fall in love?* Not one in every ten thousand, I am convinced. Not one married pair in ten thousand have felt for each other as two or three couples do in every novel. There is the sexual instinct, of course, but that is quite a different thing; the novelists daren't talk about that. The paltry creatures daren't tell the one truth that would be profitable. The result is that women imagine themselves noble and glorious when they are most near the animals. This Miss Royston—when she rushed off to perdition, ten to one she had in mind some idiot heroine of a book.[38]

Yet if there is an element of exaggeration creeping into the tone with which Gissing invests Rhoda Nunn's fervour on this subject, its impact is qualified by his treatment of Monica, who marries the elderly, narrow-minded Edmund Widdowson on the premiss that 'between the prospect of a marriage of

---

[37] George Gissing, *The Odd Women* (1893; repr. Virago, 1980), 54.
[38] Ibid. 58.

esteem'—for, if dull and demanding, Widdowson is at least socially thoroughly respectable—'and that of no marriage at all there was little room for hestitation'.[39] But the ideal reader of either gender whom Gissing is addressing has little trouble in foreseeing unhappiness for Monica in a marriage when it had never occurred to the husband that 'a wife must remain an individual, with rights and obligations independent of her wifely condition', and who advises her 'You shall read John Ruskin; every word he says about women is good and precious'.[40] Too late, Monica realizes that Rhoda Nunn's strictures on the subject of marriage had been perfectly justified, and resents the narrow intellectual and domestic confines in which she now finds herself. Widdowson, reluctantly, takes out a subscription to Mudie's, and 'Monica found more attraction in books as her life grew more unhappy'. She seems, however, unable to perceive that the two different types of reading in which she indulges contradict each other, rather than being conflatable. Monica absorbs some 'modern teaching': she 'sought for opinions and arguments which were congenial to her mood of discontent, all but of revolt'. But what are, by inference, feminist works are, fatally, consumed alongside fiction in which the love-interest predominates:

Sometimes the perusal of a love-story embittered her lot to the last point of endurance. Before marriage, her love-ideal had been very vague, elusive; . . . Now that she had a clearer understanding of her own nature, the type of man corresponding to her natural sympathies also became clear. In every particular he was unlike her husband. She found a suggestion of him in books . . . [41]

Yet when Monica tries to write Bevis, her candidate for romance, into her own live plot of running away with him to France, she finds him weak-willed, ready enough to flirt with her and flatter her up to a point, but bound by convention when she throws herself upon his mercy. To some extent, Gissing is showing her to have been as deluded as Miss Royston, but his incorporation of Monica's story into the main plot of his own book enables him to use the trope of reading not just for an isolated moralistic end, but as part of his whole protest against a system which constrains under-educated middle-class women into leading unfulfilling lives.

The fact that Monica takes to reading both 'new woman' fiction and more racy romantic texts, and contemplates acting on what she absorbs, is not put down to an innate disposition to an over-active imagination which needs to be tempered by a recognition of social and moral obligations to one's self and to others. Rather, it is presented as a direct result of her stultifying social circumstances. Such a form of escape is presented as being as understandable as the routes chosen by her unmarried sisters: Alice takes to hot gin, 'the bottle

---

[39] Ibid. 68.   [40] Ibid. 152–3.   [41] Ibid. 202.

beside her, and a novel on her lap';[42] Virginia sought nightly solace in the Bible: 'This was *her* refuge from the barrenness and bitterness of life.'[43] To think about the practice of reading, for Gissing, was also to make his readers think about the society from which readers come, and the position of women, in particular, within it. The references to reading in *The Odd Women*, like those in *Shirley*, also carry with them the effect of leading the reader to think about what is involved in the process of reading, and of encouraging them to recognize the simultaneous power and falsity of fictional expectations. They function to warn the reader against accepting a happy ending to this novel: even the possible liaison between Rhoda Nunn and the apparently forward-thinking Everard comes to nothing.

But the majority of novels which incorporate literary references do so in order to manipulate a different topos, that of assuring the reader of the realistic probability, rather than the fictionality, of a text. For example, Margaret Oliphant, in *Hester* (1883) emphasizes the straightforward, pleasant plainness of her heroine through a pointed fictional contrast. Hester is made to conclude that she 'is never likely to produce the effect which heroines in novels—even though comparatively plain—did produce', and, the authorial voice continues:

it is a pity, for the sake of young readers, that all the girls in novels, with so very rare exceptions—and Jane Eyre, if not pretty, probably was less plain than she thought, and certainly was *agaçante*, which is much more effective—should be beautiful and should have so much admiration and conquest. The girls who read are apt to wonder how it is that they have not the same fortune.

This, of course, is a ploy to gain sympathy for Hester's 'fine scorn of feminine victories in this sort', and admiration for her deeper, more emulatable moral qualities, thus allowing a reader who may doubt her own attractiveness a positive point of entry into the identificatory reading of this fiction.[44] Moreover, the contrived ending, whereby Hester is granted not just one, but two suitable suitors to choose between, is thereby rhetorically guaranteed against outright fictional improbability.

None the less, the frequency of the repetition of this device means that we should never take it at its face value within any individual text. It should be recognized for what it is, a literary convention; its very presence reassuring the reader not only that she is within fictional territory, but that she is aware of this fact. It is an example of what Roland Barthes puts forward as one of the pleasures of reading: the enjoyment of perversity, of knowingly believing in contradictions. 'Just as the child knows its mother has no penis and simultaneously believes she has one', Barthes writes, 'so the reader can keep saying: *I know these are only words, but all the same* . . . (I am moved as though

---

[42] George Gissing, *The Odd Women*, 302.
[43] Ibid. 305.
[44] Margaret Oliphant, *Hester*, 3 vols. (1883), i. 150.

these words were uttering a reality).'[45] Yet this trope, too, can be manipulated. In Trollope's *The Small House at Allington* (1864), Lily Dale, recovering from being jilted by the snobbish and self-centred Augustus Crosbie, discusses the 'exquisite new novel' she has been reading with her sister Bell:

'I am quite sure she was right in accepting him, Bell,' she said, putting down the book as the light was fading, and beginning to praise the story.

'It was a matter of course,' said Bell. 'It always is right in the novels. That's why I don't like them. They are too sweet.'

'That's why I do like them, because they are so sweet. A sermon is not to tell you what you are, but what you ought to be, and a novel should tell you not what you are to get, but what you'd like to get.'

'If so, then, I'd go back to the old school, and have the heroine really a heroine, walking all the way up from Edinburgh to London, and falling among thieves; [the reader is tacitly expected to recognize this as a reference to Scott's *The Heart of Midlothian*]; or else nursing a wounded hero, and describing the battle from the window. We've got tired of that; or else the people who write can't do it now-a-days. But if we are to have real life, let it be real.'

'No, Bell, no!' said Lily. 'Real life sometimes is so painful.'[46]

The reader is here led, in the short term, to sympathize with Lily's desire to read for escapism. But what of the relation of this passage to the novel as a whole? Crosbie, although physically attractive, was manifestly an unsuitable match for Lily; another suitor, Johnnie Eames, waits in the wings, with the narrator charting his progress from 'hobbledehoyhood' to Civil Service success. The dynamics of the narrative appear for a long while to be leading us towards the contradiction of Lily's belief that real life is painful, and that it may provide a happy ending in a way which would prove, as in the case of *Hester*, that romantic fiction does not always mislead. But instead, the reader's own expectations are confuted, since Lily's continued determination to remain true to the vows of love which she made towards the unworthy Crosbie is unshakeable. Fiction, rather than consoling, is used in this case to interrogate the desirability of holding to a rigorous code of female constancy even to the point of self-sacrifice, and also, in the process, to suggest to the reader that a 'real' happy ending, worthy of the pages of fiction, may well be the product of compromise rather than of idealism.

Right at the end of the period covered by this book, Virginia Woolf, in *The Voyage Out* (1915), presented the figure of Rachel Vinrace.[47] At twenty-four, she knows a good deal about music, but extremely little about adult behaviour.

---

45 Roland Barthes, *The Pleasure of the Text*, trans. by Richard Miller (1976), 47.

46 Anthony Trollope, *The Small House at Allington*, 2 vols. (1864), ii. 121–2.

47 For an extended discussion of the part which reading plays in the lives both of Rachel Vinrace and Helen Ambrose, see Beverly Ann Schlack, *Continuing Presences: Virginia Woolf's Use of Literary Allusion* (University Park, Penn. and London, 1979), 15–28.

An only child, she was brought up, after her mother's death, by two aunts in Richmond, with excessive care paid first to her health, and then to her morals. The resulting state was one of ignorance, which she sought to amend through reading: 'She groped for knowledge in old books, and found it in repulsive chunks . . . '.[48] Rachel was not, in any case, we are told, particularly fond of literature. But another aunt, Helen Ambrose, takes her abroad, determined that she should learn more about life. Reading more widely was part of this process, and Helen observes with interest the degree to which Rachel starts to identify herself with textual figures. Rachel works her way through Ibsen:

Far from looking bored or absent-minded, her eyes were concentrated almost sternly upon the page, and from her breathing, which was slow but repressed, it could be seen that her whole body was constrained by the working of her mind. At last she shut the book sharply, lay back, and drew a deep breath, expressive of the wonder which always marks the transition from the imaginary world to the real world.

'What I want to know,' she said aloud, 'is this: What is the truth? What's the truth of it all?' She was speaking partly as herself, and partly as the heroine of the play she had just read.'

Although the landscape outside looks very solid and clear, by contrast to the page of the book:

for the moment she herself was the most vivid thing in it—an heroic statue in the middle of the foreground, dominating the view. Ibsen's plays always left her in that condition. She acted them for days at a time, greatly to Helen's amusement; and then it would be Meredith's turn and she became Diana of the Crossways. But Helen was aware that it was not all acting, and that some sort of change was taking place in the human being.

Reading away, taking on board textual strategies with 'the curious literalness of one to whom written sentences are unfamiliar': 'In this way she came to conclusions, which had to be remodelled according to the adventures of the day, and were indeed recast as liberally as anyone could desire, leaving always a small grain of belief behind them.'[49] But literature, as Woolf tacitly expects her reader to recognize, can only be a partial guide to life. For when Rachel starts to feel a certain amount of first-hand interest in men, she finds the experience perplexing, and 'none of the books she read, from *Wuthering Heights* to *Man and Superman*, and the plays of Ibsen, suggested from their analysis of love that what their heroines felt was what she was feeling now'.[50]

Acknowledgement of the degree to which an individual can get absorbed by fiction is coupled in *The Voyage Out* with a recognition (which the reader is expected to share) that such habits of identification, of slipping into the skin and mind of a fictional character, can go hand in hand with a self-awareness of the process which is taking place. To read well is, for all the authors cited in this

[48] Virginia Woolf, *The Voyage Out* (1915), 32.
[49] Ibid. 142–144.
[50] Ibid. 272.

section, to read with various kinds of awareness, not just to be a passive being, unthinkingly losing oneself in a story, vicariously experiencing the life of another and sharing her aims and values.

It is not that the authors failed to recognize that this loss of self-consciousness could be an important part of the pleasure of reading, and that such absorption could even be linked to part of their own concept of what it meant to be a woman.'Sometimes', wrote Woolf to Ethel Smyth:

> I think heaven must be one continuous unexhausted reading. Its a disembodied trance-like intense rapture that used to seize me as a girl, and comes back now and again down here [at Rodmell] with a violence that lays me low . . . the state of reading consists in the complete elimination of the *ego*; and its the ego that erects itself like another part of the body I dont dare to name.[51]

But in this section as a whole, what emerges strongly is that various well-established assumptions about how women read could be turned to a variety of ends which ultimately contradicted prevalent stereotypes and attempts at prescriptive categorization, whether or not the attitudes of the authors might be said to be conservative in their gender politics or not. As we shall see in the two following chapters, the development of the idea of woman as rational as well as emotional, simultaneously alert to the development of her own subjectivity and to her position within society, can be illustrated through the deliberate exploitation and refutation of commonly held preconceptions about the relationship of gender and reading behaviour. Recognition of the subversion of these norms can be turned, moreover, into a means of establishing a bond between readers which is rooted not just in a shared body of knowledge and second-hand experience, but in shared methods of reading.

[51] Virginia Woolf to Ethel Smyth, 29 July 1934, *The Letters of Virginia Woolf*, ed. Nigel Nicolson and Joanne Trautmann, 6 vols. (1975–80), v. 319.

10   Sensation Fiction

In Wilkie Collins's *The Queen of Hearts* (1859), the twenty-year-old Jessie goes to stay for six weeks in the country. Her elderly guardian considers how best to amuse her: he hires a piano, borrows a pony, orders a box of novels. He inquires, cautiously, whether the novels are to Jessie's liking, and receives a complaint:

'They might do for some people,' she answered, 'but not for me. I'm rather peculiar, perhaps, in my tastes. I'm sick to death of novels with an earnest purpose. I'm sick to death of outbursts of eloquence, and large-minded philanthropy, and graphic descriptions, and unsparing anatomy of the human heart, and all that sort of thing. Good gracious me! isn't it the original intention or purpose, or whatever you call it, of a work of fiction to set out distinctly by telling a story? And how many of these books, I should like to know, do that? Why, so far as telling a story is concerned, the greater part of them might as well be sermons as novels. Oh, dear me! what I want is something that seizes hold of my interest, and makes me forget when it is time to dress for dinner; something that keeps me reading, reading, reading, in a breathless state to find out the end. You know what I mean—at least you ought.[1]

Collins, through the vehicle of Jessie's guardian and his brothers, uses this as an opening for launching his earliest tales of sensationalist suspense. More particularly, the demands which he is here recognizing are those which, when fulfilled, most perturbed reviewers faced with the phenomenon of sensation fiction in the 1860s: fiction which deliberately catered to compulsive forms of consumption, and which especially, although not exclusively, the reviewers presented as being devoured by women.

The critical attention paid to the sensation novel in the 1860s makes no bones in showing what it was about these fictions which gave cause for alarm.[2] Its frames of reference are drawn from familiar suppositions about woman's affective susceptibility. Above all, the presence of sexual desire and sexual energy within the fictions was singled out. This disruptive potential was greeted with particular anxiety when it was located in novels written by women, notably

---

[1] Wilkie Collins, *The Queen of Hearts*, 3 vols. (1859), i. 95–6.

[2] For sensation fiction, see Patrick Brantlinger, 'What is "sensational" about the sensation novel?', *Nineteenth-Century Fiction*, 37 (1982), 1–28; Elizabeth K. Helsinger, Robert Lauterbach Sheets, and William Veeder, *The Woman Question: Society and Literature in Britain and America, 1837–1883*, 3 vols. (Chicago and London, 1983), iii. 122–44; Winifred Hughes, *The Maniac in the Cellar: sensation novels of the 1860s* (Princeton, NJ, 1980); Elaine Showalter, 'Subverting the Feminine Novel', ch. 5 of *A Literature of their Own: British Women Novelists from Brontë to Lessing* (Princeton, NJ, 1977; repr. 1978), 153–81; Jenny Bourne Taylor, *In the Secret Theatre of Home: Wilkie Collins, Sensation Narrative, and Nineteenth-Century Psychology* (1988).

Mary Braddon, Rhoda Broughton, and Mrs Henry Wood. Inevitably, it also reflected on the perceived status of those women readers who borrowed and devoured these fictions so hungrily. Not only did the heroines—or female villains, depending on one's point of view—challenge the ideological premiss that the middle-class woman should be pure, innocent, and relatively passive, and suggest that desire might be directed towards channels other than the family, but their creators exhibited extremely unladylike familiarity with the scenes about which they wrote. E.S. Dallas, in *The Gay Science* (1866) claimed that 'it is curious that one of the earliest results of an increased feminine influence in our literature should be a display of what in women is most unfeminine:'[3] these novelists trangressed what was expected of a social chaperone. Henry James took Braddon to task on these grounds. She:

deals familiarly with gamblers, and betting-men, and flashy reprobates of every description. She knows much that ladies are not accustomed to know, but that they are apparently very glad to learn. The names of drinks, the technicalities of the faro-table, the lingo of the turf, the talk natural to a crowd of fast men at supper, when there are no ladies present but Miss Braddon, the way one gentleman knocks another down—all these things—the exact local colouring of Bohemia—our sisters and daughters may learn from these works.[4]

The most serious sources for alarm were succinctly overstated by Margaret Oliphant, writing in *Blackwoods* in 1867, when she claimed that the novels feature women who:

marry their grooms in fits of sensual passion; women who pray their lovers to carry them off from husbands and homes they hate; women, at the very least of it, who give and receive burning kisses and frantic embraces, and live in a voluptuous dream.[5]

'Marry their grooms in fits of sensual passion': this would readily have been recognized as an allusion to Mary Braddon's Aurora Floyd, daughter of a wealthy banker who, at seventeen, eloped to the continent with her father's groom, Conyers: not a successful or lasting match. Her absence on the continent is covered over by references to time spent in a finishing school abroad; she reads in the paper of her husband's death in a steeplechase, and, much relieved, marries a current suitor: a solid, sensible Yorkshire landowner. Inevitably, however, the groom is not dead, only seriously injured, and turns up again, employed to run her new husband's stable. Conyers blackmails Aurora: it is hardly surprising that she is suspected when he is found murdered. Ultimately exonerated, the woman faces a trouble-free future with her remaining husband, receiving no textual retribution, and expressing no remorse, for her bigamy: 'a little changed, a shade less defiantly bright, perhaps,

---

[3] E. S. Dallas, *The Gay Science*, 2 vols. (1866), ii. 298.

[4] Henry James, 'Miss Braddon', (first pub. *Nation* (1865); repr. *Notes and Reviews* (Cambridge, Mass., 1921)), 115–16.

[5] [Margaret Oliphant] 'Novels', *Blackwood's Edinburgh Magazine*, 102 (1867), 259.

but unspeakably beautiful and tender, bending over the cradle of her first-born.'[6]

Yet it was not the bigamy, distressing though some found it, which most perturbed reviewers, but Aurora's capacity for spontaneous action, and violent anger. The scene which critics found especially shocking was that in which she horsewhips a groom (ultimately disclosed to be her first husband's murderer) whom she finds ill-treating her dog. The *North British Review* condemned Braddon's treatment: 'We are certain that, except in this novel, no lady possessing the education and occupying the position of Aurora Floyd could have acted as she is represented to have done.'[7] As this remark suggests, one of the further grounds on which this type of fiction was chastized was that it contravened standards of realism as well as of idealism: sensation novels, complained the *Temple Bar*'s critic, 'represent life neither as it is or as it ought to be'. The writer made further indignant capital out of the imaginative threat which they offered to the perceived sanctity of the middle-class home:

It is on our domestic hearths that we are taught to look for the incredible. A mystery sleeps in our cradles; fearful errors lurk in our nuptial couches; fiends sit down with us at table; our innocent-looking garden walks hold the secret of treacherous murders; and our servants take a year from us for the sake of having us at their mercy.[8]

Even if this can be read as journalistic hyperbole, this rhetoric of anxiety could be found in other contexts. In 1864, for example, the Archbishop of York spoke against sensation fiction in similar terms, attacking those tales which aim at:

exciting in the mind some deep feeling of overwrought interest by the means of some terrible passion or crime. They want to persuade people that in almost every one of the well-ordered houses of their neighbours there [is] a skeleton shut up in some cupboard.[9]

The novels themselves drew attention to the frisson produced by the idea of deceptive façades, as when Robert Audley remarks: 'What do we know of the mysteries that may hang about the houses we enter? . . . Foul deeds have been done under the most hospitable roofs; terrible crimes have been committed amid the fairest scenes, and have left no trace upon the spot where they were done.'[10]

In many ways, this fiction's most disruptive potential lay not on the emphasis which it placed on woman's capacity to express powerful, emotional reactions, but in the degree to which it made its woman readers consider their positions within their own homes and within society. Either, albeit in a symbolic fashion, it suggested exactly what hypocrisy, manipulation, and concealed desires lay

---

[6] Mary Braddon, *Aurora Floyd* (1863; repr. 1984), 384.

[7] [W. Fraser Rae] 'Sensation Novelists: Miss Braddon', *North British Review*, 43 (1865), 98.

[8] [Alfred Austin] 'Our Novels: The Sensational School', *Temple Bar*, 29 (1870), 424.

[9] Quoted by Fraser Rae, 'Sensation Novelists', 203. There is a full report of the Archbishop's talk to the Huddersfield Church Institute in *The Times* (2 Nov. 1864), 9.

[10] Mary Braddon, *Lady Audley's Secret* (1862; repr. Oxford, 1987), 140.

present behind the socially respectable façade of decorum; or the structures of anticipation and abrupt revelation which characterize the novels served to show up the very boredom of this existence. A critic writing in the *Christian Remembrancer* of 1863 makes this explicit, tying in his fears about women's mental impressionability with assumptions about their physiological constitutions. He complained that the sensation novel played on the nerves, rather than on the heart; that it drugged thought and reason, and acted instead on woman's power of intuition. It took advantage, in other words, of an assumed innate faculty which might under certain circumstances be regarded as one of woman's strengths, but which should not be exploited at the expense of her simultaneously held rational capabilities, and, above all, at the cost of the necessary exercise of self-control. For in the case of sensation novels, the reviewer believed, the attention was stimulated 'through the lower and more animal instincts'. Chief among the dangers of this fiction was the fact that, for its young woman readers, it could 'open out a picture of life free from all the perhaps irksome checks that confine their own existence'. The novels were seen by him as a sign of the times, 'of impatience of old restraints, and a craving for some fundamental change in the working of society'.[11]

It was indeed the case that a striking, often-remarked on feature of the sensation novel was its contemporaneity, unlike the settings of earlier Gothic fiction. Henry James made this point in relation to *Lady Audley's Secret*:

The novelty lay in the heroine being, not a picturesque Italian of the fourteenth century, but an English gentlewoman of the current year, familiar with the use of the railway and the telegraph. The intense probability of the story is constantly reiterated. Modern England—the England of to-day's newspaper—crops up at every step.[12]

But although the *Christian Remembrancer*'s critic did not elaborate on precisely what constituted contemporary change, 'husbands and fathers' were advised to act as guardians of their own family futures, to begin to:

look around them and scrutinize the parcel that arrives from Mudies, when young ladies are led to contrast the actual with the ideal we see worked out in popular romance; the mutual duties, the reciprocal forebearance, the inevitable trials of every relation in real life, with the triumph of mere female fascination, before which man falls prostrate and helpless.[13]

Unacknowledged, but evident here is an expression of anxiety at men's own inability to control their emotions should ever woman start to act like the independent-spirited, passionate heroine of a sensation novel.

The threats to domestic order which, according to this critical rhetoric, these novels posed were not just perceived as exisiting, however, in relation to gender

---

[11] 'Our Female Sensation Novelists', *Christian Remembrancer*, NS 46 (1863), 210, 212.
[12] James, 'Miss Braddon', 112–13.
[13] 'Our Female Sensation Novelists', 234.

relations: they extended into the arena of class propriety.[14] This is particularly understandable when one recalls the frequency with which the comparison between reading the right books, and keeping the right company, was made. Such concern was made apparent in various ways. Sometimes it was expressed metaphorically, suggesting a disruption of domestic hierarchies through the transgression of tacitly demarcated reading spaces: thus Mary Braddon 'may boast, without fear of contradiction, of having temporarily succeeded in making the literature of the kitchen the favourite reading of the Drawing-room', claimed Fraser Rae.[15] 'Unhappily, the sensational novel is that one touch of anything but nature that makes the kitchen and the drawing-room kin', complained the *Temple Bar*, as if its perpetrators were disrupting the workings of evolution.[16] This is the other side of the coin to warnings in servants' manuals against borrowing their employers' fiction. A *Punch* cartoon of 1868 (Fig. 18), showing a maid-servant asking a (male) lodger about the ending of a particular story which she had been reading on the quiet, is indicative of an acceptance, at a popular level, of the cross-class (and, for that matter, the cross-gender) appeal of such novels.[17]

Yet despite the convenient target which the startling subject-matter offered, sensational novelists were not without their defenders. G. H. Lewes, writing in the *Cornhill*, claimed that one should be thankful for any novel which, like *Lady Audley's Secret*, amused the vacant or wearied mind without developing any kind of sympathy with crime or criminals. Not mentioning the gender of such fiction's readers, Lewes seemed to take the presence of such minds for granted in current society.[18] Justin MacCarthy, in the *Westminster Review*, commended sensation novelists (on this occasion George Meredith, with *The Ordeal of Richard Feverel* and *Emilia in England*, Caroline Norton's *Lost and Saved*, and an anonymous novel, *Recommended to Mercy*) for maintaining a type of psychological realism:

[14] Jonathan Loesberg's linkage of the discourse of sensation fiction with the debates surrounding the Second Reform Bill draws attention to the possible connections between these novels and political instability: 'The Ideology of Narrative Form in Sensation Fiction', *Representations*, 13 (1986), 115–38.

[15] 'Sensation Novelists: Miss Braddon', 204.

[16] 'Our Novels: The Sensational School', 424.

[17] This cross-over happened not just among readers, but among writers. Mary Braddon, as well as composing her well-known three-decker novels, turned out endless stories for cheap magazines. As she put it in a letter to Bulwer Lytton: 'I do an immense amount of work which nobody ever hears of, for halfpenny and penny journals . . . The amount of crime, tragedy, murder, slow poisoning and general infamy required by the halfpenny reader is something terrible. I am just going to do a little parricide for this week's supply.' Quoted by Robert Lee Wolff, 'Devoted Disciple: The Letters of Mary Elizabeth Braddon to Sir Edward Bulwer-Lytton, 1862–1873', *Harvard Library Bulletin*, 22 (1974), 11. The widespread presence of servants who act as observers and interpreters of sensational events in Victorian fiction has been analysed by Anthea Trodd, who sees them as being 'convenient to the writer seeking to use sensational material while acknowledging his own, or his readership's doubts about the sensational vision of the home', *Domestic Crime in the Victorian Novel* (Basingstoke, 1989), 95.

[18] [G. H. Lewes] 'Our Survey of Literature and Science', *Cornhill Magazine*, 7 (1863), 135.

SENSATION NOVELS.

Mary. "PLEASE, SIR, I'VE BEEN LOOKING EVERYWHERE FOR THE THIRD
VOLUME OF THAT BOOK YOU WAS READING."

Lodger. "OH, I TOOK IT BACK TO THE LIBRARY THIS MORNING, I——"

Mary. "OH! THEN WILL YOU TELL ME, SIR, IF AS HOW THE 'MARKIS'
FOUND OUT AS SHE'D PISONED 'ER TWO FUST 'USBANDS?!"

18. *Punch* cartoon, 28 March 1868

There is no good end attained by trying to persuade ourselves that women are all incorporeal, angelic, colourless, passionless, helpless creatures, who are never to suspect anything, never to doubt anyone, who regard the whole end and passion of human life as ethereal, Platonic love, and orderly, parent-sanctioned wedlock. Women have especial need, as the world goes, to be shrewd, self-reliant, and strong; and we do all we can in our literature to render them helpless, imbecile, and idiotic.[19]

Others went so far as to claim that certain lessons might be learnt from reading this type of fiction, or, at any rate, that its contents were going to add little circumstantial knowledge to women already familiar with certain other sorts of printed material. Thus the *Medical Critic*'s correspondent wrote of Mary Braddon's *Aurora Floyd* that 'the whole novel may be regarded as an admonition to young ladies not to let their fancies run away with them', and continues:

although a sensation novelist must step a little over the bounds of probability, although clandestine marriages with grooms are unfrequent, and although, when contracted, they usually involve a totally different chain of consequences from those imagined by Miss Braddon—still, young ladies who read newspapers will not, on the whole, learn much previously unknown evil from the romance.[20]

In general, the writer claimed that it was not just in the novel alone that standards were changing: 'the popular craving for excitement' was pandered to in the columns of the daily papers, fast 'becoming formidable rivals to quiet novels'.[21] Contemporaries would have recognized in this an allusion to the fact that since 1857, detailed reporting of divorce cases had been allowed in the newspapers, and dead-pan descriptions of bigamy, domestic violence, forced marriages, and marriages contracted under false pretences could be read alongside accounts of other crimes.[22]

[19] Justin MacCarthy, 'Novels with a Purpose', *Westminster Review*, NS 26 (1864), 48.

[20] 'Sensation Novels', *Medical Critic and Psychological Journal*, 3 (1863), 519.

[21] Ibid. 514. Other critics occupied themselves with offering reasons why standards seemed to have changed so rapidly. In the *Temple Bar*, for example, the hypotheses were advanced that the 1851 exhibition gave an impetus to British communications with the Continent; the Limited Liability Act encouraged financial speculation in those who would previously have shown caution, and the Divorce Bill 'familiarized the public mind . . . with conjugal infidelity'. [Alfred Austin] 'Our Novels: The Fast School', *Temple Bar*, 29 (1870), 179.

[22] For sensationalism and newspaper reportage, see Thomas Boyle, *Black Swine in the Sewers of Hampstead: Beneath the Surface of Victorian Sensationalism* (1990). The 1861 Yelverton bigamy-divorce trial, in particular, attracted a great amount of publicity, and after the revelations of this case the public became aware of a complicated accumulation of laws which made bigamy—just—legally possible. See Jeanne Fahnestock, 'Bigamy: The Rise and Fall of a Convention', *Nineteenth Century Fiction*, 36 (1981), 47–71; Arvel B. Erickson and John R. McCarthy, 'The Yelverton Case: Civil Legislation and Marriage', *Victorian Studies*, 14 (1971), 275–91; Mary Lyndon Shanley, ' "One Must Ride Behind": Married Women's Rights and the Divorce Act of 1857', *Victorian Studies*, 25 (1982), 355–76. The topicality of the subject is reflected not just in Braddon's *Lady Audley's Secret*, *Aurora Floyd*, and *John Marchmont's Legacy* (1863), in Wilkie Collins's *No Name* (1862) and *Man and Wife* (1870) and in a number of less-well-known texts, but in the 'Hon Mrs Yelverton' (as she called herself)'s *Martyrs to Circumstance* (1861): she turned her private difficulties into further active capital by hiring herself out to give readings from this.

Dickens, writing in *All the Year Round*, was, however, among those who pointed out that there is nothing new about sensation—he profers as early prototypes Oedipus, Satan in *Paradise Lost*,

Additionally, the writer of this article acknowledged the popular view that these fictions offered escapism and vicarious excitement: 'girls and women who are restrained by the fear of consequences from giving the rein to their own passions, still find a fictitious excitement in reading about, and also imagining, the gratified passions of others.'[23] Excitement, indeed, but not without its own self-imposed limitations. For other contemporary reviewers felt obliged to stress that however undesirable the subject-matter of the sensation novel might be, the resolution of its plot invariably supports prevalent social and moral values and formations. Winifred Hughes, in her thorough study of the sensation novel genre, usefully brings in Peter Brooks' discussion of the fact that the plotting of sensation fiction tends to be characterized by a consolidation of social norms. In *The Melodramatic Imagination* (1976), albeit largely writing about the development of melodrama in France, Brooks suggests that the form is particularly appropriate to a time of rapid and confusing social change:

Melodrama starts from and expresses the anxiety brought by a frightening new world in which the traditional patterns of moral order no longer provide the necessary social glue. It plays out the force of that anxiety with the apparent triumph of villainy, and it dissipates it with the eventual victory of virtue . . . it strives to find, to articulate, to demonstrate, to 'prove' the existence of a moral universe which, though put into question, masked by villainy and perversions of judgment, does exist and can be made to assert its presence.[24]

Lady Audley may exhibit an unusual, fascinating degree of powerful assertiveness as she pushes her first husband down a well, sets fire to an inn in which the man who threatens to unmask her calculating nature is staying, and contemplates poisoning her second husband. But ultimately she goes, or pretends to go, mad, and is sent to an asylum in Belgium where she eventually dies. This fate suggests a form of moral retribution working from within Lady Audley's own constitution rather than being imposed by the judiciary. Hence it is ultimately completely inescapable. Isabel Vane, the more directly sympathetically presented heroine of *East Lynne* (1861), is made to die (although whether of a broken heart at the prolonged stress of looking after her children without being able to make herself known to them, or of the consumption which kills

Raphael's *Massacre of the Innocents*, and Macbeth, with his 'bold, bad woman for his wife'. None the less, he refers to the 'vulgar species of sensationalism', 'the halfpenny tales of murder and felony' which currently proliferate, and which have only a tenuous relationship with those who treat thoughtfully of 'the psychology of crime and terror'. [Charles Dickens] 'The Sensational Williams', *All The Year Round*, 11 (1864) 14–16. An article in the same magazine some six months earlier had also pointed out that there was little novelty in sensationalism *per se*, looking back some seventy years to the popularity of Matthew Lewis's play *The Castle Sceptre*, and Thomas Holcroft's *Tales of Mystery*: 'Not a New "Sensation" ', *All The Year Round*, 9 (1863), 519–20.

[23] 'Not a New "Sensation" ', 517.

[24] Peter Brooks, *The Melodramatic Imagination: Balzac, Henry James, Melodrama, and the Mode of Excess* (New Haven, Conn., 1976), 20. These words of Brooks are quoted in part in Hughes, *The Maniac in the Cellar*, 176.

her son, is not entirely clear). This is both a extrication from an awkward domestic situation involving bigamy, and the culmination of a warning in which the woman reader has earlier been forcefully addressed:

Oh, reader, believe me! Lady—wife—mother! should you ever be tempted to abandon your home, so will you awaken! Whatever trials may be the lot of your married life, though they may magnify themselves to your crushed spirit as beyond the endurance of woman to bear, *resolve* to bear them; fall down upon your knees and pray to be enabled to bear them: pray for patience; pray for strength to resist the demon that would urge you so to escape; bear unto death, rather than forfeit your fair name and your good conscience; for be assured that the alternative, if you rush on to it, will be found far worse than death![25]

Nell, the extremely likeable heroine of Rhoda Broughton's *Cometh Up as a Flower* (1867), also is killed off by the author, for death seems the only means by which she can be saved from committing adultery. By the same means the reader is also mildly rebuked for enjoying the daring of going along with the impetus towards illicit passion.

But, as we shall see, the fact that a reader may be implicated, placed in a position of complicity with a heroine's transgressive, yet highly understandable desires, confirms that sensation fiction in fact did not take the stability of this moral universe entirely for granted. This is particularly true of many of the novels written by women. In these, the ready equation of the moral world of the novel (despite the exaggeration of some aspects of the action) with that of the reader is brought home not just by the broad contemporaneity of the fictions, but by the allusions which they contain, and which are used to establish a specific cultural ambit shared by both reader and central characters.

A common accusation levelled against the sensation novel was that it encouraged a taste only for more of the same: that it jaded the palate for more demanding works. Yet the writers of these novels, especially Mary Braddon and Rhoda Broughton, firmly did not limit their own literary frames of reference to contemporary fiction, nor did they expect those of their readers to be thus limited.[26] The novels of these two writers in particular are studded with quotations from writers ranging from Shakespeare to Victor Hugo, Chaucer to Milton, Longfellow to Frances Ridley Havergal. To them may be attributed the desire not to have their literary productions dismissed as utterly frivolous, particularly when one considers their prolific quoting alongside the advice manual writers's exhortations to the Victorian girl reader to check all unfamiliar

[25] Mrs Henry Wood, *East Lynne*, 3 vols. (1861), ii. 107–8.
[26] Categorizing Rhoda Broughton as a 'sensation novelist' is not as easy a piece of pigeon-holing as it is in the case of Braddon, or Ellen Wood, or their male counterparts, such as Wilkie Collins and Charles Reade. But her early novels, especially *Not Wisely But Too Well* (1863) and *Cometh Up as a Flower* (1867) unmistakably employ sensationalist elements, such as potential bigamy, and works of the 1870s certainly presented women more daringly critical of men than many of their fictional contemporaries. This factor, coupled with the reputation of her earlier novels, probably ensured that critics continued to refer to her as a sensationalist.

quotations that she comes across. Simultaneously, of course, this employment of quotations acts as a means of flattering the reader, tacitly assuming her acquaintance with this relatively wide range of references. The references to shared reading material certainly functions as a means of reinforcing the effect of the characters and readers occupying the same cultural space.

The visual arts are employed in an analogous way. Although not usually given to paraquotation, Ellen Wood intensifies the emotion towards the end of *East Lynne* when the sick William tells Madame Vine (whom he knows not to be Isabel Vane, his true mother) that he has seen the bright flowers of heaven in John Martin's pictures of *The Plains of Heaven* (which had toured England in 1855 and 1857). She thus invokes a familiar concretization of celestial beauty not just as an indicator of William's impending destination, but to occasion a poignant dialogue about whether or not his mother is to be found there. More provocatively, in *Lady Audley's Secret*, Braddon describes the portrait of Lady Audley as being painted with the exaggeration of colour and expression associated with Pre-Raphaelitism. This allows her to suggest that the techniques of an artist of that movement, emphasizing 'every attribute of that delicate face as to give a lurid lightness to the blonde complexion, and a strange, sinister light to the deep blue eyes',[27] bring out a hard, almost wicked look in the sitter. Relying on the reader's familiarity with current art in order to describe the effect created by Lady Audley, she also draws on the moral equivocation of art critics commenting on the unorthodox attractions of Pre-Raphaelite female models.

Mary Braddon and Rhoda Broughton's novels are particularly notable in their references to literary reading, however, since they encourage their consumers not just to take cultural references as part of a social backcloth, but to enter into an active process of interpretation which invites recognition of their own active, rather than passive, role as readers. At times, it is implicitly suggested to them that they would surely be more discriminating readers than the heroines themselves. Thus Kate, in Rhoda Broughton's *Not Wisely, But Too Well* (1863)—its very title drawing attention to its metatextuality—has most foolishly fallen in love with a clearly unsuitable man, Colonel Dare Stamer. The naïveté of her responses to his practised flirtatious strategies are heavily underscored by Broughton. Returning home after taking a walk with him, she turns to her books, but soon lets drop Lamb's *Essays*—'too healthy and wholesome to tempt a diseased palate'—and instead chooses a familiar narrative which takes the dangers of reading as its subject-matter, Byron's translation of Book V of Dante's *Inferno*, 'Francesca of Rimini':

That exquisite tale of hopeless, boundless passion spoke to her soul a language that it loved, and she never thought of taking to herself the warning—

[27] Braddon, *Lady Audley's Secret*, 70.

'How many sweet thoughts, what strong ecstasies,
Led these their evil fortune to fulfil?'

'He who from me shall be divided ne'er'

was the line that she took to herself; and she said it over softly, with a confident smile.[28]

More reprehensibly presented than the foolishly preoccupied Kate, Emma, the would-be literary woman at the centre of Broughton's much later novel, *A Beginner* (1899), reveals the shaky ground of her pretensions by chatting over dinner to the author of a book of essays she's admired:

'Where do you get your snatches of out-of-the-way verse from?—quotations that set one hunting for days? Where does "Blind Orion hungry for the morn" come from?'

'That is not so very out-of-the-way.'

'Is not it? I searched almost all through Milton for it. I thought it had a Miltonic cadence.' She makes use of this last phrase with a certain self-satisfaction.

'It was no use searching Milton for what belongs to "bright Keats," ' replies he a little bluntly.

'Keats! How dull of me not to have thought of him!'[29]

With little subtlety, Broughton is positioning her reader against this over-confident author of *Miching Mallecho*, a 'New Woman' novel dealing with 'hereditary vice', a genre and fashion for which Broughton evidently felt little sympathy.

Inevitably, in sensation fiction, sensitivity to poetry, and the ability to have an apposite quotation spring to one's lips, is equated with sensitivity to life in general. In Broughton's *Cometh Up as a Flower*, the fact that the autobiographical prose of the heroine/narrator Nell is as studded with pertinent quotations as a well-compiled commonplace book is a certain guide to her own worth. After her handsome, but penniless army suitor, Richard, says goodnight to her in the lane at evening: 'Then, like a blast away I passed | And no man saw me more.'[30] When she considers her family's declined financial fortunes, and the absence of an heir, it is an apt moment to comment: 'The old order changeth; giving place to new, | And God fulfils himself in many ways.'[31] The frequency of poetic references; the enjoyable, self-conscious employment of 'literary' vocabulary; the occasional insertion of a *recherché* French phrase, all contribute to a bond of shared culture. This serves to emphasize, for example, quite how wrong Sir Hugh is for Nell as a husband. As she drives back with him, reluctantly, from a picnic, he exclaims:

'Jolly and big the moon looks, doesn't it? like a Cheshire cheese!'

The moon, the sacred moon, the be-songed, be-sonneted moon, the moon that Romeo sware by, and that Milton saw 'Stooping thro' a fleecy cloud,' like a *Cheshire cheese*!

[28] Rhoda Broughton, *Not Wisely, But Too Well*, 3 vols. (1863), i. 161.
[29] Ead., *A Beginner* (1899), 40.
[30] Ead., *Cometh Up as a Flower*, 2 vols. (1867), i. 124.
[31] Ibid. 201.

'How poetical,' I said, sardonically.

'No, it isn't poetical, I know. I'm not up to the dodge of poetry. I don't go in for these kinds of things.'[32]

None the less, financial pressures force Nell—unhappily, and tragically—to marry him.

Similar assumptions concerning poetic sensibility are employed in a range of other contemporary texts. Not all of these are, strictly speaking, sensation novels. Matilda Hays's *Adrienne Hope* (1866), reviewed as a sensation novel, and influenced by prevalent fashions in some of the elements of its plot (Adrienne unwisely enters into a secret marriage with a man who subsequently publicly marries another woman) is actually far more overtly feminist than the novels of Braddon, Broughton, and Wood, with the two women eventually finding mutual support in one another after their husband's death.[33] But it, too, incorporates a sustained section indicating how foolish Adrienne is to believe in the plausible flatteries of her deceiver, whilst ignoring the real sensitivity and devotion of the crippled, and deliberately feminized Lord Horton. The latter at length declaims and proclaims the beauties of Longfellow's 'Evangeline' and Clough's 'The Bothie of Toper-na-Fuosich', a poem which might be recognized as acting as a tacit warning to Adrienne, if she had been alert enough to its tale of seduction. The attraction between Cecil, the heroine of Mary Braddon's *The Lady's Mile* (1866), and her cousin Hector Gordon is cemented by the fact that they read poetry, especially Tennyson, together. However, Hector is already engaged to another woman in India whom he had met before encountering Cecil, and dutifully leaves to marry her, although not without reading Tennyson's 'Love and Duty' to his cousin in tones of 'deep feeling':

> Should my shadow cross thy thought
> Too sadly for their peace, remand it thou
> For calmer hours to memory's darkest hold,
> If not to be forgotten—not at once—
> Not all forgotten.[34]

When Cecil marries the successful, hard-working lawyer Laurence O'Boyneville, she does it because she acknowledges and appreciates his love for her, but he is not a kindred spirit:

After telling him about a new book—a fresh view of Mary Queen of Scots, by a French historian; an anti-Carlyleian essay on Frederick of Prussia; a passionate, classic tragedy, by a new poet—Cecil would look hopefully for some answering ray of interest in her husband's face, and would behold his eyes fixed and staring, and hear his lips murmuring faintly to himself, 'The defendant seems to me to have no case, and the

---

[32] Ibid. 302–3.

[33] Matilda Hays was strongly influenced in her attitudes towards men and society by her membership of the Langham Place circle: she jointly edited the *English Woman's Journal* with Bessie Rayner Parkes.

[34] Braddon, *The Lady's Mile*, 3 vols. (1866), i. 110.

plaintiffs will be entitled to recover if Giddles and Giddles can show them that the letter was posted on the twenty-first . . . '.[35]

The reader is left in no doubt which of the two men is the more attractive, the fitter partner for Cecil, and is left somewhat disappointed when the author's propriety provides a twist of circumstances which prevent him running off with Cecil on his return to London.

If *The Lady's Mile* is, strictly speaking, a society novel with a melodramatic near-elopement in it which could readily belong to sensation fiction, Braddon's *Aurora Floyd* is, as my earlier summary indicates, sensational from beginning to end, and was frequently taken as a paradigm of the genre. The entire text is underpinned by paraquotation, from Thackeray, Dickens, Macaulay, a variety of Shakespeare plays, *Frankenstein*, Victor Hugo, Tennyson, George Eliot, Charlotte M. Yonge. Precisely what level of literary competence Braddon is anticipating is unclear. On occasion, one has the impression that she is encoding references likely to be picked up only by those whose range of reading goes beyond that customarily expected of young girls. Chapter 16, for example, ends with Mrs Powell, Aurora's sinister housekeeper-companion, sneaking a look at a letter which her mistress had written to the stable manager—the man who was, of course, Aurora's legal husband: 'It was this second page which Mrs Powell saw. The words written at the top of the leaf were these:—"Above all, express no surprise.—A.' There was no ordinary conclusion to the letter; no other signature than this big capital A.[36] Braddon is surely referring to the badge of adultery in Hawthorne's *The Scarlet Letter*, a novel which, even if quite widely noted in England (Margaret Oliphant, for example, had written of 'the unwholesome fascination of this romance'[37]) was hardly recommended to the young woman reader. *Aurora Floyd* does, however, contain plenty of side-swipes at such a reader's presumed diet of leisure material, and at the dullness of both High Church novels and conventional romances, especially those in which the pattern is for the curtain to drop on the heroine's marriage. For, asks Braddon:

is it necessary that the novelist, after devoting three volumes to the description of a courtship of six weeks' duration, should reserve for himself only half a page in which to tell us the events of two-thirds of a lifetime? Aurora is married, and settled, and happy; sheltered, one would imagine, from all dangers, safe under the wing of her stalwart adorer; but it does not therefore follow,

adds Braddon ominously, promisingly, 'that the story of her life is done'.[38]

This type of reference offers a bond between narrator and reader which is composed of presumed shared literary knowledge and tastes. Fiction plays an important part in determining this particular narrative's frame of reference, yet

[35] *The Lady's Mile*, ii. 110.
[36] *Aurora Floyd*, 155.
[37] [Margaret Oliphant] 'Modern Novelists—Great and Small', *Blackwood's Edinburgh Magazine*, 77 (1855), 563.
[38] Braddon, *Aurora Floyd*, 137.

the hint is offered that despite its sensationalism, this novel will be somewhat more true to the actual world which the reader inhabits. This reader is assumed, moreover, to be an alert interpreter, not one who will be content with passive consumption, but whose literary knowledge is called upon, and challenged, in the process of unravelling the complexities of the text. She is allowed to pick up on references to the familiar, and then has her expectations undermined. For example, Aurora is frequently compared to Cleopatra, called 'that Egyptian goddess, that Assyrian queen, with the flashing eyes and the serpentine coils of purple black hair'.[39] But she is hardly the sexual temptress, leading a noble man to his ruined doom, as Cleopatra was presented on the Victorian stage of the time.[40] Nor does she meet a tragic, if dignified end herself, but is last seen, still happily married, on her husband's comfortable Yorkshire estate. Similarly, the novel is full of references to *Othello*. Both Aurora's first and second husbands feel agonizing pangs of jealousy and bitterness, and Braddon makes the parallel with Shakespeare's play in both cases. Yet unlike Othello, Mellish refused to think 'ill of his wife. He resolutely shut his eyes to all damning evidence. He clung with a desperate tenacity to his belief in her purity.'[41] The first husband envies the satisfaction of revenge that 'the chap in the play' got 'for his trouble when the blackamoor smothers his wife', but is murdered himself. Mrs Powell also harbours Iago-like resentment, but, unlike Iago, meets only defeat. Some of these subverted parallels between play and novel have been noted by Robert Wolff, who comments that 'most important, Desdemona is innocent and yet is killed; Aurora is guilty but gets away scot-free'.[42] Literary allusions, in other words, need not necessarily lead in the direction which they would seem to anticipate. They can be used, as here, to ensure that the reader is alert to the dangers of taking the familiar for granted: a didactic formula relevant to the wider dynamics of sensation fiction.

Women sensation novelists, like many of their contemporaries, employed the convention of the French novel as an instant signifier of immorality, yet the very levity with which they treated it threw into question the tendency for more solemn commentators to condemn it out of hand. Robert Audley, the hero of *Lady Audley's Secret* is used to receiving his stimulation from yellow-backed French novels. But once he becomes embroiled with the facts of his close friend's disappearance and presumed murder, he is not only haunted by the implications of the situation which, he says, appear the more sinister when viewed in the light of Alexandre Dumas and Wilkie Collins, but 'the yellow papered fictions on the shelves above his head seemed stale and profitless'.[43]

---

[39] Ibid. 182.
[40] See Margaret Lamb, *'Antony and Cleopatra' on the English Stage* (Toronto and London, 1980), ch. 4.
[41] *Aurora Floyd*, 265.
[42] Robert Wolff, *Sensational Victorian: The Life and Fiction of Mary Elizabeth Braddon* (New York and London, 1979), 151.
[43] Braddon, *Lady Audley's Secret*, 156.

Rhoda Broughton, in *Red as a Rose is She* (1870), exploits the topos even more subversively. Here Esther, the heroine, staying with old family friends, is found by Gerard, the handsome son of the house:

deeply buried in the unwonted luxury of a French novel.

He looks at the title, and a slightly shocked expression dawns on his features: men are always shocked that women should *read about* the things that they *do*.

'Where did you get this?' (Quickly).

'I climbed up the ladder in the library; pleasant books always rise to top shelves, as the cream rises to the top of the milk.'

'Will you oblige me by putting it back where you took it from?'

'When I have read it? Of course.'

'*Before* you have read it.'

'Why should I?' (rather snappishly.)

'Why should you,' he repeats, impatiently—not much fonder of contradiction than are most of his masterful sex. 'Why because it is not a fit book for a—a *child* like you to read.

Esther daringly challenges Gerard, letting him know that she is going to continue reading—'Do you suppose that Eve would have cared to taste the apple if it had been specially recommended to her notice as a particularly good, juicy, Ribstone pippin'—though once he has left the room, Broughton, in language which foregrounds the connection between certain types of reading and sexual transgression, has her deposit it 'in the hole whence she had ravished it, between two of its fellows, as agreeably lax and delicately indelicate as itself'. Esther repairs to Gerard's study, where, Broughton pointedly indicates, French novels are much in evidence, to boast of her obedience. The narrator leaves the reader to weigh up whether less harm might have come from the inexperienced Esther continuing with a course of not uneducational reading, rather than inviting a tête-à-tête with this young man. At the close of the scene, the couple are left conversing with heads close together over the petals which they are glueing to the centre of a geranium flower which Esther will wear to a ball that evening.[44] The knowingness of the tone of this passage would seem to presuppose not just a familiarity with the contents of French fiction from Broughton's own readers, but plays on their acknowledgement of the ridiculous and hypocritical nature of masculine prohibition in this area.

It is, however, in Mary Braddon's *The Doctor's Wife* (1864) that we meet with the most sustained investigation of reading in relation to sensation fiction. As has already been noted, the plot of this novel owes something to *Madame Bovary*. A respectable, morally worthy, yet eminently dull young country doctor falls in love with Isabel, a suburban girl with a haphazard formal education (although she had picked up 'a little Italian, enough French to serve for the reading of novels that she might have better left unread'),[45] notwithstanding a large number of tastes and assumptions picked up from her membership of the

44 Broughton, *Red as a Rose is She*, 3 vols. (1870), i. 278–83.
45 Braddon, *The Doctor's Wife*, 3 vols. (1864), i. 53.

nearest circulating library. Her own life was 'altogether vulgar and commonplace, and she could not extract one ray of romance out of it, twist it as she would . . . She wanted her life to be like her books; she wanted to be a heroine'.[46] She waits 'for the prince, the Ernest Maltravers, the Henry Esmond, the Steerforth—it was Steerforth's proud image, and not simple-hearted David's gentle shadow, which lingered in the girl's mind when she shut the book'.[47]

It is unsurprising that her marriage to George Gilbert, the doctor, whilst apparently more attractive than being a governess for ever, fails to satisfy her. Even his swift, matter of fact proposal and wedding preparations are inadequate by her internalized standards, for 'were there not three volumes of courtship to be gone through first?'[48] It is not just that she wishes to postpone as long as practically possible the moment which her romance reading has taught her should be the apex of a young girl's life, mimicking the prolongation of desire on which romance reading depends. Braddon foreshadows Nancy Miller's understanding of a nineteenth-century woman's plot being one in which closure is resisted as long as possible in order to allow heroine, and reader, a sense of power and autonomy,[49] when Isabel reflects, glumly, that 'Her life had never been her own yet, and never was to be her own, she thought.' First ruled over by her stepmother, she now must acknowledge George, 'with his strong will and sound common-sense,—oh, how Isabel hated common-sense! . . . as her master'.[50]

The reader is never encouraged to identify directly with Isabel: it is assumed that she will be wiser, with a far more self-critical attitude towards the fiction she reads. It is not that Braddon is putting forward a hypocritical diatribe against novel-reading in general. The overall stance of the novel is encapsulated in the views of Sigismund Smith, a writer of hack sensation fiction, whose experience at cobbling together plots from other writers and doubling their exaggerations and improbabilities seems to owe a great deal to Braddon's own career writing for the penny novelette market: 'A novel's a splendid thing after a hard day's work, a sharp practical tussle with the real world . . . No wise man or woman was ever the worse for reading novels. Novels are only dangerous for those poor foolish girls who read nothing else, and think that their lives are to be paraphrases of their favourite books'.[51] Yet we are never directly told that Isabel should submit willingly to life with George. A kind, sympathetic doctor he may be, but so traditional in his way of life, so convinced that the ways of his father's generation were right, that he has no understanding of Isabel's attempts to

[46] Ibid. 57, 56.
[47] Ibid. 160.
[48] Ibid. 225.
[49] Nancy K. Miller, 'Emphasis Added: Plots and Plausibilities in Women's Fiction', *Subject to Change: Reading Feminist Writing* (New York, 1988), 34.
[50] Braddon, *The Doctor's Wife*, i. 239.
[51] Ibid. 60–1.

brighten their home, 'to infuse some beauty into her life—something which, in however remote a degree, should be akin to the things she read of in her books.'[52] When she reads him poetry, he yawns; when she places flowers on his dressing-table, he complains that the blossoms are liable to generate carbonic acid gas. The novel just predates *Our Mutual Friend* (1864–5), but it can be used as a comment on the fact that following *The Complete British Family Housewife* is unlikely to provide a recipe for domestic happiness unless one's husband is as caring as a John Harmon. To Isabel the making of pastry 'was a wearisome business. It was all very well for Ruth Pinch to do it for once in a way, and to be admired by John Westlock, and marry a rich and handsome young husband in next to no time'.[53] But in any case, Gilbert has his long-standing housekeeper, Mrs Jeffson, so Isabel is as likely to be bored and dissatisfied within the home as Isabel Vane, who found, in her turn, that all the ordering of East Lynne was executed by her resident sister-in-law. It is hardly surprising that Isabel should come very close to being seduced by Roland Lansdell, master of Lansdell Priory and author of some exaggeratedly world-weary poetry ('a sort of mixture of Tennyson and Alfred de Musset').[54] None the less, the reader's understanding rather than sympathetic identification is sought, since Lansdell's selfishness, and inability to appreciate Isabel's innocence of real life, as opposed to fiction, is increasingly exposed. Indeed, we are told unequivocally that he is 'a beautiful useless, purposeless creature; a mark for manoeuvering mothers; a hero for sentimental young ladies,—altogether a mockery, a delusion, and a snare'.[55] Isabel's own standards of judgement are mocked, particularly since she finds herself only able to describe her sensations through reference to fiction. Thus when Roland first talks with her, 'she was stricken and dumbfounded . . . a Pamela, amazed and bewildered by the first complimentary address of her aristocratic persecutor'.[56]

Yet Isabel is not deprived of the hand of the novelist intervening to rescue her. The reader is warned, repeatedly, against the dangers of confusing fiction with reality, as Isabel is shown lost in daydream: 'It was better than reading, to sit through all the length of a hot August afternoon thinking of Roland Lansdell. What romance had ever been written that was equal to this story; this perpetual fiction, wih a real hero dominant in every chapter.'[57] She learns painfully that Roland is far from a romance hero, and that being in love with a live, experienced man is quite different from loving a nobleman in a novel. Moreover, she comes to see that melodrama provides a destructive rather than a welcome factor in life. When her father re-emerges after many years' absence,

---

[52] Braddon, *The Doctor's Wife*, 263.
[53] Ibid. ii. 40.
[54] Ibid. i. 299. In subsequent additions, the name of Edgar Allen Poe was added to the list of authors.
[55] Ibid. ii. 3.
[56] Ibid. i. 316.
[57] Ibid. ii. 104.

he is revealed to the reader as a forger: moreover, one who was jailed due to the evidence of Roland Lansdell, and who emerges from prison determined to gain his revenge. Roland dies from the injuries Isabel's father inflicts just at the moment when she would have been free to marry him, George having fatally caught typhoid fever from the villagers he had been nursing. Isabel is left a rich woman (Roland had bequeathed his estate to her, falsely assuming that she would have been prepared to elope with him to the continent), but Braddon determinedly refuses to show her receiving any ultimate satisfaction based on romantic premisses. Instead, she is finally seen an excellent manager of her estate, erecting model cottages and a substantial schoolhouse, the 'chastening influence of sorrow' having 'transformed a sentimental girl into a good and noble woman—a woman in whom sentiment takes the higher form of universal sympathy and tenderness'.[58]

Isabel is still alive, even happy in her widowed, yet thoroughly useful state at the end of the novel. Novel-reading remains uncondemned as an activity in itself: what is seen to matter is the cultivation of a self-knowing, responsible attitude towards it. Despite all that has happened to her as a result of her misplaced assumptions, there is no admonitory conclusion, in contrast, say, to the sermon which follows the almost parodic catalogue of disasters which befalls the romance addict at the centre of the Reverend Paget's parodic, overstated Christian diatribe against the sensation genre, *Lucretia* (1865). But as well as debunking the expectations of any contemporary reader who might be attempted to put her trust in romance fiction (although Braddon's novel clearly predicates a reader who, although well enough versed in nineteenth-century novels and poetry to pick up the many allusions she makes, would not fall into the trap of assuming that her life could parallel their plots), *The Doctor's Wife*, like other fictions by Braddon and Broughton, raises questions which throw into contention current commonplaces about sensation fiction.

D. A. Miller, in his stimulating essay '*Cage aux folles*: Sensation and Gender in Wilkie Collins's *The Woman in White*' sees the mode of reading which the genre encourages as depending on a 'hysterical' response, mobilizing our sympathetic nervous system at the expense of our rational faculties, reinforcing a bodily split between *psyche* and *soma*. Miller's late twentieth-century terms are, in fact, uncomfortably close to the physiological explanation of sensation fiction's effects which was put forward in the 1860s. Moreover, he describes the genre as 'obsessed with the project of finding meaning—of staging the suspense of its appearance—in everything except the sensations that the project excites in us'.[59] But whilst this may be true in terms of the male writers of the

---

[58] Ibid. iii. 300.

[59] D. A. Miller, '*Cage aux folles*: Sensation and Gender in Wilkie Collins's *The Woman in White*', in Jeremy Hawthorn (ed.), *The Nineteenth-Century British Novel* (1986), 96. Interestingly, Miller notes (p. 100) that the text of *The Woman in White* explicitly assumes that the reader is male, hence someone who 'falls victim to an hysteria in which what is acted out (desired, repressed) is an essentially female "sensation"'.

genre, especially Collins and Charles Reade, the idea that the uncovering of meaning is unequivocally at the centre of the female sensation novel cannot be upheld. Certainly, some of Mary Braddon's works, especially *Lady Audley's Secret* and *Aurora Floyd*, depend on the narrator withtolding information from the reader which she only later fully comprehends: what is it that Lady Audley whispers to Phoebe that was 'so simple that it was told in five minutes', and why does George show no sign of recognition when he sees his wife's portrait? But Rhoda Broughton's novels, although they contain potential bigamists, betrayals, and the possibility of elopement, derive their sensationalism from explicit situation, rather than from mystery.

Above all, the women sensation writers invite their readers to join in a process which involves the active construction of meaning, rather than its revelation. This construction does not necessarily depend on the validation of the narrator, for their fictions often leave one with moral, interpretative problems. Lady Audley may herself suggest that her greedy, selfish, murderous nature is something which she has inherited, and may—indeed must—be classified as insanity. But is madness a sufficient explanation for her actions, particularly since (as Miller points out) the bigamy, arson, and attempted murder are 'motivated . . . by impeccably rational considerations of self-interest'?[60] May the crimes, at least at a symbolic level, not have something to do with the social and economic position of women in mid-Victorian England? Does the neat narrative uniting of the novel's benevolent characters at *Lady Audley's* close act as a sufficient bulwark against the threat that disruption and disorder may lie inside the most apparently happy homes? Can the independence, the enjoyment of manipulative skills, and the self-awareness of sexual magnetism associated with Cleopatra remain perpetually subdued when a woman possessing these characteristics is none the less apparently happily married, as in the case of Aurora Floyd? What are the implications of the fact that two men have to die in *The Doctor's Wife*—the worthy doctor and the rakish Byronic would-be seducer—in order for Isabel, unworthy in many ways, to achieve a far happier fate than that of Emma Bovary, who is consumed by her own romantic preoccupations rather than rescued by the narrator for an independent woman's life?

In all these, and many other examples of women's sensation fiction, external proprieties are maintained, enabling their authors' indignant self-defence against charges of immorality. But as Laura Mulvey has commented in relation to Douglas Sirk's movies of the 1930s: 'Ideological contradiction is the overt mainspring and specific content of melodrama, not a hidden, unconscious thread to be picked up only by special critical processes.'[61] It is difficult to read

---

[60] Miller, '*Cage aux folles*', 110.

[61] Laura Mulvey, 'Notes on Sirk and Melodrama', *Movie*, 25 (1977–8); repr. Christine Gledhill (ed.), *Home is Where the Heart Is: Studies in Melodrama and the Woman's Film* (1987), 75.

these fictions without becoming aware of the tensions which are built up between those social assumptions which structure the facts of the plot, and the sympathies which are called out towards the transgressive heroines. Sometimes these sympathies are invoked spasmodically, as in the case of Lady Audley, sometimes across the grain of overt authorial comment, as in the case of Isabel Vane, represented on the surface as carrying a cross through life because of her adultery. But what these novels share is a posing of moral questions, rather than a dictating of the answers. Whilst the manipulation of a reader's desire, through the suspended outcome, the concealment of clues, the frustration of a heroine's wishes is a continual part of the fictions, so, too, as we have seen, are both references to literature, and addresses to a reader's presumed knowledge of life. The reader is habitually acknowledged as possessing a wider, more subtle interpretative system than that granted to the heroine. The ability to read literature carefully is equated (as in so many advice manuals) with the ability to read life. This attention which is demanded on the part of the reader, not to mention the command which she is implicitly expected to uphold over a wide range of literary references, goes some way towards giving the lie to the dangerously uncritical mindlessness which so many critics chose to present as being induced by the opiate of sensation fiction.

II 'New Woman' Fiction

At first sight, the controversy induced by the emergence of the 'New Woman' fiction in the 1890s bears a close similarity to the wave of anxiety expressed about the sensation novel some thirty years earlier: should girls be allowed to read such fiction? what would be its effects upon them? Detractors from the sensation novel found support in contemporary physiological and psychological theory, and their successors did not abandon the justifications with which such hypotheses still continued to provide them. But increasingly, they attacked the new fiction from a largely sociological perspective, believing that such writing would cause women to question marital and family values, and hence would damage society's necessary structures. They also tended to see the sub-genre as a symptom of wider social decay, in which blame fell on acquiescent reader as well as author.

As in the case of sensation fiction, it is easy to identify the specific elements which made this fiction controversial, and which ensured that writing about it led, in turn, to good journalistic copy. Such elements include protests against the restrictive upbringing of girls and the inadequacies of their education; the challenging of the assumptions that woman's best possible future lay in marriage, that the only place to bear and bring up children was within such a marriage, and that, indeed all women possessed a 'maternal instinct'; the importance placed upon women's struggles and achievements in their working lives, whether as journalist or doctor, teacher, or musician; and the questioning of double sexual standards. There was nothing new in the last, of course, but the writers of the 1890s laid particular stress on the part played by men in spreading venereal disease, and on indicating that this was just one of the aspects of sexuality about which girls were unlikely to learn anything before they were married—if then. Underlying many of these issues, as Ann Ardis has noted, the question of 'where sexuality figures into the whole of human character' not only appears as central to such novels, but links them with a proliferation of contemporary discourses discussing sexuality.[1]

Form, as well as content, distinguishes 'New Woman' fiction from the sensation novel. Its plotting is rarely complex in the sense of involving the reader in concealment and suspense: it is not predicated upon the reading process gratifying a desire for clarification and resolution. Its preferred form is the *Bildungsroman*, and it shares a certain number of characteristics with nineteenth-century women's autobiography. Frequently, it privileges childhood, both as a nostalgic realm which cannot be recaptured, and as a recognized site of gendered injustices. More noticeably, it presents a woman's

---

[1] Ann Ardis, *New Women, New Novels: Feminism and Early Modernism* (1990), 50.

life as process, stressing the value of continuity, even endurance, and of adhering to often painfully learnt principles: principles which are self-generated and rationally arrived at, rather than being imposed by dominant social beliefs. Death, whether as punishment or evasion, is rarely employed (although Emma Frances Brooke, in *A Superfluous Woman* (1894) has Jessamine die from the syphilis which her husband has also passed on to her sickly children, and in an early example of the genre, Mona Caird's *The Wings of Azrael* (1889), legal justice is evaded, in true sensationalist style, by having the heroine fall backwards over a cliff just after she has—quite justifiably—stabbed her sadistic husband).[2] Yet potentially happy partnership is very rarely the solution proferred by the novelists, either.[3] An exception to this might initially seem to be found at the conclusion of Sarah Grand's *The Beth Book* (1897). After an appalling marriage to Dr Dan Maclure (the superintendent of the local Lock Hospital, where prostitutes were examined under the terms of the Contagious Diseases Act; a vivisectionist; and a man with extremely conservative views about woman's position within marriage who himself has an affair with a woman patient), Beth encounters a potential 'New Man' from the New World, an American artist. She nurses him through sickness. They temporarily lose touch, and then, in the final paragraph of the novel, Beth sees a horseman riding towards her across the fields:

She watched him, absently at first, but as he approached he reminded her of the Knight of her daily vision, her saviour, who had come to rescue her in the dark days of her deep distress at Slane—

> 'A bowshot from her bower-eaves,
> He rode between the barley-sheaves.'

'The barley-sheaves!' suddenly Beth's heart throbbed and fluttered and stood still. The words had come to her as the interpretation of an augury, the fulfillment of a promise. It seemed as if she ought to have known it from the first, known that he would come like that at last, that he had been coming, coming, coming through all the years. As he drew near, the rider looked up at her, the sun shone on his face, he raised his hat. In dumb

---

[2] One of the most frequently cited examples of 'New Woman' fiction, Grant Allen's *The Woman Who Did* (1895) concludes with the heroine, Herminia, poisoning herself with prussic acid. But the plot of the novel calls into question its right to be considered in the same terms as feminist works. The Girton-educated Herminia is determined to avoid marriage, and finds a partner, Alan Merrick, who is happy to go along with her decision. He dies of typhoid in Italy, where they have gone for the birth of their daughter. The very fact that this daughter is called Dolores does not augur well. Herminia is determined to bring Dolores up on her own, despite society's general disapproval on the one hand and the offer of marriage from a sympathetic Fabian on the other. Allen's point is made when Dolores grows up holding extremely conventional views, and returns to her paternal grandfather in order to facilitate her engagement.

[3] To have the heroine ultimately settle down in relative contentment with a husband, like Gwen Waring at the end of Iota's *A Yellow Aster* (1894) is to restore the value of conformity, and hence query the categorization of such a novel, after all, among other 'New Woman' fictions. The fact that many reviewers were determined to isolate early aspects of Gwen's character and to label her as a 'New Woman' is indicative of the usefulness of the stereotype for the elaboration of a reviewer's own opinions about the desirable characteristics of contemporary womanhood.

emotion, not knowing what she did, Beth reached out her hands towards him as if to welcome him. He was not the Knight of her dark days, however, this son of the morning, but the Knight of her long winter vigil—Arthur Brock.'[4]

But despite Elaine Showalter's contention that, unusually, Grand allows Beth 'to survive and succeed',[5] an alert reader, used to the fact that quotations may be incorporated to serve more than one end, might well query the wisdom of Beth putting so much faith into her knight in shining armour. Certainly, this ending gives 'sunny imaginations hope',[6] but anyone knowing 'The Lady of Shalott' is unlikely to feel confident in prophesying a happy, active future, when rescue is couched in terms of the sight of a chivalric horseman.

As this example indicates, the 'New Woman' fiction of the 1890s shared with sensation fiction (despite their other differences) the expectation that its readers would take the actual activity of reading seriously, however much their attention might be claimed by the nature of the subject-matter. Yet notwithstanding the use which we have just seen Sarah Grand making of Tennyson, the reading material which really counts is not the standard poetic repertoire of the Victorian young woman, but non-fiction, or fiction which poses provocative social questions. Many earlier uses of quotation in fiction primarily aimed at women assume that they will use pre-established associations in order to interpret a particular fictional scenario. But here, the emphasis falls not so much on texts with which the reader will necessarily be already familiar, but on those which she may be encouraged to go and read. Above all, the novels themselves encourage an interrogative manner of reading, not just developing one's rational powers in relation to the printed word, but in relation to society more widely.

This emphasis on rationality and interrogation does not involve jettisoning the imaginative faculties, and disavowing the importance of emotion. The employment of the *Bildungsroman* as a mode of narration is, after all, one which encourages sympathetic identification on the reader's part. The reader's growth in knowledge is made to parallel that of the protagonist: as Rita Felski has put it, in relation to recent twentieth-century woman's fiction: 'the feminist *Bildungsroman* is a didactic genre which aims to convince the reader of the legitimacy of a particular interpretative framework by bringing her or him to a cumulative and retrospective understanding of the events narrated in the text.'[7]

---

[4] Sarah Grand, *The Beth Book* (1897; repr. Virago, ed. Elaine Showalter, 1983), 527.

[5] Showalter, introd. to ibid. [xi].

[6] Lucy Snowe's words, at the conclusion of Charlotte Brontë's *Villette* (1853; repr. Oxford, 1984), 715, when she addresses those who wish to believe, against all the other evidence, that M. Paul indeed returns from his stormy voyage home. The ending of *Villette*, incidentally, was softened from its initial unequivocal shipwrecking of M. Paul in order to satisfy the fictional desires of a *male* reader, the Revd Patrick Brontë.

[7] Rita Felski, *Beyond Feminist Aesthetics: Feminist Literature and Social Change* (1989), 137. See also Susan Suleiman, *Authoritarian Fictions: The Ideological Novel as Literary Genre* (New York, 1983), for an expanded discussion of problems concerning reading and interpretation raised by the *roman à thèse*.

Such fiction simultaneously invites intimacy, particularly through its incorporation of telling details (although it rarely approaches the confessional confidence of tone popularized by Rhoda Broughton) and, in its adherence for the most part to realist principles, it claims typicality.[8] Yet the relatively downbeat endings of the novels ensure that the reader is not lured into total identification with the central character: these novels are not dramas of wish-fulfilment. A space is thus set up between the heroine's resigned or compromised fate and the creation of the desire either that she could internally have been stronger and have stuck more bravely to her principles; or that social pressures did not render principled stances almost impossible to maintain. Readers are thus alerted to the simultaneous operation of both unconscious and societal factors upon an individual: acknowledging, and regretting the effects on a fictional character is the first step, these novels suggest, in the readers's own critical examination of their own position within society.

Recognizing this combination of factors allows one to see that whilst the reading of the 'New Woman' may be portrayed as primarily rational in its demands, the novelists themselves continued to build on the belief that emotional response could be a valuable tool in acquiring knowledge. They saw, as Alison Jaggar phrases it in an essay which indicates quite how challenging such assumptions are to the Western philosophical tradition, that: 'Critical reflection on emotion is not a self-indulgent substitute for political analysis and political action. It is itself a kind of political theory and political practice, indispensable for an adequate social theory and social transformation.'[9]

Two questions preoccupied antagonistic reviewers: why was this new type of fiction so popular, and, as W. T. Stead asked in a long article in the *Review of Reviews*, 'What will be the end of all this kind of writing upon the girls who are just flowering into womanhood?'[10] 'The sale of these books by thousands is not a healthy sign', warned Hugh Stutfield in his *Blackwood's* article 'The Psychology of Feminism'. 'People read them because they are interested in them, and the interest arises from the fact that what they read corresponds to something in their own natures.'[11] However, rather than turning to the

---

[8] There are, of course, some notable exceptions to the tendency of 'New Woman' fiction to adopt a realist style. Some of George Egerton's stories, and the section of Grand's *The Heavenly Twins* entitled 'The Tenor and the Boy', utilize a quasi-mystical tone, similar to that already employed in Olive Schreiner's *Dreams* (1891). Other works, such as Florence Dixie's *Gloriana; or the Revolution of 1900* (1890) adopt a Utopian mode, although this was more favoured by American feminist novelists, such as Marie Howland, Elizabeth Corbett, and Charlotte Perkins Gilman, than by British writers.

[9] Alison M. Jaggar, 'Love and Knowledge: Emotion in Feminist Epistemology', in Ann Garry and Marilyn Pearsall (eds.), *Women, Knowledge, and Reality: Explorations in Feminist Philosophy* (1989), 149.

[10] [W. T. Stead] 'The Book of the Month: The Novel of the Modern Woman', *Review of Reviews*, 10 (1894), 73.

[11] Hugh Stutfield, 'The Psychology of Feminism', *Blackwood's Edinburgh Magazine*, 161 (1897), 115.

changing educational and employment opportunities for women to provide at least a partial explanation for this, he once again resorted to the body as a site of explanation. Highly influenced by Max Nordau's *Degeneration* (1895; translation of *Entartung*, Berlin, 1892–3), he saw this condition in quasi-medical terms as a 'morbid pessimism, subdued or paroxysmal': a condition of inseparably linked body and brain which fed off reading, quoting the German's belief that 'the influence of polite literature on life is much greater than that of life on polite literature'.[12] Blame for disease is thus shifted back from the syphilitic men of Grand's fiction or of Emma Frances Brooke's *A Superfluous Woman*, on to the unhealthy condition of womanhood itself. As well as a manifestation of mental disease, Stutfield also lamented the wide circulation of this literature for tending 'to widen the breach between men and women, and to make them more mutually distrustful than ever'.[13] This breach is dramatized by Stutfield through his characterization of the different responses of women and men to the new literature. 'These searching studies in the sexual emotions of young ladies are, I fear, a source of merriment to the masculine mind', he noted.[14] By way of example, he claims that while at a matinée of Ibsen's *Little Eyolf* which he attended, some of the women in the audience were much affected, sobbing at the 'lugubrious' parts, while 'the males, I regret to say, were more disposed to chuckle irrelevantly', being less sympathetic to 'the whinings of sexual hysteria'.[15]

Stead's anxieties about the changing positional relations of women and men were a mirror image of Stutfield's. Despite his acknowledgement of the justice in protesting against loveless marriage, enforced motherhood, sexual ignorance, and second-hand bridegrooms, he was concerned that this fiction would promote divorce, and would shatter the pedestal on which stands the ideal of womanhood. Rather than exaggerating sexual difference, this writing inflicted damage, in Stead's opinion, precisely because it obliterated the criteria by which one might establish such difference: 'All this natural and legitimate use of genuine but lawless love as a foil to bring into stronger relief the hatefulness of loveless marriage will operate, is now operating in the direction of debasing the moral standard of the ordinary woman to the level of the ordinary standard of the ordinary man.'[16]

What these two representative articles manifest is a phenomenon familiar from earlier discussion of women and their taste in fiction: that despite Stead's acknowledgement that: 'the Modern Woman novel is not merely a novel written by a woman, or a novel written about women, but it is a novel written by a

---

[12] Hugh Stutfield, 'The Psychology of Feminism', 114.
[13] Ibid. 116.
[14] Ibid. 107
[15] Ibid. 113.
[16] [Stead] 'The Novel of the Modern Woman', 73.

woman about women from the standpoint of women',[17] the debate was inevitably conducted in terms of women's relations with men. Stutfield noted that it was the introspection of Egerton's writing, or of the tubercular artist Marie Bashkirtseff's immensely popular Journal, which constituted much of their appeal for women. But such 'morbid ego-mania' was, for him, merely another symptom:

The book sold like wild-fire. 'All the tired and discontented women of the time recognised themselves on every page, and for many of them Marie Bashkirtseff's Journal became a kind of secret Bible, in which they read a few sentences every morning, or at night before going to sleep.'
  Not a very satisfactory Bible, to be sure, but the literature of hysteria is always sure of its public, and she was symptomatic of a restless and fretful age.[18]

In describing frustration, indignation, and reformist enthusiasm in terms of pathological symptoms (restlessness, nerves, hysteria, drives towards self-induced misery)—'the most morbid symptoms of erotomania', according to James Ashcroft Noble—[19] what these anxious, antagonistic commentators failed to give weight to is the rewriting of affectional relationships within these works. This writing is conducted in terms which strengthen the possibilities for binding women together through shared subjectivity.

These comments I have just quoted are notable for the confidence with which men write of the workings of women's bodies, for at the forefront of women's complaints in the 1890s was the degree to which they were frequently kept in ignorance about corporeal facts, whether concerning themselves, or the men whom they might marry. At this time, women increasingly came to locate their gender's susceptibility to real-life events, as well as to fiction, not within physical and psychological 'facts' about their make-up, but within ignorance. 'Innocence' and 'purity' were synonyms for dangerous gaps in their knowledge concerning social, and in particular sexual, relations. The feminist movement of the late nineteenth century and early twentieth century was, as has been noted, 'a campaign for free speech in a double sense: not merely to propagate woman suffrage or repeal of the C.D. Acts at public meetings, but to widen the range of the topics which women could discuss in public'.[20] Such discussion partially took place through organized channels, like Josephine Butler's Ladies' National Association, which encouraged women when speaking in public meetings to break through the suffocating mysticism which surrounded sexual issues. Partially, it was aired through the dissemination of written material, including

[17] Ibid. 64.
[18] Stutfield, 'The Psychology of Feminism', 109.
[19] James Ashcroft Noble, 'The Fiction of Sexuality', *Contemporary Review*, 67 (1895), 493.
[20] Brian Harrison, 'Women's Health and the Women's Movement in Britain: 1840–1940', in Charles Webster (ed.), *Biology, Medicine and Society 1840–1940* (Cambridge, 1981), 21.

fiction. To write of such topics as venereal disease, or the chains forged by maternity, in novels which circulated widely was to bring controversial discussion into the drawing-room, into the sphere of mother-daughter relations, and into the very institution of marriage. Contemporary commentators noted this development with varying degrees of enthusiasm or disdain. Blanche Leppington, in the *Contemporary Review*, claimed that even the:

social-problematical novel or drama, with its flippancy, its garish crudity, its deification of selfishness, is probably not without its use as at least a carrier of questions to which it may provoke, if it cannot give, an answer. With all its contempt for the accepted moralities, it is helping to carry the pressure of the moral question into the sacred enclosure of marriage itself, from which all questioning has been too long excluded; and it is perhaps hardly too much to say no service could well be greater than this.[21]

We already saw, in Part II, how romantic fiction fell under increasing suspicion for the falsification it engendered. Such a point was made further by Maude Wheeler, in *Whom to Marry or All About Love and Matrimony* (1894) when she complained that: 'Our girls are suffered to read trashy novels, steeped in false romantic sentiments and unreal attempts to picture love, not as it is, but as the erratic fancy of the novelist would have it seem; but how many mothers are there who would consider a knowledge of anatomy and physiology as necessary,or even desirable, elements of their daughters'education.'[22]

Yet in a decade when *David Copperfield* and *Adam Bede* could still be considered *risqué* reading, the degree of explicitness involved in informing a young woman about sexual issues was highly variable. This is indicated in passing by a doctor specializing in electric-shock cures, J. Beresford Ryley, who in *A Few Words of Advice to Young Wives* (1895) remarked that many of the gynaecological problems about which he was consulted would never have reached so severe a state if his patients had had a better understanding of the 'physical and moral risks in marriage': 'Instead of . . . dangerous reticence . . . I would encourage every young man and woman to read such books as "The Manxman," and "Tess of the D'Urbervilles", which deal so truthfully and powerfully with that all-vital question of the relation between the sexes.'[23] Tess herself, incidentally, Hardy makes clear, would have benefited from some first-hand sex education. We hear him speaking through her when she returns home, pregnant, and berates her mother: 'Why didn't you tell me there was danger in men-folk? Why didn't you warn me? Ladies know what to fend hands

---

[21] Blanche Leppington, 'The Debrutalisation of Man', *Contemporary Review*, 67 (1895), 742.

[22] Maude Wheeler, *Whom to Marry or All About Love and Matrimony* (1894), p. xvii. See Kate Flint, 'Reading the New Woman', *Browning Society Notes*, 17 (1987–8), 57–8, however, for illustration of how Wheeler herself becomes trapped within pre-existing literary formulae when she comes to define 'love'.

[23] J. Beresford Ryley, *A Few Words of Advice to Young Wives* (1895), 44. Hall Caine's *The Manxman* (1894) includes two generations of illegitimate births and a mother turning to prostitution among its melodramatic turns of plot.

against because they read novels that tell them of these tricks; but I never had the chance o' learning in that way, and you did not help me!'[24] Ironically, however, these informative fictions which Tess is postulating are doubtless the very books which other commentators would be warning the young lady against reading.

If the issue of women's reading in the 1890s becomes most active around the question of access to knowledge, particularly sexual knowledge, then it follows that the attainment of that knowledge can effectively be described and dramatized in ways which challenge the conventions used to delineate the tastes and capacities of the woman reader. Such challenges were located not just in articles and reviews, but within the fiction itself.

Among the so-called 'New Woman' novelists, Sarah Grand made the most sustained use of reading as a topos.[25] The didactic early pages of *The Heavenly Twins* (1893) introduce the heroine, Evadne, beginning with the question 'Why are women such inferior beings', 'and then she asked herself doubtfully: "Are women such inferior beings?" a position which carried her in front of her father at once by a hundred years . . . '.[26] Looking for answers, she moves through fiction to read John Stuart Mill on *The Subjection of Women*, medical books, anatomy, and physiology, just as the heroine of Grand's earlier novel, *Ideala* (1888) reads Thomas Huxley's *Elementary Physiology*. Evadne has firm tastes, eschewing, for example, the masculinism of the picaresque novel, though Grand plays on her readers' knowledge of such fiction in order to indicate that which perhaps is too controversial to articulate explicitly. As Evadne returns from her wedding, she receives a letter making clear that her new husband, Colonel Colquoun, has had a dissipated past. She leaves immediately to live with her aunt and, as she explains in a letter to her parents (the nearest we ourselves come to learning the details of her husband's background) 'his mode of life has very much resembled one of those old-fashioned heroes, Roderick Random or Tom Jones, specimens of humanity whom I hold in peculiar and especial detestation.'[27] In the copious reading notes which Grand introduces into the early chapters of the novel, as though ensuring this part of the novel has the authority of a documentary, Evadne had commented that: 'The two books taken together show well the self-interest and injustice of men, the fatal

[24] Thomas Hardy, *Tess of the D'Urbervilles* (1891; Wessex edn., 1912), 104. Hardy succinctly stated his own views on the matter of sex education for girls in a debate on the subject in the columns of the *New Review*, 10 (1894), 681: 'a plain book on natural processes, specially prepared, should be placed in the daughter's hands, and later on, similar information on morbid contingencies'.

[25] For critical discussion of 'New Woman' fiction, see Ardis, *New Women, New Novels*; Penny Boumelha, *Thomas Hardy and Women* (1982), ch. 4, 'Women and the New Fiction 1880–1900'; Gail Cunningham, *The New Woman and the Victorian Novel* (1978); Linda Dowling, 'The Decadent and the New Woman in the 1890s', *Nineteenth-Century Fiction*, 33 (1979), 434–53; Showalter, *A Literature of their Own*, ch. 7, 'The Feminist Novelists', 182–215; ead., *Sexual Anarchy: Gender and Culture at the 'Fin de Siècle*, ch. 3, 'New Women', 38–58.

[26] Sarah Grand, *The Heavenly Twins*, 3 vols. (1893), i. 16.

[27] Ibid. 104.

ignorance and slavish apathy of women; and it may be good to know such things, but it is not agreeable.'[28] Grand thus gives, in passing, an argument against those who would seek to prevent girls reading these eighteenth-century novels.

Although in time Evadne returns to the Colonel, it is only on the condition that they never have sexual relations. It is in describing how the Colonel tries to tempt Evadne away from this decision that Grand makes explicit use of the difference between a man's expectation of the effects which reading certain material would have on a woman, and the actual outcome. He furnishes their married home with bait, filling the shelves with all her old books, including Herbert Spencer and Francis Galton, and adds some new material: 'He had arranged the books himself, placing Zola and Daudet in prominent positions, and anticipating much entertainment from the observation of their effect upon her. He expected she would end by making love to him.'[29] But the Colonel is disappointed in his expectations. It is as though, through Evadne, Grand is confuting anxiety that women may be unduly stimulated by salacious reading material. ' "By-the-way," ' asks her husband:

'have you read any of those books I got for you—any of the French ones?'
    Her face set somewhat, but she looked up at him, and answered without hesitation: 'Yes. I have read the *Nana*, *La Terre*, *Madame Bovary*, and *Sapho*.'
    She stopped there, and he waited in vain for her to express an opinion.
    'Well,' he said at last, 'what has struck you most in them?'
    'The suffering, George,' she exclaimed—'*the awful, needless suffering!*'[30]

This phrase turns into a refrain: Evadne's habitual comment during the rest of the novel at the sad state of humanity.

Grand's next novel, *The Beth Book* (1897), presents another heroine who suffers from her husband's literary assumptions, but a different point is being made. Dr Dan makes Beth, for his own pleasure, read conventional love stories aloud to him. When he is in male company, he may claim to enjoy modern French writers for the picture of 'real life' that they give, but his private taste is much less demanding. Beth finds a sympathetic auditor for her complaints against her husband's choice of books in Sir George Galbraith: *she* values works which provide 'food for thought' since 'the mind craves for nourishment', and she also acknowledges that 'good fiction' may play a considerable part in improving the mind, enlarging the sympathies and educating judgement. Unsurprisingly, the catalogue of faults which she finds in her husband's selection of reading material is turned into a justification for the type of fiction which the reader is at that very moment consuming: the novels which she would like to write sound just like Grand's own:

[28] Sarah Grand, *The Heavenly Twins*, 23.
[29] Ibid. 217.
[30] Ibid. 277.

I never will have a faultlessly beautiful heroine, for instance. I am sick of that creature. When I come to her, especially if she has golden hair yards long, a faultless complexion, and eyes of extraordinary dimensions, I feel inclined to groan and shut the book. I have met her so often in the weary ways of fiction! I know every variety of her so well! She consists of nothing but superlatives . . . I would not write plotty-plotty books either, nor make a pivot of the everlasting love-story, which seems to me to show such a want of balance in an author, such an absence of any true sense of proportion, as if there was nothing else of interest in life but our sexual relations.[31]

Yet despite the heavily autobiographical element in *The Beth Book*, Beth does not herself become a novelist. Rather, it is on going to the library for her husband's reading material that Beth discovers the non-fiction which is to help her in her own career as writer and speaker: Emerson, Macaulay, de Quincey, Carlyle. Even if their verbal mannerisms temporarily clog her own 'natural faculty', she is, Grand makes clear, serving her apprenticeship, and learning to expand her mental horizons, unlike her husband. The inclusion of his reading, it would seem, both serves to show that men use fiction as an escape route, and that conventional fictional types help to establish male, rather than female, ideals. This is a point which was to be made again in H. G. Wells's *Ann Veronica* (1909), notwithstanding the highly equivocal line which the novel takes on the subject of women's independence. Here, Ann Veronica's father complains that his daughter's desire for a less restricted lifestyle is derived from her reading: 'It's these damned novels. All this torrent of misleading, spurious stuff that pours from the press. These sham ideals and advanced notions. Women who Dids, and all that kind of thing . . . '.[32] Yet his own reading material, 'healthy light fiction with chromatic titles, "The Red Sword," "The Black Helmet," "The Purple Robe,"' consumed 'in order "to distract his mind"',[33] gives him substantially less guidance in confronting the world.

There was nothing new in suggesting that men, like women, derive expectations from what they read. A writer in the *Saturday Review* could ask, in half-jocular fashion: 'Who can follow with attention the adventures of a heroine whose personal appearance he objects to? or who can enter with rapture into the aspirations and ambitions of a young man whom he would studiously avoid if he came across him at his club?'[34] Men were presented, like women, as being vulnerable to the effects of French fiction. The Revd. C. B. Tayler's *Mark Wilton* (1848) chronicles the downfall of a merchant's clerk to a life of gambling, theatre-going, drunkenness and reading French novels, and the irresponsible, corrupt central figure of Walter Besant's *In Deacon's Orders* (1895) is also given to reading this genre. But to indicate explicitly that men are less discriminating readers than women: that, indeed, they happily consume

[31] Grand, *The Beth Book*, 373.
[32] H. G. Wells, *Ann Veronica* (1909), 30.
[33] Ibid. 16.
[34] 'To Those About to Write a Novel', *Saturday Review* (22 Jan. 1887), 122.

precisely those romantic works which were popularly believed to limit women's perspectives on life, is to reverse popular expectations about each gender's reading habits.

These small-scale, but pointed references to women's and men's reading practices and expectations should be seen in the context of the challenges which the novels' central themes present in themselves. Grand's more conservative reviewers were shocked by the very elements which made her works such notable interventions for progressively thinking women. The *Spectator*, for example, complained that 'Sarah Grand explicitly or implicitly raises a number of questions which cannot be adequately discussed in *any* column with a mixed clientele',[35] precisely the kind of concealment of sexual issues against which Grand protested. Evadne spoke for her creator when she is made to say: 'I would stop the imposition, approved of by custom, connived at by parents, made possible by the state of ignorance in which we are carefully kept . . . of a disreputable man for a husband.'[36] The *Spectator* may be contrasted with Mary Fordham, writing in *Shafts*, who records with sorrow a conversation she had had with a girl to whom she had just lent the book, and who had maintained that 'it lay in Evadne's power to have made her husband better; she neglected her duty to him in not living with him as his wife'. But Fordham maintains that Evadne did right: she had married her husband under false pretences, believing him to be as pure as she was, and 'we have the power to insist upon pure men as the husbands of pure women'. This will only be achieved, she insists (in common with many of *Shafts'* correspondents) if mothers send girls, and boys too, out into the world with the knowledge of sexual matters which is 'both power and purity'.[37]

Nowhere is this ignorance more dangerous than in the matter of venereal disease, as Grand demonstrated, to many reviewers' disgust, in both her major novels. In *The Heavenly Twins* Edith, a bishop's daughter, is initially presented as a complete foil to the independent Evadne. When we encounter her, this archetypal pink and white heroine is demurely reading that most decorous of biographies, the *Life of Frances Ridley Havergal*, the popular, and extremely pious poet. Brought up in 'complete' ignorance of life, however, Edith is Grand's sacrificial lamb, marrying a rakish, diseased man in Colonel Colquoun's regiment, giving birth to a sickly child, and herself dying insane. Venereal disease figures prominently in *The Beth Book*, too. After her marriage, Beth initially fails to understand why she should be so shunned by other women: gradually it dawns on both her and the reader that her husband is in charge of a Lock hospital for prostitutes suffering from venereal disease. Beth perceives, slowly: 'that so-called civilised men, who boast of their chivalrous protection of

---

[35] *Spectator* (25 Mar. 1893), 395.
[36] Grand, *The Heavenly Twins*, i. 97.
[37] Mary Fordham, 'Knowledge is Power', *Shafts*, 2 (1893), 137.

the "weaker sex," had imposed upon women a special public degradation, while the most abandoned and culpable of their own sex were not only allowed to go unpunished, but to spread vice and disease where they listed.'[38] When Beth asks her husband 'What do you do to the men who spread it? What becomes to diseased men?', he replies, 'Oh, they marry, I suppose. Anyhow that is not my business': crude in its didacticism, perhaps, but designed to shock.

Grand's fiction was immensely popular. In the first year of its publication Heinemann reprinted *The Heavenly Twins* six times: by the time it came out in one volume, the following year, nearly 20,000 copies had been sold in this country.[39] The image of a woman reading this novel became, together with references to her fondness for Ibsen, E. F. Benson's *Dodo*, and learning by heart quotations from *The Second Mrs. Tanqueray*, a cliché in the description of the 'New Woman'.[40] A *Punch* cartoon of 1894 (Fig. 19) shows a bespectacled, plainly dressed woman of the type, brandishing aloft the key of her emancipation, surrounded by book-spines and papers labelled *Dodo*, 'Ibsen', 'Tolstoi', 'The Revolt of the Daughters', and 'Mona Caird'. Behind her is one woman brandishing a banner bearing the legend 'Divided Skirt' in the face of the Dragon of Decorum, another wielding a double-headed axe at the figure of Mrs Cerberus, with her three heads labelled Mrs Grundy, Mamma, and Chaperon, and a female knight tilting at the windmill of marriage laws. These represent the fantasies with which *Punch*'s cartoonist populates 'Donna Quixote's head. She lives, according to the supporting quotation from Cervantes, in 'A world of disorderly notions *picked out of books*, crowded into his (her) imagination.' But the correspondence received by Grand and her contemporaries—George Egerton, Mona Caird, Emma Frances Brooke, Edith Johnstone, and so on—testify to their popularity among woman readers, and to the influence of their work in the growing feminist movement. The 'New Woman' fiction, far more even than the sensation novels earlier in the century, may be said to have created and consolidated a community of woman readers, who could refer to these works as proof of their psychological, social, and ideological difference from men.

However, although these publications, fictional and journalistic, may represent both the actuality and self-construction of one conspicuous group of women readers of the 1890s, an alternative set of images was created, in both review articles and novels, by those who were in opposition to their stance. Such opposition was certainly not limited to men. Eliza Linton dedicated her novel *The One Too Many* (1894) to 'the SWEET GIRLS STILL LEFT AMONG US | who have no part in the new revolt | but are content to be | Dutiful, Innocent, and

---

[38] Grand, *The Beth Book*, 401.

[39] These figures are given by Gillian Kersley, *Darling Madame: Sarah Grand & Devoted Friend* (1983), 72.

[40] Kathleen Cuffe, 'A Reply From the Daughters I', *Nineteenth Century*, 35 (1894), 437.

DONNA QUIXOTE.

[" A world of disorderly notions *picked out of books*, crowded into his (her) imagination."—*Don Quixote*.

19. *Punch* cartoon, 28 April 1894

Sheltered'. Linton's review article 'The Philistine's Coming Triumph' sympathizes with those male reviewers, such as W. T. Stead, the proud bearer of the nom de plume 'Philistine', who found that the new fiction blasphemed the sanctities of domestic life.[41] Annie Swan, contributing to a debate on 'What should women read?' in her fashionable, conservative magazine *The Woman at Home* in 1896, claimed that she was looking at the question from the point of view of a mother who would wish her daughter to 'grow up wise, discriminating, simple-hearted and pure-minded': 'She will be a wise woman who seeks to keep much of modern fiction out of her young daughter's hands, else she will have her standing handicapped at the very threshold of life.'[42]

And protests against current fictional trends could be found within fiction itself. A young woman in Marie Corelli's *The Sorrows of Satan* (1895) attributes her downfall to a combination of modern novels, and Swinburne. If anything, the poet, overtly interrogative of Christianity, comes off worse than the novelists: 'I believe there are many women to whom his works have been deadlier than the deadliest poison, and far more soul-corrupting than any book of Zola's or the most pernicious of modern French writers.' Lady Sybil acknowledges the seductive power of the ornate language and persuasive rhymes to implant the notion that Christ was no more than 'carrion crucified'. At first causing her to shudder, at length this poetry, working its fascination upon her, removed for ever all sense of sacredness from her soul. Whilst at first glance the fiction also, with its 'horrible lasciviousness', filled Sybil with 'genuine disgust', the amount of praise which it received in the leading journals of the day—'its obscenities were hinted at as "daring",—its vulgarities were quoted as "brilliant wit" '—led her to try again, and, gradually, she was hooked: 'little by little the insidious abomination of it filtered into my mind and *stayed there*. I began to think about it,—and by-and-by found pleasure in thinking about it. I sent for other books by the same tainted hand, and my appetite for that kind of prurient romance grew keener.'[43] When the hero of the novel falls in love with her, she claims to feel nothing in return, for she is 'one of your modern women,—I can only think,—and analyse'. What more might he expect:

I ask you, do you think a girl can read the books that are now freely published, and that her silly society friends tell her to read,—'because it is so dreadfully *queer*! and yet remain unspoilt and innocent? Books that go into the details of the lives of outcasts?—that explain and analyse the secret vices of men?—that advocate almost as a sacred duty 'free love' and universal polygamy?—that see no shame in introducing into the circles of good wives and pure-minded girls, a heroine who boldly seeks out a man, *any* man, in order that she might have a child by him, without the 'degradation' of

[41] E. Lynn Linton, 'The Philistine's Coming Triumph', *National Review*, 26 (1895), 40–9. For Linton's conservative attitudes, see Nancy Fix Anderson, *Woman Against Women in Victorian England: A Life of Eliza Lynn Linton* (Bloomington, Ind., and Indianapolis, 1987).

[42] Annie S. Swan, in 'What Should Women Read?', *The Woman at Home*, 37 (1896), 31.

[43] Marie Corelli, *The Sorrows of Satan* (1895), 405–6.

marrying him? I have read all those books,—and what can you expect of me? Not innocence, surely!⁴⁴

The tone here, as throughout, is self-consciously 'literary' and melodramatic, creating a gothic horror story out of the very process of reading, and consolidating, simultaneously, the value and appeal of Corelli's own romantic fictions.

Not all the emphasis on women entering adult life with adequate sexual knowledge centred on what to avoid in men, however. Woman's relationship towards maternity also faced reassessment. Much of the fiction portrays women as having the physical impulse to bear children, but indicates that motherhood should involve more rational considerations as well, since the role has social as well as personal implications. 'Motherhood', to quote Hadria, the heroine of Mona Caird's *The Daughters of Danaus* (1894), 'in our present social state, is the sign and seal as well as the means and method of woman's bondage. It forges chains of her own flesh and blood; it weaves cords of her own love and instinct.'⁴⁵ In Ménie Muriel Dowie's *Gallia* (1895), both the heroine's reading of newspaper articles on 'the state regulation of vice' and of social ethics—particularly Mill and Herbert Spencer (and, reading between the lines, the eugenics of Galton) determine her pragmatic attitudes. Parenthood, for Gallia, should be a matter for beautiful, healthy physical specimens, producing strong, finely bred children. This would serve to remove the physical stress of motherhood from marriage, and, far more shockingly, to separate the issue of love between adults from parentage. The implications are somewhat different in Emma Frances Brooke's *A Superfluous Woman* (1894). Jessamine, the woman of the title, takes her ideas about woman's independence, we are led to believe, from a highly selective and exaggerated reading of John Stuart Mill, Thoreau, and Browning's 'Waring'. But 'correct' texts were not enough in themselves, this 'New Woman' fiction suggests: what matters is the thought which goes into reading them. Although Jessamine attempts to escape from London society and goes to live on a Scottish farm, her residual social allegiance is revealed all too closely through the absorbed interest with which she reads the gossip pages in the newspapers. Despite the fact that she 'longed definitely and deeply after motherhood',⁴⁶ her snobbism does not let her accept the offer of marriage which she receives from a healthy, handsome Scottish peasant. Physically attracted by him, prepared to seduce him both for the pleasure this would bring her *and* in order to get pregnant, Jessamine is allowed no such course of action by Brooke. Rather, she returns to London, bears syphilitic children to the dissolute Lord whom she marries, and dies insane. The novel has a gloomy 'Catch-22' structure. Brooke does not advocate parenthood outside wedlock,

⁴⁴ Marie Corelli, *The Sorrows of Satan*, 201–2.
⁴⁵ Mona Caird, *The Daughters of Danaus* (1894), 341.
⁴⁶ [Emma Frances Brooke] *A Superfluous Woman*, 3 vols. (1894), ii. 165.

but demonstrates how the pressures of fashionable society prevent women from choosing a socially sanctioned route to motherhood outside the terms of their own conditioning. However, submission to the orthodoxies of this conditioning kills them. The novel demands that its readers consider the relative importance to a woman of motherhood on the one hand, and that staple of romance, high social status, on the other. The two, it suggests, may not be compatible.

Reading, and its implications for sexual knowledge, is presented differently again in Ella Hepworth Dixon's *The Story of a Modern Woman* (1894). Throughout the novel, the heroine, Mary, defines herself and her life against forms of story-telling. Retrospectively, she can be understood as a blend of two of her favourite childhood books: she both 'thrilled with the lurid emotion' of *Wuthering Heights* and was moved by the 'poor drab, patient, self-contained' Lucy Snowe in *Villette*.[47] Like so many Victorian girls, Mary, once in her teens, had to use books rather than live mentors to enable her to make up her mind on subjects crucial to women: 'the questions of marriage, of maternity, of education'.[48] The vast majority of the books which she read were by men:

It was not, of course, till years afterwards, that Mary became conscious of the fine irony of the fact that man—the superior intelligence—should take his future companion, shut her within four walls, fill that dimly lighted interior with images of facts and emotions which do not exist, and then, pushing her suddenly into the blinding glare of real life, should be amazed when he finds that his exquisite care of her ethical sense has stultified her brain.

The girl was reading *David Copperfield* when she descended one day, with knitted brows, to the room where her governess was laboriously copying in water-colours a lithographed bunch of roses.

'What is a lost woman really, Miss Brown?' demanded the girl, with her tense look. 'Dickens says that little Em'ly is a lost woman, because she goes to Italy with that Mr. Steerforth. Was Mr. Steerforth a lost man, too?'[49]

As *The Story of a Modern Woman* progresses, so, however, does Mary's consciousness of the gap that exists between fiction and life. The narrator notes, briefly, the escapist function that fiction can play, remarking on the faces of nursemaids bent over penny novelettes as they push their prams through Regent's Park. It is a superior version of this market which, when she becomes a hack writer, Mary earns her living through supplying. She claims that she would like to write a realist novel, with 'twenty-seven years of actual experience in it' but that such an 'idea was too sad—too painful, all the publishers said. It wouldn't have pleased the British public', with their demand for a ball in the first volume of their three-decker novel, a picnic and a parting in the second,

[47] Ella Hepworth Dixon, *The Story of a Modern Woman* (1894; repr. 1990), 23.
[48] Ibid. 25.
[49] Ibid. 26.

and an opportune death in the third. 'The *banal*, the pretty-pretty, the obvious! This is what she was to write—if she wanted to make any money, to keep her head above water.' Marketable fictional standards are hypocritical ones. Although headlines and street-corner placards may scream the details of the latest scandalous divorce case, her publisher tells her that the public want 'thoroughly healthy reading': no form of sexual realism would be economically, let alone morally, respectable. He condemns current trends in continental fiction—'These novelists are getting so morbid. It's all these French and Russian writers that have done it'—and recommends that she write 'a thoroughly breezy book with a wedding at the end' to counteract such tendencies, and make her, and himself, a profit.[50]

The Story of a Modern Woman itself resolutely avoids a happy ending, whether a romantic one or, for that matter, one which celebrates the triumph of the independent woman. Not that it is without love-interest, even if Mary's suitor, Vincent Hemming, is treated by the narrator with considerable ironic disdain. Despite his persuasive eloquence on the subject of women's rights; despite his promise to marry Mary when he returns from his world trip investigating the position of women, he proves shallow, selfish, ambitious, and weak-willed. He allows himself to be trapped into marrying a 'vulgar', commonplace, lumpy Northern heiress in order to gain funds which will ensure his return to Parliament. Mary, despite her patient waiting, is left alone at an age when it would be considered unlikely that she could obtain a husband, and with all her long-term imaginings, and internalized social expectations, having been fixed on Hemming. Yet when he comes to her, near the close of the novel, holds her in his arms, and implores her to flee to France with him, and be what he has never had, a 'real' wife, Mary refuses. This, however, is no conventional act of moral self-assertion. Nor, as had been the case when adultery looked on the cards in the sensation fiction of Mary Braddon or Rhoda Broughton, is some fortuitous narrative twist needed to extricate the heroine. Rather, Mary claims, 'I can't, I won't, deliberately injure another woman'. She urges Hemming to think not just of his wife, but of his daughter. 'I could not bear that she should grow up and hate me. All we modern women mean to help each other now.'[51] Dixon claimed that the 'keynote of her book, lay in the phrase 'All we modern women mean to help each other now. If we were united, we could lead the world.' It was, she said, 'a plea for a kind of moral and social trades-unionism among women'.[52]

It would be misleading to leave this chapter, however, as though the fiction of the 'New Woman' ushered in an enduring new genre of the novel, in which not only were sexual and marital issues discussed with frankness, but, more

---

[50] Ella Hepworth Dixon, *The Story of a Modern Woman*, 183.
[51] Ibid. 255.
[52] Ella Hepworth Dixon, quoted W. T. Stead, 'The Novel of the Modern Woman', 71.

importantly, in which women were offered images of articulacy and efforts at self-determination. Even if such 'New Woman' novelists did not reward such efforts with fairy-tale happy endings, thus emphasizing the struggles ahead, these fictions served, potentially, as confirmation of the fact that independently-minded women readers were not without others who thought and felt along the same lines.

Yet the 'New Woman' fiction was swiftly presented in the light of a *passé* publishing phenomenon. H. G. Wells, reviewing Hardy's *Jude the Obscure* in February 1896, was already eager to announce that 'it is now the better part of a year since the collapse of the "New Woman" fiction began'.[53] To some Edwardian writers, it seemed strange that it, and the novels of Ouida, say, should have provoked so much anxiety among the parents of growing daughters, whereas fifteen years later works dealing with adultery, mistresses, and seduction were relatively commonplace, and, many critics worried, provoked a demand for stronger stuff yet. 'It is no unusual thing to-day', wrote Basil Tozer in 1905, 'to hear women of a certain set asking one another what books they have read and can recommend that are "really *haut-goût*," a phrase meaning . . . books that verge as closely as possible upon the immoral'—confessing to reading, indeed, only the 'equivocal passages'.[54] The prolific popular novelist 'Rita' described how fashion switched to the 'society' novel, with its 'stamp of religion and mysticism; of sex frailty, and of strange cults; of odious vices and habits . . . a sauce *piquante* for jaded palates'.[55] Such works as Hubert Wales's *The Yoke* (1907), in which the forty-year-old Angelica chooses to sleep with Maurice, her attractive young ward, until he marries, in order to protect him from venereal disease, and Elinor Glyn's *Three Weeks* (1907), where the English heroine notoriously seduces the Arab sheikh on a tiger-skin, typified what was, on the surface, a new openness in writing about sexuality in popular fiction.[56]

'Victoria Cross' (Vivien Cory)'s *The Greater Law* (1914) shows how the topos of reading as educator could be woven into such works. But although, by this time, it had become a commonplace to show the woman taking the initiative, the choice of reading material indicates the underlying social conservatism of much of this superficially daring writing. Helena has had a child by the married man whom she loves: in order to please her family and bring the child up in respectability, she agrees to marry a young man who has been kept in a local asylum because of his apparent lack of any moral judgement, and his resultant susceptibility to any suggestion. As she comes to feel an increasing amount of romantic interest in him, she is afraid of making too overt a sexual move, in case this were to release, through suggestivity, uncontrollable erotomania. Rather,

53 H. G. Wells, *Saturday Review*, 81 (1896), 153.
54 Basil Tozer, 'The Increasing Popularity of the Erotic Novel', *Monthly Review*, 20 (1905), 54.
55 'Rita' [Eliza Margaret Humphreys] *Personal Opinions Publicly Expressed* (1907), 141–2.
56 See David Trotter, 'Edwardian Sex Novels', *Critical Quarterly*, 31 (1989), 92–105.

she makes an entirely successful attempt to develop his moral sense, hence turning him into the most desirable of handsome husbands. She puts love before him:

as it had always been to herself, something exquisite, pure, divine; a gift to this world straight from the hands of the gods. They read those books chiefly in which it is so portrayed. So does the image of love and passion stand out in white light in the pages of Plato and the Attic dramatists, and these were constantly in his hands.

Amongst the latter writers she chose out those for him in which there was depth and philosophical work, where the language was refined and the images beautiful, and filled a revolving bookcase in his room with the works of Milton, Victoria Cross and Bulwer Lytton.[57]

An attentive reader might well wonder whether Plato's writing was going to enable Hilda to make much headway with Clive, or could question the impact of Milton's portrayal of Eve. But such attentiveness is not invited, unless it is to note from the novel's very opening the narrator's approval of the ease with which Hilda knows her way around classical writers. Yet ultimately even here, woman is hardly reading for her own benefit, but to ensure that she can turn her classical knowledge into the apparatus through which to maintain traditional gender roles.

Although suffrage is unmentioned in the novel, *The Greater Law* can, appearing in 1914, be interpreted as a deliberately conservative gesture, on a par with Mrs Humphry Ward's *Delia Blanchflower* (1915), or W. Barton Baldry's *From Hampstead to Holloway* (1909), or Ford Madox Hueffer's *Mr Fleight* (1913). In each of these, the heroines, who come into direct contact with the suffrage movement, all recognize the errors of their ways. Their femininity reasserts itself against the representatives of this movement, who are inevitably presented as strident and shabbily dressed. It is not at all surprising, therefore, to find that it is in the relatively small handful of suffrage novels that the importance accorded to reading in 'New Woman' fiction finds its true immediate successor.

Reading, in these novels, is treated in a straightforward way. Since the emphasis falls on activity (speaking, marching, demonstrating, debating with those in one's domestic circle, going to prison), reading for pleasure or the general expansion of one's knowledge hardly figures at all. In Gertrude Colmore's documentary conversion novel *Suffragette Sally* (1911), it is referred to in order to add circumstantial detail to the mimetically realistic narrative, and employed with calculated didacticism. The maid-servant Sally is shown enthusiastically reading, and then helping to sell, *Votes for Women*. The novelist chronicles the combination of harassment and rewards of a day spent on a street corner, encountering a stream of reactions from 'the maiden ladies who spoke to each other of "these creatures" as they went by' to 'the timid woman who

[57] Victoria Cross [Vivien Cory] *The Greater Law* (1914), 272–3.

hastened past, paused, hesitated and scuttled back, thrust a penny into Sally's hand, murmured: "Just to see," and hid her *Votes for Women* under her coat'.[58]

Charlotte Despard and Mabel Collins's *Outlawed* (1908) shows Beryl, the heroine, to be a lover of liberty through her enthusiasm for Shelley and Mazzini, but in fact it is the 'gallant' procession of women whom she sees on her release from Holloway (where she has been imprisoned not for suffrage activities, but on a falsely premissed murder charge) which converts her to the Cause.[59] Likewise, in Constance Elizabeth Maud's *No Surrender* (1911), the upper-class woman, Alice Walker, can bear it no longer when she watches the procession of 'those pioneers down the ages who had fought for Freedom, Justice, and Truth in some form or another, whether in religion, politics, science or art': Joan of Arc, Miriam, Deborah, Sappho, Hypatia, Boadicea, Elizabeth Fry, Mary Wollstonecraft, Mrs Somerville, Vittoria Colonna, Jane Austen, George Sand, Charlotte and Emily Brontë, Elizabeth Barrett Browning, Angelica Kaufmann, Mme le Brun, Rosa Bonheur, and Florence Nightingale. She rushes down from the balcony where she had been watching, and falls in beside a woman who can only be Mrs Pankhurst:

> 'May I walk behind you? Do you mind?' she gasped out breathlessly.
> The kind grey eyes smiled down on this unexpected companion.
> 'Do, my dear—do walk with us. Where did you come from?'
> Alice fell into line as she answered with a little line which was almost a sob.
> 'I was looking on just as an outsider, till I couldn't bear being an outsider another minute—I want to belong!'[60]

In suffrage fiction, communal activity is represented as playing a far greater part in the establishment of feminist solidarity than the solitary occupation of reading.

Yet one should not forget the emphasis placed on the idea that women should read thoughtfully and critically, and act on what they learn, through the encouragement given by writers in *Votes for Women* and *The Vote*, as well as by certain other critics, particularly Rebecca West in the *Freewoman* (founded 1911) and the *New Freewoman* (founded 1913). These magazines strongly supported the suffrage whilst dealing with broader social and political issues as well.[61] Their writers laid the foundations for later twentieth-century feminist criticism, and they looked back to the 'New Woman' novelists as representing an important development, since they typified the fact, as Elizabeth Robins put

---

[58] Gertrude Colmore, *Suffragette Sally* (1911), 66.

[59] Mrs Despard and Mabel Collins, *Outlawed: A Novel on the Woman Suffrage Question* (1908), 300.

[60] Constance Elizabeth Maud, *No Surrender* (1911), 328.

[61] See the reviews collected in Jane Marcus (ed.), *The Young Rebecca: Writings of Rebecca West 1911–1917* (1982), 12–238: this also includes West's writings for the *Clarion*. West's pseudonym (she was born Cicily Isabel Fairfield) is borrowed from the name of the strong-minded heroine of Ibsen's *Romersholm* (1885–6): a conspicuous example of a real woman assuming identity *via* literary example.

it, that women writers were no longer playing the 'sedulous ape', imitating 'as nearly as possible the method, but above all the point of view, of man'.[62] Looking retrospectively, Robins complained about a lack of literature which celebrated womanhood not from a male perspective, but from an angle which acknowledged woman's range of capacities and interests. Many girls resent:

being put off with mere goody-goody, and variants of the Patient Griselda theme. They wish to hear about other girls who feel as they themselves feel, and who do some of the things they long to do.

The average woman, too, takes an interest in other women, and in other women's achievements—an interest which, in the average man, seems largely confined to the love-story. The woman likes the love-story too. But she knows very well that isn't all there is to be said about a woman's life.[63]

Addressing the League of Women Writers, Robins advocated more biographies and autobiographies which point roads to follow; which praise girls' 'courage, good temper, wit, resourcefulness, endurance' as do books for boys when extolling their heroes, and she looked forward to the women's writing of the future, which will fulfil the ancient Euripedean prophecy of a day when the old bards' stories

> Of frail brides and faithless shall be shrivelled as with fire,
>
> .   .   .   .
>
> And woman, yea, woman shall be terrible in story.
> The tales, too, meseemeth, shall be other than of yore
> For a fear there is that cometh out of women and a glory,
> And the hard hating voices shall encompass her no more.[64]

Robins had in mind not just readers of the present, but of the future. The writers whom she addresses, in representing woman as they perceive her, will be writing: 'So that her children's children reading her story shall be lifted up—proud and full of hope. 'Of such stuff,' they shall say, 'our mothers were! Sweethearts and wives—yes, and other things besides: leaders, discoverers, militants, fighting every form of wrong.'[65]

By the 1890s, no longer were forbidden books the main issue in themselves, despite Rossi's picture, and despite the querulous complaints of some reviewers

---

[62] Elizabeth Robins, 'Women Writers', *Way Stations* (1913), 5. Originally published by the WSPU as a pamphlet entitled 'Woman's Secret', this important piece of feminist criticism outlines the reasons why women writers so frequently adopt the standards and techniques of dominant male literary forms: their publishers, critics, and readers are men; money and reputation are vested in men. Robins then describes how standards of literary judgement differ, since books written by women are universally presumed to bear some reference to her actual experience, whereas breadth of emotion and action in male writing is attributed, more desirably, to a powerful imagination.

[63] Elizabeth Robins, 'The Women Writers', *Way Stations* (1913), 233–4. This paper was originally given at the Criterion, 23 May 1911, and was printed in *Votes for Women*, 4 (30 June 1911), 639.

[64] Ibid. 235.   [65] Ibid. 236.

and journalists. Ella Hepworth Dixon included freer access to reading material among her catalogue of social changes affecting young women's lives when she wrote in 1899:

If young and pleasing women are permitted by public opinion to go to college, to live alone, to travel, to have a profession, to belong to a club, to give parties, to read and discuss whatsoever seems good to them, and to go to theatres without masculine escort, they have most of the privileges—and others thrown in—for which the girl of twenty or thirty years ago was ready to barter herself for the first suitor who offered himself and the shelter of his name.[66]

Rather, what counted was the development of writers' perceptions about the relationship between fictional texts and the society of their readers, and the ways in which readers could be invited to use similar techniques when approaching both novels and their lives. What, further, is particularly significant about 'New Woman' fiction, for the purposes of this study, is the degree to which it denied what so much of the theory surrounding women's reading insisted upon: the interdependency of mind and body. Earlier in the century, the restrictions placed upon the woman reader, the anxieties surrounding her reading (so frequently couched in terms of concern for her body) resembled a means of controlling her physical responses. The dangerous frissons of excitement which she might obtain from certain texts rendered her vulnerable at best to accusations of frivolity, and they might, it was thought, send her at worst in search of more tangible pleasures. But by the 1890s, these anxieties and prohibitions were directed towards, among other things, attempts to control her conscious *knowledge* of sexuality: her understanding of its threats, and its role within patriarchal society, as well as its delights. Many of the strictures, like the strictures earlier in the century, rely on the unquestioned assumption that reading is a subjective, identificatory process, and that the majority of women readers lack the power to perform the very act which, as we have seen, the reading of much Victorian women's fiction demands: commenting on the body through the mind. Whilst, as we have noted, these novels frequently encouraged recognition between consumer and character, thus implicitly appealing to certain structures of desire, they also could stress the importance of knowledge, of rationality, and of critical alertness in reading.

Above all, as I mentioned above, readers were encouraged to apply the criteria that they would emply when reading a novel to the society around them. When the model for interpreting non-literary texts and scenarios was a romance or fantasy one, such a project could only lead to misinterpretation and relative catastrophe, as Henry James dramatized in *In the Cage* (1898). Here, the unnamed heroine devours novels, 'very greasy, in fine print and all about fine folks, at a ha'penny a day'.[67] She prides herself on 'her gift for keeping the clues

---

[66] Ella Hepworth Dixon, 'Why women are Ceasing to Marry', *Humanitarian*, 14 (1899), 394.
[67] Henry James, *In the Cage* (1898; repr. Harmondsworth, 1972), 11.

and finding her way in the tangle' as she pieces together fragments about the society women and men who send telegrams through the office where she works. This is done by means of the literal scraps of text which they give her, 'and she read into the immensity of their intercourse stories without end'.[68] Her error is to trust that her mastery of her favourite fictions means that she can enter confidently into the lives of her customers.[69] But when fiction, such as that by New Women novelists, suggests that reading may be a route to gaining crucial knowledge rather than escaping from social realities, it encourages the interpretation of society in quite a different light.

[68] Ibid. 23.

[69] For an excellent extended reading of this novella which brings out the theme of reading within it, see Jolly, *History and Fiction*, 112–32.

Part V

20. *Carte de visite: Mrs Coventry Patmore*

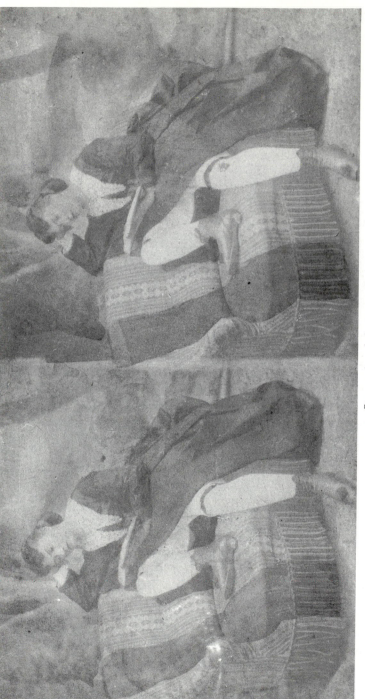

21. *Stereoscopic card of woman reader*

12   Conclusion

Two photographs present two entirely differing aspects of the woman reader (Figs 20 and 21). In the first, a respectably dressed middle-aged lady poses for the camera, reading a book which functions as a sign in a variety of ways. It suggests class status, proclaiming that she has leisure time enough to read. We have the choice of believing that it holds spiritual or practical advice on which she is pondering; factual knowledge which she is absorbing; or that the woman is appreciating the beauties of the literary sentiments which it contains. Emphatically, this is not reading for escapist relaxation, since even the option of reposing on a straight-backed chair has been eschewed. Although the lace mantilla suggests a devotional volume, the book might, plausibly enough, be a volume of poetry, since the woman in question is Mrs Coventry Patmore.[1] Here, indeed, is the proof that a book is a perfectly appropriate prop for the Victorian Angel in the House.

The other image, however, proclaims no such message of respectability. This stereoscopic card may well be French in provenance, something which would only underline still further the message that French literature is a dangerously corrupting force. But the intention in this case is not to warn, like the stern voice of the governess in *Sybil Lennard*, but to titillate. The woman is respectably enough dressed; her hair is tied neatly back, she wears a plain dark dress with a white lace collar, and robust lace-up boots. Her features could best be described as homely and sensible: above the waist, she is, as she concentrates on her reading, a model of propriety, the pattern, even, of a governess. Her absorption in her reading suggests a fictitious oblivion of what is going on below the waist, for in fact, her dress is swept back, revealing her substantial, white-stockinged legs and the touch which gives away the calculatedly inviting nature of the pose, a pair of pink garters. The fact that the positioning of her legs is reminiscent of the posture a woman would adopt when riding side-saddle rather than when lolling on a sofa offers a further pointer to her potential for activity, even control and domination.

The book that improves the spiritual or moral condition of the reader, confirming, rather than challenging assumptions about her social role, and the provocative book which stimulates sexual impulses: these are the two polarized stereotypes of women's reading in the Victorian and Edwardian periods. The images we have just been considering dramatize two types of scopophilia (as

[1] Although not, I think, Coventry Patmore's first wife, Emilia Augusta Andrews, but the second Mrs Patmore, the Catholic, Marianne Caroline Byles, whom Patmore married in 1864, following the death of his first wife two years earlier.

defined by Freud in his *Three Essays on Sexuality*, where, taking scopophilia as one of the component instincts of sexuality which exists independently of the erotic zones, he associates it with the practice of taking others as objects and subjecting them to a controlling, and inquisitive gaze).[2] In the first instance, the image, or the idea, of the woman reader is fetishistic, reassuring rather than dangerous, ensuring that woman is contained within recognized domestic categories. Our postulations about her own reading serve to confirm the image which we see, ensuring that it exists outside of linear time, that it represents an enduring ideal. On the other hand the second image, of the girl on the sofa, invites a voyeuristic reading. It presumes a narrative, whether of corruption and transgression or of redemption and forgiveness: either is dependent on the establishment of guilt, hence reinforcing the spectator's sense of control.[3]

Yet between these two types of image of the woman reader fall a range of further alternatives, many dramatized, in their turn, by the *carte de visite*. In these, books can function as props in the most literal of senses (Fig. 22), mere parts of the furnishings of the home; they are a means of uniting a mother with her daughters, sharing stories or educating them (Fig. 23); they co-join wife and husband (Fig. 24). Women glance at the photographer as though he is a more interesting distraction than the illustrated volume open on their lap (Fig. 25); or seem reluctant to be interrupted by him (Fig. 26); or refuse to register him at all, either because they are absorbed in their reading (Fig. 27), or apparently lost in the contemplation of its implications, locked into their own reverie, their own mental space, day-dreaming of romance or mentally following the journey of a pioneering woman explorer. Further images have throughout this study been compiled from other sources: the servant who, as in William Hay's picture of 1868, abandons her housework for the lures of fiction (Fig. 28); the self-improver, copying extracts into her commonplace book and looking up unfamiliar words in the dictionary; the spinster surrounded by ostentatiously worthy feminist volumes or the 'New Woman' with Ibsen in hand; the self-educator, translating Latin texts, learning astronomy, or reading Gibbon. It is impossible to speak of the woman reader as though she ever held a consistent, stable identity: she is herself fragmented both into many sets of rhetorical patterns, each serving particular ideological ends, and into an endless variety of actual reading practices. In the face of this, the question 'what difference does the hypothesis of a woman reader make to our understanding of the writings of this period?' also, inevitably, disintegrates.

What are the implications of this? Does the recognition of the heterogeneity of the woman reader add up to no more than the common-sense statement that

---

[2] Freud, *Three Essays on the History of Sexuality* (1905), *Pelican Freud Library*, 7, 69–70.

[3] I have drawn heavily in this paragraph on the positions advanced by Laura Mulvey in her article 'Visual Pleasure and Narrative Cinema', *Screen*, 16 (1975; repr. Constance Penley (ed.), *Feminism and Film Theory* (1988), 57–68), esp. 64.

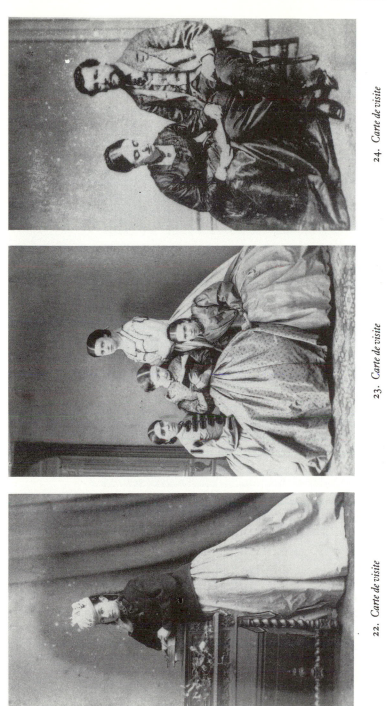

22. *Carte de visite*

23. *Carte de visite*

24. *Carte de visite*

27. *Carte de visite*

26. *Carte de visite*

25. *Carte de visite*

28. William Hay, *A Funny Story*, (1868)

we are all different,[4] therefore each of us has different reading experiences: another example of currently fashionable anti-essentialist feminist criticism? To some extent, this is true. The variety of evidence put forward in this book demonstrates that despite the recurrence of certain stereotypes throughout the period, and the way in which these stereotypes functioned to determine attitudes about reading in the home, in education, and in the provision of public library facilities which would serve a growing number of readers, individuals frequently read across the grain of such expectations. On occasion they explicitly recognized them and deliberately challenged them from within. By the 1890s, a relatively small, but growing number of novels, such as Ethel M. Arnold's *Platonics* (1894), Edith Johnstone's *A Sunless Heart* (1894), and Emma Frances Brooke's *Transition* (1895), had begun to exploit the fact that not every woman's primary sexual orientation is a heterosexual one, a factor which destabilizes yet further the ease with which one may write of 'the woman reader'. Additionally, I have not had the space to do more than touch on the ways in which patterns of identification or resistance in relation to their reading material might differ between a Yorkshirewoman and a woman from London; a girl of sixteen or a grandmother of sixty; a governess or an iron-manufacturer's wife; a young woman who has been educated at home and 'finished' in Switzerland or a product of a high school and Girton. Each of these readers might be imagined, providing a means to interrogate a text and its assumptions, a hypothetical position which can help to lay bare the ideological structuring of a nineteenth- or early twentieth-century work. Such a hypothetical reader simultaneously functions as a necessary reminder that the question of gender in reading cannot be considered apart from questions of class, of education, of religious belief, and of other social and ethnic factors.

Yet may the question of a 'woman reader' not be a question of positionality, as I argued in Chapter 2, rather than an issue which invites one to consider the materiality of individual readers, as I have just been doing? Yes and no. For from one point of view, 'Readers, like texts, are constructed; they inhabit reading practices rather than create them *ex nihilo*', as Diana Fuss has put it with admirable clarity. Such practices develop, as she also notes, according to historic and cultural variables: this book supports her assertion that there is no

---

[4] See Eve Kosofsky Sedgwick, *Epistemology of the Closet* (Berkeley, Calif., and Los Angeles, Calif., 1990), 22, where she glosses her axiom *'People are different from each other'*: 'It is astonishing how few respectable conceptual tools we have for dealing with this self-evident fact. A tiny number of inconceivably coarse axes of categorization have been painstakingly inscribed in current critical political thought: gender, race, class, nationality, sexual orientation are pretty much the available distinctions. They, with the associated demonstrations of the mechanisms by which they are constructed and reproduced, are indispensable, and they may indeed override all or some other forms of difference and similarity. But the sister or brother, the best friend, the classmate, the parent, the child, the lover, the ex-: our families, loves, and enmities alike, not to mention the strange relations of our work, play, and activism, prove that even people who share all or most of our own positionings along these crude axes may still be different enough from us, and from each other, to seem like all but different species.'

such thing as a 'natural' way to read a text.[5] One might, therefore, plausibly argue that the practice of nineteenth- and early twentieth-century women readers had nothing to do with their biological sexuality, but rather with the demands particular texts made upon them; with the expectations which they internalized or withstood, and with the modes of reading which they consciously employed. These resulted, in their turn, from the differing discourses in which the topic of reading and gender were encountered during this period.

But, as with any conclusion which attempts to link ideological criticism with psychoanalytic considerations, this acknowledgement of constructed positionality is not sufficient, partly since it fails to address, perhaps inevitably, the mechanisms through which any particular individual may come to accept or question ideological assumptions. In any case, the conclusions I am advancing cannot ultimately be said to be anti-essentialist, since they are predicated on the fact that recognizing herself *as* woman when she reads, and hence acknowledging, even if seeking to transform, the social circumstances which the woman reader must inevitably negotiate, was a crucial form of self-affirmation during this period.

Two self-portraits by Gwen John, *A Lady Reading* (1910–11) and *Girl Reading at the Window* (1911) (Figs. 29 and 30) can be used to symbolize the woman reader's growth in self-confidence. In the first of these, the figure stands in a sombre, sparse room, her reading apparently confirming the sense of self-enclosure emanated by her physical surroundings. I termed the painting a self-portrait, but in fact Gwen John refused to give the woman's figure her own face. 'I tried to make it look like a vierge of Durer, it was a very silly thing to do', she wrote to a friend. 'I did it because I did not want to have my own face there.'[6] But in the second work, the artist is no longer afraid of being the object of her own gaze as she reads. Moreover, although she is still totally absorbed in the small fat volume which she holds, she is turned towards the window. The outside world is no longer blocked by a check curtain, but a thin gauze veil is the only filter for the light which comes into the room, lifting the heavy ochre colour of the earlier painting into a lighter, more optimistic pale yellow. The painting is narcissistic, but not claustrophobically so: that unpaintable gap between woman as painter and the reading woman (for how can one paint with accuracy what one looks like when one's eyes are averted from one's own gaze?) is a gap of self-reflection, in both senses of the term.

Reading, in the Victorian and Edwardian period, as now, was an activity through which a woman could become aware of the simultaneity of the sensations of difference and of similarity. Moreover, her own reading could seldom fail to make it clear to her that her own choice of reading position

[5] Diana Fuss, *Essentially Speaking* (1989), 35.
[6] Gwen John to Ursula Tyrwhitt, 1 Oct. [probably 1911], quoted by Cecily Langdon, *Gwen John* (New Haven, Conn., and London, 1987), 141.

29. Gwen John, *A Lady Reading*, (1910–11)

30. Gwen John, *Girl Reading at the Window*, (1911)

(where to differ, where to acknowledge a bond) was, in the broadest sense, a political choice. Reading, in other words, provided the means not only, on occasion, for the Victorian woman to abnegate the self, to withdraw into the passivity enduced by the opiate of fiction. Far more excitingly, it allowed her to assert her sense of selfhood, and to know that she was not alone in doing so.

We are left with a problematic relationship: one between theories concerning the formation of the individual subject, and the part which reading may play in this, and the positioning of this same subject within, and against, both dominant and oppositional discourses which theories of reading simultaneously drew upon and informed. This is not a relationship in which the two sides can be dissolved into one another, although it is one in which the continually shifting terms can be described. The practice of reading, at once pointing inwards and outwards, to the psychological and the socio-cultural, is an ideal site for the examination of this intersection of Victorian, Edwardian, and contemporary preoccupations: bodies, minds, and texts.

Bibliography

PERIODICALS

Academy
All The Year Round
Athenaeum
Belgravia
Blackwood's Edinburgh Magazine
Chambers' Journal
Child-Study
Christian Remembrancer
Church of England Quarterly Review
Contemporary Review
Cornhill Magazine
Eclectic and Congregational Review
Englishwoman
Englishwoman's Review
Foreign Quarterly Review
Fortnightly Review
Fraser's Magazine for Town and Country
Galaxy
Girl's Own Paper
Graphic
Humanitarian
Illustrated Family Novelist
Illustrated London News
Journal of the Women's Education Union
Lancet
Library
Library Journal
London Journal
Macmillan's Magazine
Magdalen's Friend and Female Homes Intelligencer
Medical Critic and Psychological Journal
Monthly Review
National Review
Nineteenth Century
North British Review
Our Mothers and Daughters
Princess's Novelettes
Provincial Medical Journal

Quarterly Review
Review of Reviews
Saturday Review
Shafts
Spectator
Temple Bar
The Times
T. P. 's Weekly
Victoria Magazine
Vote
Votes for Women
Welcome Guest
Wesleyan-Methodist Magazine
Westminster Review
Woman at Home
Young Woman

BOOKS AND ARTICLES

Place of publication of books is London unless otherwise indicated

History and Theory of Reading

ALLESTREE, R., *The Ladies Calling. In two parts* (Oxford, 1673).
ALTICK, RICHARD D., *The English Common Reader* (1957; repr. 1963).
BACON, FRANCIS, 'Of Studies', *The Essayes or Counsels, Civill and Morall*, ed. Michael Kiernan (Oxford, 1985), 152–4.
BALSILLIE, DAVID, *The National Home Reading Union* (Edinburgh, 1889).
BARNICOAT, CONSTANCE A., 'The Reading of the Colonial Girl', *Nineteenth Century*, 60 (1906), 939–50.
BOSANQUET, HELEN, 'Cheap Literature', *Contemporary Review*, 79 (1901), 671–81.
BRADDON, M. E., 'My Daughters', *Welcome Guest*, 3 (1861), 79–82.
BROWNSTEIN, RACHEL M., *Becoming a Heroine* (1982; repr. Harmondsworth, 1984).
BURKE, KENNETH, *The Philosophy of Literary Form* (Berkeley, Calif., 1973).
CHISHOLM, HUGH, 'How to Counteract the "Penny Dreadful"', *Fortnightly Review*, NS 58 (1895), 765–75.
COLLINS, CHARLES ALLSTON, 'Our Audience', *Macmillan's Magazine*, 8 (1863), 161–6.
CULLER, JONATHAN, *On Deconstruction: Theory and Criticism after Structuralism* (1982).
DAWSON, Captain, *Give Attention to Reading: A Talk on the Reading of Books* (1892).
'DECEM' [Edward Dowden], 'Fiction and its Uses', *Fraser's Magazine* 72 (1865), 746–60.
'DOUBLEDAY' [Alfred Ainger], 'Books and their Uses', *Macmillan's Magazine*, 1 (1859), 110–13.
ELLIS, Mrs (ed.), *The Young Ladies' Reader* (1845).
FLYNN, ELIZABETH A., 'Gender and Reading', *College English*, 45 (1983), 236–53.

GOSSE, EDMUND, 'The Tyranny of the Novel', *National Review*, 19 (1892), 163–75.

GREG, W. R., 'False Morality of Lady Novelists', *National Review*, 8 (1859), 144–67.

HAKE, EDWARD, *A Touchestone for this time present . . . Whereunto is annexed a perfect rule to be observed of all Parents and Scholemaisters, in the trayning up of their Schollers and Children in learning* (1574).

HARDY, THOMAS, 'The Profitable Reading of Fiction', first published *Forum* (1888); repr. *Life and Art* (New York, 1925), 56–74.

HASLAM, JAMES, *The Press and the People: An Estimate of Reading in Working-Class Districts* (Manchester, 1906).

HITCHMAN, FRANCIS, 'Penny Fiction', *Quarterly Review*, 171 (1890), 150–71.

HOLLAND, NORMAN, *The Dynamics of Literary Response* (New York, 1968).

HUEY, E. B., *The Psychology and Pedagogy of Reading* (Boston, 1908).

'LEE, VERNON' [Violet Paget], 'A Dialogue on Novels', *Contemporary Review*, 48 (1885), 378–401.

LOW, FLORENCE B., 'The Reading of the Modern Girl', *Nineteenth Century*, 59 (1906), 278–87.

LUCAS, CAROLINE, *Writing for Women: The Example of Woman as Reader in Elizabethan Romance* (Milton Keynes and Bristol, Pa, 1989).

MAXWELL, HERBERT, 'The Craving for Fiction', *Nineteenth Century*, 33 (1893), 1046–61.

MITCHELL, SALLY, 'Sentiment and Suffering: Women's Recreational Reading in the 1860s', *Victorian Studies*, 21 (1977), 29–45.

—— *The Fallen Angel: Chastity, Class and Women's Reading 1835–1880* (Bowling Green, Ohio, 1981).

OLIPHANT, MARGARET, 'The Byways of Literature: Reading for the Million', *Blackwood's Edinburgh Magazine*, 84 (1858), 200–16.

—— 'Novels', *Blackwood's Edinburgh Magazine*, 102 (1867), 257–80.

PALGRAVE, F. T., 'On Readers in 1760 and 1860', *Macmillan's Magazine*, 1 (1860), 487–9.

PAYN, JAMES, 'Penny Fiction', *Nineteenth Century*, 9 (1881), 145–54.

'Penny Novels', *Macmillan's Magazine*, 14 (1866), 96–105.

—— *Spectator* (18 Mar. 1863), 1806–8.

RADWAY, JANICE, *Reading the Romance: Women, Patriarchy, and Popular Literature* (Chapel Hill, NC, 1984).

REEVE, CLARA, *The Progress of Romance*, 2 vols. (1785).

RIDDING, Lady Laura, *et al.*, 'What Should Women Read?', *The Woman at Home*, 37 (1896), 29–32.

ROSENBLATT, LOUISE' *The Reader, the Text, the Poem: The Transactional Theory of the Literary Work* (Carbondale, Ill., 1978).

'S', 'What is the Harm of Novel-reading?', *Wesleyan-Methodist Magazine*, 78 (1855), 932–4.

SALMON, EDWARD G., 'What Boys Read', *Fortnightly Review*, NS 39 (1886), 248–59.

—— 'What Girls Read', *Nineteenth Century*, 20 (1886), 515–29.

—— 'What the Working Classes Read', *Nineteenth Century*, 20 (1886), 108–17.

SALTER, THOMAS, *A Mirrhor mete for all Mothers, Matrones, and Maidens, intituled the Mirrhor of Modestie* (1574).

SCHWEICKART, PATROCINIO P., 'Reading Ourselves: Toward a Feminist Theory of Reading', in Elizabeth A. Flynn and Patrocinio P. Schweickart (eds.), *Gender and Reading: Essays on Readers, Texts, and Contexts* (Baltimore, Md. and London, 1986), 31–62.

STRAHAN, [ALEXANDER], 'Bad Literature for the Young', *Contemporary Review*, 26 (1875), 981–91.

SOULSBY, LUCY, *Stray Thoughts on Reading* (1895).

SOULSBY, LUCY H. M., *Record of a Year's Reading* (1903).

SULEIMAN, SUSAN R., and CROSMAN, INGE (eds.), *The Reader in the Text: Essays on Audience and Interpretation* (Princeton, NJ, 1980).

'T. C.', 'Novel Reading: A Letter to a Young Lady', *Christian's Penny Magazine and Friend of the People*, 14 (1859), 155–6.

TOMPKINS, JANE P. (ed.), *Reader-Response Criticism: From Formalism to Post-Structuralism* (Baltimore, Md. and London, 1980).

VIVES, JUAN LUIS, *The Instruction of a Christian Woman* (trans. Richard Hyrde *c.*1540), repr. in *Vives and the Renascence Education of Women*, Foster Watson ed. (1912).

WELLDON, J. E. C., 'The Art of Reading Books', *National Review*, 23 (1894), 213–18.

WILLMOTT, R. A., 'Book-Love', *Fraser's Magazine for Town and Country*, 36 (1847), 199–203.

WOLLSTONECRAFT, MARY, *Vindication of the Rights of Women* (1792; repr. Harmondsworth, 1975).

'A Working Woman', 'Do Public Libraries Foster a Love of Literature Among the Masses?' *Chambers' Journal*, 6th ser. 3 (1899), 134–6.

WRIGHT, J. J., *So Many Books! So Little Time! What to Do?* (Birmingham, 1892).

YATES, MARGARITA, 'Do Our Girls Take an Interest in Literature?' *Monthly Review*, 23 (1906), 120–32.

YONGE, Miss, 'Children's Literature, Part III: Class Literature of the Last Thirty Years', *Macmillan's Magazine*, 20 (1869), 448–56.

YONGE, CHARLOTTE M., *What Books to Lend and What to Give* (1887).

Literary Criticism

ALLOTT, MIRIAM. (ed.), *The Brontës: The Critical Heritage* (1974).

ARDIS, ANN, *New Women, New Novels: Feminism and Early Modernism* (1990).

ARMSTRONG, NANCY, *Desire and Domestic Fiction: A Political History of the Novel* (New York and Oxford, 1987).

—— and TENNENHOUSE, LEONARD (eds.), *The Ideology of Conduct: Essays on Literature and the History of Sexuality* (1987).

ARNOLD, MATTHEW, 'The Study of Poetry', introd. to *The English Poets: Selections with Critical Introductions*, ed. Thomas Humphry Ward (1880).

AUSTIN, ALFRED, 'Our Novels: The Fast School', *Temple Bar*, 29 (1870), 177–94.

—— 'Our Novels: The Sensational School', *Temple Bar*, 29 (1870), 410–24.

AVERY, GILLIAN, *Childhood's Pattern: A Study of the Heroes and Heroines of Children's Fiction, 1770–1950* (1975).

BARTHES, ROLAND, *The Pleasure of the Text*, trans. Richard Miller (1976).

BESANT, WALTER, LINTON, E. LYNN, and HARDY, THOMAS, 'Candour in English Fiction', *New Review*, 2 (1890), 6–21.

BOUMELHA, PENNY, *Thomas Hardy and Women* (1982).

BRANTLINGER, PATRICK, 'What is "Sensational" about the Sensation Novel?', *Nineteenth-Century Fiction*, 37 (1982), 1–28.

BRATTON, J. S., *The Impact of Victorian Children's Fiction* (1975).

BRISTOW, JOSEPH, *Empire Boys: Adventures in a Man's World* (1991).

BRODZSKI, BELLA, and SCHENCK, CELESTE, 'Introduction', *Life/Lines: Theorizing Women's Autobiography* (Ithaca, NY, and London, 1988), 1–15.

BROOKS, PETER, *The Melodramatic Imagination: Balzac, Henry James, Melodrama, and the Mode of Excess* (New Haven, Conn., 1976).

CADOGAN, MARY, and CRAIG, PATRICIA, *You're a Brick, Angela! The Girls' Story 1839–1985* (1986).

COE, RICHARD, *When the Grass was Taller: Autobiography and the Experience of Childhood* (New Haven, Conn., 1984).

COHN, JAN, *Romance and the Erotics of Property: Mass-Market Fiction for Women* (Durham, NC, 1985).

CORTNEY, W. L., *The Feminine Note in Fiction* (1904).

CUNNINGHAM, GAIL, *The New Woman and the Victorian Novel* (1978).

DARTON, F. J. HARVEY, *Children's Books in England: Five Centuries of Social Life* (3rd edn. rev. Brian Alderson, Cambridge, 1958).

DE BOLLA, PETER, *The Discourse of the Sublime: History, Aesthetics and the Subject* (Oxford, 1989).

DECKER, CLARENCE R., 'Balzac's Literary Reputation in Victorian Society', *PMLA* 47/2 (1932), 1150–7.

DICKENS, CHARLES, 'The Sensational Williams', *All the Year Round*, 11 (1864), 14–16.

DOUGHAN, DAVID, and SANCHEZ, DENISE, *Feminist Periodicals 1855–1984: An Annotated Critical Bibliography of British, Irish, Commonwealth and International Titles* (Brighton, 1987).

DOWLING, LINDA, 'The Decadent and the New Woman in the 1890s', *Nineteenth-Century Fiction*, 33 (1979), 434–53.

ELIOT, GEORGE, 'The Natural History of German Life', *Westminster Review*, NS 10 (1856), 51–79.

FAHNESTOCK, JEANNE, 'Bigamy: The Rise and Fall of a Convention', *Nineteenth-Century Fiction*, 36 (1981), 47–71.

FELSKI, RITA, *Beyond Feminist Aesthetics: Feminist Literature and Social Change* (1989).

FLINT, KATE, 'Trollope and Sexual Politics', introd. to Anthony Trollope, *Can You Forgive Her?* (1864–5; repr. Oxford, 1982), pp. xv–xxx.

—— 'Reading the New Woman', *Browning Society Notes*, 17 (1987–8), 55–63.

FRIEDMAN, SUSAN STANFORD, 'Women's Autobiographical Selves: Theory and Practice', in S. Benstock (ed.), *The Private Self: Theory and Practice of Women's Autobiographical Writings* (1988), 34–62.

GAGNIER, REGENIA, *Subjectivities: A History of Self-Representation in Britain* (New York and Oxford, 1991).

GALLAWAY, W. F., Jr., 'The Conservative Attitude Toward Fiction, 1770–1830', *PMLA* 55 (1940), 1041–59.

GARDINER, JUDITH KEGAN, 'On Female Identity and Writing by Women', *Critical Inquiry*, 8 (1981), 347–61.

GRAHAM, KENNETH, *English Criticism of the Novel 1865–1900* (Oxford, 1965).

GREG, PERCY, 'Mr Trollope's Novels', *National Review*, 7 (1858), 416–35.

GREG, W. R., 'False Morality of Lady Novelists', *National Review*, 8 (1859), 144–67.

—— 'French Fiction: The Lowest Deep', *National Review*, 11 (1860), 400–27.

HAYS, MARY, *Letters and Essays, Moral and Miscellaneous* (1793).

HENNELLY, MARK, 'Jane Eyre's Reading Lesson', *English Literary History*, 51 (1984), 693–717.

HEY, VALERIE, 'The Necessity of Romance', *Women's Studies Occasional Papers*, 3 (1983).

HOBBY, ELAINE, *Virtue of Necessity: English Women's Writing 1649–88* (1988).

HOWARTH, WILLIAM L., 'Some Principles of Autobiography', in *Autobiography: Essays Theoretical and Critical*, ed. James Olney (Princeton, NJ, 1980), 84–114.

HUGHES, WINIFRED, *The Maniac in the Cellar: Sensation Novels of the 1860s* (Princeton, NJ, 1980).

HULL, SUZANNE, *Chaste, Silent and Obedient: English Books for Women, 1475–1640* (San Marino, Calif., 1982).

JACOBUS, MARY, *Reading Woman* (1986).

JAMES, HENRY, *Notes and Reviews* (Cambridge, Mass., 1921).

JAMES, LOUIS, *Fiction for the Working Man 1830–50: A Study of the Literature Produced for the Working Classes in Early Victorian Urban England* (1963; repr. Harmondsworth, 1974).

—— 'The Trouble with Betsy: Periodicals and the Common Reader in Mid-Nineteenth-Century England', in Joanne Shattock and Michael Wolff (eds.), *The Victorian Periodical Press: Samplings and Soundings* (Leicester, 1982), 349–66.

JELINEK, ESTELLE C., 'Introduction: Women's Autobiography and the Male Tradition', in ead. (ed.), *Women's Autobiography: Essays in Criticism* (Bloomington, Ind., and London, 1980), 1–20.

JOLLY, ROSLYN, 'History and Fiction: Modes of Narrative in the Works of Henry James', (D. Phil. thesis, Univ. of Oxford, 1990).

JONES, ANN ROSALIND, 'Nets and Bridles: Early Modern Conduct Books and Sixteenth-Century Women's Lyrics', in Nancy Armstrong and Leonard Tennenhouse (eds.), *The Ideology of Conduct: Essays on Literature and the History of Sexuality* (1987), 39–72.

KELSO, RUTH, *The Doctrine for the Lady of the Renaissance* (Urban, Ill., 1956, 1978).

KINGSLEY, CHARLES, 'On English Literature': Introductory Lecture given at Queen's College London, 1848, *The Works of Charles Kingsley*, xx. *Literary and General Lectures and Essays* (1880), 245–65.

KNOX, VICESIMUS, *Essays Moral and Literary*, 3 vols. (Basle and Strasburg, 1800).

KRISTEVA, JULIA, 'The Adolescent Novel', in John Fletcher and Andrew Benjamin (eds.), *Abjection, Melancholia and Love: The Work of Julia Kristeva* (1990), 8–23.

'Lady Novelists', *Eclectic and Congregational Review*, 15 (1868), 300–15.

LAMB, MARGARET, *'Antony and Cleopatra' on the English Stage* (Toronto and London, 1980).

LEVINE, PHILIPPA, ' "The Humanising Influences of Five O'Clock Tea": Victorian Feminist Periodicals', *Victorian Studies*, 33 (1990), 293–306.

LEWES, G. H., 'Balzac and George Sand', *Foreign Quarterly Review*, 33 (1844), 265–98.

—— 'Ruth and Villette', *Westminster Review*, 59 (1853), 474–91.

—— 'Our Survey of Literature and Science', *Cornhill Magazine*, 7 (1863), 132–9.

LOESBERG, JONATHAN, 'The Ideology of Narrative Form in Sensation Fiction', *Representations*, 13 (1986), 115–8.

'M', 'French Novels', *Belgravia*, 3 (1867), 78–82.

MACCARTHY, JUSTIN, 'Novels with a Purpose', *Westminster Review*, 82 (1864), 24–49.

MARCUS, JANE, 'Invincible Mediocrity: The Private Selves of Public Women', in Shari Benstock (ed.), *The Private Self: Theory and Practice of Women's Autobiographical Writings* (1988), 114–46.

MARTIN, ROBERT K., 'Jane Eyre and the World of Faery', *Mosaic*, 10 (1977), 85–95.

MILLER, D. A., '*Cage aux Folles*: Sensation and Gender in Wilkie Collins's *The Woman in White*', in Jeremy Hawthorn (ed.), *The Nineteenth-Century British Novel* (1986), 94–124.

MILLER, NANCY K., *Subject to Change: Reading Feminist Writing* (New York, 1988).

MODLESKI, TANIA, *Loving with a Vengeance* (1982).

MOORE, GEORGE, 'A New Censorship of Literature', *Pall Mall Gazette* (10 Dec. 1884), 2.

—— *Literature at Nurse, or Circulating Morals* (1885).

'Moral and Political Tendency of the Modern Novels', *Church of England Quarterly Review*, 11 (1842), 286–310.

MORAWSKI, STEFAN, *Inquiries into the Fundamentals of Aesthetics* (Cambridge, Mass., 1974).

MULOCK, DINAH, 'To Novelists – and a Novelist', *Macmillan's Magazine*, 3 (1861), 441–8.

MULVEY, LAURA, 'Visual Pleasure and Narrative Cinema', *Screen*, 16 (1975); repr. Constance Penley (ed.) *Feminism and Film Theory* (1988), 57–68.

—— 'Notes on Sirk and Melodrama', *Movie*, 25 (1977–8); repr. Christine Gledhill (ed.), *Home is Where the Heart Is: Studies in Melodrama and the Woman's Film* (1987), 75–9.

MYERS, MITZI, ' "A Taste for Truth and Reading": Early Advice to Mothers on Books for Girls', *Children's Literature Association Quarterly*, 12 (1987), 118–24.

—— '*Harriet Martineau's Autobiography*: The Making of a Female Philosopher', in Estelle C. Jelinek (ed.), *Women's Autobiography: Essays in Criticism* (Bloomington, Ind. and London, 1980, 53–70.

MYERS, SYLVIE HARSTACK, *The Bluestocking Circle: Women, Friendship, and the Life of the Mind in Eighteenth-Century England* (Oxford, 1990).

NOBLE, JAMES ASHCROFT, 'The Fiction of Sexuality', *Contemporary Review*, 67 (1895), 490–8.

'Not a New "Sensation" ', *All the Year Round*, 9 (1863), 517–20.

OGDEN, C. K., *Bentham's Theory of Fictions* (1932).

OLIPHANT, MARGARET, 'Modern Novelists – Great and Small', *Blackwood's Edinburgh Magazine*, 77 (1855), 554–68.

—— 'Novels', *Blackwood's Edinburgh Magazine*, 102 (1867), 257–80.

'Our Female Sensation Novelists', *Christian Remembrancer*, NS 46 (1863), 209–36.

PETERSON, CARLA L. *The Determined Reader: Gender and Culture in the Novel from Napoleon to Victoria* (New Brunswick, 1986).

POOVEY, MARY, *The Proper Lady and the Woman Writer: Ideology as Style in the Works of Mary Wollstonecraft, Mary Shelley, and Jane Austen* (Chicago, 1984).

—— *Uneven Developments: The Ideological Work of Gender in Mid-Victorian England* (Chicago, 1988).

QUALLS, BARRY, *The Secular Pilgrims of Victorian Fiction* (1982).

RAE, W. FRASER, 'Sensation Novelists: Miss Braddon', *North British Review*, 43, NS 4 (1865), 180–205.

REPPLIER, AGNES, *Points of View* (1893).

RIGBY, ELIZABETH, 'Children's Books', *Quarterly Review*, 74 (1844), 1–26.

ROBINS, ELIZABETH, *Way Stations* (1913).

ROGERS, WINFIELD H., 'The Reaction against Melodramatic Sentimentality in the English Novel, 1796–1830', *PMLA* 49 (1934), 98–122.

ROWBOTHAM, JUDITH, *Good Girls Make Good Wives: Guidance for Girls in Victorian Fiction* (Oxford, 1989).

SCHLACK, BEVERLY ANN, *Continuing Presences: Virginia Woolf's Use of Literary Allusion* (University Park, Penn. and London, 1979).

SEDGWICK, EVE KOSOFSKY, *Epistemology of the Closet* (Berkeley, Calif., and Los Angeles, Calif., 1990).

SEGAL, ELIZABETH, ' "As the Twig is Bent . . . ": Gender and Childhood Reading', in Elizabeth A. Flynn and Patrocinio P. Schweickart (eds.), *Gender in Reading: Essays on Readers, Texts, and Contexts* (Baltimore, Md., and London, 1986), 165–86.

'Sensation Novels', *Medical Critic and Psychological Journal*, 3 (1863), 513–19.

SHEVELOW, KATHRYN, *Women and Print Culture: The Construction of Femininity in the Early Periodical* (1989).

SHOWALTER, ELAINE, *A Literature of their Own: British Women Novelists from Brontë to Lessing* (Princeton, NJ, 1977; repr. 1978).

—— *Sexual Anarchy: Gender and Culture at the 'Fin de Siècle'* (1991).

SIMCOX, EDITH, 'Autobiographies', *North British Review*, 101 (1869), 383–414.

SMITH, NIGEL, *Perfection Proclaimed: Language and Literature in English Radical Religion, 1640–1660* (Oxford, 1989).

SMITH, PAUL, 'Men in Feminism: Men and Feminist Theory', in Paul Smith and Alice Jardine (eds.), *Men in Feminism* (1987), 33–46.

SMITH, SIDONIE, *A Poetics of Women's Autobiography: Marginality and the Fictions of Self-Representation* (Bloomington, Ind., and Indianapolis, 1987).

SPACKS, PATRICIA MEYER, 'Stages of Self: Notes on Autobiography and the Life Cycle', in Albert E. Stone (ed.), *The American Autobiography: A Collection of Critical Essays* (Englewood Cliffs, NJ, 1981), 44–60.

STANG, RICHARD, *The Theory of the Novel in England 1850–1870* (1959).

STEAD, W. T., 'The Book of the Month: The Novel of the Modern Woman', *Review of Reviews*, 10 (1894), 64–74.

STEPHEN, LESLIE, 'Rambles among Books (No. II): Autobiography', *Cornhill Magazine*, 43 (1881), 410–29.

STODART, M. A., *Female Writers: Thoughts on their Proper Sphere, and on their Powers of Usefulness* (1842).

STUTFIELD, HUGH, 'The Psychology of Feminism', *Blackwood's Edinburgh Magazine*, 161 (1897), 104–17.

SULEIMAN, SUSAN, *Authoritarian Fictions: The Ideological Novel as Literary Genre* (New York, 1983).

TAYLOR, HELEN, 'Romantic Readers', in Helen Carr, (ed.), *From My Guy to Sci-Fi: Genre and Women's Writing in the Postmodern World* (1989), 58–77.

TAYLOR, JENNY BOURNE, *In the Secret Theatre of Home: Wilkie Collins, Sensation Narrative, and Nineteenth-Century Psychology* (1988).

TAYLOR, JOHN TINNON, *Early Opposition to the English Novel: The Popular Reaction from 1760 to 1830* (New York, 1943).

THURSTON, CAROL, *The Romance Revolution: Erotic Novels for Women and the Quest for a New Sexual Identity* (Urbana, Ill., and Chicago, 1987).

TOMPKINS, JANE, *Sensational Designs: The Cultural Work of American Fiction, 1790–1860* (New York, 1985).

TOZER, BASIL, 'The Increasing Popularity of the Erotic Novel', *Monthly Review*, 20 (1905), 53–9.

TRODD, ANTHEA, *Domestic Crime in the Victorian Novel* (Basingstoke, 1989).

TROLLOPE, ANTHONY, *Four Lectures*, ed. Morris L. Parrish (1938).

TROTTER, DAVID, 'Edwardian Sex Novels', *Critical Quarterly*, 31 (1989), 92–105.

TUCHMAN, GAYE, *Edging Women Out: Victorian Novelists, Publishers, and Social Change* (1989).

WARHOL, ROBYN R., *Gendered Interventions. Narrative Discourse in the Victorian Novel* (New Brunswick and London, 1989).

WAYNE, VALERIE, 'Some Sad Sentence: Vives' *Instruction of a Christian Woman*', in Margaret Hannay (ed.), *Silent But For the Word: Tudor Women as Patrons, Translators, and Writers of Religious Works* (Ohio, 1985).

WEST, REBECCA, *The Young Rebecca: Writings of Rebecca West 1911–1917*, ed. Jane Marcus (1982).

WHEELER, MICHAEL, *The Art of Allusion in Victorian Fiction* (1979).

WILLIAMS, IOAN, (ed.), *Novel and Romance 1700–1800: A Documentary Record* (1970).

WOOLF, VIRGINIA, *A Room of One's Own* (1929; repr. Harmondsworth, 1973).

WORTON, MICHAEL, and STILL, JUDITH, 'Introduction', *Intertextuality: Theories and Practices* (Manchester and New York, 1990), 1–44.

Fiction

AGUILAR, GRACE, *Home Influence: A Tale for Mothers and Daughters*, 2 vols. (1847).

ALLEN, GRANT, *The Woman Who Did* (1895).

AUSTEN, JANE, *Northanger Abbey* (1818; repr. 1971).

—— *Sanditon* (written 1817) (1954).

BRADDON, MARY, *Lady Audley's Secret* (1862: repr. Oxford, 1987).

—— *The Doctor's Wife*, 3 vols. (1864).

—— *Aurora Floyd* (1863; repr. 1984).

—— *The Lady's Mile*, 3 vols. (1866).

BRABY, MAUD CHURTON, *Downward: A 'Slice of Life'* (1910).

BRONTË, CHARLOTTE, *Jane Eyre* (1847; repr. Oxford, 1969).

—— *Shirley* (1849; repr. Oxford, 1979).

—— *Villette* (1853; repr. Oxford, 1984).

BROOKE, EMMA FRANCES, *A Superfluous Woman*, 3 vols. (1894).

BROUGHTON, RHODA, *Not Wisely but Too Well* (1863).

—— *Cometh Up as a Flower* (1867).

—— *A Beginner* (1899).

—— *Red as a Rose is She* (1870).

CAINE, HALL, *The Manxman* (1894).

CAIRD, MONA, *The Daughters of Danaus* (1894).

CAREY, ROSA NOUCHETTE, *Nellie's Memories*, 3 vols. (1868).

COLLINS, WILKIE, *The Queen of Hearts*, 3 vols. (1859).

COLMORE, GERTRUDE, *Suffragette Sally* (1911).

CORELLI, MARIE, *The Sorrows of Satan* (1895).

CORY, VIVIEN, 'Victoria Cross', *The Greater Law* (1914).

DESPARD, Mrs, and COLLINS, MABEL, *Outlawed: A Novel on the Woman Suffrage Question* (1908).

DICKENS, CHARLES, *The Pickwick Papers* (1837; repr. Oxford, 1986).

DIXON, ELLA HEPWORTH, *The Story of a Modern Woman* (1894, repr. 1990).

ELIOT, GEORGE, *The Mill on the Floss* (1861; repr. Oxford 1980).

—— *Middlemarch* (1874 edn.; repr. New York and London, 1977).

EWING, JULIANA HORATIA, *Six to Sixteen: A Story for Girls* (1876).

'FALCONER, LANOE' [Mary Elizabeth Hawker], *Mademoiselle Ixe* (1890).

FLAUBERT, GUSTAVE, *Madame Bovary* (Paris, 1857).

GISSING, GEORGE, *The Odd Women* (1893; repr. 1980).

GRAND, SARAH, *The Heavenly Twins*, 3 vols. (1893).

—— *The Beth Book* (1897; repr. 1983).

GREY, CAROLINE, *Sybil Lennard*, 3 vols. (1846).

HAMILTON, ELIZA, *Translation of the Letters of a Hindoo Rajah*, 2 vols. (1796).

HARDY, THOMAS, *Tess of the D'Urbervilles* (1891; Wessex edn., 1912).

'IOTA' (Kathleen Caffyn), *A Yellow Aster* (1894).

JAMES, HENRY, *In the Cage* (1898, repr. Harmondsworth, 1972).

JEBB, H. G., *Out of the Depths* (1859).

KENEALY, ARABELLA, *Dr Janet of Harley Street* (1893).

LENNOX, CHARLOTTE, *The Female Quixote* (1752; repr. 1986).

MAUD, CONSTANCE ELIZABETH, *No Surrender* (1911).

MELMOTH, COURTNEY, *The Pupil of Pleasure* (1777).

NIGHTINGALE, FLORENCE, *Cassandra* (1852, rev. 1859; repr. in Ray Strachey, *The Cause* (1928).

OLIPHANT, MARGARET, *Hester*, 3 vols. (1883).

REEVE, CLARA, *The School for Widows*, 3 vols. (1791).

SCHREINER, OLIVE, *The Story of an African Farm*, 2 vols. (1883).

—— *Dreams* (1891).

SEWELL, ELIZABETH, *Margaret Percival*, 2 vols. (1847).

SYRETT, NETTA, *The Victorians* (1915).

TROLLOPE, ANTHONY, *The Small House at Allington*, 2 vols. (1864).

—— *Is He Popenjoy?* 3 vols. (1878).

VATCHELL, H. A., *The Hill* (1905).

WELLS, H. G., *Ann Veronica* (1909).

WOOD, Mrs HENRY, *East Lynne*, 3 vols. (1861).
WOOLF, VIRGINIA, *The Voyage Out* (1915).
YONGE, CHARLOTTE M., *The Daisy Chain* (1856; repr. 1988).
—— *The Clever Woman of the Family* (1865).
ZOLA, ÉMILE, *Piping Hot!* (1885).

Advice Texts

ABERDEEN, Countess of, *Mistresses and Maid-Servants: Suggestions towards the Increased Pleasure and Permanence of their Domestic Relations* (Aberdeen and London, 1884).
ADAMS, W. H. DAVENPORT, *Women's Work and Worth* (1880).
BAINTON, GEORGE, *The Wife as Lover and Friend* (1895).
BARNARD, AMY B., *The Girl's Encyclopaedia* (1909).
BAYLY, Mrs., *An Old Mother's Letter to Young Women* (1884).
BELL, MARY, *A Book of Counsels for Girls* (1888).
—— *The Lowly Life: A Simple Book for Girl-Workers* (1892).
BOWMAN, ANNE, *The Common Things of Every-Day Life: A Home Book of Wisdom for Mothers and Daughters* (1857).
BRABY, MAUD CHURTON, *Modern Marriage and How to Bear It* (1909).
BROWNE, PHYLLIS, *What Girls Can Do* (1880).
CHILD, LYDIA MARIA, *The Girl's Own Book* (1869).
ELLIS, Mrs., *The Mothers of England: Their Influence and Responsibility* (1843).
FARNINGHAM, MARIANNE, *Girlhood* (1869).
GISBORNE, THOMAS, *An Enquiry into the Duties of the Female Sex* (1797).
GREY, MARIA, and SHIRREFF, EMILY, *Thoughts on Self-Culture Addressed to Women*, 2 vols. (1850).
The Habits of Good Society: A Handbook of Etiquette for Ladies and Gentlemen (new edn., 1890).
HARDY, EDWARD JOHN, *The Five Talents of Woman* (5th edn., 1895).
HELPS, SIR ARTHUR, *Friends in Council: A Series of Readings and Discourse Thereon*, 2 vols. (1847).
JAMES, Mrs ELIOT, *Our Servants: Their Duties to us and Ours to Them* (1882).
JAMES, JOHN ANGELL, *Female Piety: or the Young Woman's Friend and Guide through Life to Immortality* (1852).
MACKARNESS, Mrs HENRY (ed.), *The Young Lady's Book : A Manual of Amusements, Exercise, Studies, and Pursuits* (1876).
MASON, CHARLOTTE M., *Home Education: A Course of Lectures to Ladies* (1886).
MULOCK, DINAH, *A Woman's Thoughts About Women* (1858).
'One Who Knows Them', *Girls and their Ways* (1881).
PULLAN, MATILDA, *Maternal Counsels to a Daughter* (1855).
SEDGWICK, C. M., *Means and Ends; or, Self-Training* (1839).
—— *Morals or Manners; or, Hints for Our Young People* (1846).
SHIRREFF, EMILY, *Intellectual Education and Its Influence on the Character and Happiness of Women* (1858).
Society for Promoting Christian Knowledge, *A Mistress' Counsel; or A Few Words to Servants* (1871).

SOULSBY, LUCY, *A Home Art, or Mothers and Daughters* (Oxford, 1890).

—— *Happiness* (1899).

STODART, M. A., *Every Day Duties: in letters to a young lady* (1840).

——*Principles of Education Practically Considered; with an especial reference to the Present State of Female Education in England* (1844).

STRUTT, ELIZABETH, *The Feminine Soul: Its Nature and Attributes, with Thoughts Upon Marriage, and Friendly Hints Upon Feminine Duties* (1857).

SWAN, ANNIE S., *Courtship and Marriage and the Gentle Art of Home-Making* (1893).

E. A. W. [Walker, E. A.], *Friendly Hints to Our Girls* (1889).

—— *Womanhood; or Thoughts for Young Women* (1891).

WELBY, ELLA, *Every Day: Thoughts on the G. F. S. Rules of Life* (1895).

WHEELER, MAUDE, *Whom to Marry or All About Love and Matrimony* (1894).

The Young Servant's Own Book, intended as a Present for Girls on First Going Into Service (1883).

Medicine and Psychoanalysis

ALAYA, FLAVIA, 'Victorian Science and the "Genius" of Woman,' *Journal of the History of Ideas*, 38 (1977), 261–80.

ANDERSON, E. GARRETT, 'Sex in Education: A Reply', *Fortnightly Review*, NS 15 (1874), 582–94.

BASTIAN, HENRY CHARLTON, *The Brain as Organ of Mind* (1880).

'Miss Becker on the Mental Characteristics of the Sexes', *Lancet*, 2 (1868), 320–1.

'Miss Becker's Paper read before the British Association for the Advancement of Science: The Equality of Women', *Englishwoman's Review*, 9 (1868), 48–55.

BLACK, GEORGE, *The Young Wife's Advice Book* (1st pub. 1880; issued as an 'entirely new edition' 1910).

BLACKWELL, Dr ELIZABETH, *Counsel to Parents on the Moral Education of their Children in Relation to Sex* (2nd edn., 1879).

BONAVIA, E. M., 'Women's Frontal Lobes', *Provincial Medical Journal*, 11 (1892), 358–62.

CARPENTER, WILLIAM, *Principles of Human Physiology* (1842).

CARTER, A. B., *Diseases of the Nervous System* (1855).

CARTER, ROBERT BRUDENELL, *On the Pathology and Treatment of Hysteria* (1853).

CHODOROW, NANCY, *The Reproduction of Mothering: Psychoanalysis and the Sociology of Gender* (Berkeley, Calif., 1978).

CLARKE, EDWARD H., *Sex in Education* (Boston, 1875).

CLOUSTON, THOMAS SMITH, *Female Education from a Medical Point of View* (Edinburgh, 1882).

—— *Morals and Brain* (1912).

DARWIN, CHARLES, *The Descent of Man, and Selection in Relation to Sex*, 2 vols. (1871).

—— *The Expression of the Emotions in Man and Animals* (1872).

DRAYTON, H. S., 'Is the Brain of Woman Inferior?', *Englishwoman*, 3 (1896), 463–6.

DUFFIN, LORNA, 'Prisoners of Progress: Women and Evolution', in Sara Delamont and Lorna Duffin (eds.), *The Nineteenth Century Woman: Her Cultural and Physical World* (1978), 57–91.

ELLIS, HAVELOCK, *Man and Woman: A Study of Human Secondary Sexual Characteristics* (1894).

FERRIER, DAVID, *Functions of the Brain* (2nd edn. 1886).

FOSTER, MICHAEL, *A Text-Book of Physiology* (2nd edn. 1878).

FREUD, SIGMUND, *Three Essays on the History of Sexuality* (1905), *Pelican Freud Library*, 7 (1977), 33–169.

—— 'On Narcissism: An Introduction' (1914), *Pelican Freud Library*, 11 (1984), 61–97.

—— 'The Relation of the Poet to Day-Dreaming' (1907), *Pelican Freud Library*, 14 (1985), 131–41.

—— *Papers on Psycho-Analysis* (2nd edn., 1918).

GEDDES, PATRICK, and THOMSON, J. ARTHUR, *The Evolution of Sex* (1889).

GLLIGAN, CAROL, *In a Different Voice: Psychological Theory and Women's Development* (Cambridge, Mass., 1982).

HARRISON, BRIAN, 'Women's Health and the Women's Movement in Britain: 1840–1940' in Charles Webster (ed.), *Biology, Medicine and Society 1840–1940* (Cambridge, 1981), 15–71.

JORDANOVA, LUDMILLA, 'Natural Facts: A Historical Perspective on Science and Sexuality', in Carol MacCormack and Marilyn Strathern (eds.), *Nature, Culture, and Gender* (Cambridge, 1980), 42–69.

KIRK, E. B., *A Talk with Girls About Themselves* (1905).

KLEIN, MELANIE, 'A Contribution to the Theory of Intellectual Inhibition' (1931), in *Love, Guilt and Reparation and Other Works 1921–1945* (1975); repr. 1988, 236–47.

LADD, GEORGE, TRUMBULL, *Elements of Physiological Psychology* (1887).

LAQUEUR, THOMAS, *Making Sex: Body and Gender from the Greeks to Freud* (Cambridge, Mass., and London, 1990).

LAYCOCK, THOMAS, *A Treatise on the Nervous Diseases of Women* (1840).

LEWES, G. H., *The Physiology of Common Life*, 2 vols. (1859; 1860).

—— 'Editor', 'The Heart and the Brain', *Fortnightly Review*, 1 (1865), 66–74.

—— *Problems of Life and Mind*, ser. 1, 2 vols. (1873); ser. 2 (1877); ser. 3, 2 vols. (1879).

MADDOCK, ALFRED BEAUMONT, *Practical Observations on Mental and Nervous Disorders* (1854).

MAUDSLEY, HENRY, *The Physiology and Pathology of the Mind* (1867).

—— 'Sex in Mind and in Education', *Fortnightly Review*, NS 15 (1874), 466–83.

MEISSNER, W. W., 'Notes on Identification. III. The Concept of Identification', *Psychoanalytic Quarterly*, 41 (1972), 224–60.

MILLINGEN, J. G., *Mind and Matter, illustrated by Considerations on Hereditary Insanity and the Influence of Temperament in the Development of the Passions* (1847).

MOSCUCCI, ORNELLA, *The Science of Woman: Gynaecology and Gender in England, 1800–1929* (Cambridge, 1990).

ROMANES, GEORGE, J., 'Mental Differences between Men and Women', *Nineteenth Century*, 21 (1887), 654–72.

RYAN, MICHAEL, *The Philosophy of Marriage* (1837).

RYLEY, J. BERESFORD, *A Few Words of Advice to Young Wives* (1895).

SHOWALTER, ELAINE, *The Female Malady: Women, Madness and English Culture, 1830–1980* (1985).

SPENCER, HERBERT, *Education: Intellectual, Moral and Physical* (1861).

—— *The Principles of Ethics*, 2 vols. (1892–3).

STRACHEY, JAMES, 'Some Unconscious Factors in Reading', *International Journal of Psychoanalysis*, 11 (1930), 322–31.

SULLY, JAMES, *The Human Mind: A Text-book of Psychology*, 2 vols. (1892).

TILT, E. J., *On the Preservation of Health of Women at the Critical Periods of Life* (1851).

YOUNG, ROBERT M., *Mind, Brain and Adaptation in the Nineteenth Century: Cerebral Localization and its Biological Context from Gall to Ferrier* (Oxford, 1970; new introd. 1990).

WALKER, ALEXANDER, *Woman Physiologically Considered as to Mind, Morals, Matrimonial Slavery, Infidelity and Divorce* (1840).

Education

ANDERSON, K., 'Frances Mary Buss, the Founder as Headmistress, 1850–94', in R. M. Scrimgeour, (ed.), *The North London Collegiate School 1850–1950: A Hundred Years of Girls' Education* (1950), 25–54.

ARCHER, R. L., *Secondary Education in the Nineteenth Century* (Cambridge, 1921).

ATKINSON, PAUL, 'Fitness, Feminism and Schooling', in Sara Delamont and Lorna Duffin (eds.), *The Nineteenth Century Woman: Her Cultural and Physical World* (1978), 92–133.

AVERY, GILLIAN, *The Best Type of Girl: A History of Girls' Independent Schools* (1991).

BALDICK, CHRIS, *The Social Mission of English Criticism 1848–1932* (Oxford, 1983; new edn. 1987).

BEALE, DOROTHEA, ('A Utopian'), 'On the Education of Girls', *Fraser's Magazine*, 74 (1866), 509–24.

—— *Reports Issued by the Schools' Inquiry Commission on the Education of Girls* (1869).

—— SOULSBY, LUCY H. M., and DOVE, JANE FRANCIS, *Work and Play in Girls' Schools* (1898).

BREMNER, C. S., *Education of Girls and Women in Great Britain* (1897).

BRITTAIN, VERA, *The Women at Oxford* (1960).

BROWNE, Sir JAMES CRICHTON, 'Should Women be Educated?', *Englishwoman*, 2 (1896), 454–62.

BURSTALL, SARA A., *English High Schools for Girls* (1907).

—— and DOUGLAS, M. A., (eds.), *Public Schools for Girls: A Series of Papers on their History, Aims, and Schemes of Study* (1911).

—— *Retrospect and Prospect: Sixty Years of Women's Education* (1933).

BURSTYN, JOAN, 'Education and Sex: The Medical Case Against Higher Education for Women in England, 1870–1900', *Proceedings of the American Philosophical Society*, 117 (1973), 79–89.

BUSS, FRANCES M., *Leaves from the Note-Books of Frances M. Buss, being Selections from her weekly addresses to the Girls of the North London Collegiate School*, ed. Grace Toplis, (1896).

CLUTTON, E., *Colston's Girls' School Jubilee 1891–1941* (Bristol, 1941).

DAVIN, ANNA, '"Mind that you do as you are told": Reading Books for Board School Girls, 1870–1902', *Feminist Review*, 3 (1979), 89–98.

DOYLE, BRIAN, 'The Hidden History of English Studies', in Peter Widdowson (ed.), *Re-Reading English* (1982), 17–31.

—— *English & Englishness* (1989).

DYHOUSE, CAROL, 'Social Darwinistic Ideas and the Development of Women's Education in England, 1880–1920', *History of Education*, 5 (1976), 41–58.

—— *Girls Growing up in Late Victorian and Edwardian England* (1981).

FAWCETT, MILLICENT GARRETT, 'The Education of Women of the Middle and Upper Classes', *Macmillan's Magazine*, 17 (1868), 511–17.

FITCH, J. G., 'The Education of Women', *Victoria Magazine*, 2 (1864), 432–53.

FLETCHER, SHEILA, *Feminists and Bureaucrats: A Study in the Development of Girls' Education in the Nineteenth Century* (Cambridge, 1980).

GOODSON, IVOR F., and BALL, STEPHEN J. (eds.), *Defining the Curriculum: Histories and Ethnographies* (1984).

GRANT, JULIA M., MCCUTCHEON, KATHERINE H., and SANDERS, ETHEL F., *St Leonards School 1877–1927* (1927).

GRYLLS, ROSALIE GLYNN, *Queen's College 1848–1948* (1948).

HIGGINSON, Mrs ALFRED, *The English School-girl: Her Position and Duties. A Series of Lessons from a Teacher to her Class* (2nd edn., 1879).

JOHNSON, ROBERT, *A Lecture on Female Education* (1860).

KAMM, JOSEPHINE, *Hope Deferred: Girls' Education in English History* (1965).

KAYE, ELAINE, *A History of Queen's College, London, 1848–1972* (1972).

KINGSLEY, CHARLES, *Health and Education* (1879).

HALL, G. STANLEY, *Adolescence: Its Psychology and its Relation to Physiology, Anthropology, Sociology, Sex, Crime, Religion, and Education* (New York, 1904).

MASON, CHARLOTTE M., *Home Education* (1886).

PALMER, D. J., *The Rise of English Studies* (1965).

PASCOE, CHARLES EYRE, *Schools for Girls and Colleges for Women: A Handbook of Female Education chiefly designed for the use of persons of the upper middle classes* (1879).

PEDERSEN, JOYCE S., 'Schoolmistresses and Headmistresses: Élites and Education in Nineteenth-Century England', *Journal of British Studies*, 15 (1975), 135–62.

PHILLIPS, ANN, (ed.), *A Newnham Anthology* (Cambridge, 1979).

PURVIS, JUNE, 'The Double Burden of Class and Gender in the Schooling of Working-class Girls in Nineteenth-Century England, 1800–1870', in L. Barton and S. Walker (eds.), *Schools, Teachers and Teaching* (Lewes, 1981), 97–116.

Reports from Commissioners to the Schools' Inquiry, PP. 1867, XXVIII, Part IV.

Royal Commission on Secondary Education (1894–95), Minutes of Evidence.

SOULSBY, LUCY H. M., *School Work* (1890).

—— *Home Rule, or Daughters of To-Day* (Oxford, 1894).

STEADMAN, F. CECILY, *In the Days of Miss Beale: A Study of Her Work and Influence* (1931).

TURNER, BARRY, *Equality for Some: The Story of Girls' Education* (1974).

VERNON, MAUD VENABLES, 'How Should Women be Educated?', *Englishwoman*, 3 (1896), 177–81.

WORDSWORTH, ELIZABETH, *First Principles in Women's Education* (Oxford, 1894).

Autobiographies and Letters

ABERDEEN, Lord and Lady, *'We Twa': Reminiscences of Lord and Lady Aberdeen* (1925).

BALFOUR, LADY FRANCIS, *Ne Obliviscaris: Dinna Forget*, 2 vols. (1930).

BARING, MAURICE, *The Puppet Show of Memory* (1922).

BARLOW, AMY, *Seventh Child: The Autobiography of a Schoolmistress* (1969).

BENTLEY, PHYLLIS, *'O Dreams, O Destinations': An Autobiography* (1962).

BOOKER, BERYL LEE, *Yesterday's Child 1890–1909* (1937).

BONDFIELD, MARGARET, *A Life's Work* (1950).

BRADLEY, JOHN LEWIS, 'An Unpublished Ruskin Letter', *Burlington Magazine*, 100 (1958), 25.

BRAZIL, ANGELA, *My Own Schooldays* (1925).

BRITTAIN, VERA, *Testament of Youth* (1933) repr.; 1983).

BROWN, JEAN CURTIS, *To Tell My Daughter* (1948).

BROWN, Mrs JOHN, *Memories of a Friendship* (Cape Town, 1923).

BUTLER, JOSEPHINE E., *Recollections of George Butler* (Bristol and London, 1893).

——*An Autobiographical Memoir*, ed. George W. Johnson and Lucy A. Johnson (Bristol and London, 1909).

BUTTS, MARY, *The Crystal Cabinet: My Childhood at Salterns* (1937).

CAMBRIDGE, ADA, *The Retrospect* (1912).

CAMPBELL, MARGARET, 'Margaret Campbell (Marjorie Bowen), 1873', in *Myself When Young: by Famous Women of Today*, ed. Margot Asquith (1938), 41–64.

CARBERY, MARY, *Happy World: The Story of a Victorian Childhood* (1941).

CAVENDISH, LUCY, *The Diary of Lady Frederick Cavendish*, ed. John Bailey, 2 vols. (1927).

CHARLES, ELIZABETH, *Lady Augusta Stanley: Reminiscences* (1892).

CHOLMONDELEY, MARY, *Under One Roof: A Family Record* (1918).

CHORLEY, KATHARINE, *Manchester Made Them* (1950).

CLOUGH, BLANCHE ATHENA, *A Memoir of Anne Jemima Clough* (1897).

COBBE, FRANCES POWER, *Life of Frances Power Cobbe: as told by herself* (1904).

COLE, MARGARET, *Growing up into Revolution* (1949).

COURTNEY, JANET E., *Recollected in Tranquillity* (1926).

DAVIES, MARGARET LLEWELYN, (ed.), *Life as we have known it: By Co-operative Working Women* (1931).

DICKENS, CHARLES, *Letters of Charles Dickens*, ed. Madeline House and Graham Storey, ii. *1840–1841* (Oxford, 1969).

DIXON, ELLA HEPWORTH, *As I Knew Them* (1930).

ELIOT, GEORGE, *The George Eliot Letters*, ed. Gordon Haight, 9 vols. (1954–1978).

EVANS, JOAN, *Prelude and Fugue: An Autobiography* (1964).

EYLES, LEONORA, *The Ram Escapes* (1953).

FAITHFULL, LILLIAN M., *In the House of My Pilgrimage* (1924).

FARJEON, ELEANOR, *A Nursery in the Nineties* (1960).

FARNINGHAM, MARIANNE, *A Working Woman's Life: An Autobiography* (1907).

FOLEY, ALICE, *A Bolton Childhood* (Manchester, 1973).

FRASER, Mrs HUGH, *A Diplomat's Wife in Many Lands* (1910).

GASKELL, ELIZABETH, *The Letters of Mrs Gaskell*, ed. J. A. V. Chapple and Arthur Pollard (Manchester, 1966).

GISSING, GEORGE, *Letters of George Gissing to Members of His Family*, collected and arranged by Algernon Gissing and Ellen Gissing (1927).

GLENDINNING, VICTORIA (ed.), *A Suppressed Cry: Life and Death of a Quaker Daughter* (1969).

HAMILTON, CICELY, *Life Errant* (1935).

HAMILTON, MARY AGNES, *Remembering My Good Friends* (1944).

HAVERGAL, M. V. G., *Memorials of Frances Ridley Havergal* by her sister, M. V. G. H. (1880).

HARRISON, JANE ELLEN, *Reminiscences of a Student's Life* (1925).

HOPKINSON, EVELYN, *The Story of a Mid-Victorian Girl* (1928).

HOWITT, MARGARET, (ed.), *Mary Howitt: An Autobiography* (1889).

JACKSON, ANNABEL HUTH, *A Victorian Childhood* (1932).

JOHNSON, ELLEN, *Autobiography, Poems and Songs of Ellen Johnson, the 'Factory Girl'* (Glasgow, 1867).

KEMBLE, FRANCES ANNE, *Records of Later Life*, 3 vols. (1882).

KENNEY, ANNIE, *Memoirs of a Militant* (1924).

KNIGHT, LAURA, *Oil Paint and Grease Paint* (1936).

—— *The Magic of a Line* (1965).

LODGE, ELEANOR C., *Terms and Vacations* (1938).

LONGFORD, CHRISTINE, 'Early Snobberies', in *Little Innocents: Childhood Reminiscences*, with preface by Alan Pryce-Jones (1932), 115–18.

LUBBOCK, SYBIL, *The Child in the Crystal* (1939).

LYTTON, CONSTANCE, *Prisons and Prisoners* (1914).

—— *Letters of Constance Lytton*, selected and arranged by Betty Balfour (1925).

MARSHALL, MARY PALEY, *What I Remember* (1947).

MARTINDALE, HILDA, *From One Generation to Another 1839–1944* (1944).

MARTINEAU, HARRIET, *Harriet Martineau's Autobiography*, ed. Maria Weston Chapman, 2 vols. (Boston, 1877).

MAURICE, C. EDMUND, *Life of Octavia Hill: As Told in her Letters* (1913).

MAYO, ISABELLA FYVIE, *Recollections of what I saw, what I lived through, and what I learned, during more than fifty years of Social and Literary Experience* (1910).

MCCALL, DOROTHY, *When That I Was* (1952).

MITCHELL, HANNAH, *The Hard Way Up: the Autobiography of Hannah Mitchell, Suffragette and Rebel*, ed. Geoffrey Mitchell (1968).

MONTEFIORE, DORA B., *From A Victorian to a Modern* (1927).

One of Her Daughters, *The Life of Florence L. Barclay: A Study in Personality* (1921).

Oxford and Asquith, Countess of (ed.), *Myself When Young, by Famous Women of To-Day* (1938).

PECK, WINIFRED, *A Little Learning or A Victorian Childhood* (1952).

PETHICK-LAWRENCE, EMMELINE, *My Part in a Changing World* (1938).

PROCTER, ZOË, *Life and Yesterday* (1960).

RHONDDA, Viscountess, *This Was My World* (1933).

RITCHIE, ANNE THACKERAY, *Chapters from Some Memoirs* (1894).

RUSSELL, DORA, *The Tamarisk Tree: My Quest for Liberty and Love* (1975).

SEWELL, ELIZABETH, *The Autobiography of Elizabeth Sewell*, ed. by her niece, Eleanor L. Sewell (1907).

SHORE, EMILY, *The Journal of Emily Shore* (rev. edn., 1898).

SMITH, MARGARET, *A Different Drummer* (1931).

SMITH, MARY, *The Autobiography of Mary Smith Schoolmistress and Nonconformist* (1892).

SMYTH, ETHEL, *Impressions that Remained*, 2 vols. (1919).

STARKIE, ENID, *A Lady's Child* (1941).

STOCKS, MARY, *My Commonplace Book* (1970).

SWANWICK, H. M., *I Have Been Young* (1935).

SYRETT, NETTA, *The Sheltering Tree* (1939).

VYVER, BERTHA, *Memoirs of Marie Corelli* (1930).

THOMPSON, FLORA, *Lark Rise* (1939).

WARD, Mrs HUMPHRY, *A Writer's Recollections*, 2 vols., (1918).

WEBB, BEATRICE, *The Diary of Beatrice Webb*, i. 1873-1892, ed. Norman MacKenzie and Jeanne MacKenzie (1982).

WHITE, FLORENCE, *A Fire in the Kitchen: The Autobiography of a Cook* (1938).

WOOLF, VIRGINIA, *The Letters of Virginia Woolf*, ed. Nigel Nicolson and Joanne Trautmann, 6 vols. (1975–80).

YONGE, C. M., 'A Real Childhood', *Mothers in Council*, 3 (1893), 15–21.

Biography

ANDERSON, NANCY FIX, *Woman Against Women in Victorian England: A Life of Eliza Lynn Linton* (Bloomington, Ind., and Indianapolis, 1987).

BLACK, HELEN C., *Notable Woman Authors of the Day: Biographical Sketches* (Glasgow, 1893).

BURTON, HESTER, *Barbara Bodichon 1827–1891* (1949).

BURNS, JABEZ, *The Mothers of the Wise and Good* (1846).

CLAYTON, ELLEN, *Women of the Reformation* (1861).

—— *English Female Artists* (1876).

—— *Female Warriors* (1879).

COLLOMS, BRENDA, *Charles Kingsley: The Lion of Eversley* (1975).

DARTON, J. M., *Famous Girls Who Have Become Illustrious Women of Our Time: Forming Models for Imitation by the Young Women of England* (1880).

ELLSWORTH, EDWARD W., *Liberators of the Female Mind: The Shirreff Sisters, Educational Reform, and the Women's Movement* (1979).

EWART, HENRY, *True and Noble Women* (1888).

FARNINGHAM, MARIANNE, *Women and their Work: Wives and Daughters of the Old Testament* (1906).

FIRST, RUTH and SCOTT, ANN, *Olive Schreiner* (1980; repr. 1989).

FIRTH, C. B., *Constance Louisa Maynard: Mistress of Westfield College* (1949).

GROSSKURTH, PHYLLIS, *Havelock Ellis: A Biography* (New York, 1980).

HAIGHT, GORDON S., *George Eliot: A Biography* (Oxford, 1968).

KAVANAGH, JULIA, *Women of Christianity exemplary for acts of piety and charity* (1852).

KERSLEY, GILLIAN, *Darling Madame: Sarah Grand and Devoted Friend* (1983).

LANGDON, CECILY, *Gwen John* (New Haven, Conn., and London, 1987).

LIDDERDALE, JANE, and NICHOLSON, MARY, *Dear Miss Weaver: Harriet Shaw Weaver 1876–1961* (1970).

MacSorley, Catherine Mary, *A Few Good Women, and what they teach us: A Book for Girls* (1886).

Menzies, Louisa, *Lives of the Greek Heroines* (1880).

Millgate, Michael, *Thomas Hardy: A Biography* (Oxford, 1982).

Mitchell, Susan L., *George Moore* (Dublin, 1916).

Morley, Ann, and Stanley, Liz., *The Life and Death of Emily Wilding Davison* (1988).

Nord, Deborah Epstein, *The Apprenticeship of Beatrice Webb* (Amherst, 1985).

Raikes, Elizabeth, *Dorothea Beale of Cheltenham* (1908).

Reade, Charles L. and Reade, the Revd. Compton, *Charles Reade, Dramatist, Novelist, Journalist: A Memoir*, 2 vols. (1887).

Ross, Dorothy, *G. Stanley Hall, The Psychologist as Prophet* (Chicago, 1972).

Sutherland, John, *Mrs Humphry Ward: Eminent Victorian, Pre-eminent Edwardian* (Oxford, 1990).

Todd, Margaret, *The Life of Sophia Jex-Blake* (1918).

Trevelyan, Marie, *Brave Little Women: Tales of the Heroism of Girls. Founded on Fact* (1888).

Wolff, Robert Lee, 'Devoted Disciple: The Letters of Mary Elizabeth Braddon to Sir Edward Bulwer-Lytton, 1862–1873', *Harvard Library Bulletin*, 22 (1974), 5–35, 129–61.

—— *Sensational Victorian: The Life and Fiction of Mary Elizabeth Braddon* (New York and London, 1979).

Libraries

Barwick, G. F., *The Reading Room of the British Museum* (1929).

Brown, Jas. D., 'The Working of Clerkenwell Public Library', *Library*, (1893), 109–19.

Fitzgerald, Percy, 'A Day at the Museum Reading Room', *Belgravia*, 46 (1881), 156–64.

Friswell, Hain, 'Circulating Libraries: Their Contents and their Readers', *London Society*, 20 (1871), 515–24.

Greenwood, Thomas, *Public Libraries: A History of the Movement and a Manual for the Organization, and Management of Rate-Supported Libraries* (4th edn., 1894).

Griest, Guinevere, *Mudie's Circulating Library and the Victorian Novel* (1970).

Kaufman, Paul, *Libraries and their Users* (1969).

Kelly, Thomas, *Books for the People* (1977).

Kersey, Edward, 'A Romance of a Public Library', *Belgravia*, 18 (1889), 35–49.

Manners, Lady John, *Some of the advantages of easily accessible reading and recreation rooms and free libraries with remarks on starting and maintaining them, and suggestions for the Selection of Books* (1885).

—— *Encouraging Experiences of Reading and Recreation Rooms* (1886).

Robertson, John M., *What to Read: Suggestions for the Better Utilisation of Public Libraries* (1904).

Tedder, Henry R., 'Librarianship as a Profession', *Transactions and Proceedings of the Fifth Annual Meeting of the Library Association of the United Kingdom* (Cambridge, 1882).

WOOD, BUTLER, 'Three Special Features of Free Library Work: Open Shelves, Women Readers, and Juvenile Departments', *Library*, 4 (1892), 105–14.

Miscellaneous

BAINTON, GEORGE, *The Art of Authorship: Literary Reminiscences, Methods of Work, and Advice to Young Beginners, Personally Contributed by Leading Authors of the Day* (1890).

BELL, Lady, *At the Works* (1907).

BLACKBURN, HELEN, *Women's Suffrage: A Record of the Women's Suffrage Movement in the British Isles with Biographical Sketches of Miss Becker* (1902).

BLACKIE, AGNES A. C., *Blackie & Son 1809–1959* (Glasgow, 1959).

BLAND, LUCY, 'The Married Woman, the "New Woman" and the Feminist: Sexual Politics of the 1890s', in Jane Rendall (ed.), *Equal or Different: Women's Politics 1800–1914* (1987), 141–64.

BOURDIEU, PIERRE, 'Cultural Reproduction and Social Reproduction', Richard Brown (ed.), *Knowledge, Education and Cultural Change: Papers in the Sociology of Education* (1973), 71–112.

—— *Distinction: A Social Critique of the Judgement of Taste* (La Distinction: critique sociale du jugement (1979)), trans. Richard Nice (1984).

BOWDLER, THOMAS, *The Family Shakespeare*, 4 vols. (1807).

BOYLE, THOMAS, *Black Swine in the Sewers of Hampstead: Beneath the Surface of Victorian Sensationalism* (1990).

BRISTOW, EDWARD J., *Vice and Vigilance: Purity Movements in Britain since 1700* (1977).

BROWNING, ELIZABETH BARRETT, *Aurora Leigh* (1857: repr. 1978 with introd. by Cora Kaplan).

BUCKLE, HENRY THOMAS, 'The Influence of Women on the Progress of Knowledge', *Fraser's Magazine for Town and Country*, 57 (1858), 395–407.

CARPENTER, EDWARD, *Love's Coming of Age* (Manchester, 1896).

CRACKANTHORPE, B. A., 'The Revolt of the Daughters', *Nineteenth Century*, 35 (1894), 23–31.

—— 'The Revolt of the Daughters (No. 1): A Last Word on "The Revolt"', *Nineteenth Century*, 35 (1894), 424–9.

DALLAS, E. S., *The Gay Science*, 2 vols. (1866).

DAVIDOFF, LEONORE, *The Best Circles: Society Etiquette and the Season* (1973).

DAVIES, EMILY, *Thoughts on Some Questions Relating to Women, 1860–1908* (Cambridge, 1910).

DAVIN, ANNA, 'Imperialism and the Cult of Motherhood', *History Workshop Journal*, 5 (1978), 9–65.

DEGLER, CARL, 'What Ought To Be and What Was: Women's Sexuality in the Nineteenth Century', *American Historical Review*, 79 (1974), 1468–90.

EDELSTEIN, TERI J., 'Augustus Egg's Triptych: A Narrative of Victorian Adultery', *Burlington Magazine*, 125 (1983), 202–10.

ERICKSON, ARVEL B., and McCARTHY, JOHN R., 'The Yelverton Case: Civil Legislation and Marriage', *Victorian Studies*, 14 (1971), 275–91.

FIRESTONE, SHULAMITH, *The Dialectic of Sex* (1970).

FOUCAULT, MICHEL, *The Archaeology of Knowledge* (L'Archéologie du savoir (1969), trans. A. M. Sheridan Smith (1972).

FREEDEN, MICHAEL, 'Eugenics and Progressive Thought: A Study in Ideological Affinity', *Historical Journal*, 11 (1979), 645–71.

FRIED, MICHAEL, *Absorption and Theatricality: Painting and Beholder in the Age of Diderot* (Berkeley, Calif., 1980).

FUSS, DIANA, *Essentially Speaking* (1989).

GREER, GERMAINE, *The Female Eunuch* (1970; repr. 1971).

HARRISON, BRIAN, 'For Church, Queen and Family: The Girls' Friendly Society, 1875–1920', *Past and Present*, 61 (1973), 107–38.

HAWEIS, M. E., 'The Revolt of the Daughters (No. II). Daughters and Mothers', *Nineteenth Century*, 35 (1894), 430–6.

HEATH-STUBBS, M., *Friendship's Highway, Being The History of the Girls' Friendly Society 1874–1920* (1926).

HELSINGER, ELIZABETH K., SHEETS, ROBERT LAUTERBACH, and VEEDER, WILLIAM, *The Woman Question: Society and Literature in Britain and America, 1837–1883*, 3 vols. (Chicago and London, 1983).

HOPKINS, ELLICE, *Girls' Clubs and Recreative Evening Homes* (1887).

JAGGAR, ALISON M., 'Love and Knowledge: Emotion in Feminist Epistemology', in Ann Garry and Marilyn Pearsall (eds.), *Women, Knowledge, and Reality: Explorations in Feminist Philosophy* (1989), 129–55.

JAMESON, ANNA, *Legends of the Madonna* (1852).

JEFFRYS, SHEILA, *The Spinster and Her Enemies: Feminism and Sexuality 1880–1930* (1985).

JOYCE, Hon. Mrs, 'Need of a Mother's Union in all Classes', *Mothers in Council*, 3 (1893), 111–18.

KELLY-GADOL, JOAN, 'Did Women have a Renaissance?', in R. Bridenthal and C. Koonz (eds.), *Becoming Visible: Women in European History* (Boston, 1977), 137–64.

KERR, ROBERT, *The Gentleman's House; or How to Plan English Residences, from the Parsonage to the Palace* (3rd edn., rev. 1871).

'LEE, VERNON', *The Handling of Words, and Other Studies in Literary Psychology* (New York, 1923).

LEPPINGTON, BLANCHE, 'The Debrutalisation of Man', *Contemporary Review*, 67 (1895), 725–43.

LIDDINGTON, JILL, and NORRIS, JILL, *One Hand Tied Behind Us: The Rise of the Women's Suffrage Movement* (1978).

LINTON, E. LYNN, 'The Philistine's Coming Triumph', *National Review*, 26 (1895), 40–9.

MARTIN, FRANCES, 'The Glorified Spinster', *Macmillan's Magazine*, 58 (1888), 371–6.

MOZLEY, ANNE, 'Clever Women', *Blackwood's Magazine*, 104 (1868), 410–27.

NEAD, LYNDA, *Myths of Sexuality: Representations of Women in Victorian Britain* (Oxford, 1988).

NEWTON, JUDITH, 'Making—and Remaking— History: Another Look at Patriarchy', *Tulsa Studies in Women's Literature*, 3 (1984), 125–42.

OLIPHANT, MARGARET, 'The Condition of Women', *Blackwood's Edinburgh Magazine*, 83 (1858), 139–54.

PANKHURST, SYLVIA, *The Suffragette Movement* (1931; repr. 1977).

PANTON, J. E., *A Gentlewoman's House: The Whole Art of Building, Furnishing, and Beautifying the Home* (1896).

'RITA' [Eliza Margaret Humphreys], 'The Modern Young Person', *Belgravia*, 86 (1895), 61–4.

—— *Personal Opinions Publicly Expressed* (1907).

ROBERTS, ELIZABETH, 'Learning and Living—Socialisation Outside School', *Oral History*, 3 (1975), 14–28.

ROSCOE, WILLIAM CALDWELL, 'Woman', *National Review*, 7 (1858), 333–61.

RUSKIN, JOHN, *The Works of John Ruskin*, ed. E. T. Cook and Alexander Wedderburn, 39 vols. (1903–12).

SEMMEL, B., *Imperialism and Social Reform: English Social Imperialist Thought 1895–1914* (1960).

SHANLEY, MARY LYNDON, '"One Must Ride Behind": Married Women's Rights and The Divorce Act of 1857', *Victorian Studies*, 25 (1982), 355–76.

SHERIDAN, RICHARD BRINSLEY, *The Rivals* (1775), ed. Richard Little Purdy (Oxford, 1935).

STEPHEN, LESLIE, 'Art and Morality', *Cornhill Magazine*, 32 (1875), 91–101.

SURTEES, VIRGINIA, *The Paintings and Drawings of Dante Gabriel Rossetti (1828–1882): A Catalogue Raisonée*, 2 vols. (Oxford, 1971).

THOMAS, KEITH, 'Women and the Civil War Sects', *Past and Present*, 13 (1958), 42–62.

TICKNER, LISA, *The Spectacle of Women: Imagery of the Suffrage Campaign 1907–14* (1987).

URWICK, E. J. (ed.), *Studies of Boy Life in Our Cities* (1904).

VICINUS, MARTHA, *Independent Women: Work and Community for Single Women* (1985).

WRIGHT, PATRICK, *On Living in an Old Country: The National Past in Contemporary Britain* (1985).

Index